The Post-Reformation

Religion, Politics and Society in Britain Series

The Conversion of Britain: Religion, Politics and Society in Britain, 600–800
Barbara Yorke

Religion and Society in Twentieth-Century Britain
Callum G. Brown

The Post-Reformation

Religion, Politics and Society
in Britain 1603–1714

John Spurr

University of Swansea

Harlow, England • London • New York • Boston • San Francisco • Toronto
Sydney • Tokyo • Singapore • Hong Kong • Seoul • Taipei • New Delhi
Cape Town • Madrid • Mexico City • Amsterdam • Munich • Paris • Milan

Pearson Education Limited
Edinburgh Gate
Harlow
Essex CM20 2JE
England

and Associated Companies throughout the world

Visit us on the World Wide Web at:
www.pearsoned.co.uk

First published 2006

© Pearson Education Limited 2006

The right of John Spurr to be identified as author of this work has been asserted
by him in accordance with the Copyright, Designs and Patents Act 1988.

ISBN-13: 978-0-582-31906-6
ISBN-10: 0-582-31906-4

British Library Cataloguing-in-Publication Data
A catalogue record for this book is available from the British Library

Library of Congress Cataloging-in-Publication Data
Spurr, John.
    The post-Reformation : religion, politics, and society in Britain, 1603–1714 / John Spurr.
      p. cm. — (Religion, politics, and society in Britain)
    Includes bibliographical references and index.
    ISBN 0–582–31906–4 (alk. paper)
    1. Great Britain—Church history—17th century.   2. Christianity and politics—Great
Britain—17th century.   3. Christian sociology—Great Britain—History—17th century.   I.
Title. II. Series.

    BR756.S68 2006
    274.1′06—dc22
                              2005055584

10 9 8 7 6 5 4 3 2 1
11 10 09 08 07 06

Typeset in 10/13.5pt Sabon by 35
Printed and bound in Malaysia

The publisher's policy is to use paper manufactured from sustainable forests.

To Sam, Rene and Ivor

Contents

Series editor's preface

No understanding of British history is possible without grappling with the relationship between religion, politics and society. How that should be done, however, is another matter. Historians of religion, who have frequently thought of themselves as ecclesiastical historians, have had one set of preoccupations. Political historians have had another. They have both acknowledged, however, that both religion and politics can only be understood, in any given period, in a social context. This series makes the interplay between religion, politics and society its preoccupation. Even so, it does not assume that what is entailed by religion and politics remains the same throughout, to be considered as a constant in separate volumes merely because of the passage of time.

In its completed form the series will have probed the nature of these links from c.600 to the present day and offered a perspective, over such a long period, which has not before been attempted in a systematic fashion. There is, however, no straitjacket that requires individual authors to adhere to a common understanding of what such an undertaking involves. Even if there could be a general agreement about concepts, that is to say about what religion is or how politics can be identified, the social context of such categorisations is not static. The spheres notionally allocated to the one or to the other alter with circumstances. Sometimes it might appear that they cannot be separated. Sometimes it might appear that they sharply conflict. Each period under review will have its defining characteristics in this regard.

It is the Christian religion, in its manifold institutional manifestations, with which authors are overwhelmingly concerned since it is with conversion that the series begins. It ends, however, with a volume in which Christianity exists alongside other world religions but in a society frequently perceived to be secular. Yet, what de-Christianisation is taken to be depends upon what Christianisation has been taken to be. There is, therefore, a relationship between topics which are tackled in the first volume, and those considered in the last, which might at first sight seem unlikely. In between, of course are the 'Christian Centuries' which, despite their label, are no less full of 'boundary disputes' both before and after the Reformation. The perspective of the series, additionally, is broadly pan-insular. The Britain of 600 is plainly not the Britain of the early twenty-first century. However, the current political structures of Britain-Ireland have arguably owed as much to religion as to politics. Christendom has been inherently ambiguous.

It would be surprising if readers, not to mention authors, understood the totality of the picture that is presented in the same way. What is common, however, is a realisation that the narrative of religion, politics and society in Britain is not a simple tale that points in a single direction but rather one of enduring and by no means exhausted complexity.

Keith Robbins, November 2005

Preface

Writing this book presented a double challenge. My account had to reveal a world that is very different from our own, especially in its religious and political preoccupations. But it also had to convey something of the seventeenth century's dynamism, of the changes and struggles that had by 1714 left British society more recognisably modern than it was in 1603. Religion was at the heart of the story. Religious beliefs, values and practices cannot easily or helpfully be separated from the social, political and personal life of the period. But that does not mean religion can be explained in terms of something else. Religion is not a vehicle for liberty, democracy, progress, tolerance, patriarchy or the bourgeois work ethic. It is primarily the bundle of human beliefs and practices about and towards the supernatural, the creator, the next life, and the significance of this life. Religion is expressed in the personal and private form of piety. It takes on institutional form in the shape of churches, clergies, doctrines and church services. So there are numerous ways of writing the history of religion in seventeenth-century Britain. In what follows I have not pursued a narrow ecclesiastical or denominational history, but neither have I subsumed the spiritual experience of the seventeenth century to the political narrative.

This is a book for the general reader and the student as much as it is for the specialist in the period. It is a hybrid of my own reading in primary materials, both printed and in manuscript, and the published research of many scholars. I am particularly fortunate to be working in a field – religious history – and a period – the seventeenth century – that have attracted the attention of some outstanding historians and writers. I owe much to those scholars upon whose work I have drawn so heavily, and since the format of this book does not permit full acknowledgement of my debt (even if that were possible), I am very happy to recognise it here. All quotations, whether from seventeenth-century manuscript or printed sources or secondary authorities, have been ruthlessly modernised. It is not appropriate in a book of this scale to supply references for every quotation or fact. Nor, more contentiously perhaps, have I felt it necessary to describe at any length some of the more tangential issues when this would have distracted me from the task of providing a clear account of the mainstream of religious life and the evidence from which we can reconstruct it. The select bibliography will repay careful attention by those interested in following up some of the themes of this book or in pursuing subjects that I have passed over in silence: I would urge those interested in witches, science, atheism or other important topics to read some of the excellent works that are listed there. It is a daunting task to render the complex events and values of the seventeenth century into a single, straightforward and fairly brief book. Whether I have achieved this without unduly compromising the realities of the seventeenth century or the nuances of modern historical scholarship is, thankfully, for others to judge, but I have certainly enjoyed the attempt. The processes of writing and seeing the book into print have been greatly eased by the saintly patience and sympathetic guidance of the series editor Keith Robbins and the professionalism of the editorial staff at Pearson.

Personal thanks are due to my colleagues, students, friends and family. I have received many kindnesses from Mark Goldie, Ian Green and John Miller. John Morrill and Blair Worden have been supportive beyond measure. I am constantly grateful for the love, help and tolerance of Eileen and Fred Spurr, Rene and Ivor Colville, Ed, Kay and Daniel Colville, Joanna Spurr and Ian, Edward and Eleanor Sisley. And, as I often ask them, where would I be without Harry, Alice, Will, Sam and Anne?

John Spurr

Abbreviations

Abbott   W.C. Abbott (ed.), *The Writings and Speeches of Oliver Cromwell* (4 vols, Cambridge, Mass., 1937–47; reprinted Oxford, 1988).

BL   British Library

Bodl. L.   Bodleian Library, Oxford

CSPD   *Calendar of State Papers Domestic*

CUL   Cambridge University Library

Durham   *Durham Parish Books* (Surtees Society, 84, 1888)

DWL   Dr Williams's Library, Gordon Square, London

Evelyn   *The Diary of John Evelyn*, ed. E.S. de Beer (5 vols, Oxford, 1955)

Gardiner   S.R. Gardiner (ed.), *The Constitutional Documents of the Puritan Revolution 1625–1660* (3rd edn, Oxford, 1906)

Heywood   *The Autobiography of Oliver Heywood*, ed. J.H. Turner (4 vols, Brighouse, 1882–5)

HJ   *Historical Journal*

HLQ   *Huntington Library Quarterly*

JBS   *Journal of British Studies*

JEH   *Journal of Ecclesiastical History*

Josselin   *The Diary of Ralph Josselin 1616–1683*, ed. A. Macfarlane (1976)

Kenyon   J.P. Kenyon (ed.), *The Stuart Constitution 1603–1688: Documents and Commentary* (Cambridge, 1966)

P&P   *Past and Present*

17C   *The Seventeenth Century*

SCH	*Studies in Church History*
Spurr, *EP*	J. Spurr, *English Puritanism 1603–1689* (Basingstoke, 1998)
Spurr, *RC*	J. Spurr, *The Restoration Church of England, 1646–1689* (New Haven, Conn., 1991)
Sussex	*Churchwardens Presentments (Seventeenth Century): Part I. Archdeaconry of Chichester*, ed. H. Johnstone (Sussex Record Society, 49, 1947–8)
TRHS	*Transactions of the Royal Historical Society*
Watts	M.R. Watts, *The Dissenters: From the Reformation to the French Revolution* (Oxford, 1978; reprinted 1985)

Introduction:
the Post-Reformation

The Post-Reformation is a novel term and, perhaps, a new idea. While it is generally appreciated that the Protestant Reformation was a momentous challenge to religious, political and social life in the middle of the sixteenth century, there may be less awareness of how the effects of that confrontation made themselves felt in subsequent decades. So historians have begun to use the idea of the Post-Reformation to direct attention towards the long-term implications of the Reformation. Currently, the label is used in two ways. First it refers to the period and the process by which people moulded the messages of the Protestant Reformation and the Catholic Counter-Reformation. For one eminent historian, John Bossy, the term has the 'benefit of putting due weight on the state of affairs, on both sides of the confessional fence, as the seismic upheavals of the sixteenth century settled down into everyday continuity': in other words, it is all about the way that people got used to the Reformation and started to live with it.[1] This usage has the great advantage that it allows historians to sidestep crude questions about whether the Reformation had succeeded or failed by 1600 and to explore instead the reality of religious belief and behaviour. They can evaluate that reality in its own terms without worrying too much if what people actually said and did measured up to all the definitions and demands laid down by theologians and clergymen. It is, therefore, of genuine value to those like the present author who write about religion in the seventeenth-century British Isles. However, Britain in the seventeenth century was anything but a place where life had 'settled down into everyday continuity'. The second modern use of the term 'the Post-Reformation' is a straightforward recognition of the continuing repercussions of the 'seismic upheavals' of the English and Scottish Reformations. 'The Reformation almost permanently destabilised the religion of England, and with its religion its politics,' observe Collinson and Craig. 'The religious history of the seventeenth century, in particular, consists of a series of reverberations, not so much ripples as waves, disturbing the surface of a pond broken by the first stone: Laudianism in reaction against an almost dominant Jacobean Calvinism, a politically reactivated Puritanism rising up against Laudianism, reactive processes within resurgent Puritanism, Independency setting itself up against Presbyterianism, both Presbyterians and Independents taking fright from the sects; and then the Anglican revanche of the Restoration and all that followed from that.'[2] To describe how these and other waves rocked Britain and Ireland during the seventeenth century is one of this book's main purposes: another is to bring to life the diverse religious experiences of this dramatic century.

The Post-Reformation was a phase of British history shaped by competition over the meaning and legacy of the Reformation. The contest was about completing, defining, redefining, defending or even reversing the Reformation. These were highly political arguments. The Church of England's jurisdiction, organisation and government, its theological complexion, and its very origins as a true, saving, church were in themselves controversial, as was the nature of royal authority over the church and the nation's spiritual well-being, especially in the three distinct but interconnected territories of England and Wales, Ireland, and Scotland. It is hard to imagine a question of more fundamental political importance than, for instance, whether people should be allowed to choose their own religion. 'The state would never be in safety, where there was toleration of two religions,' fulminated William Cecil, the principal councillor of Queen Elizabeth. 'For there is no enmity so great as that of religion, and they that differ in the service of God can never agree in the service of their country.'[3] What was unthinkable to a Tudor Englishman was common sense to an Augustan Briton. In 1716 Dudley Ryder was delighted with John Locke's *Letter on Toleration*: 'the whole affair about toleration in religion is put into so clear and strong a light that I think it cannot but convince any man that reads it. He is for a universal unlimited toleration and that a magistrate has nothing at all any more than any other man to interfere or meddle in religious matters.'[4] This was a mental revolution of huge significance and it began, although it was not completed, during the seventeenth century. So, too, did the saturation of political life and language with religious ideology and terminology: religion was a prop of the Stuart monarchy and the interregnum regimes; political groupings were consistently confused with religious and denominational labels, as in the case of Presbyterians,

Arminians, Independents, Whigs and Tories; and, through notions like 'antipopery' and the 'godly prince', religion shaped fundamental political concepts such as nationhood and monarchy. Rulers and politicians were quick to identify a political threat in specific types of theology or worship; they doubted the sincerity of those who claimed religion as a motive for opposition or dissent, but they happily presented themselves as pursuing religious goals.

The passage from 'England' to 'Great Britain' was one of the salient developments of the seventeenth century. Our understanding of that process and of its implications has been enriched by the emergence of the 'new British history' in recent decades. A succession of historians have shown us that the political identities and histories of the three Stuart kingdoms, England and Wales, Scotland, and Ireland, were simultaneously distinct and closely interrelated. At the level of the political elites and aristocracy, in the fast-moving world of high politics, and especially in the crisis years of the mid-century, decisions in Whitehall or Westminster were shaped by and in turn influenced what was going on in Cork and Aberdeen, Argyll and Ulster, and even Boston and New York. Some aspects of religious life were similarly 'British' in their dimensions. Royal policies on church government or worship pursued in one corner of the Stuart dominions were frequently watched with a wary eye from another. Religious life far from Whitehall was shaped by any number of mundane factors ranging from personal connections and visits to the distribution of books and pamphlets. The role of emigration across the North Sea or the Atlantic is another obvious example, as are the many population movements within the British archipelago. Hard times in Scotland in the 1690s led to a wave of emigration to Ulster and a consequent fillip to Ulster Presbyterianism: reinvigorated Presbyterianism not only established an effective synod to govern its burgeoning meetings, but it also sent out missionaries into hitherto neglected areas such as Drogheda. The 'British' approach can also prove enlightening because it encourages a comparative viewpoint: it has often been remarked, for example, what different consequences flowed from the decision of Protestant reformers to spread the message in Wales through the Welsh language, while in Ireland the Protestant church resolutely stuck to English as the language of worship and instruction. The covenanting and conventicling movement that emerged in Presbyterian Scotland in the early seventeenth century was paralleled by a spiritual revival and mass communions in the north-east of Ireland. It also had unmistakeable similarities to the notion of a covenanted community that was being developed in New England. Of course, some of the lessons taught by a British approach about provincial variation can be applied on a smaller scale: the regions of England did not all advance towards Protestantism at the same pace; while remote and poverty-stricken areas could not always command the attention of reformers and clergy, the local 'ecology' of political power and resources, settlement patterns, landowner-ship, educational opportunities, patterns of employment, and other unique factors, often proved decisive in determining the religious character of a town, a county or a region. As we shall see, the politics of the local community was at the heart of the Post-Reformation.

Religion in seventeenth-century Britain was not a modern political 'problem'; it was not an issue, like inflation or the use of resources in the health service, to be managed or solved through the application of political strategies. Religion was part of the way that society and politics were con-stituted. Political and moral ideas ranging from the nature of civil obedi-ence to the treatment of those of other faiths were framed in religious terms. In 1599, for example, the Privy Council was alarmed that in the north of England the Queen's subjects were 'declining . . . from the reli-gion established and their due allegiance': they did not attend church and were led astray by Jesuits and Catholic missionaries to 'the great dishonour of almighty God, the discontentment of her majesty, and danger of the state'.[5] Most people found it so difficult to conceive of politics without a religious or spiritual dimension that anyone who did advance a secular view of politics automatically found themselves tarred as an 'atheist'. As John Bossy reminds us, the root meaning of the word 'religion' is to bind, it is what makes people into a community and creates authority within that group. Yet, as Bossy also observes, during the early modern centuries this older sense of religion was being supplanted by the idea of rival religions, hard-edged entities competing with each other for followers and for domin-ance.[6] That process is visible in seventeenth-century Britain and it will be a major theme of the following chapters. It involved not just the advent of rival churches in the traditional sense, but also the emergence of unfamiliar forms of religious association such as sects and separatist congregations. These are terms to which we will return repeatedly, both in the narrative chapters and at greater length in Chapter 12, but the crucial distinction is that while 'churches' are generally committed to geographically based units such as parishes, to the notion of serving the entire community, and to operating within the world as they find it, 'sects' are groups of indi-viduals who voluntarily associate together and are often at odds with the world around them. A sect will typically display an introverted character, its members marked out by distinctive dress, speech or behaviour, perhaps repudiating the conventional religious formalities, such as set patterns of worship or a separate class of ministers, and frequently espousing a belief, a prophecy or a practice which sets it on a collision course with the community around it or with the political authorities. Such sects have often aspired to remake the world in their own image.

The significance of these developments can perhaps only be comprehended in the light of an assessment of the nature and depth of mainstream religious belief. Scholars now judge that seventeenth-century popular religion in England and Wales was a hybrid, a religious culture better labelled Post-Reformation than Protestant. Many of the population were able to absorb the Protestant message and remould it along the lines of their abiding preoccupations with death and salvation, neighbourliness and morality, fate and the extra-ordinary. Others, of course, embraced Protestant teaching wholeheartedly or rejected it entirely. Did a gap develop in the seventeenth century between the religiously committed – the zealots of all denominations, 'popish', 'puritan' and sectarian – and the mass of the population? While the opening of such a gulf between the religious aspirations and behaviour of devout minorities and the apathy, ignorance or hostility of the majority would be significant in itself, it would also raise crucial questions about how the country stumbled into civil war and revolution during the seventeenth century. It would form part of the story of the developing religious and cultural pluralism of Britain and Ireland. For the seventeenth century saw the development and institutionalisation of distinct religious cultures, both as formal denominations and as cultural identities such as 'the godly', 'free-thinkers' or 'churchmen'.

In broad terms, then, the Post-Reformation has both a political and a social dimension. The two halves of this book are devoted to each of these different aspects. Although the first half is a political narrative and the second an account of the social and cultural place of religion in the seventeenth century, both are intended to portray change: the first through the narration of events and policies and the second in a more thematic discussion designed to help readers understand why and how religion mattered to 'ordinary people'. In the second half of the book I deliberately concentrate upon the mainstream, upon the all-too-silent majority, as much as possible (and in this, the century of the vocal Christian, it *is* possible to hear many ordinary voices). In addition to its own intrinsic interest, the mainstream was where radicalism began. Whether they reacted violently against the routine religion of the parish or fell away more gradually, whether they wanted to follow their own prophet, tailor their own practice, or eschew religion altogether, those given to change all started from these commonplace practices and institutions. I hope that running through this whole book is an awareness of the role of religion in opening people to the possibility of change and innovation. In due course religion surrendered that leading role as a catalyst of political and social change and became a matter of almost purely private concern, but even at the end of the seventeenth century that shift was as yet only dimly apparent.

Notes

1   J. Bossy, *Peace in the Post-Reformation* (Cambridge, 1998), p. 3; F. Heal, *Reformation in Britain and Ireland* (Oxford, 2003), p. 479; J. Spurr, 'The English "Post-Reformation"?' *Journal of Modern History* 74 (2002).

2   P. Collinson and J. Craig, *The Reformation in English Towns 1500–1640* (Basingstoke, 1998), p. 17.

3   C. Russell, *The Crisis of Parliaments* (1971), p. 149.

4   *The Diary of Dudley Ryder 1715–1716*, ed. W. Matthews (1939), p. 82.

5   M.J. Braddick, *State Formation in Early Modern England c.1550–1700* (Cambridge, 2000), pp. 287–8.

6   J. Bossy, *Christianity in the West 1400–1700* (Oxford, 1985), pp. 170–1.

CHAPTER 1

England, Ireland and Scotland in 1603

In 1603 James VI, King of Scotland, succeeded Elizabeth I and became King of England and Wales and King of Ireland. Among the tributes, petitions and advice that showered down on the new King were several surveys of the state of religion in his new realms. Some were reports on the education and capabilities of the clergy of the Church of England and others assessed the strength of various religious minorities; some sought to reassure him, others to inspire him to further reform of the church. Unlike these contemporary commentators, historians find it difficult to take a snapshot of religion at the beginning of the seventeenth century. It is not simply the usual problem of freezing what is really a dynamic process, it is much more a fundamental question of where to focus the picture. Should one concentrate on the Church of England? But the English church was contested ground from its very inception and it was still very far from being a uniform institution with a single clear message. Should we privilege the well-recorded views of the church's clergy or would we be better advised to explore the less well-documented attitudes of the laity? What of Roman Catholics and their co-religionists in Scotland and Ireland? Or the Presbyterians in Scotland? Beyond all these considerations, there is a need to explain why religion should occupy the foreground of our picture. So, before introducing some of the arguments surrounding the clergy's religious outlook and the religion of the laity, let us consider why religion was of such political and social importance in 1603.

Protestant kingdoms

At the beginning of the seventeenth century the three kingdoms of England and Wales, Ireland, and Scotland had been Protestant for several decades.

The English and Welsh Reformation began as an act of state in the 1530s when Henry VIII used Parliament to sever all links with the papacy and establish his own position as 'supreme head' of the church in his realms. This was rapidly followed by the dissolution of the monasteries and the seizure of their valuable lands. The subsequent sale and distribution of these broad acres among the gentry and aristocracy did much to ensure the commitment of this politically crucial class to the break from Rome. The 1536 Act of Union, which extended the English pattern of shires to Wales, coincided with Henry's Reformation and presented the Welsh gentry with opportunities in Parliament and in their localities to participate in and profit from enforcing the new religious arrangements.

Whereas England and Wales were effectively one political and religious unit, Ireland was a complex dominion where Henry's authority and ambitions were limited. Technically only the Lord of Ireland, Henry's control, especially beyond 'the Pale', the area around Dublin, was dependent upon the precarious good will of the great Irish lords. An abortive rebellion by these lords compelled Henry to intervene and in 1536–37 the Irish Parliament passed legislation that mirrored the statutes of the English Reformation. In 1541 Parliament acknowledged Henry as King. The Irish Reformation was, in the words of Alan Ford, 'an English affair, imposed from England, dependent upon events in England, and led in Ireland by officials and ecclesiastics who were members of the Church of England'.[1] Its impact, moreover, was slight. Whatever might be decided in Dublin made little difference to religious practices in Gaelic Ulster or Connacht.

In England, although the papacy had been repudiated under Henry and the church plundered, theologically little had changed. It was the reign of his son Edward VI that saw the process of Protestant Reformation move up a gear: the 1549 Uniformity Act obliged the population to attend English-language services according to the new Book of Common Prayer, but the decisive turn towards a Swiss-style Reformed Protestantism came with the 1552 Uniformity Act and the revised Prayer Book. Edward's premature death the following year allowed his Catholic successor Mary to throw the machine into reverse. Hampered by the lukewarm attitude of the papacy and English aristocracy, and by her own temperament – she foolishly created three hundred Protestant martyrs or, as she saw it, dispensed exemplary punishment to three hundred obstinate heretics – Mary did not win England back to Catholicism before her death in 1558. At this point, thirty years of upheaval and suffering had confirmed the zealots of both sides, but resolved nothing. A religious spell had been broken: the unity of the church had been breached; the mass transformed; purgatory denied;

the clergy polluted by marriage; the monasteries dissolved; the beauties of
the church destroyed by iconoclasts. And yet the world had not stopped
turning. God had not intervened. To see all that Catholicism held dear
destroyed may have weakened the faith of some Catholics. But it did not
necessarily strengthen the faith of Protestants. Too many of the English
obeyed the new religion grudgingly, while the reformers concentrated their
energies on rooting out the old, on de-Catholicising rather than evangelising
the land. It seems likely that many of the English were left with their faith
in medieval Christianity, in the saving intercession of the church and the
value of good works, shattered, but with little to replace it.

The task of spreading the new faith was undertaken during the long
reign of Elizabeth I. Provocatively, Collinson has claimed that 'the
Reformation was something which happened in the reigns of Elizabeth and
James I. Before that everything was preparative, embryonic. Protestantism
was present, but as a kind of subculture, like Catholicism later.'[2] The
Elizabethan Act of Uniformity and Prayer Book of 1559 were designed
with an eye to reconciliation. Earlier versions of the liturgy were conflated
and theological issues were left vaguely defined, rather as they were in
the Thirty-nine Articles of 1563, the Church of England's basic doctrinal
statement. Putting this Elizabethan 'settlement' into effect, ironing out
problems and accommodating different interests, was a slow business.
It was not until late in Elizabeth's reign that the English church had
an effective Protestant preaching clergy and the bishops could be sure of
commanding respect. Even then there was, under the umbrella of the
official church, a diversity of religious practice and belief across the
parishes. Equally importantly, there were groups of disaffected Protestants
and Roman Catholics who remained a thorn in the church's flesh.

Those who were convinced that the Elizabethan church could and
should go faster in evangelising the nation have usually been dubbed
'puritans'. Although, as we shall see, there were to be many different
'puritanisms', the Elizabethan puritans were principally those clergy and
their supporters who formed the vanguard of official efforts to spread
Protestantism. While they applauded much in the Church of England, it
remained, in their eyes, 'but halfly reformed', especially in the areas of
worship and church government. Worship according to the 1559 Prayer
Book offended puritans because it was redolent of popery and trespassed
on the consciences of both ministers and their flocks. Even a stalwart of the
Elizabethan church like John Foxe felt compelled to point out that the
Word of God is the final arbiter of divine worship and 'it is certain that
there are several matters in this book which seem too little exactly to

correspond to complete reformation of the Church, and which perhaps might be radically changed for the better'. Others were less polite: it is 'an unperfect book, culled and picked out of that popish dunghill, the mass-book full of all abominations'. Calls for reform of the church's government sprang from disillusionment with the current crop of bishops and from comparisons drawn with Scotland and Geneva where 'discipline' had been imposed within a Presbyterian system. The Presbyterians' case was strengthened by scholars who could find no warrant in scripture for church government by bishops, but much to support a Presbyterian system of congregations governed by pastors and elders, each sending representatives to district assemblies (or classes) and those in turn contributing to provincial or national meetings (synods). For all their pamphleteering and parliamentary lobbying, Elizabethan Presbyterians had no success in revising the constitution of the episcopal Church of England. Even the Presbyterian experiments in English counties in the 1570s and 1580s were more a way for the clergy to compare notes and encourage one another than a means of enforcing discipline on the laity. Yet in the 1590s Archbishop Whitgift became convinced of the danger posed by the Presbyterians. Presbyterian satirical pamphlets had exposed the bishops and the church to popular ridicule. A small number of separatists who had denied the power of the prince in religion turned out to have connections among the Presbyterians. In reaction, puritan leaders were dragged before the courts and intimidated into silence. Their movement had been driven underground, but their cause had not been defeated.

The Post-Reformation Roman Catholic community adapted uneasily to conditions under Elizabeth I. In the 1560s the signs were all of compromise on both sides. The authorities exhibited a degree of leniency or even unofficial tolerance of traditional religious practices – especially in those areas, such as Lancashire or Durham, where visitations were less thorough – and many priests continued to say mass for semi-secret Catholic congregations. By the same token, many Catholics appear to have attended parish church, but to have abstained from receiving the communion, simply to escape the twelve-pence fine for non-attendance stipulated by the Uniformity Act. Within a few years, things went sour. A succession of Catholic plots and risings in favour of Mary, Queen of Scots, and the pope's declaration that Elizabeth was excommunicate and deposed, provoked the regime. Fines of £20 per month could now be imposed on those who stayed away from the parish church. Conversion to Roman Catholicism was equated with treason and priests could be punished simply for saying mass. In the 1570s missionary priests began to infiltrate

England and Wales, followed in the 1580s by Jesuits. These were English Catholics who had fled to seminaries in Rome or Flanders to receive training and ordination. Identified with the Counter-Reformation, these missionaries saw the Catholic reconquest of England, both spiritually and militarily, as their ultimate goal. In 1588 they called, without success, for English Catholics to rise up in support of the Armada.

The history of English Catholicism is controversial. One account is that English Catholicism was dwindling into insignificance before it was rescued by the arrival of the missionaries who constructed an underground church that was deeply influenced by Tridentine practices and ideals. The missionaries, however, have been criticised for sticking rather too closely to the existing Catholic communities and failing to take their message to potential new converts. The scholarly controversy about the degree of change and continuity within Catholicism is now looking rather tired and in danger of oversimplifying the nature of the community. Some of this debate is simply a matter of perspective. Too much concentration on a certain kind of source, especially for the last decades of the sixteenth century when both Elizabeth and the Jesuits were prepared to fight fire with fire, leads to an excessively confrontational view of Catholic–conformist relations. Questier, for example, has urged us to view the 1580s and early 1590s as an anomaly in the general pattern, 'a Catholic "puritan" experiment with separatism, an experiment in which the language of evangelical fervour, mission, blood, suffering and, above all, martyrdom had, for a short time, coincided with, perhaps been assisted by, the war with Spain'.[3] The more normal pattern prevailing in the sixteenth and certainly in the seventeenth century is of a variety of possible Catholic positions, some hardline or evasive, but others flexible, politically astute, and open to compromise. It may be possible to relate this diversity to the quarrel between Jesuits and the 'Appellants' or secular clergy over the structure of the Catholic church in England. The former regarded England as a missionary field and therefore suited to rule by the regular clergy directly answerable to Rome, while the latter recommended a diocesan structure – however clandestine and limited in effect – and government by bishops. In the political context of the later 1590s, these represent different views of how the Catholic community and church might adapt themselves to life under a Protestant monarch, especially if such a monarch was prepared to concede toleration to Catholics. Many in the Appellant camp saw themselves as both good Catholics and good subjects of the Queen. They talked of taking oaths of loyalty and were courted by Bishop Bancroft and other Protestant leaders. They entertained high hopes that James VI of Scotland, son of a

Catholic martyr, might succeed to the English throne. In the minds of the secular clergy and Catholic aristocracy, English Catholicism was far from doomed to slow extinction.

Thanks to recent research, it is becoming apparent that the Catholic community enjoyed a broad social base, embracing humble folk as well as the traditional Catholic gentry and aristocracy, and including new converts just as much as those brought up within the old faith. Conventionally, Catholics have been allotted to the arcane categories of the 'recusant' and the 'church papist'. 'Recusancy' or a refusal to attend parish church was a criminal offence and so the extent of prosecution and conviction can be mapped fairly accurately from the records. 'Church papists', those who went to the parish church while remaining loyal Catholics in private, represent a less clearly defined group. While both categories were real enough, it may be that individuals moved between the two more easily than historians have realised and that neither category was a permanent definition of a Catholic's stance.[4] Calls by Questier and Lake for the 'reintegration of the political history of English Catholics into the mainstream narrative' remind us not to dismiss the political viability of Roman Catholicism too early.[5] In a personal monarchy, the preferences of the ruler and the complexion of the court can be highly significant – as Britons would discover before the seventeenth century was out.

*

The Scottish Reformation took place in 1560 just as Elizabeth was consolidating her religious settlement in England. The two processes were rather different, however. In Scotland, a group of nobles, inspired by John Knox the Calvinist preacher, aided by English troops, and allied to secret Protestant congregations, rebelled against Mary of Guise, the French Catholic Regent. Once a peace had been achieved, the single-chambered Scottish Parliament enacted a sweeping Reformation: papal authority was renounced; a Calvinist Confession of Faith was instituted; and work began on a scheme of church government known as the Book of Discipline. The English ambassador reported that the Scots are 'so deeply persuaded in the matter of religion, as nothing can persuade them that may appear to hinder it'.[6] The resulting Kirk or church differed markedly from its sister church south of the border. The Kirk was Calvinist, Presbyterian and free of royal control. The parish ministry was based on the four offices of preacher, deacon, doctor and elder; each parish congregation exercised 'discipline' over its members; ministers and lay elders cooperated in running the weekly courts or Kirk sessions and in serving on the district committees (the pres-byteries and synods); congregations sent representatives to the General Assembly of the Kirk which therefore had a strong lay presence. There were no bishops in the Kirk and no royal governor over it. The ministers maintained the principle of a separation of authorities between the 'two kingdoms' of church and state, although this did not prevent the Kirk offering its advice where relevant to the pursuit of godliness. Congregations enjoyed freedom within limits to organise their own worship and adopted the plain style of worship to be seen in European Calvinist churches.

There is no denying the popularity of the Scottish Reformation. Within a generation at the most, the Scottish Lowlands had been purged of Catholicism and its profane and superstitious ways: indeed, a 'cultural re-volution' had been achieved, and the foundations laid for the abstemious, morally repressive, sermon-centred, and dour Calvinist religion which was to characterise Scotland for several centuries. Strict in morality, censorious in punishing the sinner – every Kirk had a stool of repentance – devoted to keeping the whole of the Sabbath day for the works of religion, Bible-reading and sermon-noting, suspicious of images and gaiety, in thrall to the minister, self-righteous – it is perhaps too easy to caricature this form of Protestantism. It was a religion that moved people: it spawned spiritual 'revivals', brought people together in large numbers for open-air worship and prayer meetings, and lent itself to apocalypticism. Todd has recently attributed its success to two related factors: one is the local basis upon which Protestantism took root and the other is its willingness to absorb and adapt traditional Scottish ways. Working from the Kirk sessions records, she is able to show how theology could be tempered in practice by ministers and elders who knew those standing before them, who appreciated their moral, spiritual and practical frailties.[7]

The Calvinist Kirk dominated the Scots-speaking Lowlands and the North-East, towards Moray, Banff and Aberdeen, but Calvinism also made inroads into the Gaelic-speaking Highlands and Islands. Patronised by the Clan Campbell and the fifth Earl of Argyll, and adapting to local conditions, this Gaelic Calvinism operated through teams of itinerant Gaelic-speaking ministers, dressed in plaids and bonnets rather than the conventional Geneva gowns.[8] In general, of course, the Gaelic Isles and Highlands retained their traditional ways and beliefs, their distinctive dress and kin-based society, their highly developed oral culture, and their own version of Catholicism: the Calvinist James VI pungently described them as 'wild savages void of God's fear and our obedience'. When Catholic missionaries such as the Franciscans or Dominicans reached these remote areas, they found that 'these people are neither Catholic nor heretical, since they detest Protestantism as a new religion and they listen to the preachers out of sheer necessity, straying in matters of faith out of ignorance caused by the lack of priests'.[9] Highlanders wedded to the ancient practices of Celtic Christianity were suspicious of these priests with their Tridentine notions of the Catholic faith: when the missionaries did succeed, as on Islay or Harris, it was often thanks to the sponsorship of clan chieftains.

Sixteenth-century Scotland was an impoverished, largely agricultural country with difficult communications and pronounced regional variations. Power lay in the hands of the nobility who not only owned the land but also dispensed justice and provided what passed for local government. The weak monarchy of the Catholic Mary, Queen of Scots, was followed by a period of insecurity and strife under successive regents. Mary's claim to Elizabeth's throne was one reason why the English government never took its eye off Scotland. Mary's son and successor James VI was brought up a Calvinist and endured a rough political schooling – at one point the young King was held prisoner for a year in Ruthven castle by a band of Protestant lords – but he emerged with real skills in political management, adept at both the grand gesture and the necessary compromise. So far as he could, James kept his options open. He refused to dispense with the service of leading Catholic lords such as the Earls of Huntly and Erroll. Although he could not prevent the spread of Presbyterianism, he attempted to balance it by displays of royal authority: he held on to his right to summon the General Assembly and succeeded in maintaining a shadow church structure of bishops. These bishops were an anomaly. They had no position in the Kirk – although James was later to impose them on the General Assembly – and limited diocesan revenues or authority. But episcopacy was to be a useful adjunct to royal power in the seventeenth century: the Scottish episcopate, comprising the archbishops of St Andrews and Glasgow, along with another twelve bishops, were to grow in authority whenever the monarchy was in the ascendant; episcopacy existed in Scotland until 1638 and then again, more effectively, between 1661 and 1689. In the late sixteenth century, however, the bishops cut a poor figure in comparison with the Presbyterian Kirk. During the 1590s, James clashed regularly with the Kirk's leaders. On one notorious occasion in 1596 the eminent Presbyterian Andrew Melville plucked at the King's sleeve and called him 'God's silly [weak] vassal'. Little wonder that James later wrote 'some fiery spirited men in the ministry . . . finding the gust [taste] of government sweet, they began to fantasy to themselves, a democratic form of government' and delude themselves that they might rule 'in a popular government by leading the people by the nose'.[10]

*

Mainland Britain's commitment to Protestantism was both practical and ideological. In England, the Tudor Reformation had enshrined the relationship between church and state in the royal supremacy exercised over the Church of England. The monarchy was a clear winner from the arrangement. But the use of Parliament to legislate this new arrangement had effectively bound the political elite to the Reformation. This was made easier, thanks to the extraordinarily small elite of England and Wales – not much more than 20,000 gentlemen, esquires, knights and peers out of a population of over four million in 1603. This group dominated Parliament, where 120 peers and 26 bishops made up the House of Lords and 90 knights of the shires and 372 burgesses comprised the Commons. They also dominated the provinces. In return for their unpaid and often unsupervised help in the administration of local government and justice, the landed class enjoyed very low levels of royal taxation. They had profited directly from the Reformation, thanks to the sale of monastic lands and the distribution of impropriated tithes and advowsons. Yet, as we have noted, there were still gentlemen and nobles, and indeed humbler individuals, who retained their Catholic faith, and some of these, too, played a part in the political and administrative life of the country. Scotland's commitment to Protestantism was no less rooted in practical issues. But here there were signs of more obvious antagonism between the different social groups and regions. The landowners vied with the Kirk for control of the lands of the medieval church and there was competition between aristocratic and ecclesiastical jurisdictions. Yet at a local level the Presbyterian ministers and elders were clearly fulfilling a social need as they took upon themselves the job of tackling problems of vagrancy, education, and poor relief, alongside their pastoral and moral oversight of the community. Ireland, of course, was another story. It was 'overwhelmed with the palpable darkness of idolatry', in the words of one Protestant bishop.[11] The Catholic population was still married, christened and buried by Catholic priests and continued to pay their tithes to them. The Reformation had no impact on most of the country.

The ideological commitment to Protestantism operated at several levels. Most fundamentally, religion, especially Protestant religion, was concerned with human depravity and the need to curb and control sin.

Many of its teachings were recommended in precisely these terms. The fear of hell, observed John Owen, was the 'great engine of the providence of God to preserve mankind from wickedness which would undermine society'.[12] Religion sustained the hierarchical structure of society, teaching everyone the rights and obligations that belonged to their proper place on the social ladder. Patriarchy was woven into the fabric of Christianity at every point, from God the father to Noah, the first father and first king, down to the injunctions of St Paul to obey the powers that be (Romans 13: 6). Preachers, especially on anniversaries such as 5 November, Gunpowder Plot Day, or in prominent public pulpits, would stress the divine origin of royal authority: 'majesty is a deputy-divinity . . . God having proposed to man the visible Godhead of a King, as his own proportional and lawful image'.[13] Scripture offered examples of godly princes, 'nursing mothers' and 'nursing fathers' of God's church (Isaiah 49: 23), and laid down the rules by which they governed. Kings enjoy a divine right, argued James I, but God is 'the surest and sharpest schoolmaster that can be devised for them'.[14] Scripture told not only of the fate of bad kings but of rebels: for instance, Robert Cecil saw the Earl of Essex's rebellion in terms of Absalom's rebellion against King David just as readily as he did in terms of historical precedents such as the risings of Wat Tyler or Jack Cade.

English Protestantism can almost be defined as a repudiation of popery: it was an ideology and identity created in opposition to the Church of Rome. Antipopery began in the Reformation's rejection of Roman Catholic doctrines and institutions. That original denunciation of Catholic idolatry, superstition, formalism and error was full of malice and invective. But the brew turned toxic with the addition of other ingredients such as prophecy and millenarianism. Post-Reformation English antipopery drew on the mysterious biblical prophecies in the Books of Daniel and Revelations to interpret the history of Christianity. This involved identifying symbols and figures such as 'the beast' and 'the five monarchies' with specific churches, institutions and phases of history and offering a timetable for the final confrontation between good and evil, Christ and Antichrist, after which there would be Judgement Day and human history would come to an end. John Foxe, the author of the *Acts and Monuments* of the English martyrs, peddled a version of this Christian history that identified the pope with Antichrist and argued that the countdown to Armageddon had begun. This schema gave a leading role to the godly prince, the new Constantine, whose task it was to further the Reformation, take on Antichrist and hasten the final apocalypse. Foxe's book was officially required to be on display in every parish church and his brand of apocalyptic and millenarian thinking became a major component of English Protestantism.

International events were accommodated to this reading of history and Roman Catholicism. The Counter-Reformation followed by the revival of Catholicism in Central Europe, the global dominance of Spain and its determined campaign against the Protestant Dutch, the papal excommunication of Elizabeth and the Armada, all reinforced the conviction, amounting in some cases to paranoia, that the cosmic struggle was coming to a climax and that England stood alone against the forces of Antichrist. At its more precise, the fear was that England would be invaded from abroad, possibly via Ireland, in conjunction with a Jesuit-inspired rising of English Catholics, and accompanied by massacres, the firing of cities, the deposition and murder of the monarch, the abolition of parliaments, and the installation of a brutal and rapacious foreign ruler. The Church of Rome would be restored to its authority and lands, an Inquisition would be erected, monks, nuns and domineering priests would arrive, and, worst of all, the pure milk of the Protestant gospel would be banned with all that that implied for the salvation of the English. Such nightmares were so vivid to seventeenth-century English people, and were kept so fresh in their minds by preachers and publicists, that they prompted repeated scares and spasms of anti-popish violence throughout the century. They coloured attitudes towards some of the century's most fundamental political issues – in foreign policy and domestic matters – and shaped the most crucial political events, in 1640–42, 1679–81 and 1688–89. Antipopery was, however, a flexible ideology that several rival parties could and did deploy to great effect.

'Anti-catholicism,' observes Collinson, 'became the sheet anchor of England's nationhood.'[15] Protestantism supplied several of the ideological materials from which Post-Reformation national identities could be constructed. Among the English, it encouraged talk of England's peculiarly favoured status and destiny; its scriptural emphasis fostered the idea of a 'godly prince'; and antipopery underscored the need for national vigilance and unity. Yet, as Collinson has also remarked, 'Protestantism complicated the religious sense of nationhood even while intensifying it.'[16] This is true of England where much of the seventeenth century was devoted to quarrels between opposing notions of the goals and progress of the Protestant Reformation. In Wales some lamented the dilution of national identity and the threat to the Welsh cultural heritage, while others crowed over the rich pickings of the union with England and its Protestant church: in 1716, one Welsh Nonconformist preacher congratulated the Welsh on sloughing off their nationhood and becoming 'one and the same people and body politic, happily incorporated with the English'.[17] Protestantism underpinned the English 'civilising mission' to Ireland and inevitably came into conflict with native definitions of the 'true religion' as well as those of Scottish immigrants in Ulster. The situation in Scotland was more complex still. Protestantism of the Presbyterian Calvinist brand had already become the main vehicle of Scottish national identity – and the capstone to this edifice would be the National Covenant of 1638. Yet Scottish Protestantism was part of a wider international Protestantism. The Kirk did not disguise its sense of mission: 'other Kirks abroad . . . have not been favoured with [our] measure of reformation,' remarked the ministers in 1618, 'the Lord has been more liberal to us and requires of us that we give example and encouragement to them to aspire to our perfection'.[18] No doubt they hoped to inspire their brethren south of the border. After 1603 the union of the two kingdoms in the person of James VI and I led some to dream of a closer union, the foundation of 'the most opulent, strong and entire empire of the world', and a real alignment of the two churches. As one preacher pictured it, every man sat content under his vine and fig tree 'from Kent to Kintyre, from the south of England to the north of Scotland'.[19]

All of these aspirations and anxieties should be seen against the backdrop of contemporary social conditions. In 1603 England was a jittery country. Long-term trends such as inflation and population growth had unsettled the nation: prices roared ahead of wages, and a national population of 4.1 million in 1603 would reach 5 million by mid-century; racked by plague, crime and disorder, London was becoming a huge city, home to 185,000 people in 1600 and to 355,000 just forty years later. The last fifteen years of Elizabeth's reign had been overshadowed by economic depression, costly and fruitless wars with Spain and in Ireland, social tensions and political instability. Yet this was also a vibrant society, full of young people, leavened with entrepreneurs and adventurers, and with a pronounced interest in what was going on elsewhere in the British Isles and beyond. This was simultaneously a literate and an oral culture. Around 30 per cent of the male population could write and a much higher proportion was able to read. The printed sermon, pamphlet and broadside were already staples of metropolitan life and familiar in provincial towns and cities. News and opinion were spread by gossip, rumour, and ballad-singers just as easily as they were by handwritten newsletters or printed tracts. And religion was a favourite topic of conversation, not least because it was part of the very fabric of life. It will take the rest of this book to portray the religious life of the country, but as a starting point let us turn to the English clergy.

The clergy of the Church of England

In 1603 an optimistic view of the Church of England's nine thousand ministers would suggest that they were a predominantly graduate and preaching clergy, committed to spreading the gospel, which for the majority meant a deep attachment to their pastoral role and their Calvinist teachings. At university they had imbibed the predestinarianism of the Calvinist theologians of Heidelberg and Geneva and of some native teachers such as William Perkins: they saw themselves and the English church as part of the European Reformed tradition. The ministers were fervently anti-Catholic and many were lukewarm about the rituals prescribed in the Prayer Book. This at least was the image, but there were of course many differences depending on age and ambition, ability and taste, location and wealth: ministers in parts of Wales or Lancashire might have a very different grasp of the theology of the church or the traditional rituals of worship from that of thrusting young clergymen serving urban parishes in the south-east. Archbishop Whitgift's survey of the state of the church in 1603 produced a total of 4,840 clergymen who were licensed as preachers. Nearly 4,000 of these ministers were graduates. Yet it was still possible to work one's way up from a post like parish clerk to ordination and a parish living without going anywhere near the university.

One common, but not universal, characteristic of these ministers was their Calvinist theology. Most historians accept that there was a 'Calvinist consensus' in the English church at this time. Its central principle was the doctrine of predestination, that God, without respect to human merit, had preordained some of humankind to salvation and these 'elect' could never fall from grace. This teaching was unexceptional; it was based on scripture and avowed in Article 17 of the Thirty-nine Articles; and many preachers and lay people regarded it as 'a comfortable doctrine'. Naturally, it gave rise to further questions. Does God consciously choose other souls for damnation? Was the decision made before or after the Fall? Did Christ die on the Cross for all mankind or only the elect? But these were disputable and best left to theologians (as is the question of whether Calvin himself held Calvinist views or whether they are really the teachings of his successor Beza). Indeed, even the main doctrine of predestination was carefully qualified by the convention that it is impossible in this life to know who the elect are. We should all live as if we are one of those destined for salvation, but the mysterious eternal decrees of God are not something about which human beings are equipped to speculate. Kendall has called this intellectual conviction, this devout hope, *credal predestinarianism* and distinguished it from the far more intense, personal, sense of election as one of the saved that he calls *experimental predestinarianism*: the former is a matter of belief or credence, the latter is a profound experience.[20]

One source for experimental predestinarianism was the search by individuals for assurance of their own salvation. They looked in their hearts and actions for signs of their elect status and some began to equate a godly life with proof of election. The danger was that this might lead to presumption and hypocrisy among those convinced of their election and anxiety and despair on the part of those who were uncertain of their own standing with God. Many clergymen wrestled with these pastoral problems in trying to comfort their congregations while maintaining the theological coherence of their Calvinist doctrine. Some modified their message: John Overall, preaching at Epping in the 1590s, found his flock so troubled by predestination and so unsure that Christ died for them that he began to teach that Christ had died for all men – a position known as 'hypothetical universalism' because it did not mean that the *saving effect* of Christ's death would actually be universal. Samuel Harsnett preached against Calvinism at Paul's Cross in 1584 and was silenced by Whitgift. A handful of clergymen questioned predestination in its very heartland, the University of Cambridge: Baro and Barrett provoked uproar in the 1590s when they argued that election was conditional on human faith. Not only were they reprimanded by the university: their views prompted Whitgift to publish the Lambeth Articles (1595), a clear assertion that the Church of England taught that God had predestined some to salvation and others to damnation without any reference to their faith or merits. Ominously, Queen Elizabeth declined to put her weight behind the Lambeth Articles and they never became an official statement of doctrine. Although such minor setbacks did little to shake the overwhelming contemporary conviction that the Church of England's theology of salvation was Calvinist, the troubles of the 1590s were straws in the wind: this was to be a divisive issue in the seventeenth century.

The English church took a stern line against the Church of Rome. Subverted by Satan, the Roman church had become antichristian, the opposite of a true religion. Rome's doctrines were erroneous and condemned its followers to damnation: the worship of saints, the Virgin Mary, and the consecrated bread and wine, were all idolatry; the doctrine of justification by works was effectively a repudiation of Christ's sacrifice on the Cross; and the elevation of papal authority over the Word of God was blasphemous. Roman Catholicism pandered to debased human nature, to superstition, formality and hypocrisy; it was the tool of self-interested clergymen and an overbearing papacy. The pope tyrannised individual consciences and invaded the rights of princes. Although few of the English clergy doubted that the pope was Antichrist, there was room for disagreement about what this implied. Did it mean, for instance, that no one who died in the communion of the Church of Rome could be saved? What then of those earlier generations who had had no choice because they had died before the Reformation? This also touched on whether English Protestantism had emerged from the pre-Reformation church or whether its roots lay in underground medieval heresies. Several features of the Church of England, such as its bishops and courts, had been inherited from its medieval predecessor, and if that medieval church was irredeemably antichristian then it followed that those institutions must be tainted.

Sabbatarianism was another clerical preoccupation. One might think that the fourth commandment – 'remember the Sabbath day, to keep it holy' – was plain enough, but in the 1580s puritan ministers began to formulate a new teaching based on their reading of Reformed theologians such as Bucer, Bullinger, Beza, and Zanchius, and on their pastoral experience. Greenham, for example, presented his view of the Sabbath as a reply to the papists on one side and the separatists on the other since both of them argued that the obligation to respect the Sabbath was simply a ceremonial ordinance imposed by the church or inherited from Jewish superstition. But to Greenham and his brethren, the inclusion of the Sabbath in the Ten Commandments meant that it was an obligation of the moral rather than the ceremonial law. Moreover, they taught that the Sabbath is a fast rather than a feast, that the fast lasts twenty-four hours and prohibits all non-religious activities, and that the judicial law of Moses should apply to Sabbath-breakers. Sabbatarianism was a distinctly puritan position and drew a sharp and practical line between those clergy who espoused it and those for whom Sunday was a day set apart for both worship and other necessary and pleasant activities.

The details of public worship divided the clergy. Arguments over liturgical conformity had not abated. Some ministers bitterly resented the 'rags of Rome' and the ceremonies, others simply preferred to devote their energies to alternatives, such as preaching or bible discussion, that they and their parishioners valued more highly. Nor was there any effective mechanism for ensuring that in their parish churches ministers were complying with the rubrics and forms of the Prayer Book. However, just as some clergy cut corners and adapted the liturgy, there were other ministers and congregations who found the liturgy and its rituals a satisfying and helpful experience. Indeed, some clergymen, such as Lancelot Andrewes in the privacy of Ely House chapel, had begun to experiment with more elaborate ceremonial, while Westminster Abbey under successive deans retained old-fashioned practices, vestments and rituals in defiance of prevailing expectations.

These four issues – Calvinism, Rome, Sabbatarianism and worship – created tensions between the clergy and occasionally erupted into controversies. Yet they do not neatly match other clerical divisions of the time. Nor indeed were all differences of viewpoint equally contentious. In the 1580s and 1590s several apologists for the Church of England had sketched out a defence of episcopacy in reply to Presbyterianism. They had suggested that God had indicated a preference for churches to be governed by bishops (what was known as a *iure divino* or divine right argument) but this explosive claim had ignited no controversy within the church. Understanding complex groups such as the clergy of the Church of England inevitably forces us to classify ministers according to principles and parties, but we must never forget that there are always other ways of categorising the clergy and that there will always be individuals who burst out of the boxes into which we try to cram them.

One taxonomy of the clergy at the start of the seventeenth century can be constructed around the issue of conformity. Thus at one extreme might lie the group of ministers who could not compromise over their refusal to use Prayer Book ceremonies – men who had been suspended from office or even deprived of their living for nonconformity. These were zealous gospellers and usually keen Calvinists, sharing an outlook with a broader group of evangelical ministers who can be labelled 'conformable' because they were able to bring themselves to conform, albeit with no enthusiasm for the ceremonies, if that was to be the price of maintaining their ministry. Such 'moderate' or 'evangelical' churchmen placed a higher value on preaching, catechising, spreading the doctrine of justification by faith alone and combating the Roman Antichrist, than they did on jumping the hoops held up by the authorities. The third grouping of clergy was the Calvinist conformists who genuinely respected the right of the king and bishops to order 'indifferent' matters such as vestments and ceremonies. They saw conformity as a hedge against disorder which was offensive to both God and king and they distrusted the motives of those who refused conformity. Finally, on the other wing of the church were those conformist clergy, still a small number in 1603, who repudiated Calvinism both as doctrine and as a style of piety. They have been described as 'avant-garde conformists', as 'anti-Calvinists', or as forerunners of the 'Arminian' and 'Laudian' groups that emerged in the 1620s, but their characteristics were diverse, ranging from a rejection of predestinarianism to an elevation of prayer, from a dislike of excessive preaching to an emphasis on the sacrament of the Eucharist.

There are some trends – experimental predestinarianism is more characteristic of the radical Nonconformists or the conformable Calvinists than the other groups – and some striking exceptions. The point of such a breakdown is not to pigeonhole every clerical position but to highlight the issues around which individuals moved. As the work of Lake, Fincham and Webster has shown, individuals combined their views in different ways at different times.[21] Attitudes towards conformity changed as the definition of conformity changed. There is no better example of such change, or of the fluidity of religious labels, than the term 'puritan'. Puritanism in the 1570s and 1580s was applied to that radical element among the clergy who advocated quite specific reform of the church in a Calvinist and Presbyterian direction. Historians, notably Lake and Collinson, have also discerned a 'moderate puritanism' that promoted clerical conformity as the price of fighting off Antichrist and advancing the Reformation, a position, moreover, which could be espoused quite comfortably by a bishop. Often identified with the views and name of Archbishop Grindal, the archbishop who stood up to Queen Elizabeth to defend preaching conferences or 'prophesyings', this ideal of an evangelical episcopate persisted well into the seventeenth century. Collinson argues that after organised Presbyterianism was crushed in the 1590s, some of its values fed a diffuse spiritual tendency among lay and clerical individuals and in certain localities and towns: this godly outlook, centred on the Bible, preaching, predestination and the Sabbath, had become the leading edge of the conformist church by 1603. Collinson has also suggested that puritanism was largely reinvented as an attributed set of characteristics, a hostile stereotype of eye-rolling, hypocrisy and cant, by the satirists and yellow press of the 1590s. This was a polemical construct that led to the stock figure of the puritan on the Jacobean stage, to Malvolio and Tribulation Wholesome, but had little connection with the realities of the Jacobean church. As a product of controversy, the label 'puritan' would always enjoy a double life as a term of abuse and a descriptive label. If we judge from letters and diaries, rather than the more obviously public sources such as plays, pamphlets and sermons, then we are left in little doubt that the Jacobean English could spot a real puritan when they met one and that they did meet such people both among the clergy and lay folk. Seventeenth-century puritanism was a form of religious expression and one that attracted a sizeable minority of the English.

The religion of the lay people

The Elizabethan divine Richard Hooker asserted that 'there is not any man of the Church of England, but the same man is also a member of the commonwealth; nor any man a member of the commonwealth which is not also of the Church of England'. This was a pious wish or a political fiction rather than a statement of reality. Despite the legal obligation to attend the parish church, a sizeable minority of the population stayed away. Roman Catholic recusants were fined and listed and so we can say that nationally 2 per cent of the adult population fell into this category. But this is a worrying statistic. There were presumably other Catholic absentees, too poor and insignificant to warrant prosecution. Closer attention to recusancy returns has raised the possibility that recusants who were fully involved in the life of their community, perhaps holding office or with other responsibilities, may have been tactfully overlooked when the constables or churchwardens were making their reports.[22] The church papists can hardly be judged regular or serious supporters of the parish church; they saw themselves as Catholics. Sir John Petre, who maintained a Catholic household in Essex, still went to the parish services: 'do you think there are not [those] that go to the church that bear as good a mind to Godwards as those that refuse, yes, and if occasion serve, will be able to do better service than they which refuse to go to the church?'[23] A larger but more amorphous group of absentees were the young, the feckless, the quarrelsome, the dissolute and the drunk, some of whom were officially cut off from the church by a sentence of excommunication, others simply skulking out of sight of the churchwardens and their neighbours. The difficulty of estimating the size of this group will be discussed in Chapter 9, but it may have been somewhere in the order of 10 per cent of the adult population. Buried within this group, there were undoubtedly those who we might call separatists, individuals whose Protestant religious principles led them to form their own congregations and not to worship alongside the ignorant and profane sinners in the parish church. The persecution of Brownists and Anabaptists under Elizabeth, including the execution of 'frantick Hacket', a self-proclaimed Messiah, in 1591, and Barrow, Greenwood and Penry in 1593, temporarily cowed the separatists.

Recently historians have begun to recognise that there was another strand of radical sectarianism that did not hive off from the parish church. For a variety of reasons, including the belief that there was no obligation to volunteer for persecution or that ceremonies were of no real significance, some individuals and groups with spectacularly unorthodox ideas conformed quite happily. John Etherington, a London box-maker, whose story has been pieced together by Peter Lake, was a meticulous conformist in attending church and respecting the rituals, yet he was also mixed up in the heretical Family of Love and London antinomianism.[24]

Notwithstanding the drunks, recusants and separatists, most of the population were conforming members of the Church of England. They attended church routinely and it is a fair bet that most were God-fearing folk who sought to live as good Christians in this world and hoped to enjoy eternal life as one of the saved in the next. As we will see in later chapters, they identified with the parish and the church building, with the churchyard where their ancestors were buried, and with the community whose values and rites were celebrated by the church. None of this *necessarily means* that they took any notice of what the clergyman taught in the pulpit or the catechism class or that they were fascinated by the details of predestinarian doctrine. The character of popular conformist belief is one of the most impenetrable problems facing historians of the seventeenth century. Where did the religious allegiance of the ordinary man or woman in the pews lie? What did they understand and accept of the Reformation and the Protestant gospel?

The answers rather depend on whom you ask. The godly clergy generally took a downbeat line. A meeting of ministers in 1604 judged that there were three types of lay people in their congregations: 'those effectually called by the preaching of the gospel to the more sincere profession of religion'; those who despite all preaching were 'ignorant and superstitious' and regretted the loss of the mass; and the 'indifferent' who 'greatly regard not of which religion they be'.[25] But then this was the standard view of the evangelical clergy who suspected that the Reformation had failed to work a transformation of the nation. They had precise expectations of their flocks. Christians should understand and live by the central Protestant doctrine of justification by faith alone. But, as William Perkins complained, too many of the English believed that faith was no more than an individual's good intentions, that the core of religion was loving our neighbours as ourselves, and that however a man lived 'yet if he call upon God on his deathbed, and say *Lord have mercy upon me* . . . he is certainly saved'. In 1602 Josias Nichols examined four hundred communicants in one Kent parish and found that there was 'scarce one but did affirm that a man might be saved by his own well-doing, and that he trusted that he did so live, that by God's grace he should obtain everlasting life by serving of God and good prayers'. These stereotyped complaints were aimed at deficient clergymen as well as the apathetic laity. Richard Kilby, a Derby minister, believed that his own superficial religious education was all too typical. 'I was a little taught outward religion. That is, to say the Lord's Prayer and the Creed by rote, to go to church upon Sabbath days and hear service, yea and, after I could read, to answer the minister in the saying of Psalms etc. Having done thus, what? . . . Oh I thought I had done enough.' It was the clergy's duty to inculcate a more profound and inward religion in their flocks, to preach powerfully, to pray with them, to catechise and advise them. The effective minister was always self-critical and responsive to the needs and abilities of his flock. Kilby was keenly aware of the danger of preaching over the people's heads; his advice was to use the Bible and keep it simple and short: 'most people for some three quarters of an hour if they understand the words and perceive the matter concerning their salvation to be plainly proved out of the word of God . . . will give very diligent ear'.[26] The suggestion that Protestant doctrine, even in its Calvinist formulation, was inherently too difficult for ordinary people is palpably absurd: plenty of uneducated individuals took these ideas to heart in the seventeenth century. The different question of whether such doctrines could ever win a mass following is not so easily answered. This system of belief required a commitment to Bible study and sermon-going; it needed a high degree of spiritual self-confidence; and, of course, Calvinism was based on the idea that only some people were 'elect'. There was much in it that implied it was destined to be a minority faith.

On the strength of gloomy clerical comments, some scholars have argued that there was a common-sense attitude among the English peasantry that God would not turn his back on those who lived by the basic Christian rule of 'do unto others as you would be done by'. Fostered over generations by the simple moral instruction of the medieval church, in keeping with the reciprocal duties of agrarian communal life, such principles were far deeper rooted in most individuals than the paradoxical theology of justification by faith and predestination could ever hope to be. If the moral and theological certainties of older ways still lingered, then perhaps so too did a preference for traditional forms of worship. Haigh has made a case that even in 1603 a large part of the population was still subconsciously attached to the old popish ways, thanks to the ease with which traditional worship could be grafted on to the forms of the Prayer Book.[27]

It was precisely all those aspects denounced by puritans as reminiscent of popery – the vestments, the sign of the cross, kneeling, communion wafers – which attracted the conservatives. The inherent difficulty of proving such a case, given the available evidence, has been one reason why Haigh's views have not commanded widespread assent. But such arguments focus attention on the perplexing problem of how we might gauge popular appreciation of Prayer Book worship. Maltby has reported parishioners' complaints about ministers who did not read the service well or at all: for instance, the churchwardens of Kimcoate, Leicestershire, complained in 1602 that their parson 'breaks the order of the church and the Book of Common Prayer'.[28] Although we can rarely be certain why such allegations were launched, they do at least show that some parishioners possessed a good knowledge of the Prayer Book.

It is unlikely that popular belief can ever be the subject of systematic quantitative study: historians have largely abandoned the search for precise measures of explicit religious allegiance – such as the opening clauses of wills – and instead have begun to concentrate on seeing religious belief and behaviour in the wider context of lay ideas and attitudes.[29] The laity's ideas about what went on in church are not easily detached from their ideas about ghosts and witches, apparitions and charms, dreams and astrology, fortune and fate. What we might call 'superstition' and 'folk belief' were powerful forces shaping individuals at every level of society in the seventeenth century, as were those deeply internalised notions about what was appropriate to particular age groups or to the different sexes. The insights and the interpretive difficulties that arise from this kind of approach are easily demonstrated by considering some of the ways that religious beliefs meshed with contemporary notions of male and female.

The Protestant Reformation has often been portrayed as strengthening prevailing patriarchal assumptions. It repudiated the ideal of celibacy and elevated marriage as a religious calling, it emphasised the role of the father and amplified the more misogynistic messages of scripture – 'remember, thy sex is crazy, ever since Eve sinned' – and it invested the godly household with a spiritual purpose as the nursery of true religion.[30] Relentlessly repeated from the pulpit, this ideology was also conveyed in a distinct and popular genre of conduct books with titles like *A Godly Form of Household Government* or *Domesticall Duties*. However, another facet of this patriarchal propaganda idealised the godly wife and mother, the virtuous female 'saint'. As we will see in a later chapter, many women did value and seize the spiritual opportunities available to them within the domestic sphere. In some cases, they also embraced the underlying suggestion that, whereas the male sex was ruled by rationality and intellect, the female sex was better able to sublimate personality and intellect and surrender more completely to the will and love of God. Common notions of women as 'ardent' or as 'empty vessels' channelled female piety towards experiences of 'rapture' and 'possession by God'. This was dangerous talk: on the one hand, it provided a distinct, even enviable, form of piety that suited the socially and educationally subordinate position of women; on the other, it could be used to explain away the deluded women who followed the sects and prophets, and by invoking their alleged susceptibility to emotional appeals, it merely served to confirm the irrational nature of such heterodox movements. Even the language of religion was gendered in various ways. While the terminology of theology, religious controversy, and even many sermons was resolutely masculine – think of all the kings, battles, tribes and martial imagery of the Old Testament so beloved of seventeenth-century preachers – the vocabulary of devotion took a different turn. The Christian soul, irrespective of the individual's gender, adopted a sexualised language of physical love, of marriage to Christ, that also drew on scriptural exemplars such as the *Song of Songs*: 'many a sweet, sweet soft kiss, many perfumed well smelled kisses and embracements have I received of my royal master', wrote one Scottish minister, 'we cannot rest till we be in other's arms.'[31] It seems apparent, then, that questions of gender, so fundamental to the exploration of any past society, will illuminate religious attitudes and vice versa.

In recent years, students of popular religion in the early modern period have increasingly taken a new tack by reversing traditional priorities. So instead of defining 'Protestantism' at the outset of their investigation, they have suspended judgement and pursued their material, whether it is folk belief or the trade in cheap pious books, until it has offered up an idea of what it was to be a Protestant in the Post-Reformation. In one of the most fruitful examples of this principle in practice, Walsham has tracked the notion of divine providence through ballads, chapbooks, prodigies and woodcuts as well as sermons and theological works. She follows her sources into the world of cheap print, hack authors and booksellers in order to identify and map a sensibility which was a major part of the early seventeenth-century popular world-view. Such astute research has suggested that at the popular level the Reformation was less the simple replacement of Catholic doctrine by Protestant doctrine than 'a gradual modification of traditional piety'. So we can say that even in 1603 the piety of many individuals was still intensely visual, still attached to heroes, albeit now Protestant martyrs rather than Catholic saints, and still preoccupied with notions of morality as 'good neighbourliness'. 'The resulting patch-work of beliefs may be described as distinctively "post-Reformation",' concluded Tessa Watt, 'but not thoroughly "Protestant".' No one would dispute the quotation marks around 'Protestant', even if they might argue that contemporaries saw themselves as 'Protestant' *whatever that meant.* Some historians would perhaps want to lay more emphasis on the word 'patchwork' to draw attention to the sheer number of different versions of belief, every one of them an idiosyncratic, provisional, personal 'take' on religion, and all of them jostling for space and a hearing.[32] It was that contest which animated the political story that follows.

Notes

1 A. Ford, 'Dependent or Independent? The Church of Ireland and its Colonial Context, 1536–1649', *17C*, 10 (1995), 166.

2 P. Collinson, *The Birthpangs of Protestant England* (Basingstoke, 1988), p. ix.

3 M.C. Questier, 'What Happened to English Catholicism after the English Reformation?' *History*, 85 (2000), 41.

4 M. Rowlands (ed.), *English Catholics of Parish and Town 1558–1778* (Catholic Record Society, 1999); A. Walsham, *Church Papists* (1993).

5 P. Lake with M. Questier, *The Antichrist's Lewd Hat: Protestants, Papists and Players in Post-Reformation England* (New Haven, Conn., 2002), p. 321.

6 F. Heal, *Reformation in Britain and Ireland* (Oxford, 2003), p. 364.

7 M. Todd, *The Culture of Protestantism in Early Modern Scotland* (New Haven, Conn., 2002), p. 409.

8 J. Dawson, 'Calvinism and the Gaidhealtachd in Scotland', in A. Pettegree, A. Duke and G. Lewis (eds), *Calvinism in Europe 1540–1620* (Cambridge, 1994).

9 M. Mullett, *Catholics in Britain and Ireland, 1558–1829* (Basingstoke, 1998), p. 53.

10 D.G. Mullan, *Scottish Puritanism, 1590–1638* (Oxford, 2000), p. 259.

11 A. Ford, *The Protestant Reformation in Ireland, 1590–1641* (Frankfurt, 1987; reissued Dublin, 1997), p. 27.

12 C. Hill, *A Turbulent, Seditious, and Factious People: John Bunyan and his Church* (Oxford, 1989), p. 183.

13 M. McClure, *The Paul's Cross Sermons 1534–1642* (Toronto, 1958), p. 245.

14 P. Croft, *King James* (Basingstoke, 2003), p. 132.

15 Collinson, *Birthpangs*, p. 10.

16 Collinson, *Birthpangs*, p. 17.

17 G.H. Jenkins, *The Foundation of Modern Wales: 1642–1780* (Oxford, 1987), p. 214.

18 Todd, *Culture of Protestantism in Early Modern Scotland*, p. 404.

19 A.I. MacInnes, *The British Revolution, 1629–1660* (Basingstoke, 2005), p. 31; Collinson, *Birthpangs*, p. 18.

20 R.T. Kendall, *Calvin and English Calvinism to 1649* (Oxford, 1979); also see P. Lake, 'Calvinism and the English Church 1570–1635', *P&P*, 114 (1987).

21 K. Fincham, *Prelate as Pastor: The Episcopate of James I* (Oxford, 1990); P. Lake, *Moderate Puritans and the Elizabethan Church* (Cambridge, 1982); P. Lake and M. Questier (eds), *Conformity and Orthodoxy in the English Church c.1560–1660* (Woodbridge, 2000); T. Webster, *Godly Clergy in Early Stuart England: The Caroline Puritan Movement, c.1620–1643* (Cambridge, 1997).

22 W. J. Sheils, 'Household, Age and Gender among Jacobean Yorkshire Recusants', in M. Rowlands (ed.), *English Catholics*.

23 Walsham, *Church Papists*, p. 82.

24 P. Lake, *The Boxmaker's Revenge: 'Orthodoxy', 'Heterodoxy' and the Politics of the Parish in Early Stuart London* (Manchester, 2001).

25 Spurr, *EP*, p. 41.

26 Perkins, Nichols and Kilby are quoted in C. Haigh, 'Success and Failure in the English Reformation', *P&P*, 173 (2001), 31, 47–8; also see Haigh, 'The Taming of Reformation: Preachers, Pastors and Parishioners in Elizabethan and Early Stuart England', *History*, 85 (2000); P. Lake, 'Richard Kilby: A Study in Personal and Professional Failure', *SCH*, 26 (1989); E.J. Carlson, 'Good Pastors or Careless Shepherds? Parish Ministers and the English Reformation', *History*, 88 (2003).

27 See C. Haigh, *English Reformations* (Oxford, 1993), pp. 290–3.

28 J. Maltby, *Prayer Book and People in Elizabethan and Early Stuart England* (Cambridge, 1998), pp. 42–3.

29 On the limitations of wills see C. Marsh, '"Departing Well and Christianly": Will-making and Popular Religion in Early Modern England', in E.J. Carlson (ed.), *Religion and the English People 1500–1640* (Kirksville, Mo., 1998).

30 B. Capp, *When Gossips Meet: Women, Family and Neighbourhood in Early Modern England* (Oxford, 2003), p. 3.

31 S. Hardman Moore, 'Sexing the Soul: Gender and the Rhetoric of Puritan Piety', *SCH*, 34 (1998), p. 177.

32 A. Walsham, *Providence in Early Modern England* (Oxford, 1999), p. 5; T. Watt, *Cheap Print and Popular Piety, 1550–1640* (Cambridge, 1991), p. 327; N. Jones, *The English Reformation* (Oxford, 2002), p. 6; P. Lake with M. Questier, *The Antichrist's Lewd Hat*, pp. 318, 715.

PART ONE

Religion and politics

Introduction

The Reformation brought religion to the centre of the British political stage. It set in train changes that were to be felt long after the supposed 'settlements' of the 1560s. It left questions unanswered and hopes unfulfilled. Much of the history of seventeenth-century politics can be told in terms of competing impulses to advance, complete or reverse the Reformation: in the 1630s, Archbishop Laud wanted to return the Church of England to its first reformation; in the early 1640s preachers exhorted Parliament 'to finish this much-desired Reformation', to complete the 'perfecting of the Reformation', and 'to bring us back not only to our first Reformation in King Edward's day, but to reform the Reformation itself'.[1] The abolition of the Church of England in the 1640s was justified in the *Directory for the Public Worship* (1645) by 'the gracious providence of God, which at this time calls upon us for further reformation, and may satisfy our own consciences, and answer the expectation of other reformed churches, and the desires of many of the godly among ourselves'. In 1688 William of Orange invaded England and toppled James II to save Protestantism and liberty and to advance the Reformation. Protestantism was once again in danger when the Jacobite Rebellion of 1715 raised the spectre of a popish ruler who would tear up the laws, destroy liberty, and persecute 'all his subjects into the exercise of his own superstitious, idolatrous and cruel religion'.[2]

Protestantism inspired messianic ideals about national destiny and mission. The English were God's chosen people, England was another Israel, Scotland was the bride of Christ. The religion of the British kingdoms was of international significance. In the 1640s, John Milton believed that England was chosen before any other nation so 'that out of her, as out of Sion, should be proclaimed and sounded forth the first tidings and trumpet of Reformation to all Europe'. Reformation was not only institutional and national, it was also moral and personal: 'first reform your own families,' urged a parliamentary fast preacher in 1641, 'and then you will be the fitter to reform the family of God. Let the master reform his servant, the father his child, the husband his wife.'[3] 'If ever we expect a national reformation,' a preacher told one Nottingham congregation in 1698, 'it must take its first rise from our persons and families.'[4] The Elizabethan William Perkins complained that 'in many places of our land there is by God's blessing much teaching, yet there is little reformation in the lives of most'. And in 1688, English preachers told their congregations that 'a national reformation is now expected by the Lord'.[5] Burnet's *Discourse of Pastoral Care* (1692) aimed at 'the completing of our Reformation, especially in the lives and manners of men'.[6] The personal was political in the seventeenth century. Divine providence saw to that. God's oversight of the world included indisputable messages for the nation as a moral entity. Wars, fires, plagues and second chances were dished out to the English, Irish and Scots as if they were so many errant children in need of well-meant correction from a stern, yet loving, father. In the eyes of many, this was precisely what they were: 'Where is our reformation in one point,' asked John Evelyn in 1679, 'after all the powerful preaching, sacred ordinances, and a million distinguishing favours accumulated on us?'[7]

Yet for all this, the seventeenth century did not undergo 'a long Reformation', a single campaign to create a Protestant nation and church. The seventeenth century experienced a Post-Reformation contest between several versions of Reformation.[8] Disagreeing with each other about the most fundamental questions such as the constitution of the true church, the economy of salvation, or the nature of meaningful worship, and vying with each other for freedom and primacy, the zealous of all denominations naturally laid claim to the legacy and rhetoric of Reformation. They were just as strident in denouncing its abuse by their opponents. 'The devil of rebellion doth commonly turn himself into an angel of reformation,' warned *Eikon Basilike*, the voice of the martyred Charles I, 'it is no news to have all innovations ushered in with the name of reformations in church and state.'[9] But the game had moved on since the Tudors and their Reformation. The distinctive characteristics of the Post-Reformation century were to be religious innovation and competition.

Notes

1   Edmund Calamy, *England's Looking Glass* (1642), preface; Cornelius Burges, *Two Sermons Preached to the Honourable House of Commons . . . 17 Nov. 1640* (1641), sig. A3v; Edmund Calamy, *A Sermon Preached before the House of Commons . . . November 17 1640* (1641), p. 40.

2   C. Haydon, *Anti-Catholicism in Eighteenth-century England* (Manchester, 1993), p. 93.

3   Calamy, *England's Looking Glass*, p. 60.

4   Daniel Chadwick, *A Sermon Preached in the Church of St Mary in Nottingham* (1698), pp. 45–6.

5   T. Claydon, *William III and the Godly Revolution* (Cambridge, 1996), p. 60.

6   Gilbert Burnet, *Discourse of Pastoral Care* (1692), sig. A3r.

7   BL, Add. MS 78299, fo. 1.

8   The essays in N. Tyacke (ed.), *England's Long Reformation 1500–1800* (1998), document some of these rival notions of 'reformation' in detail. Reformation is also a prominent theme of recent work by Gary De Krey, now reprised in his *London and the Restoration 1659–1683* (Cambridge, 2005).

9   *Eikon Basilike*, ed. P.A. Knachel (1966), pp. 94, 160.

CHAPTER 2

James I (1603–25)

At the death of an English monarch, the authority of most officials 'is expired with the prince's breath' and the fortunes of ministers, courtiers, policies and even churches hang on the needs and whim of the new sovereign. So no wonder the English were anxious when Elizabeth Tudor finally relinquished her hold on life in 1603, for her successor was a foreigner, James Stuart, James VI of Scotland. Despite all the political machinations of Robert Cecil, the architect of James's succession, many were unsure what to expect of their new monarch, who was a vigorous adult with sons, a tried ruler, a Calvinist but no Presbyterian, and the son of Mary, Queen of Scots, a Roman Catholic 'martyr' who had died at the hands of Elizabeth I. In London, where 'there was a diligent watch and ward kept at every gate and street, day and night, by householders', the proclamation of the King was greeted with 'silent joy, no great shouting'. Thomas Wentworth later recalled 'all men expecting upon the death of our late famous Queen Elizabeth that we should have been forced like Rachel to have fled with our God and with Jacob to have been fugitives too with our wives and families'. Even allowing for rhetorical exaggeration, Wentworth captures something of the wariness with which the English regarded their new king.[1]

James immediately sought to reassure his new subjects. Within days of Elizabeth's death, there appeared in London a new edition of James's book *Basilikon Doron*, his 1599 manual on kingship addressed to his son Prince Henry. James pronounced himself 'ever for the medium in everything'. He regarded the ceremonies in the public worship of the church, the wearing of surplices by the clergy, and government of the church by bishops as 'indifferent things', matters undecided by God and left to human authority. Moreover, he would respect clergymen who took different views on such matters. What he would not tolerate were those he called puritans, in other words those such as Anabaptists, sectaries, and unbending Presbyterians who opposed royal authority. As he advised his son, 'cherish no man more than a good pastor, hate no man more than a proud puritan'. Roman Catholics were similarly beyond the pale if they upheld the doctrine that the pope had the right to depose heretical rulers. He abhorred the 'two extremities' of religion: 'to believe with the papists, the church's authority, better than your own knowledge' or 'to lean with the Anabaptists, to your own conceits and dreamed revelations'.[2] Yet James also let it be known that there would be opportunities and rewards on offer, and soon people were full of expectations 'of our nation's future greatness; every one promises himself a share in some famous action to be hereafter performed for his prince and country. They assure themselves of the continuance of our church government and doctrine.'[3] Archbishop Whitgift wrote to the bishops that James 'is received with as great unity and applause as ever prince was into any country'.[4]

As anxieties subsided, they were succeeded in some minds by a crazy optimism. A London-based commentator observed that 'these bountiful beginnings raise all men's spirits and put them in great hopes, insomuch that not only Protestants, but papists and puritans, and the very poets with their idle pamphlets promise themselves great part in his favour'.[5] The situation bred high, often conflicting, expectations of the new king. Taking their cue from James's own book, the puritans who petitioned him as he journeyed south portrayed themselves 'neither as factious men affecting a popular parity in the church, nor as schismatics aiming at the dissolution of the state ecclesiastical', but as faithful ministers 'all groaning as under a common burden of human rites and ceremonies'.[6] They turned James's own metaphor back on him by calling on the King 'as a good physician' to heal the church and they supplied a long list of its ailments in every area from the liturgy and ceremonies, to the way that the clergy were appointed and paid, and the operation of the church court system. Catholics who had been making overtures to the Elizabethan regime for toleration in return for a commitment of political loyalty saw the accession of James as a heaven-sent opportunity: 'they had loved the mother [Mary, Queen of Scots] therefore they would with all gladness have embraced the son'. Their hopes soared: as Robert Cecil complained to the Venetian ambassador in March 1605, 'the King's excessive clemency has ended in this, that priests go openly about the country, the city, and private houses saying mass, and this gives great offence'.[7]

Jacobean policy

The Hampton Court Conference of January 1604 was convened in response to puritan petitioning. Some have seen it as a forum on the deficiencies of the Church of England, while for others it was the church's showdown with a recalcitrant puritan faction. The representatives of the bishops and of the puritans were hand-picked by the government and there is more than a suspicion that the event was stage-managed so that James could make his antipathy to Presbyterianism plain: his famous maxim, 'no bishop, no king', meaning that Presbyterianism was inimical to monarchy, was uttered twice at the gathering. But this was also a genuine effort at reform. The Prayer Book was revised in small ways, the catechism was extended, a new translation of the Bible was initiated, the laws on excommunication and the practice of pluralism received attention, and the bishops were exhorted to provide resources for 'the planting of a learned and painful minister in every parish'. The meeting closed amicably, but several issues remained unresolved and later in the year the Commons returned to them by offering bills to provide a learned and godly ministry, tackle pluralism, remove scandalous and unworthy ministers, and prevent the appointment of clergy as JPs. James saw this initiative as a breach of MPs' oath of supremacy: 'in things that are against the word of God I will with as great humility as any slave fall upon my knees or face; but in things indifferent they are seditious which obey not the magistrate'. The King was prepared to treat with clemency those troubled by scruples of conscience, 'but let them meet me with obedience'. This was the abiding message from James to religious dissidents. If they obeyed him, then he would respect their conscience so far as was possible. The Jacobean Church of England was to embrace as many as possible but on the King's terms.

On 16 July James issued a proclamation which reminded the scrupulous ministers of the reforms agreed at Hampton Court and ordered the bishops to 'reclaim' such clergy 'by conferences, arguments, persuasions, and by all other ways of love and gentleness'. Yet there was a sting in the tail. 'But if our hope herein fail us, we must advertise them that our duty towards God requires at our hands that what intractable men do not perform upon admonition they must be compelled unto by authority.' The mechanism for compulsion was subscription to three articles originally drawn up by Whitgift in 1583. Ministers had to recognise the King's temporal and spiritual supremacy, acknowledge that the Prayer Book contained nothing contrary to the word of God, and accept that all of the Thirty-nine Articles were 'agreeable to the word of God'. In September

1604 under the new canons or by-laws for the church agreed by Convocation and licensed by James, all entering the ministry or taking a new living were required to sign this acknowledgment. To the King this was a way of discerning 'the affections of persons, whether quiet or turbulent', and a means of encouraging wavering ministers to side with the church. Once the clergy had demonstrated their commitment by subscribing to the articles, their subsequent conformity to the liturgy was of less concern to the King and his bishops. Subscription was a hurdle to jump. James was making a point about clerical obedience. Provided that ministers had acknowledged his authority, he would not enquire too closely into their conformity thereafter.

Over the next few years the bishops used their discretion to extract subscription from the clergy. There was no wholesale purge of puritan ministers from the church. Fincham has estimated that between seventy-three and eighty-three beneficed clergy were deprived for non-subscription between 1604 and 1609, and the majority of them before 1607. Several found alternative employment as chaplains in sympathetic godly households. Both the Privy Council under Cecil's leadership and many of the bishops consciously sought to moderate the policy of conformity. Bishops Hutton of York and Rudd of St David's doubted the wisdom and even the legality of the policy: they questioned the underlying assumption that the 'puritans' represented as serious a threat as the papists; and they were reluctant to silence some of the most effective and popular preachers in their dioceses. 'There hath been a great deal of cunning used by the bishops,' observed Samuel Hieron, 'to blind the eyes of higher authority, and to stop the clamours of the people.'[8] The depth and breadth of the commitment to an evangelical preaching ministry and the relative indifference towards strict ceremonial conformity can be seen in the attitudes of men like worldly-wise Cecil, of the evangelical bishops, and of those gentlemen who pulled strings or openly petitioned in defence of the nonconforming clergy or lobbied in Parliament.

Meanwhile the King attempted to make good the promises of Hampton Court. He repeatedly instructed the bishops to take action against non-resident clergymen and to order every pluralist to provide a preaching curate in the parishes where the incumbent did not reside. His archbishop proposed a bill to restore impropriated tithes to vicars and curates but could not get it through Parliament. The authorised version of the Bible, the 'King James Bible', appeared from the printing press in 1611. Its preface proclaimed the King's intention to advance religion 'by frequenting the house of God, by hearing the word preached, by cherishing the teachers thereof, by caring for the church, as a most tender and loving nursing father'.

*

James applied the same policy of distinguishing between dangerous dissidents and loyal subjects to the English Catholic community. He had good reason. His leniency and the passive obedience of the majority of the 40,000 English Catholics was compromised by the minority of zealots who dreamed of restoring Roman Catholicism by force of arms and with Spanish help. James ordered the enforcement of recusancy fines in response to the continual plotting of the frustrated fringe groups. While some of these conspiracies such as the Main and Bye plots of 1603 were real enough, others like the rising of a thousand men in Wales led by a priest and Morgan Clynnog, 'a cunning man in prophecy', were little more than rumours and scares. Then a plot was discovered which would have seen King, Lords and Commons blown sky high at the opening of Parliament on 5 November 1605. James became all the more precious to his shocked subjects on account of his narrow escape. Parliament voted him a large grant of taxation; the 5 November became an annual national day of thanksgiving for the happy deliverance of James and Parliament 'from the most traitorous and bloody intended massacre by gunpowder'; and antipopery became even further entrenched in the national psyche. Preachers argued that 'if papists were not blinded by superstition and hardened in idolatry' they would have recognised the failures of 1588 and 1605 as proof that God fights on the Protestant side.[9] Almost immediately two penal statutes were passed by Parliament. One banned Catholics from holding public office or living within the vicinity of London. The other, an 'act for the better discovering and repressing of popish recusants', re-enacted the Elizabethan penal laws and instituted an oath of allegiance. This act was explicitly aimed against those with 'evil affections to the King's majesty and the state of this his realm'. James claimed that he sought to identify the disloyal from those of his 'subjects, who although they were otherwise popishly affected, yet retain in their hearts the print of their natural duty to their sovereign'. The oath of allegiance included an acknowledgement of the lawfulness of James's sovereignty and a repudiation of the pope's alleged right to depose rulers. English Roman Catholics debated among themselves the weight to be given to this papal 'deposing power'. Many certainly did not see it as part of the essential doctrines of the Catholic faith. James could therefore be seen as distinguishing quite legitimately between civil allegiance and religious loyalty and even as moving towards finding some way of tolerating the religion of his Catholic subjects. On the other hand, it has been argued by J.V. Gifford and Michael Questier that the oath was a far more objectionable imposition on Catholic consciences than James pretended. Sensitive to the ways in which the oath was received by Catholics and used by the authorities, Questier suggests that it was a deliberate attempt to confuse several issues – notably in requiring the denial as 'impious and heretical [of] this damnable doctrine and position that princes which be excommunicated or deprived by the pope may be deposed or murdered by their subjects or any other' – and that some Catholics would view this as a denial of the pope's primacy. If so, and if deliberate, James was being far less accommodating to the English Catholics than he has often been painted.[10]

James certainly detested the Jesuits, those 'venomed wasps and firebrands of sedition', but he and his councillors were reluctant to unleash the full terror of the law even against the missionaries. In 1608 he told the judges that he wanted 'no torrent of blood': a grand total of nineteen Catholic priests were executed during his reign.[11] At court, James was surrounded by secret or not so secret Catholics: he had been advised in Scotland by the Catholic Huntly; in England he permitted the Earl of Northampton, Edward Lord Wotton and Sir George Calvert to exercise influence. In the Privy Council, Archbishop Bancroft repeatedly fulminated against the influence of these and others such as the Earls of Shrewsbury, Suffolk and Worcester. Northampton was certainly able to restrain the persecution of the English Catholics. It would be fair to say that James's ambiguous attitude towards Rome confused many. He recognised the Roman Church as a true church but one that contained errors of belief and practice. He entertained hopes of reuniting the Christian churches and repairing the divisions caused by the Reformation. He unsuccessfully lobbied the papacy for a general council of Christian princes to promote reunion based on scripture and the practice of the early church. Yet as the oath of allegiance made clear, James found the papal deposing power unacceptable, even impious, heretical and damnable. In his contributions to the international debate over the oath of allegiance, James stressed that at bottom this was a matter of secular politics but he also denounced the pope as Antichrist. James's notoriously loquacious manner caused trouble. It was rumoured that the pope had complained to the French King that James 'misuses him continually in table-talk and calls him Antichrist at every word: which doth so incense his holiness that some papists fear it may drive him to thunder and lighten with excommunication'. Catholic priests scratched their heads as they wondered how this abuse of the papacy could be reconciled with James's other statements about recognising the pope as one of the four patriarchs of the church. James even admitted to the Spanish ambassador that he had only identified the pope as Antichrist in print because of papal claims 'in deposing and setting up Kings at his will'.[12]

The assassination of Henri IV of France, a convert from Protestantism, by a Catholic monk in 1610 deepened English anxieties about Catholic extremists. An alarmed James pursued Catholic priests under the penal laws and a handful were executed. A crackdown against recusants was ordered, but, as so often, the impact of recusancy fines was compromised by the fact that their collection had been delegated to the Exchequer, a cumbersome and inefficient system that was open to abuse. The primacy of financial motives in the crown's dealings with Roman Catholics is suggested by the rumours that periodically swept the Catholic community that the King would offer them freedom from the recusancy laws in return for an annual 'composition' of £20,000. On their side, Catholic gentlemen flocked to buy the new titles of baronet in 1611 as a demonstration of their loyalty and subsequently threw themselves into the unpaid work of local government as further proof of their dependability.

The Catholic question was a more complex issue than most, not simply because of the diversity of English Catholicism, but also because of the Irish, Scottish and continental European ramifications of almost any issue involving the treatment of Catholics. Alongside his ambitions to be an international peacemaker, James was also concerned to arrange appropriate marriages for his children. For his heir, Prince Henry, James planned a marriage to a princess from France, Spain, Savoy or Florence, all of them staunchly Catholic dynasties. Henry, however, was a charismatic, able and independent prince at the heart of a circle of committed Protestants. He was not going to be pushed into any arranged marriage with an idolator. He was said to have consulted ten or twelve of the best ministers who had advised him against a Catholic marriage and to have concluded that 'he would never marry with any such'. It was also claimed that Henry had said 'religion lay a bleeding' because so many royal councillors were covert papists and tools of the Jesuits. His death from typhoid in November 1612 was a major blow to those 'forward' or belligerent Protestants who had associated their cause with him. They proclaimed their distress from the pulpit and laid the blame at the feet of religious indifference, atheism and sacrilege: 'What could have taken away that sweet prince, of fresh and bleeding memory, the expectation of all the Christian world, but our lukewarmness?' They stressed the danger of toleration, 'a Machiavellian policy', which they were certain would be the price of any popish marriage. In response, James was forced to profess 'his constancy in religion' to the Privy Council and spell out the terms that had been under discussion with Savoy.[13] Despite such pressure, James was not to be deflected from his purpose, and he now shifted the attention of the marriage negotiations to Charles, his younger son. Meanwhile, he could point to the marriage of his daughter Elizabeth to a Calvinist prince, Elector Frederick V of the Palatinate, as evidence of the religious even-handedness of his dynastic policy.

*

How did James I shape the Church of England? As supreme governor, monarchs could exert a powerful influence on the complexion of the church: royal preferences in doctrine and worship, appointments to bishoprics and other key posts, and, of course, the wider religious policies adopted by the government towards religious dissidents and minorities were all significant forces in moulding the national church. By issuing royal injunctions and other instructions, the King was able to keep up the pressure on the church and its officials for reform: in July 1610 James responded to parliamentary complaints by firing off a set of instructions to the bishops about pluralism, non-residence, recusancy, the church courts, clerical dress, the upkeep of parsonages, and the provision of learned books in each parish. The following spring, he wanted to know what progress had been achieved in these areas. As an amateur theologian and Calvinist, James could also be expected to take an interest in the theological position of the Church of England. He recognised that article 17 of the Thirty-nine Articles committed the church to the Calvinist doctrine of predestination and he sought to align the English church with the Calvinist or Reformed churches of Europe. Thus in 1611 James protested against the appointment of the Remonstrant Conrad Vorstius to the chair of divinity at the Dutch university of Leiden. When the controversy between the two wings of Dutch Protestantism, Remonstrant and the Calvinist Contra-Remonstrants, precipitated a grand conference, the Synod of Dort in 1618–19, James sent a British delegation that sided with the Calvinist majority in denouncing and suppressing the followers of Jacob Arminius. He had publicly demonstrated to the rest of Europe that the Church of England was a Calvinist church. Yet James did not see any need for theology to lead to controversy back at home. He was happy to allow several theological viewpoints to coexist provided that they did not spill over into domestic quarrels. So much was evident from the sermons that he heard in his own court. James was an afficionado of preaching. He habitually arrived at chapel midway through the service and the minister would then break off the prayers and immediately enter the pulpit to preach. Thanks to McCullough, it is now realised that the court pulpit was a forum for competing views on a whole range of ecclesiastical and doctrinal matters.[14] James was treated to a healthy clerical debate within a generously defined conformity. True, some sermons were more controversial than others. In 1611 Bishop William Barlow praised the invocation of saints, auricular confession, and fasting, 'things entirely removed from the practice of religion in this kingdom', in the words of one observer.[15] Lancelot Andrewes even used court sermons to dissuade the King from devoting quite so much attention to preaching at the expense of prayer.

Although apparently happy to hear a range of views expressed in the court pulpit, James generally appointed a certain type of minister to the episcopate. These were orthodox Calvinists and antipapists with a commitment to efficient administration, orderly church life, and solid preaching in the parishes. Fincham, the authority on the Jacobean episcopate, distinguishes men like Archbishop Toby Matthew of York, Bishops King of London, Lake of Bath and Wells, and Morton of Coventry and Lichfield, among others, as 'evangelicals', zealous preachers and staunch opponents of popery with a strong personal sense of mission. Such bishops usually had a broad degree of sympathy for those among their clergy who scrupled strict conformity. Other bishops were just as orthodox in their Calvinism, but a shade less zealous, content to balance service to their flock with attention to the demands of their monarch. Archbishop Bancroft, for example, was more in the mould of his predecessor Whitgift, an orthodox Calvinist but also a convinced opponent of the Presbyterian movement. Bancroft was determined to strengthen the church by protecting its jurisdiction against other forces and codifying its laws. In 1604, while Bishop of London, he was probably the moving spirit behind Convocation's adoption of 141 canons in less than three weeks. There are hints, in, for instance, the sermons of his chaplains, that Bancroft was less tolerant than some of his brethren of those clergymen who did not conform fully to the Prayer Book. George Abbot, who succeeded Bancroft in 1611, was more concerned with the threat from popery than from clerical nonconformity. He was also increasingly perturbed by the growing influence of a small band of bishops, notably Lancelot Andrewes, John Buckeridge and Richard Neile, whose views were significantly out of kilter with majority opinion in the church. Labelled by historians as 'anti-Calvinists' or 'avant-garde conformists', these clergymen deplored the prevailing attitudes within the Jacobean Church of England. They resented the relaxed attitude towards clerical conformity, the overemphasis on preaching and the consequent downplaying of prayer and the sacraments, and the theological presumption of Calvinists who were convinced that they were among the small number of God's elect predestined to salvation for all eternity. What mattered, of course, was whether such views could harness any political support, whether the King would listen to their siren voices.

Seventeenth-century churchmen, especially bishops, were politicians. James I presided over a revival of the clergy's political influence (although his son was to outdo him). In 1610 Archbishop Bancroft pronounced that 'the King that now is, loves his clergy as ever any'.[16] James valued clergymen for their expertise in several fields. As a Christian prince, he expected to need and receive spiritual and theological advice; as a keen controversialist, he used his bishops and other divines as his foils and aids. He appointed several bishops to the Privy Council; Abbot was made first commissioner of the treasury in 1618 and Bishop Williams became Lord Keeper in 1621; bishops took a greater role in the Court of Star Chamber. Several clergymen were keen exponents of royal absolutism in the pulpit and in print. Andrewes was fulsome in his praise of both James and the institution of monarchy: the King was God's lieutenant on earth, supreme governor of the church by divine right, to whom total obedience was due. In the 1614 Parliament, Bishop Neile's defence of the royal prerogative provoked uproar. Indeed, the twenty-six bishops sitting in the Lords formed a block of reliable government votes. Whatever the disagreements among themselves, few were going to openly oppose the will of their royal master.

Political skills were also evident among the senior clergy when it became necessary to defend the interests of the church. With James's help, the bishops defended the jurisdiction of the Court of High Commission against the criticism of the common lawyers. They blocked legislation, even reforming legislation, when they perceived Parliament to be trespassing on matters which were properly the business of Convocation, the church's own representative assembly. Bancroft, a canny defender of the church's interests as he saw them, devoted much of his energy to thwarting parliamentary bills by procedural tactics or by poisoning the King's mind against them and then to advancing his own proposals to tackle such abuses as impropriate livings.

Real political power ultimately lay at court, in the treacherous world of factions grouped around ministers and favourites. After the death of Robert Cecil, Earl of Salisbury, in 1612, court politics were dominated by a faction centred on Henry Howard, Earl of Northampton, which was suspicious of parliaments, well disposed towards Spain, and crypto-Catholic. Opposing the Howard faction was a loose alliance of consciously 'Protestant' politicians who espoused closer working relations with Parliament and anti-Spanish foreign policy. Among this group were not only the Earls of Pembroke and Southampton, Lord Chancellor Ellesmere and Sir Edward Coke, but also Archbishop Abbot and Bishops King and Montagu. Abbot was determined to defend Protestant orthodoxy against the malign influence of the Howards by any means. One means took the handsome shape of George Villiers, a young man brought to court by Abbot and Pembroke to supplant the Howard protégé, Sir Robert Carr, Earl of Somerset, in the King's favour. In more strictly ecclesiastical struggles, the Calvinist and anti-Calvinist clerical groups certainly sought to manipulate the King by playing on his fears of puritan and Catholic extremists. Thus Abbot would warn James of the popish leanings of up-and-coming young clerics such as John Howson or William Laud, while in response Abbot's adversaries smeared him as a 'puritan bishop' – a charge that would return to haunt him later in the reign. Abbot was, says Fincham, the only bishop to take his quarrels to Parliament: in 1614 he hoped that Parliament would coerce James into 'some deeper castigation than is here laid upon' the Roman Catholics.[17]

Such manoeuvres were the preserve of a small elite of court-based clergymen and bishops. Many Jacobean bishops spent much of their time in their dioceses working among their clergy to improve preaching and pastoral care in the parishes. They examined candidates for the ministry, preached and exhorted others to preach, and provided training for the clergy. They threw their weight behind campaigns to enforce regular catechising or to organise collaborative preaching 'exercises'. Some, such as Bishops Chaderton of Lincoln or Carleton of Chichester, have left behind solid records of administrative prowess. All of the bishops enforced the requirement that new ordinands subscribe to the articles but some continued to turn a blind eye to clerical nonconformity in matters of ceremony. Fincham points to the visitation articles issued by bishops: evangelical bishops such as Abbot, Morton and King enquired if the surplice was worn or 'usually' or 'commonly' worn and if the sign of the cross in baptism was omitted, whereas the anti-Calvinist and several Calvinist bishops wanted to know if the surplice was *always worn* or if the cross was *ever omitted*. There are many cases of ministers being given extra time to consider their position on conformity or being told to do better next time: in 1611 William Gouge was simply admonished to conform after admitting that he distributed the sacrament to his congregation whether they stood, sat or knelt. In 1612 Bishop James Montagu of Bath and Wells gave Richard Bernard first a licence to preach in the diocese and then a parish in Somerset despite the fact that Bernard had been ejected from his Nottinghamshire parish for nonconformity in 1605. Bernard went on to become one of Somerset's most notable puritan preachers and authors.

Royal policy could only ever be one factor among the many shaping the Church of England. The practical difficulties of policing what happened in the thousands of parish churches week in and week out were immense. The system of reporting and visitation depended upon the cooperation of clergy, parishioners and local officials and therefore demanded that the crown and the bishops worked with rather than against the grain of local sentiment. The authorities also had to negotiate the vested interests of lay patrons and parishioners and the entrenched privileges of cathedrals, universities, urban corporations and other bodies. As a result, the church was a diverse institution characterised by decentralisation and by pockets of clerical autonomy. Perhaps this is most evident in the numerous puritan ministers who did not use the Prayer Book in full, who did not make the sign of the cross at baptism, or bless the ring in marriage, or give the bread and wine only to those who knelt. Such godly ministers routinely offered more preaching and catechising than was officially required and often led their flocks in voluntary exercises such as prayer meetings or Bible discussions. If they were employed as chaplains or lecturers, these ministers might well evade the requirements of the church authorities altogether. Rather fewer clergymen deviated in what we might call the 'opposite' direction, towards a stricter use of the Prayer Book and a more 'Catholic' style of piety, but there were some who advocated more ritual and less preaching, who promoted confession, the frequent reception of the sacrament, and a greater devotion to the physical sufferings of Christ. All too often, those on both extremes were reacting against each other and attempting to stigmatise their opponents. Yet even to describe the diversity of the Jacobean church simply in terms of clerical attitudes is perhaps misleading since it was local self-sufficiency, identity and pride that sustained the intensely local character of the church.

Those in the local community who had prospered, saved or combined so as to fund a new pulpit, lectern, communion plate or stained glass, or to endow a lectureship, were investing in their parish church. Many Jacobean churches were refurbished or repaired, paved, pewed or even rebuilt at the expense of the parish. Much of this was simply making good the ravages of time, but it was also an attempt to provide sufficient space for the growing population and to reorganise the interior of churches to better suit the preaching and liturgy of Protestantism. Merritt has shown that at least sixty-three London churches were rebuilt or significantly repaired and beautified in James's reign. At St Anne's, Blackfriars, where the minister was the noted preacher and (as we have just seen) nonconformist William Gouge, the parish spent £1,500 on repairs in 1613. As Dean of Westminster, Richard Neile spent £1,128 on construction work at the Abbey and Westminster School between 1605 and 1610. Nor was this fashion restricted to the metropolis.[18] Individually or collectively, the English displayed their identification with and commitment to their local churches in the form of hard cash.

While the diversity of the Jacobean church has to be recognised – with some regions such as East Anglia, Cheshire or Northamptonshire conspicuously puritan and others, such as Lancashire and Wales, containing a higher proportion of church papists – it is not necessarily a cause for congratulation. Diversity could offer faction an opportunity. Where the local community was divided, the lack of a clear line from the centre could allow animosities to spill over into conflict.

Scotland and Ireland

As he left Scotland in 1603, James had rashly promised that he would visit his native kingdom every three years. It was in fact fourteen years before he returned to Scotland, but in the interim he kept a close eye on Scottish politics through various agents, in particular the Earls of Dunfermline and Dunbar, the enlarged Scottish Privy Council, and the Lords of the Articles, the committee that effectively conducted the business of the single-chamber Scottish Parliament. James wooed and rewarded the Scottish nobles, dealt with the clans by a mixture of coercion and non-intervention, pacified the borders, and encouraged the gradual spread of English-style JPs in the Lowlands. He continued to promote the interest of the Scottish bishops and with it, his own authority. He appointed bishops to vacant sees, returned the bishops to Parliament, and restored to them the revenues and jurisdictions lost at the Reformation. In 1610 three Scottish bishops were brought to Westminster for consecration by English bishops in what looked like an assertion of the principle of the 'apostolic succession' – the consecration of one bishop by another in an unbroken chain reaching back to the original Apostles. Two years later the Scottish Parliament recognised James as 'supreme governor'. Simultaneously the King chipped away at the pretensions of Presbyterianism and of the General Assembly. He convened the General Assembly and then refused to allow it to meet. When radicals held their own Assembly at Aberdeen, James had the ringleaders detained in England. Meanwhile, bishops were appointed as commissioners in the Assembly and as the constant moderators of the synods. The Assembly's role as the ultimate court of church discipline was usurped by Courts of High Commission on the English model.

James travelled to Edinburgh in 1617, motivated, he said, by a salmon-like instinct, but also, in truth, by the desire to escape an unsavoury court scandal surrounding his former favourite. Welcomed enthusiastically by his subjects, James proceeded to offend many of them by installing an organ and choir in the royal chapel at Holyrood Palace and hearing the English Prayer Book service. Worse still, he then proposed that the General Assembly should endorse five changes to religious practice – kneeling at communion, private baptism, private communion, confirmation by bishops alone, and the observance of holy days such as Christmas and Easter – which in the eyes of many Scots were little short of popish. The Assembly at St Andrews rejected these out of hand, and James had to intimidate another meeting at Perth in 1618 to force them through. Archbishop Spottiswood was alleged to have remarked that 'the King is pope now', but James had yet another fight before the Five Articles of Perth were ratified by the Scottish Parliament in 1621. The Five Articles undoubtedly hor-rified the Kirk and divided its members: in the words of one contempor-ary, they were 'withstood by the most considerable part of the subjects, of all qualities, both laity and clergy'. Since James took little interest in their enforcement, it is difficult to see what had been achieved other than the alienation of his Scottish subjects. One view, advanced by Morrill, is that James simply wanted to open the eyes of the Scots to the virtues of the English way of doing things. He did not aim to make the churches in England and Scotland the same, but he did want to encourage mutual understanding and respect. There is no evidence that he desired religious uniformity across his kingdoms, but he had clearly come to prefer the style and values of the English church, which he said was 'sureliest founded upon the Word of God, of any church in Christendom'.[19]

*

James's Irish kingdom was little more than a poorly understood and con-trolled colony. The Protestant Reformation had failed dismally, while the sixteenth-century influx of English Protestant settlers had provoked risings by the Catholic Gaelic population. The last of these was the Nine Years'

War that had ended with the surrender of the Gaelic leader Tyrone on 30 March 1603. The vast majority of the island's 1.4 million people belonged to one of the two Catholic communities, the Gaelic population or the Old English (or Anglo-Norman) population. Although the Catholic church in Ireland recognised James's dynastic right to the Irish throne despite his Protestantism, there was little hope of mutual understanding between the Catholic Irish and the Calvinist monarch. As if to remind their new King of the unique political alliances which operated in Ireland, in April 1603 the Old English Catholic towns of Kilkenny, Drogheda, Waterford, Limerick and Cork rose briefly in a 'loyal' rebellion, a theatrical assertion of their Catholic identity which included the claims that James was a secret Catholic and a descendant of a line of Irish kings. The real struggle, however, was going on elsewhere. For the first four years of his reign, James undermined the morale and power of the Ulster lords, until the flight of Tyrone, Tyrconnell and their followers into European exile finally allowed him a free hand in the northern provinces of Ireland. James annexed large parts of northern and central Ireland, ordered that the native population be moved to the west, and systematically granted blocks of 1,000 or 2,000 acres to Scottish and English Protestant settlers. This was an avowed policy of Anglicisation, supported by the introduction of English principles of land tenure and inheritance, English farming practices, and a version of English Protestantism. But it was also a 'British' solution as the new King of Ireland, Scotland and England exploited the opportunity to move populations between the component units of his 'multiple monarchy'. Plantations, in the words of one advocate, 'will bring wealth, civility and the form of true religion into that province [of Ulster]; which . . . hath been suffered to lie in the hands of barbarous and irreligious people for hundreds of years past'.[20] In many cases the Gaelic population remained where they were but became tenant farmers to the 'New English' settlers, a subject people under alien rule. Increasingly the authorities came to identify the Old English with the Gaelic population and to label them all as subversive, potentially disloyal, papists. In 1614 James told a delegation of Old English leaders that they were 'but half subjects . . . you that have but an eye to me one way and to the pope another way'.[21]

The process left the Church of Ireland in a peculiar position. On the one hand James saw the church as another tool for spreading civility, order and government among the barely subdued Irish, but on the other it increasingly saw itself as the church of the colonists rather than of the native population. At the Hampton Court Conference James raised the problem of how suitable clergy were to be provided for the Irish church. It was often said that the wrong Protestant ministers were sent to Ireland: 'profane men go to convert men superstitious, puritans are sent to persuade papists', complained Sir John Harington.[22] But as Ford has demonstrated, from the 1590s the English-born leaders of Trinity College Dublin began to train a new generation of more effective Protestant clergy. There were significantly more Protestant preachers in Ireland by the 1620s than there had been in 1603, although few of them were native Irishmen. An uncompromisingly Protestant Prayer Book had been provided for the Church of Ireland in 1604 and translated into Gaelic in 1608. Bishops with experience of reforming the Gaelic dioceses of the Scottish Isles, such as Alexander Knox, were translated to Ireland.

For all these initiatives, the Church of Ireland possessed neither the personnel nor the commitment to evangelise the native Irish population. The puritan outlook of many of its ministers, reinforced by the Irish Articles of 1615 (which included eight of the unofficial Calvinist Lambeth Articles of 1595), and the influence of Scottish emigrants, produced an inward-looking and pessimistic church, preoccupied with providential and millenarian ideas, determined to maintain the purity of Protestantism in the midst of an ocean of irredeemable popish superstition. The Church of Ireland was a legally distinct and often rather theologically detached sister of the Church of England, representing the more 'puritan' vision of what that church might have become, albeit in considerably more straitened circumstances. Meanwhile, Irish Catholicism remained largely untroubled during the early seventeenth century. Given the numbers of recusants and their poverty, there was no hope of enforcing conformity through fine or excommunication so the recusancy laws were a dead letter; and the tensions between those Catholics who followed the traditional ways and those, mainly the Old English, who were attracted by the values and ideals of the Counter-Reformation and the newly arrived Jesuits, remained as yet submerged.

Religion, diplomacy and politics: 1618–25

In his later years James maintained his even-handed religious policy of cultivating a moderate middle ground and stigmatising the extremists, but under the pressure of events and growing religious animosities, it was looking less and less credible. As James passed through Lancashire in 1617, he encountered a little local difficulty. Catholicism and the old ways were still strong in the county and many of the local godly believed that the papists were enticing people away from Sunday services with piping and dancing on the village greens. The godly responded by attempting to suppress Sunday afternoon recreations and to drive the people into church for much of the Sabbath day. Although obviously no friend of popery, James was concerned that such authoritarianism would in fact have the unintended consequence of alienating people from the church. He also jibbed at JPs taking the law into their own hands. So in conjunction with Bishop Thomas Morton, James issued a Declaration of Sports that permitted lawful recreations, such as dancing and archery, on a Sunday after church service. Reissued in 1618 as a national order, its impact was fairly muted beyond those few places, such as Northamptonshire, where it provided an opportunity for point-scoring between existing religious rivals. The practical effect was less important than the public rebuff to the Sabbatarianism of 'the puritans and precise people' and the encouragement this gave to their opponents.

Meanwhile, on the European stage, James's position was increasingly difficult. The dispatch of a British delegation to the Synod of Dort in 1618 had signalled the theological alignment of the Church of England with the Reformed churches of Europe. But power politics and diplomacy tugged James in another direction once war broke out in central Europe. The Kingdom of Bohemia had rebelled against its Austrian Habsburg Emperor and in 1619 James's son-in-law, the Calvinist Elector Frederick, had rashly accepted the Bohemian throne. The Austrian and Spanish branches of the Habsburg dynasty then cooperated to seek revenge. In 1620 a Spanish army occupied Frederick's Rhineland principality and another defeated his army outside Prague. In England the clamour was for military intervention in defence of international Protestantism and Stuart family honour. But James was wedded to his habitual policy of mediation. Diplomacy would be best served by a marriage between his son Charles and the Spanish Infanta. A storm of criticism broke over this ignominious policy. Not only were the brave Protestants Frederick and Elizabeth to be abandoned to their fate, but the King was also negotiating for a marriage treaty that would undoubtedly secure greater freedom for English Catholics. In the summer of 1620 it was rumoured that 'there be at least two or three hundred Jesuits, priests and friars lately come over, and grow so bold that they go up and down in some places in their habits'.[23] John Pym prophesied that 'if the papists once obtain a connivance, they will press for a toleration; from thence to an equality; from an equality to a superiority; from a superiority to an extirpation of all contrary religions'. Prominent among the critics were several churchmen including royal chaplains and even Archbishop Abbot.

By this time the Howard ascendancy was long over and George Villiers, Duke of Buckingham (as he became in 1623) was the dominant minister and favourite, enjoying unparalleled influence over both the King and his immature heir. Buckingham and Charles persuaded James that in the worsening international crisis and a deepening domestic economic depression, it would be wise to be prepared for any eventuality and so the King met Parliament in 1621. James pledged himself to maintain peace if possible and to make financial cutbacks; in return Parliament voted meagre taxes and launched investigations into royal grants of patents and monopolies, thus opening a can of worms that brought down Lord Chancellor Francis Bacon and threatened Buckingham himself. As a diversion, in the next session Buckingham stirred up demands for war and a Protestant marriage for Prince Charles. This only led to angry exchanges between King and Commons on the freedom of parliamentary speech and the composition of a Protestation asserting parliamentary privileges to be the birthright of the English, which James himself ripped out of the Commons' Journal before dissolving Parliament. This sorry episode left James without money and even more convinced that a Spanish match was the only viable option. In increasingly poor health, James negotiated with Gondomar, the Spanish ambassador, who dragged out the process so as to keep England sidelined from the European conflict.

Impatient and impetuous, Buckingham and Charles secretly set off on horseback for Madrid in February 1623. It was a doomed enterprise. Their false beards fell off at Gravesend, and a gaggle of envoys, chaplains and servants followed in their wake. On their arrival in Spain, 'they found nothing but penury and proud beggary, besides all other discourtesy'. At home the English were beside themselves with rumours of what would be conceded to Spain: 'men mutter of a toleration in religion'; and the penal laws were in fact temporarily suspended.[24] Simonds D'Ewes, a young law student, recorded the mounting criticism: 'more and more grew every man's talk, and from their talk their censure, and from their censure their dislike of this match, but especially of so dangerous and rash a journey'.[25] When, humiliated and rebuffed, the hapless pair eventually returned that autumn, they were greeted with bells and bonfires, with 'the greatest expression of joy by all sorts of people that ever I saw,' recorded William Laud, and with an anthem in St Paul's on the text 'when Israel came out of Egypt, and the house of Jacob from amongst the barbarous people'.[26]

English public opinion had been inflamed by antipopery. Despite the order that preachers should desist from anti-Catholic invective, pulpits rang with apocalyptic warnings and pamphleteers dwelt on the threat from Jesuit hellhounds and firebrands. Catholicism had indeed been enjoying a small revival under James, especially at court where there were Catholic peers and Catholic servants such as the musicians William Byrd and John Bull and the Master of the King's Works Inigo Jones. The number of Jesuits in England had grown from 40 in 1606 to 123 in 1623; the Benedictines had established an English congregation in 1619 and the Franciscans would do so six years later; and in 1621 a vicar apostolic, effectively a bishop, the aptly named William Bishop, had been appointed, along with the hierarchy of archdeacons and deans, to govern the Catholic secular clergy.

In October 1623 a floor collapsed beneath a Catholic congregation meeting in an attic adjoining the French ambassador's house in Blackfriars, London. More than ninety were killed, including the Jesuit preacher, but far from helping the survivors, Londoners taunted and pelted them, and then went on a rampage against recusants. Preachers and pamphleteers made much of the 'fatal vespers' as a sign of God's detestation of popery and as a warning to the nation and its governors against compromise or collaboration with Rome. Buckingham capitalised on this mood to form a 'patriotic' coalition with his critics. The King was persuaded to call a Parliament for February 1624. That Parliament passed a series of domestic reforms, among them some of the measures lost in 1621, swept Lord Treasurer Cranfield, an opponent of the war, from office, and made a substantial grant of taxation in return for breaking off marriage negotiations with Spain and preparing for war in aid of the Palatinate.

A long-brewing power struggle within the Church of England also spilled over into this Parliament. Archbishop Abbot's influence had waned dramatically since 1619. He had lost his old political allies at court and antagonised the King by his opposition to the Spanish match. To the King, Abbot increasingly seemed to be the 'puritan bishop' that his adversaries made him out. In August 1622 James issued directions to preachers that forbade the clergy from preaching on affairs of state – by which was understood the Spanish marriage and foreign policy. They were also to refrain from 'bitter invective and undecent railing speeches against the persons of either papists or puritans', to devote Sunday afternoon sermons to catechism topics or better still to a catechism class, and to leave 'the deep points of predestination, election, reprobation, or of the universality, efficacity, resistibility or irresistibility of God's grace' to the universities rather than to parish pulpits. Abbot distributed these instructions to the bishops with assurances that whatever 'some few churchmen, and many of the people, have sinisterly conceived', the King was not attempting to restrict preaching but rather to increase the number of solid, useful sermons. The churchmen he had in mind were those 'anti-Calvinists' who portrayed the directions as a royal curb on predestinarian preaching.

A number of these anti-Calvinists had gained promotion – Andrewes as Bishop of Winchester, Neile as Bishop of Durham, and even, against the King's better judgement, Laud as Bishop of St David's – thanks to the patronage of Buckingham or their own skills as lobbyists and polemicists. Such men disliked Calvinist theology and were suspicious of its hold on the mainstream of the Church of England. Whenever they could they redefined Calvinism, even the Calvinism of churchmen like Archbishop Abbot, as 'puritanism'. This was the tack taken, almost as an aside, by Richard Montagu, an Essex minister, when he replied to various Catholic apologists in his book *A New Gag for an Old Goose* (1624): he claimed that Catholic critics of the Church of England had mistaken puritan beliefs for Protestant ones.

The two sides squared up against each other. The publication of Montagu's book was probably organised by Augustine Lindsell and John Cosin, two of Bishop Neile's chaplains, while a petition offered to the Commons against Montagu was orchestrated by the Dean of Worcester, the Oxford Professor of Divinity, and two of Abbot's chaplains. The petition complained generally of the dangerous Arminian errors 'boldly maintained by some divines of this our kingdom', and specifically of Montagu. *A New Gag* offended in several ways. It stressed the common ground rather than the differences between the Churches of Rome and England, equated Calvinism with 'puritanism', and was, in the eyes of John Pym, 'full fraught with the dangerous opinions of Arminius'. Montagu was assured that he had the sympathy of the King and rather than recanting he published a belligerent defence of his position entitled *Appello Caesarem* – 'I call upon Caesar (or the King)'. In July 1625, Montagu told a Commons Committee that both of his books had been published with royal approval. It is quite possible that James was attracted by Montagu's call for the Church of England to distance itself from hard-line Calvinism and its vehement antipopery; he certainly resented the way that Parliament was forcing him to takes sides in the European confessional conflict, and he was fearful of what it might portend for the security of his own throne and person.

*

James I died on 27 March 1625. An astute, experienced and pragmatic politician, James had usually succeeded in balancing the different factions within his court, his Privy Council and the Church of England; he revelled in his self-appointed role as *rex pacificus*, the peaceful king, a mediator in international diplomacy and a staunch advocate of ecumenicism. In his own eyes and those of his admirers, he was a British Solomon, a 'nursing father' to the church in his realms, and a scholar prince. As his reign proceeded, he revealed a less admirable side – slavish devotion to his favourite the Duke of Buckingham and a determined pursuit of the Catholic marriage which many of his subjects found unpalatable. Religious tensions existed within England and Scotland, yet there was little to suggest in 1625 that Scotland was only eleven years away from rebellion or that England might soon descend into civil war.

Notes

1 *The Diary of John Manningham*, ed. J. Bruce (Camden Society, old series, 99, 1868), p. 147; *Wentworth Papers 1597–1628*, ed. J.P. Cooper (Camden Society, 4th series, 12, 1973), pp. 81–2.

2 *James I: Political Writings*, ed. J.P. Sommerville (Cambridge, 1994), pp. 7, 19, 27.

3 Manningham, *Diary*, p. 148.

4 *The State of the Church in the Reigns of Elizabeth I and James I*, ed. C.W. Foster (Lincoln Record Society, 23, 1926), p. xlviii.

5 *The Letters of John Chamberlain*, ed. N.E. McClure (2 vols, Philadelphia, 1939), I, 192.

6 Kenyon, p. 132.

7 M. Mullett, *Catholics in Britain and Ireland, 1558–1829* (Basingstoke, 1998), p. 23; P. Croft, 'The Religion of Robert Cecil', *HJ*, 34 (1991), p. 783.

8 K. Fincham, 'Clerical Conformity from Whitgift to Laud', in P. Lake and M. Questier (eds), *Conformity and Orthodoxy in the English Church c.1560–1660* (Woodbridge, 2000), p. 140.

9 BL, Harleian MS 633, fo. 63v.

10 M. Questier, 'Loyalty, Religion and State Power in Early Modern England: Romanism and the Jacobean Oath of Allegiance', *HJ*, 40 (1997).

11 P. Croft, *King James* (Basingstoke, 2003), p. 161.

12 *Chamberlain Letters*, I, 284; *Newsletters from the Archpresbyterate of George Birkhead*, ed. M.C. Questier (Camden Society, 5th series, 12, 1998), pp. 21–2.

13 M. McClure, *The Paul's Cross Sermons 1534–1642* (Toronto, 1958), p. 235; *Chamberlain Letters*, I, 392, 396.

14 P.E. McCullough, *Sermons at Court: Politics and Religion in Elizabethan and Jacobean Preaching* (Cambridge, 1998).

15 P. Croft, 'The Religion of Robert Cecil', *HJ*, 34 (1991), 792.

16 K. Fincham, *Prelate as Pastor: The Episcopate of James I* (Oxford, 1990), p. 41.

17 K. Fincham, *Prelate as Pastor: The Episcopate of James I* (Oxford, 1990), p. 60.

18 J. Merritt, 'Puritans, Laudians and the Phenomenon of Church-building in Jacobean London', *HJ*, 41 (1998); N. Mole, 'Church-building and Popular Piety in Early Seventeenth-century Exeter', *Southern History*, 25 (2003).

19 *James I: Political Writings*, p. 210

20 A. Ford, *The Protestant Reformation in Ireland* (Frankfurt, 1987; reissued Dublin, 1997), p. 158.

21 Croft, *King James*, p. 148.

22 A. Ford, K. Milne and J.E. McGuire (eds), *As by Law Established: The Church of Ireland since the Reformation* (Dublin, 1995), p. 52.

23 *Chamberlain Letters*, II, 315.

24 *Chamberlain Letters*, II, 480, 484, 493, 519.

25 *The Diary of Sir Simonds D'Ewes 1622–24*, ed. E. Bourcier (Paris, 1974), p. 110.

26 *The Works of William Laud*, ed. W. Scott and J. Bliss (7 vols, Oxford, 1847–60), III, 143; *Chamberlain Letters*, II, 515, 516.

CHAPTER 3

Charles I (1625–38)

The fact that the reign of Charles I was one of the most dramatic in British history is principally due to the King himself. Between his accession in 1625 and his execution by his own subjects in 1649, Charles initiated or provoked a revolution in the Church of England, rebellions in Scotland and Ireland, a crisis in the relationship between the crown and the English Parliament, and civil wars in all three British kingdoms. These events set even deeper changes in motion. During the 1640s, the religious experiences and opportunities of the British people, like much else in their lives, were to be transformed. This chapter is devoted to the years between 1625 and 1638 and to the policies pursued in England, Scotland and Ireland. In recent decades historians have abandoned long-term explanations of the crisis that led to civil war. The systemic problems of royal finance or religious diversity were not beyond political management. There is little evidence of an aggressive parliamentary or puritan class seeking to wrest power or the constitutional initiative from the hands of the monarch. Instead of a highway to civil war, there was a tightrope to be negotiated by a skilful ruler. Charles Stuart lacked the skills, the intuition, the advisers, perhaps the self-confidence, which were needed. An austere man, he took refuge in order, ritual, art and beauty, rather than dealing with the ambiguities and compromises of political life. He had too high a regard for his own opinions and judgements, especially of people: Charles was 'too resolved from what is within him', in the opinion of the poet Suckling.[1] He believed quite sincerely in his own divine right as ruler and in the royal prerogative, that power beyond the laws which God entrusts to a prince to exercise as he thinks fit for the good of his subjects. Charles's own attitudes and responses explain much that went wrong during his reign, whether it is his treatment of opponents or parliaments or favourites, and yet none of this would have led to civil war and revolution without the fuel of religious strife. Religion turned discontent into rebellion, grievances into a holy cause.

War and 'new counsels'

Shy and reserved, neither good at explaining himself nor at taking advice, Charles I came to the throne expecting to lead the nation into war. Dependent on taxes to finance this war, and believing that MPs had morally committed themselves to it in 1624, Charles met his first Parliament in the summer of 1625 and immediately ran into difficulties. The King offered no explanation of his war plans. Uncertain whether it was to be a naval campaign or a land war in Germany, MPs refused to write him a blank cheque. Whereas all previous monarchs had been granted a lifetime right to collect a tax known as tonnage and poundage, Parliament would not even confirm the King's right to collect the duty for one year. Religion was also at the forefront of many minds. The furore over Richard Montagu's writings continued. When their author was imprisoned for contempt by the Commons, the King secured his release, ordered the Commons to drop the matter, and provocatively appointed him a royal chaplain. MPs discussed ways to strengthen the preaching ministry and English Protestantism against the threat from international popery, but everyone appreciated their subtext was that popery also loomed at home. An alleged rise in the number of Catholic recusants was offensively blamed on the King's recent marriage to the French Catholic princess Henrietta Maria. God seemed to have turned his back on the English. Plague stalked the land, military and naval expeditions ended in disaster, and government lay in the hands of the mercurial Buckingham and the aloof Charles.

Charles carefully weeded potential troublemakers out of the next Parliament: some were appointed as sheriffs to prevent their election as MPs, others like Eliot, Digges and Lord Arundel were put under house arrest, or told, as was the Earl of Bristol, to stay away from Westminster. At the opening of Parliament on 6 February 1626 William Laud preached on the theme of Jerusalem as 'a city that is united in itself' through hierarchy and order. He took a swipe at those that argued for 'parity' or equality in the church and drew a political lesson: 'they, whoever they be, that would overthrow *sedes ecclesiastica*, the seats of ecclesiastical government, will not spare (if ever they get power) to have a pluck at the throne of David'.[2] It was all to no avail. Parliament would only vote taxes if the King addressed their grievances, and above all 'the grievance of grievances', the Duke of Buckingham, who was compared by one member to Sejanus, the adjutant of the tyrannical Emperor Tiberius. 'Remember', said Charles on 29 March, 'that Parliaments are altogether in my power for their calling, sitting and dissolution; therefore as I find the fruits of them either good or evil, they are to continue or not to be.'[3]

While Parliament was planning his impeachment, Buckingham was hosting a theological conference at York House between Montagu and his adversaries. John Preston and Bishop Morton, who spoke for the Calvinists, argued that the Church of Rome was fundamentally corrupt, that baptism did not confer grace, and that the predestined saints could never fall from grace. Montagu, however, asserted that Rome was a true church, that good works played a part in justification and that ceremonies were obligatory under divine law; for good measure, his second, Dean Francis White claimed that Christ died for all. The theological divergence was undeniable. Although the conference left the issues undecided, the Commons subsequently resolved that Montagu was guilty of publishing doctrines contrary to the Thirty-nine Articles.

Parliament pressed on with the impeachment of the favourite. As Laud saw it, 'after many debates, private malice against the Duke of Buckingham prevailed, and suffocated all public business'.[4] Charles was left with no alternative but a dissolution in June. Whereas, faced with such parliamentary intransigence, his father might have made a defiant gesture before conciliating, Charles responded to this setback by adopting 'new counsels'. The tone was evident in his proclamation for establishing the peace and quiet of the church. The King declared 'to the whole world his utter dislike to all those who, to show the subtlety of their wit, or to please their own humours, or vent their own passions', spread new opinions in religion. He would not countenance 'the least innovation' in religion and any who did utter such views threatened 'the circle of order' which protects church and state and should therefore anticipate exemplary punishment.[5] Affairs were tilting decisively in favour of the anti-Calvinist clergy: after York House, Buckingham threw in his lot with them; Laud and Neile became privy councillors. In this context, the June proclamation was interpreted as a ban on Calvinist preaching. 'Predestination is the root of puritanism', explained the Master of Trinity College, Cambridge, and puritanism is the root of rebellion, disobedience and schism.[6]

The puritans recognised that a chill wind was blowing both at home and abroad. They organised to help their co-religionists in places like

Bohemia, the Palatinate and the Valtelline. In 1626 a circular letter to 'all godly Christians' from Richard Sibbes, William Gouge, John Davenport and Thomas Taylor solicited contributions to help 240 godly preachers, their wives, children and followers, who had been driven 'by the fury of the merciless papists' from the Palatinate into exile in the Netherlands.[7] Their presumption in interfering with 'foreign affairs' brought them a reprimand from the Court of High Commission. That same year, a dozen Londoners, including four ministers, formed a trust to buy up impropriations, advowsons and the leases of tithes from their lay owners. This would give the trustees, known as feofees, control of clerical income and rights of appointment that they could then use to promote and aid godly ministers. Among the feofees were members of trading companies, such as the Dorchester Adventurers, Massachusetts Bay Company, and Providence Island Company, which had been established to spread the gospel to the Americas and to profit from the New World.

The 'new counsels' were evident in other areas of government. While Charles continued to collect tonnage and poundage, in the summer of 1626 he asked his subjects to contribute to a voluntary tax (with disappointing results), and then in September, citing a national emergency, imposed a Forced Loan to raise £300,000. Bishop Laud organised the accompanying propaganda: Robert Sibthorpe preached that subjects had an overriding duty to obey their monarchs whatever was asked of them; Roger Manwaring, preaching on the scripture text, *I counsel thee to keep the King's commandment, and that in regard of the oath of God* (Ecclesiastes 8: 2), offered a classic account of the doctrine of passive obedience – 'no subject may, without hazard of his own damnation, in rebelling against God, question or disobey the will and pleasure of his sovereign'.[8]

Although the Forced Loan did bring in the cash, it also provoked anger and opposition. While troops were billeted on some of those who refused to pay, the more prominent were thrown into gaol. Seventy-six gentlemen suffered imprisonment, among them twenty-seven future MPs. Five of these knights sought to win their release through a writ of *habeas corpus* but were refused on a technicality by the judges. Many concluded that the rule of law was in jeopardy from an authoritarian King who was trying to fight a war without proper parliamentary funding. Such suspicions were reinforced when it later transpired that Charles had secretly instructed the Attorney General to tamper with the ruling in the Five Knights case so that it would provide a precedent for a royal right to imprison at will. The situation was not helped by the latest round of diplomatic and military blundering. Buckingham managed to launch a war against France – in addition to the continuing war with Spain – and then to mismanage a military expedition in aid of the French Huguenots of La Rochelle. Thus were the funds produced by the Loan squandered.

An atmosphere of national crisis overtook the government and country in the winter of 1627–28. With troops in arms, the King needed money desperately. Although he was worried by a rising tide of 'popularity' or hostile public opinion, and Laud was concerned that MPs 'will fall upon church business which (in the way they have gone) is not fit for them', a meeting of Parliament was unavoidable.[9] Popular opinion was indeed critical. Thomas Scott, who won a seat in the 1628 elections, claimed that the 'dukists' had betrayed the country to Antichrist. In a pamphlet dedicated to the new Parliament Henry Burton, puritan rector of St Matthew's Friday St, London, wrote that the siren voices of Arminians had divided the King from his subjects and England from God, 'betraying us into our enemies' hands, by making God our enemy'. 'The common complaint is that popery spreads, that Arminianism spreads,' preached Jeremiah Dyke, vicar of Epping, to that same Parliament. 'As these come in, so God will go out.'[10]

The 1628 Parliament drew up the Petition of Right, a statement that English liberties included freedom from imprisonment without trial, from taxation without parliamentary consent, and from the compulsory billeting of soldiers on civilians. Originally Charles refused to accept a bill that would have given these liberties legal form, but he did, after much evasion and squirming, accept a petition which did much the same job and which also banned the exercise of martial law in the kingdom. In return he received a grant of five subsidies. Unfortunately his earlier prevarication had provoked the Commons into drawing up a remonstrance that blamed a 'popish and malignant party' for recent innovations in government and religion. This was presented to the King on 17 June with the demand that Buckingham be removed. When the Commons prepared to declare the King's collection of tonnage and poundage 'a breach of the fundamental liberties of this kingdom' and of the Petition of Right, Charles prorogued Parliament before the document could be presented. The King roundly asserted his prerogative, rejected 'false constructions' of the Petition, and gratuitously reminded members that 'I owe an account of my actions to none but God alone'.[11]

A few weeks later, the Duke of Buckingham was assassinated by a disgruntled officer at Portsmouth. This outrage was a cause of widespread popular rejoicing. The King continued on his authoritarian course but now without the shield that had been provided by his favourite. When a group of London merchants refused to pay tonnage and poundage, Charles personally instructed their goods to be seized – including those of the MP John Rolle. The King promoted Montagu to the bishopric of Chichester, Francis White to Norwich, Howson to Durham, Harsnett to York and Laud to London with a promise of Canterbury when it became vacant. The commanding heights of the church had fallen decisively into the hands of the anti-Calvinists. In June 1628 a royal proclamation had suppressed Manwaring's book and acknowledged that it had been justly censured by Parliament for its ignorance of the law, but 'its grounds were rightly laid, to persuade obedience from the subjects to their sovereign and that for conscience sake'. The King remitted Manwaring's punishment and promoted him. In November the King reissued the Thirty-nine Articles with a preface declaring that they contained the true doctrine of the Church of England, exhorting all clergy to accept 'the true, usual, literal meaning of the said articles', and commanding that 'all further curious search be laid aside, and these disputes shut up in God's promises, as they be generally set forth to us in the holy scriptures'.[12]

Charles met Parliament in January 1629 with a modest agenda of reforming legislation. But MPs had other ideas. They wanted to know how the Petition of Right had appeared in print accompanied by several royal speeches that heavily qualified their view of the Petition and reasserted the inviolability of the royal prerogative. They took up the case of Rolle and the question of tonnage and poundage became entangled with that of parliamentary immunity. Above all, they wanted to debate religion. Francis Rous MP, a zealous puritan and step-brother to Pym, urged the Commons to 'look into the very belly and bowels of this Trojan horse to see if there not be men in it, ready to open the gates, to Romish tyranny and Spanish monarchy; for an Arminian is the spawn of a Papist'.[13] Rous, Pym, Rich, Knightly and Harley were convinced that the current leaders of the church had brought popery into the heart of government. And, for the first time, they carried others with them, members like Sir Francis Seymour who believed that England's war against Spain was compromised by Arminianism. Sir Walter Earle admitted that in 1628 he had wanted to deal with liberties first and 'postpone the business of religion', but now he saw that the matters of state and religion were inextricable and in danger: 'take away my religion, you take away my life, and not only mine, but the life of the whole state and kingdom'. Popery and Arminianism walked hand in hand, while 'truths established by laws, confirmed by synods national and provincial, have been called in question'.[14] The threat was at every level. If the nation defected from the Word of God, then God would desert the cause of England; if the Arminians ruled the King they would poison his mind against Parliament.

The Commons then embarked upon a startling attempt to define the religion of the Church of England. Despite the King's declaration of November 1628, a committee led by Pym, Rudyerd and Eliot attempted to establish an authoritative interpretation of the Articles. The heads that Pym produced in the committee are an astonishing indication of the depth and breadth of the mistrust of Charles and his bishops.[15] The Calvinist heritage of the Church of England, as amplified in the Lambeth Articles, the Irish Articles and the endorsement of Dort, was restated. Arminianism was identified with popery and was held responsible for the perversion of the English church. No holds were barred: the culprits were named and their crimes identified. The litany included the failure to prosecute recusants and papists, the publications of Montagu and Cosin, the favour shown to White, Buckeridge, Neile, Laud and others who have advanced 'such papistical, Arminian and superstitious opinions and practices', all 'contrary to the former orthodox doctrine'. English developments were presented in a European and a British context. The revival of popery was part of the Counter-Reformation, which was at that very moment reclaiming large parts of central Europe for the Roman religion. The same was happening closer to home as 'Ireland is now almost wholly overspread with popery'. The prognosis was bleak for English Protestantism: 'if our religion be suppressed and destroyed abroad, disturbed in Scotland, lost in Ireland, undermined and almost outdared in England, it is manifest that our danger is very great and imminent.' This uncompromising and tendentious reading of recent history carried conviction. 'For the first time in 1629,' writes Russell, 'the Commons as a whole regarded the growth of Arminianism as a conspiracy to alter the doctrine of the Church of England.'[16] Not that the MPs achieved much. After a series of adjournments, Charles dissolved Parliament. Eliot and his allies caused a fracas in the Commons chamber during which they voted that religious innovators and advocates of the collection of tonnage and poundage were 'capital enemies' of the kingdom and those who paid the tax were betrayers of English liberties. Charles rushed out a defence of his actions and cast the blame on 'evil spirits' who had taken up the danger to religion 'as a plausible theme to deprave our government, as if we, our clergy and council, were either senseless or careless of religion'.[17] He concluded with an uncompromising promise to maintain the Church of England without concession to popery or schism.

Personal rule

The years between the dissolution of the 1629 Parliament and the convening of a new Parliament in 1640 are conventionally referred to as 'the personal rule' of Charles I. Yet it was only in England that the King dispensed with the advice of parliaments; in both Scotland and Ireland parliaments did meet during the 1630s, but as one historian has remarked, the key feature of this decade was Charles's 'reliance on the royal prerogative to enforce his will over all three kingdoms'.[18] The King took an active and personal interest in the government of each of his three kingdoms, an interest which led directly to conflict and rebellion. Having made peace with France and Spain in 1629, and free at last of the malign influence of the Duke of Buckingham, Charles perhaps had a chance to restore harmony and tranquillity to England, but his authoritarian outlook and inflexible attitude, allied to religious and cultural sympathies which many of his subjects found alien, did not help him to win the trust and loyalty of his people.

Much has been written on the 'distant kingship' practised by Charles. Unlike the accessible, informal, often seedy, court life of his father, Charles's court and household were ordered, hierarchical and dignified. It is said that Charles withdrew into the bosom of his family, into his close relationship with Henrietta Maria, and into the formality and entertainments of his court and the pleasures of his art collection. But neither Charles nor his court could be insulated from politics. Factions formed at court around figureheads and around ideological and foreign policy options. Thus Henrietta Maria's clique was naturally pro-French, while the remnants of the earlier Protestant group that gathered around the Earl of Pembroke and Archbishop Abbot were known as pro-Dutch and pro-Parliament. But the dominant faction was led by the Lord Treasurer Weston, elevated as Earl of Portland in 1633, the Earl of Arundel, Lord Cottington and Secretary Sir Francis Windebank, men with close connections to Spain and Roman Catholicism. The Earl of Dorset, who was not part of this charmed circle, ruefully named Laud, Weston, Windebank and Cottington, the inner group of the Privy Council, as 'the cabinet council'.

Charles worked hard at the business of government. He read the papers and attended meetings of the Privy Council. He took a real interest in the state of his realm and in efforts to improve it. When plague and poor harvests exacerbated underlying social and economic difficulties in the late 1620s to spark off bread riots and other disorders, the Council spurred the JPs into action with detailed sets of instructions. But the government was not content to leave matters there. The 1631 Book of Orders unveiled a scheme to reinvigorate local government. Quarter Sessions were required to report directly to the Privy Council on what was being done to deal with vagrants, alehouses, the poor, highways, and much else. Such an intrusive and time-consuming scheme ran counter to the way that English local government, staffed by unpaid amateurs and dependent on local initiative and cooperation, had evolved over the previous century. The plan – rather like parallel reforms to the county militias – reveals the government's propensity to meddle: it also suggests that its ambition often outstripped its abilities.

Charles had an over-idealised image of provincial society, a paternal-istic vision of gentlemen and nobles dispensing justice and hospitality from the gates of their mansions. Similarly archaic thinking was evident in the ingenious means that Charles and his advisers found to increase crown income. With the royal debt standing at £2 million in 1629, Charles took an understandable interest in any proposal to exploit revenues: enforcing traditional, almost forgotten, royal rights over forests, the estates of minors or wards, and fees paid by those receiving the title of knight brought in cash; so, too, did an increase in customs duties that almost doubled annual royal income from this source across the decade. Ship Money – a tax on coastal counties to provide for naval protection in times of danger – was successfully revived in 1634, and extended to all counties in the following year. As the realisation dawned on people that this was to be an annual national imposition, some shrugged and paid up, others grumbled that taxes should only be levied with the approval of Parliament, and a very few protested or even refused to pay. In 1637 the government made an example of one high-profile refuser, the former MP John Hampden. Although the judges found for the King, the slim majority of seven votes against five rendered the victory hollow; and the hyperbole of the case made on behalf of the crown, that the King *was* the law, 'a living, a speaking, an acting law', just confirmed the episode as a public relations disaster. Even so, for the time being the Ship Money continued to bring in about £200,000 a year to the Treasury and to pay for a handsome fleet. A rather different development was the emergence of a strong Roman Catholic presence at court. Under the influence of his Catholic Queen Henrietta Maria, Charles accepted a papal agent, Panzani, at court in 1634. The Queen's splendid chapel at Somerset House opened in 1636, the same year that George Con, another papal envoy, took up residence at court. Con quickly became an intimate of the King and Queen and began to win courtiers to Catholicism. Henrietta openly encouraged conversions at court, while around forty Jesuits were at work in London and large numbers of humble people attended Catholic services at various ambas-sadorial chapels. These were all alarming signs to many of his subjects, and no one would claim Charles's personal rule of England was a rip-roaring success in political terms, but then nor was it, in itself, provoking the level of discontent that would precipitate rebellion or civil war.

In Scotland the government of Charles I had showed little respect for local feelings or practice from the outset. Without prior notice or consult-ation, the King assumed to himself the power to revoke all royal grants of crown or church lands made in Scotland since 1542 and he forced the Act of Revocation through the Scottish Parliament in 1625–26. In principle the King could now dispossess the nobles and lairds of huge swathes of land, but in reality he aimed only to regularise landholding and the payment of tithes (or teinds as they were known in Scotland) and to assert royal authority. The manner of his action alarmed the Scottish elite, who claimed that it would result in 'irreparable ruin to an infinite number of families of all qualities in every region of the land', and although the policy was tempered in practice by Charles's agent the Earl of Menteith and by aristocratic obstruction, it was an inauspicious beginning to the reign.[19] It revealed Charles's poor grasp of Scottish politics and opinion, a deficiency that was never made good, not even when the King belatedly arrived in Scotland for his coronation in 1633. On this occasion Charles clumsily offended the Scots by holding the ceremony in Edinburgh rather than the traditional locations of Stirling or Scone, by using the English liturgy and coronation oath, and displaying a degree of ceremonial pomp – candles, tapestries depicting the crucifixion, bishops in white rochets and stoles of blue and gold – that was utterly foreign to Scottish worship. He stayed barely a month in Scotland, just long enough to witness parliamentary opposition to some of his new taxes and to the confirmation of the Five Articles of Perth, before heading south again. The opposition justified its stance by castigating Charles for his insensitive policies, heavy taxes, parasitic courtiers, tolerance of 'popery and Arminianism', and for arousing 'a general fear of some innovations intended in essential points of religion'.[20]

Charles I's government of Ireland turned out to be even more high-handed than his treatment of Scotland. In the first years of the reign, largely because of the need to ensure the security and loyalty of Catholic Ireland while England was at war with Spain and France, Irish landowners had been wooed. Gaelic and Old English landowners had agreed to contribute towards the costs of an expanded Irish army in return for concessions known as the Graces. These would have lifted some of the major disabilities under which Catholics laboured: individuals were to be allowed to hold public office without swearing the oath of supremacy, and the imposition of recusancy fines was to be suspended. The legal security of Catholic estates was another major concern since the unabated policy of plantation continued to threaten their lands. The Graces therefore included the proposal to extend to Ireland a recent English statute that recognised sixty years' possession of lands as establishing a valid legal title. Such concessions were resented by those, principally the New English, with a vested interest in plantations, and by the leaders of the Church of Ireland. In November 1626 Archbishop Ussher of Armagh and a dozen bishops signed a *Protestation* which claimed that suspending the recusancy fines was selling souls and that an effective toleration of Roman Catholicism was a sin. The whole scheme lost impetus as Charles began to disentangle himself from his ill-judged wars.

In 1632 Sir Thomas Wentworth, combative former President of the Council of the North, was appointed Lord Deputy of Ireland. No sooner had Wentworth arrived in Dublin than it was apparent that his plans put him on a collision course with large sections of the Irish population. He was determined that Ireland should no longer be a drain on the English Exchequer and that Irish corruption and misgovernment should be tackled. In the closely controlled Irish Parliament of 1634, Wentworth duped the Old English into a generous grant of taxation before denying them the long-promised enactment of the Graces. He had little interest in persecuting the Catholic majority for their religious beliefs, but the Graces would have jeopardised his plans for extending the plantation of Connacht. This huge disappointment drove the Old English and the Gaelic communities further together and accentuated the official tendency to regard all Catholics as the 'Irish' community in distinction from the New English, those English and Scottish settlers who formed the Protestant ascendancy. Wentworth, however, also confronted the leaders of the New English as he ruthlessly pursued what he called his policy of 'Thorough' without respect to any private or factional interests, law or principle. To many, both in Ireland and across the sea, Wentworth looked like a hatchet man advancing in the colony the draconian policies that Charles I would like to see in operation in England.

There was no more chilling instance of this tendency than Wentworth's dealings with the Church of Ireland. While the Lord Deputy saw himself as simply ensuring that the Church of Ireland conformed in its doctrine and government to the Church of England and that it enjoyed in full its property, lands and tithes, his opponents, including many in the Irish church, believed that he had transformed that institution. Wentworth and his chaplain John Bramhall, who was promoted to the bishopric of Derry in 1634, were horrified by the way that the Church of Ireland had developed its own identity and practices, based on the Calvinist Irish Articles of 1615, the influx of Presbyterians from Scotland and the consequent acceptance of those with Presbyterian ordination as ministers in this episcopal church. 'I doubt very much whether the clergy be very orthodox', Bramhall wrote to Laud in August 1633. He proposed that the Thirty-nine Articles and the 1604 canons should be established in Ireland, 'as we live all under one kingdom, so we might both in doctrine and discipline deserve an uniformity'.[21] The Convocation of the Irish clergy, which accompanied the 1634 Irish Parliament, saw a real battle between Archbishop Ussher, the architect of the 1615 articles and champion of the Church of Ireland as an autonomous national church in line with the Reformed churches of Europe, and Bramhall and Wentworth, advocates of Anglo-Irish uniformity. The Thirty-nine Articles were enacted, although some consoled themselves that the Irish Articles were never explicitly rescinded, while the new canons of 1634 managed to combine some of the existing English canons, some specific to Ireland, and some that were a compromise: thus the Church of Ireland did not require bowing at the name of Jesus, but it did stipulate that altars should be placed at the east end of the church. The changes of 1634 were not a complete victory for the advocates of uniformity and it might be more accurate to say that they brought the Churches of Ireland and England into congruity rather than conformity. Nor, of course, did the adoption of canons in Dublin mean that these were followed in practice in the churches of Ulster or Connacht. Throughout the 1630s a steady stream of complaint reached the ears of Bramhall and Laud about the refusal of ministers to wear vestments or to use the liturgy in full. However, it was generally recognised that this had been a rebuff to the puritan vision of the Church of Ireland with which Ussher was identified. He retreated to Drogheda and a life of scholarship, while Bramhall drafted legislation to curb the excessive leases of church lands and to permit lay impropriators to return their revenues to the church. Bramhall ran the church and remained in close touch with Wentworth and Archbishop Laud. The Church of Ireland was in law and theory a completely independent church, linked to the Church of England only because of the happy accident of a shared Supreme Governor, but the practical control exerted by trusted protégés and allies of Laud kept the two churches on similar paths.

'Laudianism'

Charles was the first English monarch to be nurtured from infancy in the Church of England. Within days of his accession, John Chamberlain was reporting that the King 'is very attentive and devout at prayers and sermons gracing the preachers and assembly with amiable and cheerful countenance, which gives much satisfaction, and there is great hope that the world will every way amend'.[22] Charles took a lively personal interest in ecclesiastical affairs and formed a 'unique partnership' with Archbishop Laud.[23] The cooperation between the two men is graphically revealed by the King's careful annotations on the annual reports that Laud provided on the state of each diocese. Although Laud and a group of bishops drove ecclesiastical policy forward, nothing could have been done without royal approval. Laud was always eager to have a royal order authorising his actions since it both ensured prompt obedience and offered the archbishop some protection against his enemies and critics. Ultimate responsibility lay with the King but the 'Laudians' provided the motives and means. The same question of responsibility arises over Laud's leadership of the 'Laudians'. While many other bishops had pioneered some of the policies associated with the archbishop, or took them further, it was Laud who led the Church of England during the 1630s and so it is his name which best denotes the convergence of earlier 'Arminian', 'anti-Calvinist' and ceremonialist ideas in a series of concrete initiatives for reform of the Church of England. Let us turn to the elements that made up 'Laudianism'.

*

The Laudians repudiated the predestinarian doctrines of Calvin. They believed that this doctrine, as developed by Calvin and later Reformed theologians, robbed human beings of the incentive to live good lives and made God appear tyrannical for condemning some to damnation without any regard to their lives. The doctrine that the elect, the saints, could not fall from grace was particularly offensive. 'According to this divinity, the true saints of God may commit horrible and crying sins, die without repentance, and yet be sure of salvation,' protested Laud, 'which tears up the very foundations of religion, induces all manner of profaneness into the world, and is expressly contrary to the whole current of the scripture.'[24] This was, to use a technical theological term, 'antinomianism', the principle that the saved are not able to commit sin. This principle was thought to be logically necessary because God could not be held to save someone who then falls back into sin; that would throw God's omniscience, his knowledge of all that had or would happen, into question. Antinomianism was an accusation made from many quarters in the seventeenth century. It connected an abstruse theological error with practical consequences in the lives of men and women. Laud, for example, feared that Calvinism bred pride, over-confidence and hypocrisy. Once individuals were convinced that they were among the saints, then they could no longer recognise their own dis-obedience. Preaching at Bristol, Robert Skinner ridiculed Calvinists who believed 'that all are tied up by an absolute decree and a fatal necessity and so can do no more'. He poured scorn on their hypocrisy: 'neither drunken-ness nor gluttony nor fraud nor lying nor slandering nor railing nor reviling nor (I had almost said) rebellion can cast him out of their calendar of saints; still a child of grace and one of God's dear servants for all this'.[25]

The rejection of Calvinism owed much to the teaching of Arminius, the Dutch theologian whose views were denounced at the Synod of Dort. The depth of the intellectual debts owed by English churchmen to Arminius and his followers has been explored thoroughly in Tyacke's magisterial account. Some of the Laudians were well versed in the writings of Arminius, others were not; Montagu only came to read Arminius after reaching and publishing his own conclusions; Neile claimed to have read just a few pages. It is likely that many of the Laudians were convinced of the dangers of Calvinism as much by their daily pastoral experience as they were by theological arguments. There were even some Laudians who were *not* Arminians. This is an important point to grasp about Laudianism. It was wider than any one single viewpoint. Arminianism or anti-Calvinism was a major preoccupation around which most of the Laudians gathered, but it was not the single central idea from which all else followed.

Ceremonialism was another characteristic of the group. Lake has described the Laudian 'style', an approach to worship and divinity rather than a dogmatic checklist, and one that was consciously and explicitly constructed by its followers in opposition to a caricatured 'puritanism'. Laudian divines were particularly aware of the presence of God in the church, in the building itself, the churchyard, the utensils, vestments and ornaments consecrated to worship, the congregation, and in the collective acts of prayer and worship. Their emphases on the beauty of holiness, on respect for objects and people set apart for holy purposes, and on the physical gestures of reverence and devotion, such as kneeling and bowing, arose from this intense sensitivity to the divine presence and from a close attention to the rituals described in the scriptures. Public prayer and the celebration of the sacrament were at the heart of Laudian divinity.

Laudians preached frequently on the duty and benefit of public prayer and lamented that the vogue for sermons had undermined the role of prayer in the church. They were determined to curtail preaching, even to demote it, in order to make more time for the fervent and uniform use of the Prayer Book. Public devotion, in turn, was also a means to an even greater end, the consummation of the Christian religion in the Lord's Supper. Laud famously said that the altar was the greatest place of God's residence on earth, 'yea, greater than the pulpit; for there 'tis hoc est corpus meum, "this is my body"; but in the pulpit 'tis at most but hoc est verbum meum, "this is my word"'. And a greater reverence, no doubt, is due to the body than to the word of our Lord.[26] Such reverence explains the Laudians' insistence on protecting the altar against profanation by railing it off at the east end of the church. The clergy were not simply preachers or teachers, they were also priests with a special function and access to the holy. Laudian ministers prized the continuity of the Christian church through a visible succession of bishops that reached back to the apostles. Some Laudians revived the practice of hearing confession and granting absolution. Laudian divinity had a strong sense of the liturgical calendar, of the fasts and festivals of the church as they appeared in the Prayer Book, and a correspondingly dismissive attitude towards puritan Sabbatarianism (which ignored all festivals bar the weekly Sabbath).

The Laudian vision of religion ascribed tremendous authority to the church and to the clergy. It was the church's right to order *adiaphora*, those indifferent issues, such as the circumstances of worship, which God had not explicitly laid down in scripture. This was a conventional line of argument, used by the Elizabethan church to justify its insistence that ministers wore a surplice, and one that made much of the need to worship God decently and in order. In ordering worship, the Church of England followed unimpeachable guides, the principles of reason, the precedents of scripture and the practice of the very early or apostolic church. Authoritarian Laudians seemed to believe that order and hierarchy were good in themselves. They defended order in both the sacred and secular spheres and dismissed their critics as factious spirits and partisans of 'popularity'. On occasion, Laudian defences of ceremonial uniformity implied that the actions, rites and symbols used in worship had an intrinsic religious significance. This kind of language awakened fears of covert popery.

The Laudians appeared to be less confident than their predecessors and contemporaries in identifying the papacy as 'the whore of Babylon' or pronouncing the Church of Rome to be the Antichrist. Such antipopery was simply part of the 'foul language' of controversy, said Laud, while Richard

Montagu claimed that the biblical prophecies were too obscure to permit any confident identification. It was later alleged that Gilbert Sheldon was the first in the University of Oxford to deny that the pope was Antichrist, perhaps on the occasion of his bachelor of divinity exercise or examination in 1628. These were not minor matters. They went to the heart of arguments about the location of the English church before the Reformation. Was the true church to be found in the underground heretical tradition or in the Church of Rome in which millions had lived and died? From where did the current bishops of the Church of England derive their authority? Laudian divines saw the Church of England as continuously descended from the medieval Catholic church. The apostolic succession of English bishops had been passed down through the medieval church. This meant that the medieval church and the contemporary Catholic church were corrupt, in error, misguided, but not fundamentally false. Beneath all its corruptions, the Church of Rome retained the essence of a true church in the form of valid baptism and ministry. This did not amount to crypto-popery, but not all could appreciate this fine distinction, especially when some Laudians, such as Montagu, did dabble with the theoretical possibility of a reunion of the English and the Roman churches.

The renunciation of Calvinism, the promotion of a new style of divinity, the assertion of the church's authority, and the enunciation of a novel view of the Church of Rome all amount to an impressive agenda for change in the seventeenth-century Church of England. In 1637 Laud pithily described his stewardship of the church as concerned with 'the reducing of it into order, the upholding of the external worship of God in it, and the settling of it to the rules of its first reformation'.[27] Translating these principles from the pulpit and the study into practical policies and then implementing those policies would prove challenging for the church and deeply divisive for English and Scottish society.

*

'All reformation that is good and orderly takes away nothing from the old but that which is faulty and erroneous,' asserted Laud.[28] But, in the eyes of many contemporaries, the Laudian reformation was an assault on all that was good and true. It provoked fear and animosity on a scale that eventually swept away the Church of England. While the growth of Arminianism was a serious political obsession throughout the 1620s, and one bound up with perceptions of misgovernment at home and dangerous alliances abroad, the policies for which Laud was reviled were concentrated in the mid and later 1630s. Obviously Laud did not operate in a vacuum: he had powerful allies such as Archbishop Neile and Charles I, but he also faced opponents such as the Calvinist Bishops Morton of Durham, Davenant of Salisbury and Williams of Lincoln, and the practical difficulties of enforcing his will in a decentralised and largely self-reporting church. As bishop of London from 1628, Laud was champing at the bit. His elevation to the archbishopric of Canterbury on the death of Abbot in the autumn of 1633 finally gave him the opportunity to put his plans into action. Laudian policies accelerated from 1633 and perhaps reached their apogee in the canons issued by Convocation in 1640. Yet those canons were never instituted and within months the world had fallen about Laud's ears.

Laud announced his programme in the *Instructions* of 1633 which charged the bishops to reside in their dioceses, tighten up on the quality of ordinands, enforce the royal orders of 1628 and 1629 on contentious preaching and lecturers, limit the employment of private chaplains, and provide annual reports on their progress 'so we may see how the church is governed and our commands obeyed'. He soon followed up with a 'metropolitical visitation', in which his agent, Sir Nathaniel Brent, toured the dioceses of the southern province. Any reformer needs to promote like-minded men and to weed out opponents. Laud and his allies formed a clerical elite who needed to ensure their support further down the church hierarchy. Through ecclesiastical and university patronage, they advanced believers in the cause such as Heylyn and Cosin, and those who were staunchly 'anti-puritan' although still Calvinist, such as Robert Sanderson or Samuel Fell. Other reliable men were identified through the visitation process. Bishop Wren of Norwich enlisted fifty-nine clergy as 'standing commissioners' to maintain the initiatives of his visitation. There is some evidence that draft visitation articles were circulating which may have served as a means of distinguishing between good Laudian ministers and less trustworthy clergymen. Nothing breeds success like success and as the Laudian bandwagon gathered pace many ministers began to reveal hitherto unknown zeal for ceremonies or antipathy towards Calvinism. Some of these divines may well have been at odds with the prevailing godly culture of the Church of England for several decades, others were no doubt self-interested careerists. The time had now come to nail their colours to the Laudian mast. The Laudian 'moment' had arrived.[29]

The Laudians defined themselves against their predecessors and opponents. They opposed 'puritan' ministers who spouted predestinarian Calvinism and practised partial conformity to the Church of England. Muzzling the Calvinists had been a long-standing Laudian aim. In

December 1629 royal instructions repeated the 1628 ban on preaching predestination, restricted the freedoms of lecturers and preachers, and stipulated that Sunday afternoon sermons be replaced with catechising. In 1633 Laud won a victory when the feofees for impropriations were legally dissolved. Lectureships were controlled and in some cases 'retuned' with orthodox Laudians preaching on the role of ceremonies, prayer and the sacrament. Calvinist preaching was silenced in the universities and at court: in March 1630 Bishop Davenant earned a dressing-down for trying to preach a predestinarian sermon at court. It is unlikely that obscure parish preachers were prevented from preaching in a Calvinist vein, but the major pulpits and the most eminent preachers were no longer voicing the message. The press was controlled in a similar fashion. Press censorship operated through a system of licensing. Inevitably, the human vagaries involved, the inattention, self-censorship, and sleight of hand, never mind commercial considerations, allowed works of many viewpoints to reach the booksellers' stalls. So Calvinist publications were still appearing, but with difficulty and in smaller numbers. Compromises were often required. To ensure publication, Arthur Hildersham omitted all of the material on the Sabbath from his *Lectures on Psalm 51* (1635) and Joseph Hall dropped his habit of identifying the pope as Antichrist. Backed by friends at Cambridge, Bishop Davenant published a series of Latin works that rehearsed a Calvinist interpretation of the Church of England's doctrine, but he tactfully dropped certain arguments that 'the new fangled humour of these times will not brook'.[30]

Some of Laud's initiatives were precisely calculated. The 1633 reissue of the 1618 *Book of Sports*, for example, was intended to reinforce the requirement of the *Instructions* that Sunday afternoon sermons be restricted to catechising and to strike a blow at the Sabbatarianism of the godly. Attacks on Sabbath observance 'put a knife to the throat of religion', in William Gouge's phrase, by challenging Sabbatarian notions of the day as a fast and by restricting opportunities for soul-saving sermons.[31] Whereas the original *Book of Sports* had largely sunk without trace, the 1633 reissue was vigorously promoted and ministers were expected to publish it in church. This caused many clergymen acute difficulties: some read the book while privately regarding its contents as unlawful, and others avoided the obligation or were shielded by sympathetic bishops. Bishop Davenant refused to report those who had not read the book. Other bishops used it as a test of conformity. Curle of Winchester suspended fourteen refusers and Bancroft of Oxford three. As one observer remarked, 'the state doth now take notice that the reading and the not reading this book, is becoming a mark of distinction to know a good, and a bad minister by'.[32]

A far more serious storm was unleashed by the so-called 'altar policy'. At its simplest, this was the requirement that the communion table (which in many churches was located in the chancel) be moved permanently to the east end of the church, placed 'altar-wise' with its shorter sides facing north and south, and railed off. This position was not required by the 1604 canons but there were precedents in several chapels, churches and cathedrals. Moreover, the policy was presented as no more than protecting a religious object against the unwanted and irreverent attentions of children, dogs, and other pests. This was, said Laud repeatedly, a matter of respect and good order. Even when the legal position was regularised by the 1640 canons, the relevant canon asserted that the location of the table 'is in its own nature indifferent, neither commanded nor condemned by the word of God' and implies nothing about the sacrament of the Lord's Supper. It goes on to say that since people lean, sit or put their hats on the communion table it is 'meet and convenient' to protect it with a set of rails. Such claims rang hollow in the ears of critics. The devotional context of adorned and beautified churches, of bowing at the name of Christ, and genuflecting towards the altar, indeed the unapologetic use of the term 'altar' itself, all strongly suggested that the Laudians believed that the communion was some kind of sacrifice of Christ or that the bread and wine might have somehow changed into his body and blood. The subtleties of the theology of the Eucharist need not detain us here, other than to remark that the Laudians did not espouse transubstantiation, but the policy gave people the impression that that they were leading the Church of England towards such popish doctrines.

Archbishop Neile of York was the first to require that parish officials move and rail their altars, but Laud engineered a test case before the Privy Council concerning the London church of St Gregory's by St Paul's in November 1633 and won a judgement that each bishop had the right to determine the position of the parish altars in his diocese. Zealous Laudian bishops, such as Dee of Peterborough and Piers of Bath and Wells, immediately began to demand that communion tables be moved to the east end and surrounded with rails; Laud waited some months, possibly in hope of a royal injunction, before ordering the whole southern province to follow suit in 1635. The evolution and implementation of the policy was complex and full of local variation. So far as the evidence allows us to tell, the majority of English communion tables were placed in the altar position and railed by 1640. Some of this may have happened independently of the Laudian initiative and in some counties only a minority of churches had railed altars. Bishop Hall of Exeter for example, was less than energetic in pursuit of this goal, so many of Devon's churches did not possess railed altars by 1640. On the other hand, Bishop Bancroft of Oxford was an enthusiast with the result that, in the words of one preacher, 'heretofore the evangelical altar was placed so incongruously throughout the whole diocese that a proselyte might easily mistake it for a secular table or common board: now it has that exact position which is consonant to the primitive times'.[33] The only real opposition came from Bishop Williams of Lincoln, a former politician now under a cloud, who was in a bind since his own widely publicised decision in the 1627 Grantham case had opposed an east end, altar-wise, position. In his diocese, Williams attempted to fudge the issue by recommending rails but not stipulating the position of the table. This produced a partial compliance with official policy in some parts of Lincoln diocese. Williams soon found himself under attack in the press from Laud's propagandist Peter Heylyn and then embroiled in a tortuous legal case that led to his imprisonment.

The position and railing of the altar was not the end of the matter. Some bishops or incumbents insisted on changes to the size and orientation of seats and pews, especially in the chancel, the erection of screens, partitions, and other adornments, the repair of paving and refurbishment of fabric, the building of steps and stone altars, and the provision of communion plate in the form of chalices (cups) and patens (plates). (Incidentally, many Laudians also replaced the mundane bowls used for baptisms with gilded stone fonts placed near the west door of the church.) But perhaps the most contentious issue raised by the altar policy was how people used the newly railed altar. To many, but not all, Laudian bishops, it followed from railing the altar that communicants should come to the rails to receive the sacrament and there they should kneel. So kneeling mats, kneeling boards and hassocks were purchased to place before the newly erected rails. But the English were used to receiving the bread and wine in a variety of postures and places, some in their seats, some standing, others sitting or kneeling. Therefore in some parishes, such as Market Harborough, and Epping, where the relocation and railing of the altar had grudgingly been accepted, parishioners protested when expected to receive communion at the altar rails. Even Laud appreciated that there was a need to respect these local sensitivities. Often Laudian bishops just ignored the issue, satisfied if the table had been repositioned and railed.

It was the cumulative effect of the altar policy and the other ceremonial innovations of the Laudian style that alarmed so many parishioners. Whether it touched them directly or they heard news and rumours of what was happening elsewhere, it was obvious that dramatic change was afoot in the religious life of the nation. Cressy has written of the erosion of community as mutual tolerance and local understanding began to break down under the pressure of Laudian policies. It is quite plausible that the intrusion into local practices, the expense of moving communion tables and building rails, the hectoring of some Laudian clergy, and many other prosaic irritations fuelled popular anxiety. Others were more alert to the Laudian threat to the Protestant heritage. Puritan ministers such as Charles Chauncey, who emigrated to New England in 1637, could draw only one conclusion: 'They will have priests and ministers, altars not communion tables, sacrifices not sacraments; they will bow and cringe to and before their altars, yea, they will not endure any man to enquire after what manner of Christ is in the sacrament, whether by way of consubstantiation, or transubstantiation, or in a spiritual manner; yea, they will have tapers, and books never used, empty basins and chalices there, what is this but the mass itself, for here is all the furniture of it.'[34]

The Laudian campaign to establish clerical conformity was long and hard. Diocesan visitations were a principal means of investigating liturgical and ceremonial conformity and Fincham's work on visitation articles has revealed how the Laudians moved the goalposts. The Jacobean approach had been that once a clergyman had subscribed to the articles his practice went largely unmonitored. The Laudian bishops, however, wanted to see full conformity to all of the 1604 canons concerned with worship: this included the use of the surplice, the sign of the Cross, kneeling at the sacrament, and bowing at the name of Jesus, and performing the weekday and holy-day services. Some bishops then went a step further and asked whether the ministers followed the rubrics, the marginal 'stage directions', of the Prayer Book. This involved such matters as standing at various points in the service, observing the calendar of psalms and lessons, and only allowing communion to those who had been confirmed. Laudians proclaimed their respect for the Prayer Book, but they also extended its provisions in certain directions: where the Prayer Book recommended confession as a preparation for holy communion to the sick, the Laudians made this a general recommendation to all communicants.

Every case of clerical nonconformity had to be judged on its merits. Some ministers were admonished to improve their performance, while others felt the full weight of the law. When bishop of London, Laud would summon Nonconformists to subject them to an informal harangue or reprimand, preferring to intimidate them in private rather than bully them in the public eye. But later in the decade, show trials and exemplary punishments became the order of the day. Some dissident clergy were only too willing to take a stand against the Laudian reformation and to suffer the penalties. George Walker, a London minister, was imprisoned by Star Chamber for preaching that it was 'sin to obey the greatest monarchs in things which are against the command of God'. Thomas Case, formerly of Norwich but more recently preaching to the godly in Manchester, was prosecuted for uttering privately and in the pulpit 'dangerous and unsound doctrines' and manifesting his 'great dislike of the government and discipline' of the church. In 1637 William Prynne, a puritan lawyer, had his ears cropped and 'S L' for 'seditious libeller' carved across his cheeks for his part in publishing *News from Ipswich*, a pamphlet attack on the Laudian Bishop Wren. At his trial the judge denounced Prynne for plotting with the pamphleteers Burton and Bastwick 'to set up the puritan or separatist faction'. Although he was no radical, Prynne's experience persuaded him that the bishops were a dangerous breed, an opinion shared by many of those who looked on at his sufferings with horror. As the Laudians politicised the struggle for clerical conformity, they offended a large part of the lay population. Some were simply repelled by the liturgical changes, others resented the harassment of godly Calvinist clergy and the encroachment on lay rights. Charles I demonstrated his tendency to see civil order and ecclesiastical discipline as two sides of the same coin when he intervened in the affairs of corporations such as Great Yarmouth, Salisbury, Gloucester and Shrewsbury. In the shires and the boroughs, those who fell foul of the Laudian bishops and the government's priorities brooded on their resentments and prayed for deliverance.

Rebellion in Scotland

Charles planned great changes for Scotland in the 1630s. Without consulting a General Assembly (which had not been convened since 1618), Charles set the Scottish bishops to work on a set of canons and a Book of Common Prayer for the Kirk. He insisted that the bishops take the English 1549 Prayer Book as their starting point and that they retain saints' days and texts from the Apocrypha. And when they had finished, the King, according to Laud, 'carefully looked over and approved every word in this liturgy'. He created a new bishopric of Edinburgh and ordered the transformation of St Giles's church into a cathedral, a move that rendered the three separate congregations that used the church homeless. The new Scottish Canons were published on the King's authority in January 1636. They ignored much of the reality of the Kirk. There was no mention of presbyteries, lay elders, kirk sessions, or the Assembly and bishops were simply assumed to be in charge of their dioceses. They reaffirmed the Five Articles of Perth and instructed that communion tables be placed at the east end of the church. Extempore prayers were banned and the Scots Book of Common Prayer became mandatory even though the Prayer Book was not available in print for another sixteen months.

It was on 23 July 1637 that the Privy Council trooped to St Giles's to hear the new liturgy read for the first time. The cathedral was engulfed by a riot as the crowd, led by women, pelted the clergy with stools, Bibles and stones. The bishop, dean and councillors fled for their lives. Meanwhile other coordinated demonstrations across Edinburgh reinforced the message. The Privy Council suspended the use of the Prayer Book while awaiting orders from Whitehall. Petitions against the hated Prayer Book began to flood in and a meeting of nobles, lairds, ministers and representatives of the burghs drew up a national petition which they presented to the Council on 19 September. Charles, however, was adamant that the Prayer Book must be enforced and the rioters punished, and the Council and the law courts should leave the city to avoid the disorders. In Edinburgh, events moved fast. The city council joined the protest, rioters took to the streets, and the nobles, lairds, burgesses and ministers produced the national Supplication which admitted their fear of a 'breach of our covenant with God, and forsaking the way of true religion'.[35] In organising this petition and then circulating it through the country for signatures, the noble-led Supplicants were laying the foundation for a national representative assembly. What evolved from the tumultuous meetings in Edinburgh were four committees or 'Tables' representing the four estates of nobles, lairds, burgesses and ministers. The fifth or general Table was the executive committee, dominated by nobles but representing all four Tables. The general Table had the potential to be a provisional government. What made that a reality was the King's intransigent declaration of February 1638. The Table was officially constituted as an executive and its clerk, the young Presbyterian Archibald Johnston of Wariston, was instructed to draft 'a band of mutual association for offence and defence'. The resulting National Covenant welded the traditional aristocratic 'band', a mutual pact to achieve some end, to the Protestant notion of a covenant, a solemn pledge by which the faithful bind themselves to each other and to God. The Covenant reaffirmed the nation's commitment to true religion, defined here by a series of confessions of faith from the 1580s and 1590s, and to upholding royal authority, but only in so far as the King's authority was exercised in defence of the true religion, laws and liberties of the Kingdom. The nobles and lairds signed the Covenant at Greyfriars Kirk, Edinburgh, on 28 February 1638. A solemn fast day was appointed for the people to subscribe and they did so en masse and in a state of emotional and spiritual fervour. March 1638 saw a great up-welling of evangelical zeal and an intense popular sense that Scotland was henceforth a chosen and covenanted nation, a second Israel. Charles I saw it differently. The Covenant made him no more than a Doge of Venice – the elected aristocratic leader of the Venetian Republic – and he would rather die than suffer such indignity. He played for time through the summer largely because he could not afford to mount a military campaign against the Covenanters. In a complex set of manoeuvres he called a General Assembly to meet in Glasgow in November. Charles's representative the Marquis of Hamilton soon lost control of the meeting, which had been packed full of representatives of all four estates, and when he tried to dissolve it, the Assembly ignored him. In December 1638 the Glasgow Assembly wiped the slate clean. It condemned the Prayer Book as full of popish errors, it deposed the bishops and abolished episcopacy, annulled the canons and the Five Articles of Perth, declared the Jacobean Assemblies null and void, banned clergy from civil offices, and asserted the government of the Kirk to be unequivocally Presbyterian. It ordered the Covenant to be subscribed anew, asserted the Kirk's right to call a General Assembly at least once a year, and summoned the next Assembly to meet in Edinburgh in July 1639. The Scots had thrown down the gauntlet to their King.

Notes

1 R. Wilcher, *The Writing of Royalism, 1628–1660* (Cambridge, 2001), p. 55.

2 Kenyon, p. 153.

3 A. Woolrych, *Britain in Revolution 1625–1660* (Oxford, 2002), p. 55.

4 *Works of William Laud*, ed. W. Scott and J. Bliss (7 vols, Oxford, 1847–60), III, 192.

5 Kenyon, p. 155.

6 N. Tyacke, *Anti-Calvinists: The Rise of English Arminianism c.1590–1640* (Oxford, 1987), p. 57.

7 F. Bremer, *Congregational Communion: Clerical Friendship in the Anglo-American Puritan Community 1610–1692* (Boston, Mass., 1994), pp. 70–1.

8 Kenyon, p. 15.

9 C. Russell, *Parliaments and English Politics 1621–1629* (Oxford, 1979), p. 338.

10 Tyacke, *Anti-Calvinists*, p. 159.

11 Gardiner, pp. 73–4.

12 Gardiner, pp. 75–6.

13 Russell, *Parliaments*, p. 407.

14 Russell, *Parliaments*, p. 404.

15 Gardiner, pp. 77–83.

16 Russell, *Parliaments*, p. 404.

17 Gardiner, pp. 92, 97–8.

18 A.I. MacInnes, *The British Revolution, 1629–1660* (Basingstoke, 2005), p. 75.

19 MacInnes, *British Revolution*, p. 90.

20 MacInnes, *British Revolution*, p. 95.

21 *The Works of John Bramhall* (5 vols, Oxford, 1842–5), I, lxxx–lxxxi.

22 *The Letters of John Chamberlain*, ed. N.E. McClure (2 vols, Philadelphia, 1939), II, 609.

23 K. Fincham, 'William Laud and the Exercise of Caroline Ecclesiastical Patronage', *JEH*, 51 (2000), 93.

24 Tyacke, *Anti-Calvinists*, p. 269.

25 K. Fincham, 'Episcopal Government 1603–1640' in Fincham (ed.), *The Early Stuart Church, 1603–1642* (Basingstoke, 1993), p. 82.

26 Laud, *Works*, VI, 57, 59.

27 Kenyon, p. 164.

28 N. Tyacke, 'Archbishop Laud' in Fincham (ed.), *Early Stuart Church*, p. 70.

29 The formulation is Anthony Milton's: see Milton, 'The creation of Laudianism: a new approach', in T. Cogswell, R. Cust and P. Lake (eds), *Politics, Religion and Popularity in Early Stuart England* (Cambridge, 2002).

30 A. Milton, 'Licensing, Censorship, and Religious Orthodoxy in Early Stuart England', *HJ*, 41 (1998), 639.

31 K. Fincham, 'Introduction', in Fincham (ed.), *Early Stuart Church*, p. 15.

32 K. Fincham, 'Clerical Conformity from Whitgift to Laud', in P. Lake and M. Questier (eds), *Conformity and Orthodoxy in the English Church, c.1560–1660* (Woodbridge, 2000), p. 150.

33 K. Fincham, 'The Restoration of Altars in the 1630s', *HJ*, 44 (2001), 929.

34 D. Cressy, *Travesties and Transgressions in Tudor and Stuart England* (Oxford, 2000), p. 198.

35 MacInnes, *British Revolution*, p. 113.

CHAPTER 4

Civil war and revolution (1638–49)

The regime unravels: 1638–42

The unravelling of Charles I's regime is a tale of suspicion and stubbornness, bluff and betrayal, procrastination and high-handedness, in which the personalities of individuals, particularly Charles I and John Pym, and the interplay of the three kingdoms, were as significant as disagreements over constitutional principle. Faced with the Scottish rebellion, Charles talked conciliation while planning repression: for eighteen months after the Scots first rose, he struggled to raise an army that could crush the rebels. The inadequate military machine and financial resources of his English crown prompted him to explore ways in which other parts of the composite Stuart monarchy might help him bring the Scots to heel. One option, quickly thwarted by a contemptuous and rightly suspicious Wentworth, was to accept the offer of Randall MacDonnell, the Catholic Earl of Antrim, to raise clansmen in Ulster and Scotland to aid the King. Another was to use the Catholic-officered army that Wentworth himself was slowly building in Ireland. Meanwhile, Wentworth took steps to neutralise sympathy for the Scots among their compatriots in Ulster by imposing the 'black oath', a solemn renunciation of the Covenant. Predictably, the King's opponents had also hit upon the same strategy of coordination across the three kingdoms: the Covenanters had an agent in London, the Ulster Protestants had their men in Edinburgh, and the English opposition leaders had contacts in Scotland and Ireland. Religion was a common bond among these politicians. They were united by their rejection of Laudian 'innovation' and by a genuine fear of a 'popish plot'. Fear for the safety of religion in this broad sense inspired the scares and rumours, but more specific ecclesiastical questions, such as what to do about episcopacy, would in due course create the most significant political divisions in the English Parliament. Of course, no one could forget that this was the 'bishops' war', a war provoked and prosecuted, in the eyes of many, by the proud prelates who surrounded the King. Discussing the King's declaration of war against the Scots in the summer of 1639, villagers blamed the priests and the bishops; some of the ragtag army of pressed men marching north expressed their views by burning altar rails or smashing church windows. Eventually the English army confronted a well-led, largely professional, Scots force outside Berwick in June, only to beat a quick retreat when challenged. Charles had little option but to take the advice of his nobles and cobble together a hasty truce.

Charles was still intent on suppressing the Scots even though an effective war could only be financed by a parliamentary grant of taxation. Wentworth, ennobled as the Earl of Strafford on his return to England to advise the King, encouraged Charles to call Parliament and even arranged for a meeting of the Irish Parliament to set a precedent with a generous grant of taxation. However, the English Parliament that met in April 1640 was less compliant than its Irish counterpart. MPs did not mince their words. The danger in Scotland 'stands at a distance', said Sir Harbottle Grimston, the greater danger is 'homebred' and is of Old Testament proportions: 'the Commonwealth hath been miserably torn and massacred and all property and liberty shaken, the church distracted, the gospel and the professors of it persecuted and the whole nation is overrun with multitudes and swarms of projecting cankerworms and caterpillars, the worst of all the Egyptian plagues'. The Laudian clergy were the prime targets. Those were 'bad divines' and 'ignorant statesmen' who had preached that the royal prerogative was 'that the King has an unlimited power and that the subjects have no property in their goods', said Sir Francis Seymour. 'The root of all our grievances I think to be an intended union betwixt us and Rome,' offered Francis Rous. John Pym, in a two-hour speech, produced a comprehensive summary of the nation's grievances and talked darkly of the threat from popery, for even the most apparently peaceable papists remained 'at the Pope's command at any time, who only waits for blood'.[1] Irritated by such 'preposterous courses', the King dismissed the 'Short Parliament' after less than three weeks.

Charles did not, however, interrupt the Convocation of the clergy that had, as usual, met alongside the Parliament. It may have been better if he had. The 1640 Convocation produced a set of seventeen new canons for the church which seemed almost calculated to inflame the situation: they included high-flown assertions of the divine right of monarchs and the doctrine of non-resistance, confirmation of the 'altar policy', harsh penalties for sectaries, and worst of all an oath that was intended to demonstrate that the church was opposed to innovation. The so-called *etcetera* oath required the clergy to swear 'never to alter the government of this church by archbishops, bishops, deans and archdeacons, etc., as it now stands established'. But who was to know what might be comprehended within that 'etc.'? And was it wise to rule out further reform of the church in this manner? To those already deeply alienated from the Laudian hierarchy this open-ended oath seemed an obvious trap. In Lincolnshire 'multitudes' of clergy were planning to refuse the oath and papers full of arguments against it passed 'secretly from hand to hand'; in August a meeting was held of London preachers, including John Downham and Cornelius Burges, to coordinate opposition. This 'most filthy, execrable book of Canons' struck fear into puritan hearts.[2] Some of the London godly armed themselves in anticipation of attacks by papists or by royal troops. There was disorder in the streets when Parliament was dissolved and the London apprentices, blaming Laud for the dissolution, took the law into their own hands: there were 'two insurrections in one week', recorded a diarist, an attack on Lambeth Palace, home of the archbishop, and another on one of the London gaols.[3]

The canons of 1640 helped to persuade the Scots that their Covenant would never be safe while the Laudians continued to maintain prelacy in England. So they enthusiastically set about exporting their rebellion. On 20 August a Scottish army crossed the Tweed into England. Their published purpose was unequivocal: 'The reformation of England, long prayed and pleaded for by the godly there, shall be according to their wishes and desires perfected in doctrine, worship and discipline; papists, prelates and all the members of the antichristian hierarchy, with their idolatry, superstition and humane invention shall pack them from hence; the names of sects and separatists shall be no more mentioned, and the Lord shall be one, and his name one, throughout the whole island.'[4] The Scots routed the demoralised English forces on 28 August, and occupied Newcastle and the north-east. After two months of negotiation, Charles finally signed a truce that committed him to paying the Scots £850 a day until a full agreement had been reached and guaranteed by the English Parliament. This was not the only pressure forcing Charles to summon another Parliament. Petitions from the counties, the City of London, twelve leading peers, all echoing the analysis that Pym had offered to the Short Parliament, urged the King to consult Parliament.

The Parliament that met on 3 November 1640 was to continue in one form or another until 1653. MPs and peers assembled in tense anticipation of major reforms: it was their duty, said Sir John Wray, to achieve 'true reformation of all disorders and innovations in church and religion'; but few if any could have imagined that their Parliament would find itself at war with the King in a little over eighteen months. It has often been remarked that in 1640 there was only one side, a united and overwhelming opposition to the King. Of course, this opposition in reality was a fluctuating alliance of individuals, motivated by a variety of principles, interests and personal connections. It included a group, notably Dorset, Southampton, Bristol, and Richmond in the Lords, and Edward Hyde, Sir John Culpepper and Lord Falkland in the Commons, who believed that the monarch was subject to the laws, who valued the church, the Prayer Book and bishops, but not the Laudian innovations, and who are generally known as 'constitutional royalists'. Noisier, but probably fewer in number, were the godly – Pym, Fiennes, Denzil Holles, John Hampden and Oliver St John among the MPs, and Bedford, Essex, Warwick, and Saye in the Lords – who were dubbed Pym's 'junto' by the royalist Edward Nicholas. These men were part of a network of godly activists who had cooperated during the 1630s to protect and promote puritan ministers, prepare for Hampden's trial, or participate in the Providence Island Company. It was this group that made much of the running in the Long Parliament, who set the tone of earnest godliness and hysteria, maintained the level of religious excitement, and tuned the parliamentary pulpits.

For the first six months of the Long Parliament most members were united in their opposition to Charles I's policies and advisers. Both the moderate 'constitutional royalists' and the zealous godly could agree that Strafford, Laud and other 'evil counsellors' should be removed from office and influence, that the judges who had upheld Ship Money should be investigated, that monopolies and other grievances should be redressed, and that the existence of Parliament should be guaranteed by a Triennial Act (February 1641) requiring the King to summon a Parliament every third year and providing a mechanism for this to happen if he did not. In May, Strafford 'was hurried hence / 'Twixt treason and convenience' – beheaded, in other words, after an attempt to impeach him for subverting the fundamentals laws of England and Ireland had failed due to lack of proof, and he had simply been declared guilty by a parliamentary act of attainder. 'Praised be the Lord,' exclaimed the puritan Wallington.[5] Strafford might still have escaped the scaffold if it had not been for the discovery of the Army Plot, a rash plan, in which Charles's involvement was justly suspected, by a group of officers to seize the Tower, release Strafford and dissolve Parliament by force. The subsequent tide of popular fear and fury not only panicked Charles into giving his assent to the attainder, but led Parliament to draw up the Protestation, an oath to defend the rights of King and Parliament and the true reformed Protestant religion against all popery and popish innovation. Sworn at first by MPs, the Protestation was soon extended to the entire population. The febrile atmosphere fed fears of violence, coups, massacres and risings. Pym made 'security' a central political issue and in July proposed a bill to strip the King of his control of the county militias.

The main work of Parliament, however, was in rolling back the Laudian reformation. It had been the rallying cry from the first. On 17 November 1640, the anniversary of Queen Elizabeth's accession, the preacher Stephen Marshall urged MPs to 'throw to the moles and the bats every rag that hath not God's stamp and name upon it'.[6] Parliamentary committees were rapidly established to tackle the urgent work: bishops were thrown into prison, 'scandalous clergy' were investigated, and hundreds of past cases decided in the church courts were reviewed and found wanting. As horrified MPs unearthed more and more of the excesses of the Laudian bishops, they were also presented with evidence of popular hostility towards the church policies of the 1630s. On 11 June, parishioners at St Thomas the Apostle, London, took the Protestation and heeding its words about 'popish innovations' hacked down the altar rails and made a bonfire of them in the churchyard, crying 'Dagon being now down, they would burn him.'[7] Altar rails, surplices, prayer books, images, and other Laudian targets were carefully selected for destruction by zealots, complaints against 'scandalous' and 'malignant' clergy flooded in from the parishes, and petitions arrived from the counties demanding the restoration of religion as it had been in the days of Elizabeth and James. In September, the Commons took upon themselves the authority to order churchwardens to remove innovations from the country's churches, while the House of Lords reissued their earlier instruction that church services were not to be disturbed.

There was a decisive hardening of attitudes in some quarters. Those who had once been critics of the church became implacable opponents. Confronted with evidence both of Laudian policies and of contemporary animosity, peers and MPs began to identify the office of bishop and the episcopal government of the church as the root of the problem. In December 1640, Parliament received a petition for the abolition of bishops that claimed 15,000 signatures gathered in London and the support of thirteen counties. Yet for many, abolition was still a step too far. In the subsequent debate, Digby urged, 'Let us not destroy bishops, but make bishops such as they were in primitive times.' The following June, as part of the political struggle over the exclusion of the bishops from the House of Lords, the Commons debated a bill to abolish bishops 'root and branch' and replace them with lay commissioners in each county. Since this bill would never have passed the Lords, it was a gesture, but a highly significant one; it evidenced the godly's belief that this parliament had been called 'by the immediate finger of God for this work'.[8] Under pressure, men changed their minds. The Lincolnshire MP Sir John Wray was an opponent of 'idolatry' from the outset, but disclaimed any desire to overthrow bishops; after the London petition, however, he began to argue that Parliament should at least debate church government. In May 1641 he presented a petition against episcopacy from his constituents and in November he proposed the abolition of episcopacy unless the bishops could demonstrate from the Bible that 'their spiritual primacy over the ministers of Christ be in deed and truth inferred unto them by the holy law of God'.[9]

Others moved in the opposite direction and often out of fear. They were terrified by fiery sermons calling for radical reformation. Preaching in Exeter in the summer of 1641, John Bond denounced the 'anti-reformists', those 'dull and backward to the means . . . of this reformation', who 'trample unparalleled national mercies under foot, and so are unworthy to breathe in these blessed times which we see'.[10] Popular destruction of altar rails, crucifixes, candlesticks and pictures aroused fears of the complete collapse of social order. 'The Brownists and other sectaries make such havoc in our churches by pulling down of ancient monuments, glass windows and rails that their madness is intolerable,' said one official in London. 'I think it will be thought blasphemy shortly to name Jesus Christ, for it is already forbidden to bow at his name.'[11] Bishops were part of the traditional pattern of government. Sir Thomas Aston saw the root and branchers as uprooting all order 'to shake off the yoke of all obedience, either to ecclesiastical, civil, common, statute or customary laws of the kingdom and to introduce a mere arbitrary government'. Already the effects of the collapse of their authority were visible. In the alleys of London and other towns, semi-clandestine congregations came together: constables surprised sixty people worshipping together in Deadman's Place, Southwark; six members formed the church meeting at Broadmead in Bristol in 1640, but three years later the congregation had risen to 160. Some congregations seem to have been imported by returning exiles such as Thomas Goodwin and Sidrach Simpson. William Bridge and a group of thirty exiles returned from the Netherlands to set up a church at Yarmouth. Others, such as the London congregations led by Henry Jessey,

John Duppa and John Spilsbury were the descendants of earlier underground sects. Yet, as Tolmie remarks, the London congregations probably had a thousand or so members, 'a negligible number' in such a vast city.[12] It was the reaction to these 'sects' and 'conventicles' that helped to make them so significant. The opening of Praise-God Barebon's church to the public in December 1641 provoked a riot involving thousands. Pamphleteers mocked his preaching: 'crying diverse times, as was audible heard, hell and damnation, he did speak likewise much against the Book of Common Prayer, against the bishops, and many others'.[13]

The country was now in as much danger of anarchy as it was from the rule of a misguided monarch. Sir Edward Dering, who had promoted the root and branch bill in June 1641, drew back after his experience of disorders in Kent later that summer. He was troubled to hear, too, of growing numbers of religious sects, who 'would have every particular congregation to be independent, and . . . votes about every matter of jurisdiction . . . to be drawn up from the whole body of the church . . . both men and women'.[14] The King, meanwhile, seemed to have abandoned the Laudians: in January 1641 he committed himself to restoring all matters of religion and government to what they had been 'in the purest times of Queen Elizabeth's day'; he promised to defend episcopacy – and refused to contemplate the removal of bishops from the Lords because their presence there was 'one of the fundamental constitutions of this kingdom' – but began to promote non-Laudians and Calvinists such as John Williams and Henry King. In so doing, Charles was raising a standard of moderate reform, rule according to custom and law, which many of the more traditionally minded politicians found inherently attractive. The process by which two opposing sides emerged was gaining pace.

*

In November 1641 sensational news arrived in London of a rebellion in Ulster. Gaelic leaders had attempted to seize Dublin and had called out their followers in Ulster. Primarily an attempt to regain a share in property and local power from the Protestants, this rebellion was draped in the language of loyalty to the King, and its leader Sir Phelim O'Neill even claimed to have been commissioned by Charles to mobilise in his name. Within weeks the Old English, who feared that the Scottish Covenanters and English Parliamentarians might be planning to suppress Catholicism in Ireland, had joined forces with the Gaelic rebels. The violence escalated: Protestants were murdered, driven off their lands and into exile, and something like local guerrilla war developed between the Catholic and Protestant communities. Rumour inflated the massacre of 4,000 Protestants into the massacre of tens of thousands. Everything that Pym had been saying for years about popery and plots had suddenly become all the more believable and terrifying. Wallington classed the Ulster Rising with the Armada and the Gunpowder Plot as another demonstration of 'how Antichrist, even those bloody-hearted papists, does plot against the poor Church of God'.[15]

The Ulster Rising breathed new life into Pym's campaign to curb royal powers and brought to the fore the crucial issue of whether Charles could be trusted with command of an army. Pym produced a 'Grand Remonstrance' that catalogued the misgovernment of Charles I and the fears and aspirations of the parliamentary radicals. Pointedly and controversially, it was addressed to the people and referred to Charles in the third person. It asserted the existence of a plot by 'the Jesuited papists', 'the bishops and the corrupt part of the clergy', and certain counsellors and courtiers, to subvert the constitution, 'to suppress the purity and power of religion', to promote Arminianism and accommodate popery, and 'to multiply and enlarge the difference between the common Protestants and those whom they call puritans'.[16] After a furious debate, it passed by a mere eleven votes on 23 November. Largely symbolic though it was, the Remonstrance served as a marker of the direction and pace of reform and of widening divisions. Tradition has it that Oliver Cromwell had threatened to emigrate if it was defeated, while to the more conservative it revealed that Parliament was now a more dangerous threat to the constitutional balance than the King.

Charles continued to make contradictory gestures, partly because he continued to oscillate between the advice of moderate men such as Hyde and Falkland, both of whom were now appointed to office, and the 'violent party'. The official royal reply to the Grand Remonstrance was conciliatory, appealing for reliance on the laws, mutual trust, and unity in the face of the Irish rebels, but simultaneously the King embarked on a series of provocations: he supported the bishops in a protest against votes taken in their absence in the House of Lords; he tried to install one of his own military men as Lieutenant of the Tower; and on 4 January 1642, he attempted to arrest five MPs (Pym, Hampden, Strode, Holles and Haselrig) in the Commons on a charge of treason. The five had already 'flown' to the safety of the City. Unabashed Charles went to the City authorities to demand that they be handed over, but with no success. Unfortunately for the King, the royalist mayor had lost control of the City to a radical majority returned in the recent Common Council elections. Now the radicals claimed to fear a Cavalier attack, and the City called out its militia. The two sides glowered at each other, but the weakness of the King's hand had been revealed for all to see: he withdrew first to Hampton Court, and then a few days later to the more secure base of Windsor Castle. There was an unmistakeable sense that a turning point had been reached.

On 5 March Parliament passed the Militia Ordinance that empowered its officials to raise troops – this was the first time that the Houses had claimed and exercised the power to pass legislation without royal assent. During the spring and summer, both sides sought to rally their supporters and to secure strategic towns and cities, ports, munitions, magazines – Parliament established control of Portsmouth and Hull, and the fleet, while the King gained York. There was little genuine attempt at reconciliation, but then each side believed that it could overawe the other, possibly with the help of Scottish allies, and many still thought a war unlikely. Royalism continued to gather momentum. In March a petition from Kent urged Parliament and King to renew their 'good understanding', questioned some of the powers that Parliament was taking to itself, and proclaimed the local gentry's enthusiastic support for 'episcopal government' and the 'solemn liturgy of the Church of England'. Parliament clapped the petitioners in gaol and had the petition burned by the hangman. Significantly, one of the leading petitioners was Sir Edward Dering, the one-time root and brancher. When Parliament presented the King with the *Nineteen Propositions*, he issued a masterful *Answer*, drafted by Falkland, that advanced a vision of an 'ancient, equal, happy, well-poised' constitution, based on the rule of law and a balance of Lords, Commons and Crown. Yet at the same time as making this moderate appeal to the middle ground, Charles issued commissions of array to nobles and gentlemen to raise troops in his name.

Midsummer 1642 found the nation drifting towards war. Men were genuinely perplexed when faced with the contradictory demands of Parliament and King to take up arms: the Norfolk gentleman Thomas Knyvett wrote to his wife in despair in May, explaining that he had just been commissioned by the Earl of Warwick to take command of a company under the Militia Ordinance when he encountered the King's declaration 'point-blank' against the Ordinance; in Devon the gentry struggled with their 'twofold obedience' and bewailed 'each loyal heart rent within itself'.[17] 'A plague on both your houses' was a common reaction and evidence survives of attempted neutrality pacts in over twenty counties. But the zealots, over-confident, and sometimes over-fearful of their enemies, urged on the militarisation. In early July Parliament voted to raise a volunteer army of 10,000 men under the Earl of Essex and in mid-August it declared Charles's supporters 'traitors'.

What moved people to fight? Royalists often cited the obligations of conscience and honour, as well as their detestation of rebellion: 'truly I love religion as well as any man,' explained Thomas Holles, 'but I do not understand the religion of rebellion'.[18] Enemies were demonised and reduced to crude stereotypes, 'roundhead', 'schismatic' or 'papist'. Parliamentarians were persuaded that religion was in mortal danger. They had been taught 'that Antichrist was here in England as well as in Rome, and that the bishops were Antichrist, and that all that did endeavour to support them were popishly affected, Babylonish and antichristian too, yea many professed papists'. Preachers stirred up the men: Nehemiah Wharton, a young Parliamentarian volunteer, heard Obadiah Sedgwick preach on a fast day: 'his doctrine wrought wonderfully upon many of us, and doubtless hath fitted many of us for death, which we all shortly expect'.[19] Some went to war with barely a backward glance, but most were reflective. Individuals agonised, or sought divine guidance: 'when I put my hand to the Lord's work,' remembered one West Riding parliamentarian, 'I did it not rashly, but had many an hour or night to seek God, to know my way'.[20] Many, and at all levels of society, calculated what was safest for them, their families and property, or had little choice as they were impressed for service. No generalisation does justice to the infinite complexity of allegiance in a civil war. Neither social standing, nor age, nor material interest can be used as a guide to the way that the English people took sides in 1642. Perhaps the strongest affinities were those concerned with religion. The royalists tended to attract those who still valued the Book of Common Prayer, the bishops, and the structure of the Church of England; the parliamentarians were those who believed that there was room for 'further reformation' and a need to shore up Protestantism against popish subversion.

War in three kingdoms

The inconclusive battle at Edgehill in Warwickshire on 23 October 1642 was the first pitched battle to have been fought in England since 1485. Although the Earl of Essex withdrew, the King did not capitalise on the opportunity by advancing towards London, instead he turned to Oxford which he made his base for the rest of the war and only launched an attack on the capital days later when Essex had had time to mobilise the London-trained bands. The royalist advance was halted at Turnham Green on 13 November. As campaigning ceased for the winter, there was little military achievement to report, but neither side seemed ready to make any meaningful concessions. Unrealistic peace terms were briefly discussed in the spring, before the royalists began to close in on London from three directions: the Duke of Newcastle marched from the north, defeating Sir Thomas Fairfax on the way and establishing royalist control of Yorkshire; Sir Ralph Hopton moved from Cornwall through the West Country where parliamentarian armies were defeated at Lansdown, Roundway Down and Bristol; the King meanwhile advanced from Oxford towards London. Although the King's progress was blocked at Newbury in September, the royalist victories of 1643 were proof to many that the King would now prevail; and victory, for most, was evidence of divine approval: 'look upon the King from the beginning, and think . . . if God's blessing had not gone with him, whether it had been possible he could have been in such a condition, as he is now in', urged one female royalist.[21] The other side had not completely lost heart, however. After the defeat at Roundway, Edward Harley reported 'the hand of God mightily against us, for 'twas he only that made us fly. We had very much self confidence and I trust the Lord has only brought this upon us to make us look more to him, who I am confident, when we are weakest, will show himself a glorious God over the enemies of truth.'[22] There was still everything to play for: 'two summers passed over, and we are not saved', commented Fairfax's chaplain. 'What we won one time we lost another . . . the game, however set up at winter, was to be new played again the next spring.'[23]

Charles I's other kingdoms were also racked with conflict. The general Catholic rising in Ireland had swept almost all before it, bar a small royal army under the Earl of Ormonde in the Pale and larger Scottish force commanded by Monro which had come to the aid of the Ulster Protestants. In May 1642 the Catholic rebels, lay and clerical, took an oath of association known as the Confederation of Kilkenny, by which they pledged their loyalty and their arms to the King, the Roman Catholic faith and their homeland, and renounced 'the puritans' as their enemies.[24] The Confederates moved in on Ormonde and in 1643 the King allowed him to open negotiations with the Catholic leaders. On 15 September, Ormonde and the Confederates agreed the 'cessation', a twelve-month truce, which allowed the King to bring over Irish troops to reinforce his English armies. Unfortunately this rather marginal military advantage was overshadowed by the harmful public perception in England that Charles was happy to do a deal with Catholics and to use Irish papists against English Protestants.

Events in Scotland, however, had a more decisive impact on the history of all three kingdoms. On 25 September 1643, Pym's long-nurtured Scottish alliance was finally achieved: the Solemn League and Covenant was an agreement in the name of England, Scotland and Ireland to protect the rights of the parliaments and power of the King across all three kingdoms, and to bring their churches 'to the nearest conjunction and uniformity in religion'. In England it was a commitment to extirpate popery and prelacy and to reform religion 'according to the word of God and the example of the best reformed churches'. While the Scots assumed this meant the erection of a Presbyterian church like their own, the phrase was sufficiently broad to allow the English Parliament to evade that obligation. The 'immediate political price' of the Covenant was, as MacInnes points out, 'the spread of civil war from England and Ireland to Scotland'.[25] But in the English context, the tide had begun to turn in Parliament's favour. After John Pym's death in December, even more radical MPs, such as Oliver St John, Henry Vane and Oliver Cromwell, assumed leadership of the war effort. In January 1644 a Scottish force of 21,000 under the Earl of Leven marched south to threaten Newcastle's army and in February a Committee of Both Kingdoms was created to give coordination to the joint war effort.

Trapped between Leven's army and the parliamentary forces led by Fairfax, Manchester and Cromwell approaching from the south, Newcastle's army found itself pushed back towards York. In April, the Scots and Parliamentarians laid siege to York and when Prince Rupert arrived to relieve the city some weeks later, he was forced to fight a pitched battle. The parliamentarian victory at Marston Moor on 2 July smashed Newcastle's army, destroyed the royalists' hold on northern England, made Cromwell's military reputation, and possibly decided the course of the war. It had, believed Cromwell, 'all the evidences of an absolute victory obtained by the Lord's blessing upon the godly party principally'.[26] The balance of forces was changing elsewhere. In March the parliamentarian army under Waller had heavily defeated the King's western army at Cheriton and then in conjunction with Essex's force had advanced on the King in Oxfordshire. Although Charles was forced to withdraw towards the Welsh borders, Waller and Essex threw away their successes by quarrelling among themselves and dividing their armies: Waller was subsequently to be mauled by the royalists at Cropredy in Oxfordshire, and Essex went down to serious defeat at Lostwithiel. So by the later summer of 1644, although the royalists did not look capable of mounting a credible military strategy, neither did the parliamentarians seem sufficiently organised and determined to press home their advantage to a final victory.

Parliament's problems sprang from several sources. The Scots were uneasy allies, jealous of English generals, and increasingly concerned by the campaign of James Graham, Marquis of Montrose, who had rallied royalist sympathisers in the Highlands to resist the Covenanters and their ambitious leader Argyll. Montrose had linked up with the Earl of Antrim's Catholic Irish troops, under the command of the ruthless Alasdair MacColla, and in the winter of 1644–45 he launched a war which was, seen from one perspective, a royalist rising against the Covenanters and their general Argyll, but was from another angle a clan war of the MacDonalds against the Campbells and their chieftain Argyll. In September 1644 Montrose's forces took Aberdeen and behaved barbarously; then in the depths of winter Montrose drove Argyll from his castle at Inverarary and celebrated mass there; and in February, he defeated Argyll at Inverlochry amid horrific scenes of clan vengeance. As Montrose continued to rack up victories in the summer of 1645, it was understandable that the Covenanter government in Edinburgh began to think their armies in England could be better used at home.

Parliament's own armies and generals were pulling in different directions. It had long been recognised that volunteer armies raised in and paid for by the counties were prone to strong regional sympathies, and some might refuse to march out of their own district or to winter away from their homes and families. In the hope of mitigating or overcoming this localism, Parliament had created armies based on two regional groupings, the Midland Association and the Eastern Association, in 1643. But Parliament could do little to remedy the attitudes of its generals: aristocrats and moderates such as Essex and Manchester lacked the killer instinct that was necessary to prosecute the war to a final and complete victory over the King. Manchester famously and damagingly declared that if the parliamentarians beat the King ninety-nine times, he would still be king, but if the King beat them once, they would all be hanged. Why then, asked Cromwell, did we ever take up arms? A vicious bout of political infighting in the Commons in November and December 1644 led to the purging of the half-hearted generals in the following spring through a device known as the Self-denying Ordinance and the formation of a 'New Model Army', a national army, controlled and financed from Westminster, commanded by Fairfax, Skippon and Cromwell, bringing together experienced cavalry from the Eastern Association force, a powerful artillery train, and a less-impressive infantry drawn from the old parliamentarian armies and pressed men. With regular pay, distinctive uniforms, strong leadership and discipline, the New Model soon began to take on a character unlike previous forces.

The New Model came to embody much of the godly enthusiasm of the 1640s. This was reputedly a praying army – William Dell reported that he had overheard troopers praying 'with that faith and familiarity with God that [I] have stood wondering at the grace' – its standards were adorned with 'pray and fight' and its passwords were 'God with us' and the like.[27] It was increasingly an army drawn to the principles of Independency or congregationalism, 'gathering churches' of visible professors and listening to lay preachers. In 1645 Richard Baxter found the common soldiers argued for state democracy and church democracy, against set prayers and infant baptism, 'about free grace and free will and all the points of Antinomianism and Arminianism'. He thought that 'Independency and Anabaptistry were most prevalent: Antinomianism and Arminianism were equally distributed'. The troops were also influenced by 'men that had been in London hatched up among the old separatists'.[28] But not all of the New Model was godly or godly in this style. Religious differences led to problems. The Presbyterian commander Sir Samuel Luke arrested two captains for lay preaching and was aghast when General Fairfax released them. Fleetwood, their colonel, remonstrated with Luke that 'truly in these times wherein we expect light from God our duty is not to force men, but to be tender of such as walk conscientiously, and rather to give than deprive them of liberty for we know not but those who dissent from us may be in the right'. To which Luke could only reply, 'I pray God the light you speak of proves not the darkness which hath plunged Germany into all her miseries.'[29]

The creation of the New Model was a product of the power struggles in Parliament. In the mid-1640s, loose 'war', 'peace' and 'middle parties' gave way to better-defined 'Presbyterian' and 'Independent' parties with identifiable leaders in both Houses of Parliament and fairly clear aims: the Presbyterians, led by Denzil Holles, William Strode and Sir Philip Stapleton in the Commons and Essex, Manchester and Warwick in the Lords, were close to the Scots, supported some kind of Presbyterian church, and advocated a negotiated settlement with the King. The Independents, such as the MPs Cromwell, St John, Vane and Pierrepoint and, in the Lords, Northumberland, Saye and Sele, and Wharton, were hostile to the Scots and Presbyterianism, preferring religious toleration, and convinced that the King had to be defeated militarily before national reconstruction could begin. In time, both groups would also come to be defined by their relations with the New Model Army.

As the new campaigning season began in 1645, Fairfax and the New Model still did not have the freedom of action necessary to prosecute the war. News of Prince Rupert's storming of Leicester finally convinced the

Committee of Both Kingdoms to allow Fairfax to decide his own strategy. He immediately advanced on the royalist army and took a stand south of Market Harborough. The battle of Naseby took place on 14 June. It was a brief – no more than three hours long – but comprehensive and bloody defeat for the royalists. Fifty regimental standards or colours were captured, along with the artillery, ammunition and baggage, which included some highly embarrassing royal correspondence, and a large part of the royalist infantry who were marched off into captivity. Less fortunate were the three or four hundred female camp followers or 'whores' murdered by the parliamentarians. After Naseby, Fairfax turned to the west to deal with Goring's army. Cromwell's victory against a much larger royalist force at Langport, Somerset, in July convinced the general that he had seen the face of God and inspired Major Harrison to break into rapturous praise of the Lord on the battlefield. Royalist strongholds were now picked off one after the other – Bath, Bristol, Tiverton, Basing House during the autumn – and the remaining royalist armies were tackled early in 1646; Hopton's was defeated at Torrington in January and Astley's at Stow-on-the-Wold in March. Oxford, the royalist capital, remained under siege, but in April Charles left the city and travelled northwards; on 5 May he gave himself up to the Scots encamped at Southwell as part of the encirclement of Newark; in June he ordered the surrender of his remaining garrisons.

Although at first sight the conflicts in Scotland and Ireland barely seem to be part of the same war, they were, of course, closely connected to events in England, most obviously through the King's hopes that both or either of his Celtic kingdoms would afford him the military aid that might rescue his English position. In Ireland, where Ormonde acted as the King's secret negotiator with the Confederates, the cessation of 1643 was renewed until January 1645. The King had little to offer to the Irish rebels: he was not prepared to give up his own rights in Ireland nor to sacrifice the interests of the Protestant ascendancy; but he did empower the Catholic Earl of Glamorgan to negotiate with the Confederates behind Ormonde's back. Although Ormonde won a treaty in March 1646 that promised 10,000 Confederate troops would be shipped over to fight for Charles in England, it is doubtful whether this was seriously intended and, of course, it came far too late to help the King. Meanwhile, the Confederates were still fighting the Protestant forces, mainly Monro's Anglo-Scottish army, paid for by the English Parliament. The duplicitous world of Stuart negotiations in Ireland would take another turn in 1647 when Ormonde agreed to hand Dublin over to the representatives of the English Parliament and then left Ireland. Charles had effectively lost his last toehold in Ireland.

In Scotland, the Campbells and MacDonalds continued their ferocious contest. In the summer of 1645 Leslie brought 6,000 men north from the Covenanter army in England and crushed Montrose at Phillipshaugh in September; but the MacDonalds were not finished yet, and through 1646 and into the spring of 1647 Leslie's army was forced to chase them up first the eastern and then the western coasts. Their nominal leader Montrose had fled into exile and MacColla crossed the Irish Sea only to die on an Ulster battlefield. By 1647 it finally looked as though Argyll and the Covenanters had re-established control and Scotland would offer Charles no further succour.

The wars may have been over but their scars remained. One in eight men had been involved in the wars and the best estimates suggest that 180,000 people died during the wars – a number that was roughly 3.6 per cent of the population, and which should be compared with the death toll of 2.6 per cent and 0.6 per cent of the population in the First and Second World Wars. There was a slightly higher chance that a soldier would die of dysentery, the spotted fever, or some other disease than in combat, and victims were as likely to perish in small-scale skirmishes as in battles. Petitions from veterans remind us that those who did make it home were often pitifully crippled and traumatised. Many individuals and families were broken, physically, mentally and materially, by the civil wars: they suffered casual brutality and abuse by soldiers; conscription as troops or as forced labour; the theft of property, crops and livestock; the epidemics that swept through towns or the fires that consumed them; the demolition of houses to make way for defences; and the dislocation of ordinary commerce and agriculture. War had brought far greater governmental intrusion into people's ordinary lives and far heavier taxation than anything Charles I had ever threatened. The monthly and weekly 'assessments' or taxes imposed by Parliament had followed the pattern of rates like Ship Money, but other taxes, such as the excise on foodstuffs, were unprecedented and hit the poor as much as the wealthy. While the law slept, arbitrary imprisonment and punishment were facts of life, as was the high-handed rule of the county committees, those agencies of local government that had fallen into the hands of upstarts and zealots and were quite as capable of ignoring parliamentary ordinances as riding roughshod over traditional rights and customs. One symptom of the popular hatred of the war and its effects was the rash of short-lived Clubmen Associations that emerged in 1645 across parts of the south, the south-west, South Wales, and the Welsh borders. Usually sparked by a confrontation with soldiers seeking plunder, these county movements acquired gentry leadership and an ideology of demilitarisation, the defence of local liberties and 'ancient ways', and a rhetoric of complaint about the nation's 'bleeding under the devouring sword'.[30] Although tactical needs might dictate temporary alliances with one side or the other, these associations wanted nothing more than an end to conflict and a return to the pre-war situation. There could be no going back, however. The civil wars had been a long and painful political education: individuals on both sides of the conflict and at all social levels had been forced to justify their actions; politicians, preachers and pamphleteers had fuelled the debate about why and when a parliament could take up arms against a king; and the discussion had broadened out into a discussion of the rights and duties of individuals. In no field was the debate more urgent than that of religion.

Reforming the Reformation: religion in the 1640s

Dismantling the Laudian reformation had unleashed powerful forces. The Church of England was thrown into crisis: bishops had been carted off to gaol; several parish ministers had found themselves hauled before parliamentary committees, sometimes as a result of parochial or personal feuds; in some parishes, tithes went unpaid or vestry meetings were poorly attended; and the discipline and courts of the church were grinding to a halt. Meanwhile, as we have seen, an unintended and largely unforeseen religious liberty had allowed the emergence of independent, voluntary, congregations. As so often, there are few impartial accounts of such groups: those with a pamphlet to sell or an axe to grind complained that London had become another Amsterdam or offered lurid reports of the affronts offered by the sectaries; Bishop Hall told the Lords in December 1641 that London and its suburbs hosted 'no fewer than four-score congregations of several sectaries, instructed by guides fit for them, cobblers, tailors, felt-makers, and such like trash'. In November 1643, the London clergy complained of 'the lamentable confusion of their church under the present anarchy, the increase of anabaptists, antinomians and sectaries and the boldness of some in the city and about it in gathering congregations'.[31] Parliament had never planned 'to let loose the golden reins of discipline and government in the church, to leave private persons or particular congregations to take up what form of divine service they please'. Once the 'exorbitant power' of the bishops had been curbed, the Grand Remonstrance proposed 'a general synod . . . who may consider of all things necessary for the peace and good government of the church . . . the better to effect the intended reformation'.[32]

This synod, the Westminster Assembly of Divines, made up of ninety English divines nominated by Parliament and thirty lay assessors, met in July 1643. It was, perhaps, the opportunity that Edward Calamy had imagined to 'reform the Reformation itself'.[33] The Assembly was charged with creating a new national church, with laying down its constitution, its worship and its confession of faith. Apparently the plan was to win over the middle ground of 'godly' clergy to this scheme. The learned and judicious divines summoned were a fairly representative group of puritan clergy, broadly Calvinist, sympathetic to those with scruples over conformity to the Prayer Book, and open to replacing episcopacy with some form of Presbyterianism. English Presbyterianism, however, came in many different shapes: the conventional model, as exemplified in Geneva and Scotland, included the four offices – pastor, teacher, deacon and lay elder – and an ascending series of representative assemblies, called synods and classes, to which each congregation was subject; the congregation exercised discipline over its members and the relative power of the pastor and the lay elders varied from place to place. Such a system appealed to few even in the Westminster Assembly. Robert Baillie, one of the Scottish envoys to the Assembly, was disappointed to discover only half a dozen of the divines sympathised with Scots-style Presbyterianism. Some of the English 'Presbyterian' divines argued that the Bible did not insist upon a Presbyterian government, or they proposed that each church should have a presbytery while any additional hierarchy of synods was simply a useful human addition. They were prepared to compromise if necessary, perhaps giving way on the necessity for lay elders, or recognising a role for a modified episcopacy, or allowing the civil magistrate a final say in some church matters. They regarded such matters as far less important than preserving the unity of the national church. The agreement of the Solemn League and Covenant and the influence of the Scots brought a different complexion to the Assembly. Baillie rallied support both in the Assembly and outside, especially among London's Presbyterian ministers who met at Sion College, and began to exert pressure for the full-blown Presbyterianism necessary to achieve the 'real reformation' to which the Covenant aspired.

A minority within the Assembly was uneasy about the intolerant direction that it was taking under Scottish influence. Their manifesto, *An Apologetical Narration*, which was published in January 1644, attempted to stake out a middle ground between a Scottish-style Kirk, 'the authoritative presbyterial government in all the subordinations and proceedings of it', and the separatism of the sects. The five authors deliberately fudged their own view of church government, and although they were labelled 'Independents', they actually had as much in common with the Presbyterians as they did with the gathered congregations: to some historians they were proponents of a 'decentralised Presbyterianism' in which the national church, based on existing parishes, and staffed by the four Presbyterian officers would allow congregations some control over membership. In 1644, however, they were asking for little more than exemption or a degree of tolerance on behalf of the scrupulous. Their plea was echoed by a group of Independent MPs who asked a parliamentary committee 'to endeavour the finding out some ways how far tender consciences, who cannot in all things submit to the common rule which shall be established, may be borne with'.[34] The idea that a right to toleration for dissidents should be written into the Assembly's decision on church government – effectively permitting nonconformity within the new national church – outraged many in the Assembly. After sharply fought debates, the dissenting brethren withdrew from the Assembly in April 1645.

'Independency' was an imprecise label, but a meaningful one. It signified the independence of each congregation from any other congregation or superior body, and it was the antithesis of any form of comprehensive national church. The congregation was a voluntary body, a group of Christians 'gathered' or 'called' to worship together, answerable to no other group. It admitted its own members – usually after they testified to their conversion and godly life – and chose its own pastor. Ideally, the congregation as a whole exercised discipline in the belief that members could be kept on the straight and narrow by admonition and exhortation from their 'brothers' and 'sisters', but they retained the right to expel those who would not be corrected. Those who joined such congregations paid no heed to parish boundaries, but some of them kept up their connections with their parish church, attending sermons, even filling parish office. Others were more convinced separatists. Henry Burton argued that the reformation in England was 'the new forming of a church' which was 'properly a congregation of believers called out from the rest of the world'. Since the parish congregations were not 'qualified as Christ requires', then liberty had to be granted to set up congregations 'where Christ's ordinances are administered in their purity, and so where none are admitted members of the congregation but such as are approved of by the whole assembly for their profession and conversation'.[35] The logic of their convictions led many separatist congregations to adopt the practice of 'believer's baptism'. Those who wished to join the congregation had to seal their 'covenant' or agreement with the church by undergoing baptism, often by total immersion in a nearby pond or stream. Such congregations had no time for the notion of automatically baptising babies into the universal Christian church. The rejection of infant baptism and the adoption of believer's baptism was what identified such congregations as part of the Baptist movement. Separatist and Baptist congregations often selected their pastors from among lay people, placing more weight on 'gifts' such as spiritual fervour and preaching ability than on formal education or clerical institution.

The scale of such churches was out of all proportion to the impact they had upon the religious scene of the 1640s. In that decade London appears to have been home to thirteen Independent churches led by former clergymen – such as John and Thomas Goodwin, Greenhill, Burton, and Simpson – and twelve Baptist congregations. Another ten congregations were led by laymen such as Duppa, Highland and Barbon. In a city the size of London, this was neither a large number of meetings nor of followers. Some congregations, such as Duppa's, were clearly separatist, others maintained a relationship with the parish from which they had sprung. John Goodwin was the incumbent of St Stephen's, Coleman Street, where he had probably gathered a congregation in the 1630s. In the 1640s, he effectively 'un-churched' his ordinary parishioners by restricting the sacrament to members of his gathered church. Unsurprisingly, the parishioners protested and Goodwin lost his living, but his gathered church continued to meet in his house in the parish. Outside the capital, there were gathered churches in Yarmouth, Hull, Nottingham, Chester and Bristol among other towns. Their existence was often due to the fortunes of war: parliamentarian garrisons were frequently the home of a gathered church, while Walter Cradock had to move the Llanvaches church from Bristol after that city fell to the royalists in 1643. We know little about the establishment of provincial Independent churches in the 1640s, but the origins of some of the Baptist congregations are better documented. The itinerant Baptist preacher Samuel Oates created a succession of churches in the eastern counties. Henry Denne, a graduate clergyman, who was baptised in 1643 as a member of Thomas Lambe's church in Bell Alley, off Coleman Street, became an active preacher in the army and an evangelist in Cambridgeshire. Appointed as clergyman of Eltisley, he baptised eleven members, including his wife, in 1644–45 to form the nucleus of the Fenstanton Baptist church.

However small and disparate these congregations were, they had a common identity as 'Independent' and 'separatist' churches in the mid-1640s, not least because they all had a common interest in opposing the plans of the Westminster Assembly. A comprehensive and coercive national church would have no room for gathered churches. Thus a broad 'Independent' coalition was formed which embraced many of the sects and gathered churches, the sober clerical 'Independents', much of the New Model Army, and a phalanx of Erastian and Independent MPs. It was an alliance of necessity, perhaps, and certainly a strained one: 'all sectaries are Independents', claimed one critic, but 'all Independents be not properly sectaries'. John Cotton complained that 'the anti-paedobaptists, antinomians, familists, yea, and the seekers too, do all of them style themselves Independents'.[36] To draw a fine distinction between their ecclesiastical position and that of the sects, the more conservative ministers, such as the authors of the *Apologetical Narration*, preferred to call themselves 'congregationalists'.

The struggle over the future of religion could not be divorced from the wider political questions of what kind of settlement was to be reached with the King, how the achievements of the war years were to be safeguarded, and what role the Army and the Parliament were to play. The Westminster Assembly finally offered Parliament a plan for a Presbyterian national church in the summer of 1645. Each parish was to have a congregational presbytery or eldership; these presbyteries were supervised by the classical presbyteries, courts of ministers and lay elders, whose primary function was to ensure that ministers officiated properly and that ordinances concerning the sacraments and ordination were carried out. Above these classical presbyteries were provincial and ultimately national assemblies. The eldership at each of the levels, parochial, classical and provincial, would have the power of excommunicating individuals and of keeping the ignorant and scandalous from the Lord's Supper. Parliament, however, insisted that individuals denied the sacrament should have a right of appeal from the church's authorities to a parliamentary committee of laymen. MPs showed little enthusiasm for establishing the new Presbyterian church. They passed an ordinance for the election of elders, devised a plan to divide London's parishes into twelve classical presbyteries, and for the rest of the country they simply referred the matter to the county committees.

The church settlement descended into a game of political cat and mouse: the next twelve months was 'the bustling year wherein the presbyterial and congregational governments were like Jacob and Esau struggling in the womb'.[37] The Assembly applied pressure by using its allies in London: in September the City petitioned for further action to create effective discipline since 'multitudes of unstable souls . . . have fallen off into many strange sects, maintaining most horrid and blasphemous opinions'.[38] Independents, however, made reassuring noises about mutual tolerance at every opportunity. In September Cromwell reported to the Speaker of the Commons on the capture of Bristol and commented that 'Presbyterians, Independents, all have here the same spirit of faith and prayer . . . all that believe, have the real unity, which is most glorious, because inward and spiritual . . . in things of the mind we look for no compulsion but that of light and reason.'[39] Earnest Presbyterians, such as the Scottish representative Baillie, prayed that the Assembly could persuade Parliament to give the presbyteries more coercive powers. But that was unlikely to happen. In the eyes of MPs, even Presbyterian MPs like John Harington, 'all ecclesiastical jurisdiction is in the Parliament, yea, and all spiritual'.[40] It was only after Charles's surrender that Parliament ordered London parishes to enforce their earlier instructions to create presbyteries; parish elections of lay elders followed that summer.

A partial and piecemeal Presbyterian church was created in 1646. The key was local initiative. Lancashire Presbyterians proposed a scheme to Parliament in August 1646 that was approved in December: nine classes were established and some such as Manchester and Bury functioned until 1660; a provincial assembly met at Preston from 1647. As far as we know, classical presbyteries met only in parts of London, Lancashire, Warwickshire, Derbyshire and Nottingham. Provincial assemblies met at Preston, possibly in Derbyshire, and at Sion College in London; and as a national assembly was never called, the London provincial assembly effectively acted as the national headquarters of the Presbyterian church.

So the Reformation was not to be reformed. No new Presbyterian 'Church of England' would now emerge because the religious aspirations of the English had begun to diverge in such different and potentially conflicting ways. Parliament would not tolerate the creation of a theocratic and obligatory Presbyterian church, and the Independents in Parliament and the Army were determined that the religious freedom of the sects should not be curtailed. Yet, as Lindley argues, much of the nation, and especially the capital, was weary of war and regarded the gathered churches and sects as a real threat to peace and security. Nor was it clear that what was decided in London determined what happened in the provinces. While the Assembly had deliberated at Westminster, in the shires many parishes had carried on as before, still served by ministers who had been trained and ordained within the episcopal church, perhaps still using the Prayer Book and its calendar. As a community of traditionally minded people, and as a symbol of royalist allegiance, the Church of England still existed. But it was a church without leadership or institutions. Those bishops not in prison or exile had long since retired into rural obscurity; the universities were firmly under Presbyterian control; Archbishop Laud went to the scaffold in January 1645 and on the day of his attainder, Parliament banned the use of the Book of Common Prayer and ordered parishes to purchase and use the Westminster Assembly's Directory of Public Worship. As if to underline its irrelevance, episcopacy was only formally abolished in October 1646 when financial need compelled Parliament to sell off the lands of the bishops and the cathedral deans and chapters.

The Reformation was to be fulfilled. Or so believed the visionaries, men like Henry Burton who saw reformation as the formation of new churches of spiritually pure Christians. This vision was inspired by millenarian and apocalyptic thought, long a mainstay of English Protestantism, but now, it seemed to many, on the verge of realisation. Were these not the last days when men should prepare for the calling of the Jews and the fall of Antichrist? The gathering of churches was surely evidence that God was gathering the saints together in preparation for the end of the world. 'Some apprehend that Christ shall come and reign personally, subduing his enemies and exalting his people, and that this is the new heaven and earth,' explained Thomas Collier. But he believed that 'Christ will come in the Spirit and have a glorious kingdom in the spirits of his people . . . the nature and glory of it lies in that renovation or renewing of the mind: an internal and spiritual change.'[41] The 'antinomianism' mentioned by several contemporaries was a strain of mystical puritan theology and piety. Many of the sects rejected the Calvinist doctrine that the merits of Christ were restricted only to a predestined elect. In place of the arid piety of constantly searching for signs of election, they offered a bolder confidence in the mercy and goodness of God. They were willing to 'listen to the Spirit' and critical of those they saw as 'formalists'. The ferment among religious and political radicals threw up innumerable speculations about the nature of heaven, hell, the soul, salvation and much else. Overarching all these unorthodox ideas, however, was a very simple and potentially revolutionary proposition. As William Walwyn put it, 'liberty of conscience [should] be allowed for every man, or sort of men, to worship God in that way, and perform Christ's ordinances in that manner as shall appear to them most agreeable to God's word'.[42] And this was a demand that had broad appeal. Within the army the 'most frequent and vehement disputes were for liberty of conscience . . . that the civil magistrate had nothing to do to determine of anything in matters of religion . . . but every man might not only hold but preach and do in matters of religion what he pleased'.[43]

The crisis deepens: 1647–49

An uneasy peace may have come to most of the British Isles, but the presence of numerous rival armies, with ill-defined goals and allegiances, jeopardised the chances of a secure peace settlement. Too many of the parties still believed that they could use the threat of force to get their way, and none more than Charles I who never gave up the hope that he could exploit one territory or group in his three kingdoms to impose his will on the rest. In July 1646, while Charles was in Scottish hands at Newcastle, the Presbyterian-dominated English Parliament offered him peace terms that embraced both England and Scotland. The Newcastle Propositions were an uncompromising statement that God had witnessed against the defeated Charles: the King must now swear the Solemn League and Covenant, abolish episcopacy, accept the condemnation of many of his counsellors and supporters, and surrender control of the militia for twenty years to Parliament. Charles resolutely refused to abandon his royal powers, his friends, or his religion in the form of the episcopal Church of England, and so he stalled the parliamentary commissioners. But at the end of January 1647, the Scots, who had grown tired of royal prevarication and disillusioned by the lack of English commitment to the Presbyterian church, pocketed their outstanding pay from the Parliament and marched north, leaving Charles at Newcastle, from where he was escorted by English troops to Holdenby House in Northamptonshire. There Charles continued to make small gestures – his third reply to the Propositions, dated 12 May, offered a three-year trial of Presbyterianism and parliamentary military control for ten years – while all around him a political crisis was escalating. That crisis caught up with Charles on the morning of 3 June when a party of horsemen commanded by Cornet George Joyce arrived at Holdenby to seize the King and take him to Newmarket where the New Model Army under Generals Fairfax, Ireton and Cromwell had agreed to rendezvous.

Joyce's dramatic gesture and the significant gathering of the army (which on paper was well over 20,000 strong) arose from the struggle between Holles and the Presbyterian party in Parliament and the New Model and its Independent allies. Pressed for cash, the Presbyterians wanted to disband the New Model, enlisting some of its veterans for service in Ireland, and relying on a small standing army in England, but they mishandled the business, offering little in the way of the back pay or 'arrears' owed to the troops and offensively denouncing those soldiers who insisted on petitioning for their rights as 'enemies to the state'. In April and May, the regiments had elected representatives or 'agitators' to put their case; on 5 June the army at Newmarket subscribed a 'solemn engagement' not to disband until its grievances had been met; and, on 14 June, it issued *A Representation of the Army* that famously declared: 'we were not a mere mercenary army, hired to serve any arbitrary power of a state, but called forth . . . to the defence of our own and the people's just rights and liberties'.[44] They demanded not only their arrears and an indemnity against prosecution for actions performed as soldiers, but also liberty of conscience and elections for a new Parliament. Not content with making these political and constitutional demands of Parliament, the New Model Army and the Independents now delivered their own peace terms to the King.

The *Heads of the Proposals* were presented to Charles on 23 July and published on 2 August. They offered a comprehensive settlement designed to meet the aspirations of the army, Parliament and the King. Charles was to cede military control for ten years, and accept advice on appointments, his followers were protected, bishops were retained, although shorn of any coercive power, the Covenant was not to be enforced, and use of the Prayer Book was to be legal; but just as importantly, the powers of Parliament were clearly defined by a series of procedural and constitutional limitations: parliaments were to be biennial and of fixed duration, and seats were to be redistributed so that the Commons was 'an equal representative of the whole'. Freedom of worship was established, as all penalties for absence from church or attendance at other meetings were lifted, with 'some other provision' to be made in due course to cover papists, recusants, Jesuits and priests. The *Heads* proclaimed the rule of law, the right to petition, and the importance of free and fair elections to Parliament. Generous to Charles, idealistic in many ways, and perhaps too ready to overlook the practical difficulties, these were possibly the best terms on offer to all sides. Moreover, the political dice had just fallen so as to give the New Model Army the power to back up its proposals. After hovering in the wings all summer, the army marched into London on 6 August ostensibly to restore the two Speakers of the Lords and Commons and other Independents who had fled Westminster after a Presbyterian London mob had surrounded and intimidated Parliament on 26 July. Now the Presbyterian leaders took flight, leaving Parliament in the hands of the Independents and the capital in the hands of the New Model Army.

There were tensions within the army, principally between the radic-
alised rank and file and the more conservative leaders or grandees such as
Fairfax and Ireton. The troopers and foot soldiers had been exposed to
both radical religious preaching and to the political and social ideas of men
like Lilburne, Walwyn and Richard Overton, the leaders of the Leveller
movement. In their pamphlets, these civilian activists promoted an agenda
of diverse reforms, such as reducing taxation, overhauling the legal system,
abolishing the House of Lords, creating a universal male franchise and regular elections, and introducing religious toleration. Leveller leaders and
army radicals naturally gravitated towards each other in the summer of
1647 and together they expressed their fears for the present and hopes for
the future. In mid-October, they published *The Case of the Army Truly
Stated*, which reminded the grandees and the army of its earlier solemn
engagement, denounced the *Heads* for conceding too much to Charles, and
boldly stated that 'all power is originally and essentially in the whole body
of the people of this nation'. The authors were moved by conscience: 'we
find such obligations upon our consciences, written naturally by the finger
of God in our hearts, that we cannot behold the honour of God to be
impaired'. This was a ringing assertion of the inalienable right of the individual human conscience and it was fundamentally egalitarian: 'the meanest vassal in the eye of the Lord is equally obliged and accountable to God
with the greatest prince or commander under the sun, in and for the use of
that talent entrusted unto him'.[45] It was agreed that the *Case* should be
debated by the Council of the Army meeting in Putney church at the end of
October. By the time the meeting occurred, the Levellers had boiled down
their demands into a pithy republican constitution, *The Agreement of the
People*, which became the main focus of the debates. *The Agreement*
crystallised their principles: biennial, limited-duration parliaments, whose
power 'is inferior only to theirs who choose them', but which cannot
trespass on the people's five 'native rights' – freedom of religion, freedom
from military service, indemnity for actions in the civil war, equality before
the law, and laws which are 'good and not evidently destructive to the
safety and well-being of the people'.[46]

The Putney Debates are justly famous because, thanks to the scribbled
shorthand of the army secretaries, we have a vivid, first-hand account of
what was said: the argument was full of passion, misunderstandings, and
non-sequiturs, it ranged over many issues, whether to continue negotiations with the King, the earlier commitments of the army, and the extent
of the franchise, and reached no final conclusion. Indeed, for the grandees,
the whole purpose was to keep people talking and to defuse some of the

Levellers' demands, but incidentally it revealed some of the incomprehension between the two sides – Ireton, for example, was genuinely staggered at the suggestion that those without a 'fixed interest', without real estate, should be entrusted with the vote, just as his opponents took it as axiomatic in Rainsborough's fine phrase that 'the poorest he that is in England hath a life to live as the greatest he; and therefore . . . every man that is to live under a government ought first by his own consent to put himself under that government'.[47] In the next few weeks the grandees saw off the threat from the lower ranks – ordering various regiments to different rendezvous and on one occasion court-martialling and executing a troublemaker – but the ideas and slogans enunciated in Putney church would not be suppressed as easily.

Despite all their concessions, King Charles was not to be persuaded by the *Heads of the Proposals*: he loftily told the army's representatives, 'you cannot do without me. You will fall to ruin if I do not sustain you.'[48] His efforts to play off the Independents against the Presbyterians failed, so he instead turned to potential sympathisers in Ireland and Scotland. A hazy deal with the Old English fell through, but on 26 December Charles made a secret Engagement with the Scots in which he agreed to establish Presbyterianism in England for three years and bring the two kingdoms into closer legal and administrative union in return for control of the army and appointment of his advisers. Should the English Parliament refuse to accept these terms and disband its army, the Scots promised to send forces to aid Charles. The King's part in the Engagement is perhaps adequately explained by his own inveterate plotting, his fear of the New Model, and distaste for the Four Bills, the latest demands made by Parliament. Scottish motives were more complex. They included the Covenanters' doubts about the religious commitment of their old Presbyterian allies in the English Parliament and fears of the growing influence of the Independents in the army and Parliament. It seemed quite possible that the Independents would launch an English expedition against Ireland and that they might, in time, even turn against the Scots. Yet the Scottish commissioners had no doubt conceded more than was wise in their dealings with the King and had difficulty selling the Engagement to the Committee of Estates back in Scotland. The Kirk and the Covenanter grandees such as Argyll remained unconvinced and the Scottish leadership divided into 'Engagers' and 'Protestors'.

Having just signed the Engagement, Charles rejected the Four Bills, claiming that they had effectively decided those very issues that should be the subject of negotiation between the King and Parliament. Outraged, the

Commons voted that they would make no further addresses to the King nor accept any messages from him. The country once again slid into war. The so-called 'Second Civil War' took the form of a series of uncoordinated local risings, often as much protests against the demands and intrusions of the parliamentary government as royalist rebellions, and the militarily more serious invasion by a Scottish army under Hamilton. The first signs of provincial rebellion were riots in Canterbury, Norwich and London on Christmas Day 1647 against the ban on Christmas festivities, followed by risings in South Wales in March, and shortly afterwards in East Anglia, Kent and Yorkshire. The New Model was able to deal with each in turn before turning to face Hamilton's army. Cromwell saw 'nothing but the hand of God' in the two-day running battle near Preston in which his force of 9,000 routed his opponent's army of more than 20,000. By the end of August the battles were over and the consequences were to be faced.

In Scotland the consequences were immediate. A popular Covenanter rising in the south-west swept the Engagers from office and allowed Argyll's faction to secure the government of the country. In September Cromwell's army arrived in Scotland and made certain that the Engagers had been purged from all positions of influence. In England, for all the calls for vengeance against Charles Stuart, that 'man of blood' who had invited a foreign enemy to invade his own kingdom, negotiations were once again under way between King and Parliament. With the New Model Army occupied, the Presbyterians had returned to Parliament and, fearful of what a vengeful army might do, repealed the vote of no addresses and opened talks with the King at Newport on the basis of the Newcastle Propositions. While Charles was prepared to concede control of the militia to Parliament for twenty years and offered a limited Presbyterianism, he refused to abolish episcopacy. His stubbornness was encouraged by hopes that Ormonde might yet save the day with a Catholic Irish army. Late in October, Parliament washed its hands of the Newport negotiations.

The next three months were to see the political deadlock broken by the most brutal and revolutionary means. At this distance in time, it is not always clear who was driving events or what their motives were, but it is evident that Charles had spun the web in which he was now caught. The clamour for justice against Charles was loud everywhere, but loudest among the army and its allies. They were convinced that God had witnessed against Charles Stuart, 'the capital and grand author of all our troubles', and 'since providence and necessity had cast them upon it' they were prepared to try, convict and punish their King. Ireton drafted a

Remonstrance demanding the King's trial, the dissolution of Parliament, and the establishment of supreme power in annual parliaments, elected on a wide franchise and empowered to elect a king. This radical, republican, agenda was adopted by the Council of Officers, although not without resistance from Fairfax and other conservatives, who hoped even now to win over the King, and from Lilburne and other Leveller leaders, who had no wish to exchange a royal tyrant for military tyranny; but it was snubbed by Parliament when it was presented on 20 November. The army entered London on 2 December. On 5 December the Commons voted to reopen negotiations with the King. The next morning MPs arrived at the Commons to be greeted by Colonel Thomas Pride and his troops. Pride excluded 186 MPs, imprisoned 45, and a further 56 took the hint and did not turn up: the remnant of about 150 MPs were those, mainly Independents, willing to work with the army to put Charles on trial. Pride's 'purge' of Parliament was organised by Ireton, and possibly sanctioned by Cromwell. It was a less drastic measure than the forcible dissolution of Parliament which some advocated, and it did, at least, preserve the semblance of parliamentary rule over the next few months.

All revolutions acquire an air of inevitability after the event. It was easy enough to see the trial and execution of Charles I as a sad necessity, as a foregone conclusion once the Second Civil War was under way, or the army had resolved, as it did at Windsor in May 1648, to bring 'Charles Stuart, that man of blood' to account. By November, after God had witnessed against Charles with a second defeat, Cromwell was urging his cousin, Hammond, 'to look into providences; surely they mean somewhat? They hang so together; have been so constant, so clear, unclouded.' In December and January, each stage of the process could seem almost preordained, as Pride's Purge was followed by moves to end negotiations with the King, distract the Levellers with a debate on their latest version of the *Agreement of the People*, set up a special High Court of Justice, formulate charges, and then bring Charles before the court and decide his fate. The radicalism escalated with each step. The army purged Parliament and then the purged Parliament did the same to the City of London. When the House of Lords demurred at the proposed High Court of Justice, the Commons declared that 'the people are, under God, the original of all just power' and that what the Commons enacted was law with or without the consent of King and Lords. Then the Lord's anointed, Charles I, King of England, Scotland and Ireland, was charged as 'a tyrant, traitor and murderer, and a public and implacable enemy to the Commonwealth of England'. Such revolutionary acts demand an equally revolutionary ideology to explain them, and that was at hand in the shape of puritan zeal and millenarianism. Divine providences pointed to God's judgement against Charles. The Bible provided the notion of blood-guilt – the blood that defiled the land, according to Numbers 35: 33, could only be cleansed by the blood of him that shed it – and the scheme of millenarian prophecy – Charles was readily identified as the tenth and final horn on the fourth beast described in the Book of Daniel. Preachers to Parliament stoked up the demand for justice in the name of God and at any cost: 'let justice be done, though the world be ruined'.[49]

Yet it is possible, even likely, that events did not feel quite so inevitable to those involved. Motives are rarely one-dimensional. As Kelsey has argued, calls for 'justice' could have been understood in several ways, just as many conclusions can be drawn from divine providences. Some hoped to pressurise Charles into meaningful negotiations, or force him to abdicate in favour of his youngest son, the Duke of Gloucester, or simply to tie him up in lengthy legal proceedings. A trial did not automatically mean a conviction, nor did a conviction necessarily mean a death sentence. Winning even cautious support from among the Presbyterian clergy, the City, and the Scots, obliged the proponents of a trial to present their case in such a moderate light. Early in January, for example, it was reported that some leading Presbyterian ministers would accept proceedings against the King 'in a way of justice' provided 'that he may have a legal trial, and that he may not be degraded of his titles and honours'.[50] Those, such as Cromwell, who urged on the trial could not afford, politically or psycho-logically, to present this purely as a matter of divine justice: they had to clothe the process in legal dress, however threadbare, and stress those aspects which would command the most broad support. Perhaps this is one reason for the secular nature of the charge against Charles: it concen-trated on abuse of office and trust, on war, invasion and tyranny, with never a word about popery, Arminianism or the peril of Protestantism.

Whatever the mixed motives and ultimate hopes of those involved, Charles himself took control by refusing to recognise the authority of the Court and declining to enter a plea. The King's defence was politically well judged. Not only did he point out that the proceedings had no legitimacy under God's law or English law, he portrayed himself as the true defender of the people's liberty which consisted in living under the law: if power makes law, then not only is the King wronged, but 'you manifestly wrong even the poorest ploughman'. Since he would not plead, the court could only proceed to find him guilty; on 27 January he was sentenced to death, but it took another two days before fifty-nine commissioners were ready to sign the execution warrant. Charles may have deliberately courted a martyr's death from the outset of the trial; it was plain by the last days of his life that he had embraced this option as the best and final service he could perform for his cause. He was to be executed 'in the face of God, and of all men', on a scaffold outside the Banqueting House in Whitehall on 30 January 1649. His brave death, noble speech – claiming that he died as 'the martyr of the people' – and the silent, sombre, snow-clad scene, created a traumatic moment for onlookers and the English nation. 'The blow I saw given', recalled a schoolboy witness, 'at the instant whereof . . . there was such a groan by the thousands then present as I never heard before and desire I may never hear again.' Around the country, individuals were shocked: 'Lord, lay it not as a sin to this nation', begged the puritan minister Ralph Josselin. The other Stuart kingdoms and the rest of Europe could only look on in horror at what the English had done. 'The black act is done, which all the world wonders at, and which an age cannot expiate.'[51]

Notes

1 *Proceedings of the Short Parliament of 1640*, ed. E.S. Cope and W.H. Coates (Camden Society, 4th series, 19, 1977), pp. 135, 136, 142, 146, 150.

2 C. Holmes, *Seventeenth-century Lincolnshire* (Lincoln, 1980), p. 139; P. Seaver, *The Puritan Lectureships* (Stanford, Calif., 1970), p. 264.

3 *The Diary of John Rous*, ed. M.A.E. Green (Camden Society, old series, 66, 1856), p. 90.

4 C. Russell, *The Causes of the English Civil War* (Oxford, 1990), p. 119.

5 John Cleveland, 'Epitaph on the Earl of Strafford', *Poems* (1647); K. Lindley, *Popular Politics and Religion in Civil War London* (Aldershot, 1997), p. 25.

6 Stephen Marshall, *A Sermon Preached before the Honourable House of Commons . . . 17 November 1640* (1641), p. 40.

7 Lindley, *Popular Politics*, p. 39.

8 G. Yule, *Puritans in Politics* (Abingdon, 1981), p. 107.

9 Holmes, *Seventeenth-century Lincolnshire*, pp. 143–4.

10 M. Stoyle, *From Deliverance to Destruction: Rebellion and Civil War in an English City* (Exeter, 1996), p. 169.

11 Russell, *Causes*, p. 125.

12 M. Tolmie, *The Triumph of the Saints: The Separate Churches of London 1616–49* (Cambridge, 1977), p. 37.

13 D. Freist, *Governed by Opinion: Politics, Religion and the Dynamics of Communication in Stuart London 1637–1645* (1997), p. 173.

14 R. Ashton, *The English Civil War* (1978), p. 154.

15 P. Seaver, *Wallington's World* (1985), p. 166.

16 Gardiner, pp. 202–32, esp. pp. 206, 207.

17 J.S. Morrill, *The Revolt of the Provinces: Conservatives and Revolutionaries in the English Civil War 1603–42* (Harlow, 1976), pp. 136, 162.

18 Morrill, *Revolt of the Provinces*, p. 47.

19 J. Eales, *Puritans and Roundheads: The Harleys of Brampton Bryan and the Outbreak of the English Civil War* (Cambridge, 1990), p. 176; J. Eales, 'Provincial Preaching', in T.Cogswell, R. Cust and P. Lake (eds), *Politics, Religion and Popularity in Early Stuart England* (Cambridge, 2002), p. 207.

20 W. Sheils, 'Provincial Preaching on the Eve of the Civil War', in A. Fletcher and P. Roberts (eds), *Religion, Culture and Society* (Cambridge, 1994), p. 311.

21 R. Wilcher, *The Writing of Royalism, 1628–60* (Cambridge, 2001), p. 171.

22 Eales, *Puritans and Roundheads*, pp. 168–9.

23 D.E. Kennedy, *The English Revolution 1642–1649* (Basingstoke, 2000), p. 26.

24 A.I. MacInnes, *The British Revolution, 1629–1660* (Basingstoke, 2005), p. 145.

25 MacInnes, *British Revolution*, p. 153.

26 Abbott, I, 287.

27 E.C. Walker, *William Dell, Master Puritan* (Cambridge, 1970), p. 46.

28 Richard Baxter, *Reliquiae Baxterianae*, ed. M. Sylvester (1696), I, 53.

29 J.T. Cliffe, *Puritans in Conflict: The Puritan Gentry During and After the Civil Wars* (1988), pp. 163–4.

30 Morrill, *Revolt of the Provinces*, p. 103 and pp. 98–111.

31 Watts, pp. 80, 100.

32 Gardiner, p. 229.

33 Edmund Calamy, *England's Looking Glass* (1642), p. 46.

34 Yule, *Puritans in Politics*, p. 136.

35 Tolmie, *Triumph of Saints*, p. 91.

36 A. Zakai, 'Religious Toleration and its Enemies: The Independent Divines and the Issue of Toleration during the English Civil War', *Albion*, 21 (1989), 14.

37 *Life of Adam Martindale*, ed. R. Parkinson (Chetham Society, IV, 1845), p. 61.

38 Yule, *Puritans in Politics*, p. 161.

39 Abbott, I, 377.

40 *The Diary of John Harington*, ed. M.F. Stieg (Somerset Record Society, 74, 1977), p. 20.

41 A.S.P. Woodhouse (ed.), *Puritanism and Liberty* (1938; 2nd edn, London, 1974), p. 390.

42 William Walwyn, *The Compassionate Samaritan* (1644) in D. Wootton (ed.), *Divine Right and Democracy* (Harmondsworth, 1986), p. 248.

43 Baxter, *Reliquiae*, I, 53.

44 Woodhouse (ed.), *Puritanism and Liberty*, p. 404.

45 Woodhouse (ed.), *Puritanism and Liberty*, p. 436.

46 Woodhouse (ed.), *Puritanism and Liberty*, pp. 444–5.

47 Woodhouse (ed.), *Puritanism and Liberty*, p. 53.

48 Kennedy, *English Revolution*, p. 57.

49 Kennedy, *English Revolution*, p. 126.

50 S. Kelsey, 'The Death of Charles I', *HJ*, 45 (2002), 736.

51 *The Diaries and Letters of Philip Henry*, ed. M.H. Lee (1882), p. 12; Josselin, p. 155; Bodl. L., Tanner MS 57, fo. 525.

CHAPTER 5

The Commonwealth and Protectorate (1649–60)

The 1650s was a decade of political crisis. The army established and then broke a series of parliamentary regimes and constitutions, but it could never 'sheathe the sword' and hand power over to a civilian government. Indeed, it could never establish a plausible successor to the towering figure of Oliver Cromwell: as his son asked just months before Cromwell's death, 'Have you any settlement? Does not your peace depend upon his highness's [Cromwell's] life and upon his peculiar skill and faculty, and personal interest in the army as now modelled and commanded? I say beneath the hand of God . . . there is no other reason why we are not in blood at this day.'[1] The politicians of the 1650s lurched from one crisis to another, grasping at measures that promised to heal the nation's deep divisions and then turning to expedients that could only perpetuate old animosities. Time and time again, the same political issues re-emerged: the existence and cost of the army; the relationship between parliamentary assemblies and the constitutions which called them into being; the exercise of power and responsibility in the towns and villages; and the failure to find a religious settlement. Like any other seventeenth-century government, the regimes of the 1650s were preoccupied with retaining power, but unlike other regimes they had a vision of what that power was to achieve: they had been entrusted with the defence and promotion of godly reformation, a broad term for a bundle of values and aspirations, moral and spiritual, some millenarian or apocalyptic, others more practical, but none narrowly denominational or clerical. This godly cause, a hard-won achievement of the civil wars, was not to be jeopardised by the intolerance of parliaments, the excesses of sects, or the apathy of the masses.

The godly cause had emerged from the struggle of the 1640s, a decade which, as we have seen, transformed the religious landscape of the country. Before 1640, religious conflicts had been centred on the teachings and actions of the clergy of the Church of England and on the international threat from popery. A decade later the question of liturgical conformity was irrelevant and debate on the nature of church government a sideshow since attention was focused on liberty of conscience and worship, the right of lay men (and even women) to preach, the possibility of national moral and spiritual regeneration, and the mechanisms to preserve parish-based religion. Popery remained a threat, but there was now a real possibility that the English would take the fight to the Roman Catholics and face them on their own European territory. The godly seized their moment. The failure to establish a new national church or to reach a political settlement in the later 1640s paved the way for a decade of largely unchecked religious experimentation and speculation. The number of those who joined the sects may have been small, but the sense of spiritual and intellectual emancipation was widespread. To some, this was a heady freedom; to others, it was a corrosive attack on certainty and order. The later 1640s and the 1650s are the key years in our story, the years in which religious pluralism took root and became an ineradicable fact of English life. They were also years in which the English left their stamp on Ireland and Scotland.

The Commonwealth

On 19 May 1649 England was declared 'a Commonwealth and Free State' in which supreme authority rested with 'the representatives of the people in Parliament . . . without any King or House of Lords'. This most unlikely republic had a slow birth: the Commons had only resolved to abolish monarchy as 'unnecessary, burdensome and dangerous to the liberty, safety and public interest of the people' a week after the King's head was cut off; it took another five weeks to pass acts abolishing the monarchy and House of Lords. Perhaps this just goes to show how little planning had gone into the removal of Charles I; it certainly reveals the lack of ideological republicanism in mid-seventeenth-century England. So familiar was kingship and so alien was republicanism to most people that Kelsey has described this as a period of 'unkingship'.[2]

The new Commonwealth had to clothe its nakedness in the fig leaf of known forms, familiar titles and official seals, to invent an effective machinery of government and, perhaps most urgently of all, to defend itself against military threats. Whatever its propaganda, the new Parliament – the Rump – was far from representative of the people: although its membership was over 200, only 60 or 70 of these were active participants in debates and legislation. Executive authority was exercised by a Council of State made up of MPs. The common expectation that the Rump would shortly dissolve itself and hold fresh elections was soon disappointed. Rumpers were too anxious about the security of the new Republic to risk a poll. Their anxiety was apparent in the imposition of the Engagement – an oath of loyalty to the government as it was then established without King or Parliament – first on office-holders and then extended to all adult males. Politically, the Engagement was a failure, but the arguments that swirled around it and found their way into print marked an important development in political philosophy and popular attitudes – a pragmatic distinction was increasingly drawn between the obedience due to a ruler who had the legal right to sovereignty and a ruler who in fact exercised that power, a distinction which eased many consciences both in the 1650s and later.

The military dangers to the new state were pressing. Strengthening the armed forces was a priority. First, the contest within the army between the officers and the rank-and-file radicals had to be resolved. In the spring of 1649 Cromwell broke the army Levellers by facing down a series of mutinies and having three mutineers shot in the churchyard at Burford. Meanwhile, by selling off the former royal lands, Parliament was able to pay the soldiers what was owed to them and to raise their pay; it then ordered seventy-seven new warships and conscripted thousands of seamen. None of this came a moment too soon as a new threat had emerged across the Irish Sea. The recent alliance of Ormonde, the loyal Protestant servant of the Stuarts, and the Catholic Confederates raised the threat of an Irish invasion of the new Commonwealth. The Rump took pre-emptive action. The first English troops had already defeated Ormonde's army at Rathmines, when Cromwell landed near Dublin in late August with an army of 30,000 troops. Cromwell now proceeded to subdue Ireland and to exact revenge for the 1641 rebellion from what he saw as a barbarous and guilty nation. Antipopery and a form of racist colonialism explain, but do not condone, the infamous massacres at Drogheda and Wexford that autumn: Cromwell saw the murder of 5,000 innocent civilians as 'a righteous judgement of God'. Unsurprisingly, Irish resistance soon crumbled, and by the summer of 1650 Cromwell could turn his attention to Scotland where on news of the regicide Charles II had immediately been proclaimed King. In the spring of 1650 Montrose led a royalist rising only to be captured and executed by his Scottish enemies. But in June Charles himself arrived in Scotland, ready to sign the Covenant and lead an army south. Cromwell, however, was quicker off the mark: his army reached Scotland late in July and defeated a far larger Scottish force at Dunbar on 3

September in yet another astounding victory that he attributed to God. Thereafter, without the resources to exploit his advantage and hampered by his own ill health, he could only watch and wait while the Scots absorbed the implications of their defeat and began to quarrel among themselves. The Presbyterian 'Remonstrants' now backed away from Charles, while the 'Resolutioners' pressed on with his coronation at Scone on 1 January 1651 and preparations for an invasion of England. When Charles entered England he found less support than he had anticipated – fewer than two thousand rallied to his side – and eventually he faced Cromwell at Worcester on 3 September 1651. His defeat and subsequent flight via Boscobel and the royal oak has passed into legend, as has Cromwell's verdict on Worcester as God's 'crowning mercy'. In two years, Cromwell and the army had not simply seen off the threat posed by royal armies in Ireland and Scotland, they had conquered those countries. The English Commonwealth now looked very much the British Republic.

Back at Westminster, the Rump became mired in financing the army, raising taxation, and running the country. Some of its measures were of enduring significance, such as the Navigation Act, a blow against the Dutch shipping industry, probably motivated by a fear that the Netherlands were sympathetic to the Stuart cause, that would contribute to the outbreak of a naval war with the Dutch in 1652. Other legislation simply recognised the realities: the so-called Toleration Act of September 1650 abolished the requirement to attend parish church; the more loudly trumpeted Blasphemy Act, along with other legislation against swearing, fornication and adultery, was aimed at the radical antinomian sects usually referred to as the Ranters. There was little surplus enthusiasm or energy to advance the reforms on which the army and its allies had set their hearts. For example, the proposals of Matthew Hale's Commission on Law Reform were blocked by the vested interests of lawyer MPs, while plans to increase clerical stipends were thwarted by the Rump's pressing debts. Nor were there any signs of the Rump preparing to hold fresh elections on a new franchise.

The underlying animosities between the MPs and the army, between political Presbyterianism and Independency, were deepened by arguments about the direction and pace of reform. A chorus of criticism arose from groups like the Fifth Monarchy Men, millenarian Independents inspired by the London preachers Christopher Feake and John Rogers, and by the Welsh evangelists Morgan Llwyd and Vavasour Powell, who had powerful allies in the army, notably Major General Harrison, and a power base in the Commission for the Propagation of the Gospel in Wales, a quango which effectively governed Wales. In one of their earliest manifestos, issued within days of the regicide, the Fifth Monarchists demanded that 'all worldly rule and authority' should be put down and the kingdom should be administered 'by such laws and officers as Jesus Christ our mediator hath appointed in his kingdom' in preparation for the personal rule of Christ. Political power was to be restricted to members of gathered churches, who were to rule 'till Christ come in person'. 'How can the kingdom be the Saints' when the ungodly are electors and elected to govern?' they asked.[3] The army's political inactivity was attributed to self-seeking officers and divines around Cromwell. When England went to war against the Protestant Netherlands, the Fifth Monarchists urged the government to humble the Dutch and then press home the victory, to take God's vengeance to France, Spain and the gates of Rome. Such millenarianism was frequently heard in these years – not only in sermons and tracts, but in private letters and journals, such as the diary of Ralph Josselin, a Presbyterian minister in Essex, whose 'soul pants after . . . the great work and alterations God is making and doing in the world, the advancement of his saints, the giving the nations to his Christ . . . nothing can withstand God's purpose'.[4]

God's purposes were not, however, being pursued with any vigour by the Rump. No doubt the absence of the army's leaders in Ireland and Scotland initially allowed the more conservative MPs to drag their feet, but after Worcester a confrontation became inevitable. Cromwell began to play a crucial political role from late 1651 when he could devote himself to mediating between the army and the Rump. This role required a careful balancing act between the two groups, urging further reform on one and counselling patience and caution on the other: in his meetings with MPs and officers, Cromwell canvassed opinion on the future constitution and appears to have won a commitment that the Rump would dissolve no later than November 1654. The questions then became: what kind of assembly would succeed the Rump and who would choose it? It was evident that a free election would produce a conservative parliament, full of 'Presbyters' and 'Neuters', little better than royalists in many cases and certainly unsympathetic to plans for further reform. The achievements of the Commonwealth and the aspirations of the godly could not be jeopardised in this way. Plans were therefore laid for a committee of MPs and officers to oversee the elections and to vet candidates. On 20 April 1653, learning that the Rump planned to renege on this arrangement, Cromwell stormed to the chamber with a company of troops, harangued the MPs, seized the ceremonial mace, and dissolved the Parliament, saying 'you have sat here too long for the good you do'. Cromwell later masked the whole episode with various accusations about the intentions of the MPs, but there is no reason to doubt his own account of his motives: the Rump was no longer a 'Parliament for God's people', and 'necessity and providence' demanded that he act since 'the interest of all honest men and of this glorious cause had been in danger to be laid in the dust'.[5]

The interest of the godly was served and the danger of a free election avoided by another expedient, the Nominated Assembly or 'Barebones Parliament'. After the expulsion of the Rump, the army officers created a Council of State in their own image and invited nominations from separatist congregations for the new assembly of 'persons fearing God, and of approved fidelity and honesty' to represent England and Wales, Scotland, and Ireland. In July the handpicked assembly gathered to hear Cromwell tell them that they were 'called by God to rule with him and for him' and that they stood 'on the edge of promises and prophecies'.[6] Such words were music to the ears of the Assembly's forty Baptists and Independents. The majority of the 140 members were probably less susceptible to the language of prophecy. The social and political profile of the Assembly's membership was in line with that of the Rump and it included civilian allies of Cromwell such as Cooper and Wolseley. This was not an institution designed to achieve a social revolution. Yet neither the Assembly, nor its public reputation, were managed with the necessary care, so radicals were able to make dramatic gestures and dominate the headlines – usually as wreckers and opponents of property. The dozen or so Fifth Monarchist members indulged in reckless talk of replacing the laws with the Ten Commandments or abolishing tithes without compensation to lay impropriators or alternative pay for the parish clergy. When the radicals defeated a proposal to test the abilities of those seeking a clerical position, many were convinced 'that the tithes and universities would at the next opportunity be voted down'.[7] The Assembly's days were numbered. In December the conservative majority engineered the surrender of its authority to Cromwell. 'The dissolution of this parliament and government which I apprehended would be, though not when,' came as no surprise to Josselin. But he feared that it would usher in 'evil days'.[8] Newsletters and propaganda immediately began to vilify the radicals of the Assembly as the real enemies to the laws, the ministry and tithes, and to accuse those hotheads of abolishing these institutions without providing any alternatives. The scene seemed set for stronger government.

The Protectorate

'Lord wilt thou have Oliver Cromwell or Jesus Christ to reign over us?' asked Vavasour Powell in December 1653.[9] An answer was not long in coming. Under the Instrument of Government, Britain's first written constitution, Cromwell became Lord Protector of the Commonwealth and was installed in office on 16 December. The Instrument, drawn up by John Lambert on the basis of previous army proposals going back to 1647, was presented to the public as a balanced constitution fit for all purposes and combining 'the unitive virtue (but nothing else) of monarchy', 'the admirable counsel of aristocracy' and 'the industry and courage of democracy'.[10] Supreme legislative power was shared by the Protector and 'the people assembled in parliament'. The Protector's power was limited by a strong Council (which would elect his successor), by guaranteed regular Parliaments, and by the basic principles included in the Instrument such as liberty of religion. Parliament was to meet once every three years and sit for at least five months. It was to be made up of 400 English MPs and 30 each from Scotland and Ireland: all adult males worth £200 or more a year could vote unless disqualified by Catholicism or past royalism; the seats were redistributed away from small, unrepresentative boroughs to counties.

The aims of this constitution were to settle the country and to pursue reformation. Yet, as the work of the army, could it really hope to win over popular support? The Council was full of army generals and politicians close to Cromwell. Parliament was to play a major role, but the Instrument contained a note of caution: the meeting of the first Parliament was deferred until September 1654; and the Parliaments were specifically forbidden to alter the basic settlement of the government in a single person and Parliament. There were many among both his former opponents and his allies who saw this as Cromwell's seizure of power. Levellers and 'Commonwealthsmen', as the republican supporters of the Rump were called, now turned on the Protector: Edmund Ludlow denounced the Instrument as a 'work of darkness'; Robert Overton insinuated that 'his lordship did only design the setting up of himself'; and other officers complained that so much power threatened 'to destroy Parliament, and bring us into vassalage'.[11] Cromwell, of course, believed that God had led him to this place. As Desborough had told him after Dunbar, God was the author of his successes; 'he alone is the Lord of Hosts, your victories have been given you of himself; it is himself that has raised you up amongst men, and has called you to high employments'.[12] Cromwell's own identification with

THE COMMONWEALTH AND PROTECTORATE (1649-60)   125

the divine purpose, along with the assumption that the army was the moral and political guarantor of the godly cause, were to shape political developments fundamentally: they were, above all, to determine the prospects for settlement. To the leaders of the Protectorate regime, argues Barry Coward, 'the quest for godly reformation was at least as important as the quest for settlement'.[13]

The Instrument empowered the Protector to rule by ordinance until Parliament met in September. A frenetic nine-month burst of activity by the Council saw the consideration of two hundred measures and the issue of eighty ordinances covering both bread-and-butter administration and major reforms. Ordinances provided the Protector with some king-like symbols and trappings, abolished political oaths, reformed the Court of Chancery, and established the system of triers and ejectors of the clergy. Cromwell quickly brought the Dutch war to an end, but successfully stood out in the peace negotiations for the retention of the Navigation Act. This was also the moment for the government to pursue the full union between England and Scotland that was implied by the Instrument's allocation of seats to Scottish MPs. However, the Union of April 1654 was little more than an English takeover. The Kirk was brought to heel. English law was extended to Scotland. This was part of an attack on Scottish feudalism designed, among other things, to weaken the great nobles who had supported the royalist invasions of 1648 and 1651. It provoked Scots to join the Highland rebellion of Glencairn and Middleton that in turn necessitated the dispatch of General Monk to pacify Scotland in 1654. It was only after 1655 and the arrival of Lord Broghill, former royalist and son of the Earl of Cork, as president of the Scottish Council that the situation began to improve. Ireland, too, now had parliamentary representation, but there was little pretence that it was anything other than a colony under military occupation. The Rump's Act of Settlement had provided for massive confiscations of land from the Catholics and the plantation of English soldiers and adventurers on their former lands. The Protectorate pursued this well-worn policy of making the Irish Catholics pay for their own subjugation, and encountered many of the usual problems. Transplanted Catholics suffered horribly in the poor lands of the west and turned to crime, or they remained illegally to work as labourers for the Protestant landowners. Insufficient numbers of Protestant settlers took up the lands and the Protestant missionary effort dwindled away as the newly arrived Baptist and Quaker groups jockeyed for position under the godly Lord General Fleetwood. In 1655 Fleetwood was succeeded by the more effectual Henry Cromwell, the Protector's younger son, who had less time for the religious sects and more interest in developing the commercial and fiscal potential of Ireland. Yet there was no sign in the 1650s that Ireland was becoming the prosperous, self-reliant Protestant country of which the English dreamed. It long remained a drain on the financial and military resources of the English government. The landless Irish Catholic peasants certainly gained nothing from Cromwellian rule, but a decisive shift in landownership – one estimate suggests that Catholic land-holding fell from 60 per cent of land in 1641 to just over 20 per cent in 1660 – confirmed the exclusion of all Catholics from economic as well as political power, condemning them to second-class status under the Protestant ascendancy.

In September 1654, at the meeting of his first Parliament, Cromwell recalled the parlous condition of the nation before the erection of the Protectorate: 'was not everything almost grown arbitrary?' Government and property were in danger from 'Levelling principles'; the country was at war with the Dutch; and the case of religion was even 'more sad and deplorable' with blasphemy rampant and an axe being taken to the ministry. He invited Parliament to join him in 'healing and settling' the country. Now was the moment to repudiate past excesses, to recognise the natural order of 'a nobleman, a gentleman and a yeoman', to promote true reformation and godliness, and to confirm the Instrument of Government.[14] The plea fell on deaf ears and Parliament fell on the Instrument. Although Cromwell forced out eighty or so of its most determined critics, the remaining MPs took apart the Instrument and produced their own constitution. Among other changes, their bill proposed narrower limits to religious freedom, and parliamentary control over the army. Cromwell and the Council could accept cuts in the number of troops and in funding, but would never surrender control of the army. An exasperated Protector dissolved Parliament at the first plausible opportunity. It had not passed a single piece of legislation.

In 1655 the Cromwellian government sank into what Coward has characterised as a 'siege mentality'. It had become obvious to the Protector that the majority of the population 'are persons disaffected and engaged against us', a gloomy realisation that was underlined by what Josselin described as 'the great noise of plots'.[15] Frequent rumours of assassination plots and planned risings by royalists, Levellers and disaffected officers were reaching Thurloe, Cromwell's secretary and spymaster, in the mid-1650s. Thanks to Thurloe's network, the government was prepared for any trouble that did occur and easily snuffed out the royalist Penruddock rebellion in Wiltshire in March 1655. The news from overseas was equally dispiriting: although the godly knew that the malign forces of popery were always active, the massacre of the Vaudois Protestants in the Italian Alps by the Catholic Duke of Savoy in May 1655 shocked and angered the Cromwellians; the reports that arrived later that summer of the failure of the Western Design, a naval expedition against the Spanish West Indies, threw Cromwell into a spiritual and psychological crisis. The Protector was convinced that God had turned against him and that some terrible sin needed to be expiated if divine favour was once again to shine on England. 'The Lord help us to know what our sin is, or his pleasure is, that we are so crossed and visited in Jamaica,' prayed James Berry, a godly officer.[16] 'We live in changeable and uncomposed times,' observed one preacher at St Paul's in June; 'we see distempers at home, we hear of distresses abroad; the Lord is shaking heaven and earth, churches and states.'[17]

Security and the reform of sin now overrode thoughts of settlement. Throughout 1655 the regime moved to protect and strengthen the position of its godly sympathisers in the English counties. Town councils were purged of those suspected of hostility to the cause; a proclamation was issued extolling the 'free and uninterrupted passage of the gospel running through the midst of us' and condemning those, such as the Quakers, who stirred up contention or disturbed other religious congregations; and in the autumn Major Generals were appointed as the governors of the English provinces.[18] The Major Generals scheme was an ad hoc measure to provide a quick, effective response to disorders and insurrections and to detect and deter such stirrings in the countryside. It also answered the need to cut military costs by raising a voluntary militia of county-based cavalry. Security and cost-cutting were neatly combined in the decision to fund these cavalry units from a 'decimation tax', a 10 per cent tax on all well-to-do 'royalists', by which was meant anyone who had supported the royalist cause since 1642. The whole package was presented as defensive: 'unless we would give up all for which so much blood has been spilled, and the hope of reforming the nation from the spirit of profaneness, we must secure the peace by additional forces, the charge of which ought not to be put upon those that have borne the heat and burden of the day, but on those who were the occasion of all our dangers'.[19] Yet alongside their security role, the Major Generals were required to promote godliness and discourage profanity by executing laws against Sabbath-breaking, drunkenness, swearing and betting and to suppress cockfights, horse races, brothels and illegal alehouses. As Durston has shown, these were godly men with a commitment to the cause of reformation, who came up against the intractable realities of life in the backwaters of England and Wales. 'Reformation has many enemies' in Wrexham, reported Berry. In

Monmouthshire he needed prayers and powers because here too 'reformation has many enemies', while Brecon had not a single preacher and
he feared that some of the people will 'become heathens'. But from
Carmarthen he wrote, 'I am persuaded that not only the tax, but something of reformation will be carried on in poor Wales, whom I seriously
profess, my heart pities and loves.'[20] In the Midlands, Whalley had hopes
of 'a very good outward reformation' and recognised that some aided his
work 'out of fear, some out of love'; later he reported to Thurloe that 'our
presence I find is desired in all places and gives life to all proceedings'.[21]
Individual Major Generals chalked up successes – they reanimated meetings of the ejectors, closed down alehouses by the score, arrested vagrants.
But the final assessment must be that the Major Generals lacked the
direction from the centre and the wide support in their regions that was
necessary to assure success in moral reformation, collecting the decimation
tax, or indeed in assuring political support. Even more damaging in the
long run was the harm they did to the image of the Protectorate. Their rule
was seen by many as the unacceptably authoritarian face of puritanism,
a brutal imposition of alien 'bashaws' and 'swordsmen' determined to
suppress the harmless pastimes of horse racing, and to harass royalists
even at the cost of ripping open old wounds.

In the summer of 1656 elections were held for a new Parliament –
forced on the Protector by growing debt and plans to launch a war against
Spain in alliance with France – and the damage done by the recent
heavy-handed government took its toll. In York 'they will have no swordsmen, no decimator or any that receives salary from the state to serve in
Parliament'. In Hampshire, Major General Goffe sought only 'to keep out
bad men'; in Norfolk, Haynes was staggered by the industry of the opposition; and the hardline Kelsey believed that 'the interest of God's people'
was 'to be preferred to a thousand Parliaments'.[22] The seriousness with
which God's people took these elections can be seen in Josselin's prayer
that polling day 'might have a mercy, and not a curse in it for poor
England'.[23] The election results were as bad as foreseen. The Protector had
to exclude over a hundred hostile MPs from attending the new Parliament.

At the opening of Parliament, Cromwell made a characteristically long-
winded speech which the newsletters helpfully summarised: the country
was at war with Spain, which was both an agent of Antichrist and a
supporter of the Stuarts; religious liberty was to be protected so that the
different denominations 'might not tread upon the heels or prejudice one
another'; the cause and good effects of the Major Generals were explained;
'concluding with an exhortation that all the laws and other things which

might admit of reformation might be in their thoughts, that by the pre-servation of the ministry for the worship of God, and magistracy for the keeping of people in good manners, the blessing of God might be upon the nations'.[24] At first MPs did turn their attention to reform and regulation, only to be diverted into a ten-day debate on the blasphemous activities of the Quaker James Nayler and the punishment he should receive. That debate signalled their concern over the extent of religious freedom and it drew a querulous enquiry from the Protector about the legal and con-stitutional grounds of their action, a pointed reminder that Parliament had no right to define blasphemy. It was, however, another issue that blew the Parliament off course and revealed a fundamental split within the Protector's own circle.

Cromwell had always governed through a combination of clients and allies bound to him by shared history and personal connections. Initially these had shared a single vision, but as time wore on a perceptible gap opened between the 'military' and 'civilian' Cromwellians. By 1656 the army's leaders, Lambert, Desborough and Fleetwood, were at odds with more conservative councillors such as Lord Broghill and John Claypole. The conservatives were ready to ditch the Instrument and to replace it with a civilian-authored and Parliament-approved constitution that might even include the return of a House of Lords and the title of monarch. The first act of the drama opened on Christmas Day 1656 with Desborough's attempt to smuggle a militia bill through Parliament to perpetuate the decimation tax and hence the Major Generals. Claypole and other civilian Cromwellians opposed and eventually defeated the bill. Cromwell kept his distance from the debate, but after its resolution, he told a meeting of officers that 'it is time to come to a settlement and lay aside arbitrary pro-ceedings, so unacceptable to the nation'.[25] The settlement that he had in mind was the new constitution, eventually to be known as the Humble Petition and Advice, that Broghill was promoting in Parliament. These proposals included the restoration of monarchy and a second chamber or House of Lords, some restrictions on religious liberty (aimed mainly at the Quakers and Socinians), and a few clauses that would tip the constitu-tional balance a little more in Parliament's favour. The Protector was tempted. After the fiasco of the militia bill, Parliament had shown its willingness to play ball with the Protector by voting £400,000 for the war against Spain. Now it entered into protracted negotiations with Cromwell.

The main difficulty was that Cromwell could not be persuaded to take the title of king. He knew that if he did he would lose forever the support of the army and the religious radicals, alienate many key politicians such as

Lambert and Desborough, and tie his fortunes to those of the conservative grouping. Moreover, as he said so often, monarchy had been struck down by God in 1649: 'I would not seek to set up that that providence hath destroyed and laid in the dust, and I would not build Jericho again.'[26] In May Cromwell gambled that a final refusal of the title of king would not torpedo the offer of a new constitution. The gamble paid off. The revised constitution recognised Cromwell as Protector, now with the power to name his own successor and with many of the trappings of a monarch, such as a Privy Council, and the right to nominate members of the new 'Other House'. He continued to control the army and the government received generous financial provision. Parliament meanwhile was guaranteed protection against the exclusion of MPs by the executive. Unfortunately the new arrangements did not please everyone – both Lambert and Broghill were disgruntled – and they could not guarantee harmony between the Protector and his Parliaments. The first session of Parliament with the 'Other House' and with the formerly excluded MPs was held in January 1658. It lasted a fortnight. Outraged by the attacks of republican members on the 'Other House', Cromwell dissolved Parliament with the defiant words: 'let God be judge between you and me'.[27]

Liberty or Reformation? Religion in the 1650s

'Far be it from me to nourish unthankful murmurings against the goodness of God, who hath given us so much liberty in the enjoyment of his gospel,' preached Richard Gilpin at Keswick in 1658. 'Though we have great cause to be thankful; yet still we have cause to take up a lamentation, that the sanctuary is not cleansed, and that the building is not yet perfected; how fearfully are many drunk and mad with error? . . . How have we been undone by an unlimited Christian liberty?'[28] The impetus to cleanse the sanctuary, to perfect the Reformation, was a powerful and straightforward one for the godly. 'Reformation' required the promotion of positive Christian duties such as prayer, sermon-going, catechising and godly exercises on the Sabbath. It included the suppression of superstitious practices – particularly customary festivities on 'holydays' such as Christmas and May Day – and religious offences like Sabbath-breaking or profane swearing. And it envisaged the creation of a moral community by tackling social ills such as drunkenness, gaming, bawdiness and fornication. The difficulty was that this agenda was now to be pursued within the context of 'Christian liberty' rather than of some form of national church. As Cromwell told Parliament in 1655, 'religion' – meaning the liberty of 'all species of Protestants to worship God according to their own light and conscience' – 'was not the thing first contested for, but God brought it to that issue at last'.[29] Liberty and Reformation were in tension – and to the more conservative, such as Gilpin, liberty was in danger of getting out of hand.

*

Liberty took several forms. Most striking was the liberty of those 'drunk and mad with error'. The later 1640s and the 1650s have become notorious as the period when 'the world was turned upside down' and the sects – Fifth Monarchy Men, Ranters, Baptists, Quakers and others – 'swarmed'. These were strange, unstable and usually short-lived groups. Gerrard Winstanley, a utopian and mystic, led the 'Diggers', who sought to attain true community and salvation by challenging private property: they established a precarious commune on common land in Surrey between 1649 and 1651. Some groups claimed to have been granted special revelations: the Muggletonians believed that in February 1652 God had told John Reeve, a London tailor, that he and his cousin Ludowick Muggleton were the Two Last Witnesses promised in the Book of Revelation. Other sectaries found the divine message within themselves. They cited scriptural texts such as Galatians 1: 12, *for I neither received it of men, neither was I taught it by men, but by the revelation of Jesus Christ*. Richard Coppin, an itinerant lay preacher, claimed that his preaching was commissioned by an inner revelation, not by 'Oxford and Cambridge, or the schools of Anti-Christ, by the laying on of hands of the bishop or presbytery'.[30] 'I do not expect to be taught by bibles or books, but by God,' declared Jacob Bauthumley, New Model soldier and lay preacher. Men should be 'guided by that inward law of righteousness within'.[31]

Bauthumley was reputed to be a Ranter, a label also applied to men like Abiezer Coppe and Lawrence Clarkson who talked of liberating the Spirit from within the Flesh and asserted that to the pure in spirit all things are pure. Their nebulous arguments were a reaction against the general Calvinist insistence on the sinfulness of all human actions and possibly a logical extension of Protestant ideas about justification and righteousness. Ranters were alleged to claim that since they were saved the moral law did not apply to them; no immoral or criminal action – blasphemy, adultery, drunkenness, or theft – was a sin for them: and, even more shockingly, they were charged with acting according to their principles. Such a position might represent a deviant form of the doctrine of antinomianism. That teaching was a perfectly respectable theological attempt to make sense of the doctrine of justification by faith alone and to underline the passivity of the individual in the process of salvation. In other words, it was an assertion that human works play no part in salvation. The few who explored this idea in the 1630s and 1640s had no intention of promoting licentiousness or immorality, but their speculations earned the scorn of the orthodox puritans. The accusations made against the Ranters confirmed all the worst fears of the orthodox. Indeed, the allegations may have been no more than the projected fears of the orthodox and the prurient who were too hasty to see debauchery and licentiousness as the inevitable consequence of any challenge to law and morality. In his exploration of this panic Davis argued that the 'Ranter movement' was an optical illusion caused by historians' over-reliance on the scaremongering of the yellow press.[32]

With all this talk of inner revelation or the leading of the 'Spirit', what might be called 'puritan mysticism' gained a new prominence. Mystics, almost by definition, do not form churches or adopt formulaic creeds, but those active in the mid-seventeenth century tended to elevate the Holy Spirit as experienced internally by individuals above external principles, even the Bible. They looked to the Spirit rather than outward duties, introspective piety and Bible-reading, which were part of the conventional puritan lifestyle. Many were interested in the substance rather than the forms of organised religion. Some became 'Seekers', who awaited a new race of apostles to rebuild the church. Eventually most of these people were absorbed into the largest, most successful, sect to emerge during the 1650s, the Quakers. The message of George Fox and his followers was that all men were born with a light within them which would lead them, more reliably than any other guide, be it Bible, clergy, church, or sacraments, to union with Christ. The sects and mystics were distinct from groupings like the Independents and Baptists, but numerous individuals did move between the two traditions: Gerrard Winstanley and John Lilburne were just two of the radical figures who eventually joined the Quakers.

The blurred definitions and boundaries of so many congregations make it difficult to measure the impact of sectarianism. The best documented were the Baptists who had 250 churches by the end of the decade. The Quakers expanded at an astounding rate from about 500 followers in 1652 to 20,000 five years later and somewhere between 20,000 and 60,000 in 1660. What bears repetition is that these groups never amounted to even 2 per cent of the population. Their public profile, then and now, was out of all proportion to their numbers. This was partly because of their publicity-seeking actions – interrupting church services, refusing to defer to social superiors, setting up squatter camps, or refusing to pay tithes – and partly due to the hysteria that they provoked among the majority of the population. Whatever their numbers, the Baptists, Quakers and others were an indisputable presence.

The radical religious groups offered a direct challenge to the traditional parish clergy. They argued that there was no scriptural justification for an ordained, graduate, tithe-paid clergy, or claimed that it had outlived its usefulness as the age of the gospel was giving way to that of the Spirit. Tithes, contentious at the best of times, were resented by many who were paying for services they did not or could not use. John Canne urged the clergy to follow Christ's example: 'the minister's maintenance is not any set portion of men's goods, nor to be taken from them by compulsion, but to be free'.[33] Radicals had always enjoyed the chance to harass the parish clergy, but the Quakers seem to have perfected the art in going naked for a sign, barracking the ministers in the 'steeple houses', and jeering 'woe to the false prophet' at the minister.[34] In orthodox eyes, the ministry was threatened by lay preaching, 'the shameful abuse of these times, wherein men, having no calling, presumptuously take upon them the office of God's ministers, and to preach publicly unto the people'.[35] The professional clergy looked on in horror as base mechanics, tinkers and even women usurped their own role.

The sects of the mid-seventeenth century have been explained in various ways. To some commentators, they appear to be the logical outcome of the Protestant Reformation's emphasis on the responsibility of individuals to follow their conscience, to read the Bible for themselves, and to make certain of their own salvation. To others, they represent a repudiation of the Protestant insistence on the sinfulness of human beings and the futility of human effort, and a spirited assertion of the rights of ordinary men and women to speak and write of matters hitherto restricted to the elite. Contemporaries tended to see them against their religious background and often dismissed them as a necessary evil: 'sects have most abounded when the gospel hath most prospered'.[36] Preaching an assize sermon at York, John Shaw claimed that the light of truth was spreading in America, New England, Wales and the north, 'and if it be said, so do profaneness and heresies spread, I answer, it was always so in times of reformation, till things could be settled, Satan more struggles'.[37]

*

The more insidious effect of liberty was experienced in the parishes. Since the abolition of the Church of England, and the failure to impose a Presbyterian church, there was no national church, but simply the parishes, their clergy and their congregations. Despite the fact that the Elizabethan uniformity and recusancy laws had been repealed in September 1650, which meant the end of a legally enforceable obligation to attend church, the overwhelming majority of the people still went to their own parish church each week. But what now went on there was often markedly different from the practices of the 1630s or before.

Parish worship should certainly have changed since the Book of Common Prayer was illegal and the Westminster Assembly's Directory of Public Worship was recommended as a guide to 'the general heads, the sense and the scope of the prayers', as 'some help and furniture' for the minister who should compose his own prayers. However, less than a quarter of parishes seem to have bothered to buy a copy of the Directory. In the absence of clear instructions from above, ministers probably used their own forms of worship, relying on extempory prayers, psalms, preaching, and often omitting celebration of the Lord's Supper.

The minister might have changed. One estimate suggests that 2,300 ministers were purged before 1649 on account of their royalist or Laudian leanings, their refusal to take the Solemn League and Covenant, or for ignorance and scandal. In place of these ejected ministers and of others who had died or moved on, came men with a bewildering range of beliefs about theology and church organisation. At Deptford, John Evelyn was not sure whether his parish minister was a Presbyterian or Independent, but admitted that he 'ordinarily preached sound doctrine and was a peaceable man'.[38] The preachers that Evelyn heard in his parish church included enthusiasts, former troopers, and even a 'rude mechanic'. By the same measure, although many parish clergy had been removed or had died, a significant number of those remaining in place had served in the Church of England before 1642, and were now either gratefully embracing new religious opportunities or keeping their head down until better times.

One of the most obvious effects of liberty on the parish churches was the restriction of full religious services to a small group of parishioners. Presbyterian ministers, for example, examined their flock to see who among them was fit to receive the sacrament: they were looking for 'visible worthiness, which consists in competent knowledge, profession of piety, and immunity from scandal'.[39] This always required the cooperation of parishioners and often led to large numbers absenting themselves from the parish church – as appears to have happened in Baxter's parish of Kidderminister. Another effect of this could be to restrict communion to a handful of parishioners: in Thomas Jollie's Lancashire parish only three families were thought fit to receive. When it proved impossible to restrict the sacrament to the worthy among his parishioners, Ralph Josselin simply gave up celebrating the sacrament. At the same time, however, he gathered a group of godly parishioners for private prayer meetings. This group, which he refers to as 'the society' in his diary, was probably the nucleus of those who received the sacrament when he restored it in 1651. Some Independent ministers were simultaneously responsible for a parish and for a gathered church: at St Margaret's, New Street, in London, Thomas Brooks would only serve as minister if 'fit' people from outside the parish, 'though somewhat differing in opinion', were allowed communion there and if 'the godly party' could 'gather themselves together'.[40] Independent ministers tended to restrict communion to those who had joined the congregation and to do this the candidate was expected to give 'some experimental evidences of the work of grace upon his soul'.[41] Such intrusion of voluntarily gathered congregations into the parish structure can be found as far afield as Essex and Gateshead, Stepney and Northamptonshire, but often came at a price. John Lodder's London parishioners refused his tithes because he had denied them baptism or the Lord's Supper unless they joined his gathered church. There was always a danger that people would vote with their feet and go to other parishes with less rigorous standards: the Derbyshire Presbyterian classes reproved the minister John Wiersdale for admitting his own parishioners to the sacrament 'promiscuously' and also admitting some outsiders 'who were not thought fit to be received in their own congregations'.[42]

*

Christian liberty had to be protected without allowing soul-destroying errors to spread; equally, the energies of the godly must be harnessed to the agenda of reformation without trampling on the liberty of God's people. Government therefore needed to find ways to define minimum levels of orthodoxy and promote godly preaching. One of the earliest initiatives was the Rump's Blasphemy Act of 1650 which was designed to thwart the dissemination of dangerous beliefs rather than to control an individual's private opinions. Among the errors targeted were any questioning of the existence or nature of God or Christ, the denial that the Bible was God's word or of the resurrection and final judgement, and the belief in universal salvation, free will or the adequacy of reason: in other words, the act was aimed at the errors of Socinians, antinomians and even Baptists. The Instrument of Government guaranteed freedom of belief and worship to 'such as profess faith in God by Jesus Christ (though differing in judgment from the doctrine, worship, or discipline publicly held forth)' provided they did not disturb the peace or restrain the liberty of others, and with the exception of Roman Catholicism, 'prelacy', and 'such as, under the profession of Christ, hold forth and practise licentiousness'.[43] Measures to proscribe certain radical beliefs were twinned with attempts to draw up a list of fundamentals which could serve as the benchmark for inclusion within the parish ministry or even, thought some, as the criteria for toleration.

Cromwell portrayed himself as a constable trying to preserve the delicate balance between the contending religious parties. He continually reproached the sects for their mutual intolerance: 'every sect says, oh, give me liberty. But give him it, and to his power he will not yield it to anybody else.'[44] Yet even Cromwell could not contemplate a complete freedom. The civil war had not been fought so that people could be of any religion or none. It had been fought, he believed, to make England a godly nation. Cromwell hated 'carnal divisions and contentions among Christians', especially those which arose over human forms such as liturgy or church organisation. Much better, he believed, to trust in divine providence and allow God's spirit to bring the godly to unity: godly union, not religious toleration, was his great aim. Cromwell was therefore prepared to permit conscientious belief if it did not deny the fundamental truths necessary to salvation, but he could not countenance a religious free-for-all. The fundamental truths were the remission of sins and free justification by the blood of Christ, and the core of the godly party was among the Presbyterians, Independents and Baptists. The Protector endorsed liberty while encouraging Parliament to define it to the exclusion of heresy and blasphemy. As one government propagandist explained in 1654, the regime would 'lay a healing hand to these mortal wounds and breaches, by holding forth the truths of Christ to the nation in some solid establishment, and not quite . . . lay aside or let loose the golden reins of discipline and government in the church'. Cromwell did nothing to shield the Socinian John Biddle from Parliament in 1654, and only reluctantly protected the Quaker James Nayler, but then neither did he allow MPs to mount general campaigns which might victimise godly, if misguided, individuals who were on the fringes of acceptability.[45]

The Protectorate took steps to ensure the appointment of godly preaching ministers and to guarantee their orthodoxy. John Owen and others had suggested to the Rump and the Barebones Parliaments the creation of a series of commissions composed of both clergy and laymen who would examine ministers seeking appointment and eject those who were deemed unfit. The clergy would be supported by tithes and the population would be obliged to attend worship, although not necessarily in their own parish church, every Sunday. These plans finally bore fruit in 1654 in the separate commissions of 'triers', responsible for examining and approving applicants for benefices, and 'ejectors' who judged 'scandalous, ignorant and insufficient ministers and schoolmasters'. The national board of thirty-eight triers was composed of Independent divines with a sprinkling of Presbyterians and Baptists. The ejectors were organised as thirty-eight regional boards, each with twenty or so lay commissioners and fourteen clerical assistants; although some Presbyterians served, most members were Independents or their allies. The triers were busy: they adjudicated on 3,500 nominations over five years, and Cromwell himself often took a direct interest, but it is difficult to discern a clear pattern to their appointments which often rubber-stamped the nomination made by a lay patron. The ejectors appear to have been ineffectual until the Major Generals arrived in the counties, but then, under firm guidance, the ejectors dismissed over 130 ministers in the largest clerical purge of the decade. The effectiveness of both schemes was compromised by the property rights of clergymen and laymen – a minister was legally entitled to his parish living and lay people often owned the valuable right to nominate someone to a living. The procedures also worried many. Even a minister sympathetic to the cause, such as Josselin, was apprehensive about the personal animosities and naked anti-clericalism evident in the actions of the ejectors: 'neither do I joy to see minister put under the lay power'.[46]

What was most significant about these arrangements was the absence of specific doctrinal or liturgical instructions. The triers assessed candidates' spirituality, 'holy and unblameable conversation', and 'knowledge and utterance fit to preach'. They were not required to test doctrine or impose ordination. That said, of course, the triers did tend to promote men in their own likeness – which is one reason why the triers themselves were a mixed bunch of Independents, Presbyterians and Baptists. The criteria for ejection included popish tendencies, holding opinions proscribed by the Blasphemy Act, negligence or insufficiency as a minister, and 'scandal', which covered both moral offences and support for breaches of the Sabbath, wakes, morris dancing or stage plays. No attempt was made to tell ministers how to worship, nor to oblige lay attendance at church.

Such policies could not stem the tide of sectarian and lay preaching, bring the Quakers to heel or drive the laity back to their parish churches. In the opinion of many, the price of liberty was error, distraction and ignorance among the people, and near despair among the clergy. 'We find by sad experience', admitted a group of Worcestershire ministers, 'that the people understand not our public teaching, though we study to speak as plain as we can, and that after many years preaching, even of these same fundamentals, too many can scarce tell anything that we have said.'[47] Edward Reynolds, a Presbyterian, urged the 1657 Parliament to encourage orthodox learned ministers, defend the universities and oblige the people to attend a Christian assembly to hear 'the ministry and dispensation of the gospel'. Above all, he called for efforts 'to heal and close up breaches amongst brethren, that men agreeing in faith, worship, and obedience, may be no longer strange to one another, but join hand in hand against the dangers which are threatened from a common adversary'.[48]

Some clergy did join together to combat the excesses of liberty. In at least seventeen counties ministers formed clerical associations to encourage and support one another in the work of reclaiming their flocks from heresy, blasphemy and loose living. Richard Baxter was the inspiration behind the movement which, he claimed, grew out of 'the sincere desire of concord among honest, godly, serious, humble ministers, who were of no sect or party at all, although the vulgar do call them Presbyterians'.[49] Despite their claims to be non-denominational, the county associations tended to attract support mainly from those Presbyterian and Independent divines who held parish livings. In so far as these groups were cross-denominational, the parish clergy were being brought together by a common danger: 'the Lord hath strangely made way for the long-desired union by the bitter, woeful and unutterable fruits of our divisions, which hath almost destroyed not only the ministry, but even the very heart and life of religion and godliness'.[50] These ministers were particularly eager to foster catechising among their parishioners in the hope of undoing some of the damage caused by the contentious preaching of the past decade. Without a basic understanding of Christianity dinned into them by the personal instruction of their pastor, the laity would be vulnerable to every error of the age. Baxter was a leading exponent of catechising and, through the Worcester Association, one of its main publicists; in Somerset Joseph Alleine spent five afternoons every week working his way around the households of Taunton. Catechising was not only good in itself, it also paved the way for a worthy reception of the Lord's Supper. And sometimes, to their surprise, the clergy found what they were looking for. Oliver Heywood proposed a sacrament and about 120 parishioners presented themselves for examination 'from most of which I received abundant and unexpected satisfaction, and found more knowledge, true piety, and convictions of conscience than I had before that made account of'. But this was the first communion celebrated in the parish for seven years.[51]

Anarchy and restoration

Cromwell's health and spirits began to fail in 1658. His remaining energies were absorbed by the military campaign in the Spanish Netherlands that culminated in an Anglo-French victory at the battle of the Dunes and the English occupation of Dunkirk. In August, Cromwell was taken ill. On the morning of 3 September, he died at Whitehall. 'Cromwell died. People not much minding it,' was Josselin's laconic diary entry: people would soon mind it very much, as Oliver's death precipitated a sixteen-month-long crisis. On the afternoon of 3 September the Council agreed that Richard, the eldest son of the late Protector, should be proclaimed successor. Whether this was Oliver's considered plan or deathbed decision is not known, but it was not a wise choice. Richard Cromwell could control neither the army nor Parliament. After meeting another Parliament that criticised the army and the constitution, Richard was coerced by the officers to dissolve that assembly and recall what was left of the Rump Parliament. In May the Rump set up its own Council of State, refused to recognise the Protectorate, engineered Richard's resignation and reinstated the Commonwealth. That summer Lambert and the army were busy putting down a Royalist rising in Cheshire and Lancashire, but by autumn the generals had turned on the Rump which they dissolved on 13 October. A Committee of Public Safety led by General Fleetwood was established to 'secure the people's liberties as men and Christians, reform the law, provide for a godly preaching ministry, and settle the constitution without a single person or a House of Lords'.[52] The antipathy between army and Parliament, and the rivalry between different generals, had brought government to a halt and the winter saw the country slide into anarchy.

General George Monk, commander of the army in Scotland, now acted to restore order. He demanded the return of the Rump, corresponded with leading godly figures such as John Owen, and began to move his troops towards the border. In London, chaos reigned. Unrest boiled over into riots, government disintegrated, and on 26 December troops once again restored the Rump. In January 1660 Monk and his army marched into England, dispersed Lambert's troops, reached London on 3 February, and by reinstating the MPs excluded by Pride's Purge in 1648 effectively restored the Long Parliament. But no one expected the Parliament to be anything other than a temporary measure. To a royalist like Viscount Mordaunt, the return of Charles II to his throne now seemed certain, and this was not to be attributed to Monk's intervention since 'the voice of the people is in this the voice of God'.[53] Popular, and especially gentry, attitudes were shaped by fear – rumours swept the shires that the Quakers or the Anabaptists were about to rise up – and increasingly the old ways looked safest: demands were heard for monarchy, for a full and free Parliament, and even for the Church of England.

The Long Parliament renewed the Solemn League and Covenant, revived the Presbyterian *classes*, and declared the Westminster Confession of Faith to be the religion of the land. On 21 February Monk told Parliament that 'moderate, not rigid Presbyterian government, with a sufficient liberty for consciences truly tender, appears at present to be the most indifferent and acceptable way to the church's settlement': the Presbyterian divines Calamy, Reynolds, Manton and Spurstow were despatched to Holland to negotiate with Charles Stuart. The Presbyterians rejoiced. 'Lift up thine eyes, my soul!' hymned Oliver Heywood. 'What a change has been effected in half a year! Surely there is a gracious moving wheel of providence in all these vicissitudes.'[54]

The Long Parliament dissolved itself on 16 March to make way for a newly elected Parliament. Charles Stuart now effectively laid before the country a manifesto for the restoration of the Stuart monarchy. On 4 April he issued the Declaration of Breda which proposed, subject to parliamentary approval, 'a free and general pardon' to all of his subjects, 'full satisfaction' of the army's pay arrears, the confirmation of land sales made since 1642, and 'a liberty to tender consciences'. By involving Parliament in the planned settlement, stressing his moderation and mercy, and offering not only an immediate religious freedom but also a future Act of Parliament 'for the full granting that indulgence', Charles reassured the nation. The Convention Parliament met on 25 April and soon after declared that Charles had legally been King ever since his father's execution. On 25 May Charles II landed at Dover, where the Mayor presented him with 'a very rich Bible, which he took and said it was the thing he loved above all things in the world'.[55] On 29 May, his thirtieth birthday, the King arrived in London to be greeted by 'the gentry in all their bravery and gallant splendour', by crowds and massed regiments, trumpets and drums, flowers and banners, and 'such shouting as the oldest man alive never heard the like'.[56]

Notes

1 *A Collection of the State Papers of John Thurloe*, ed. T. Birch (7 vols, 1742), VII, 217–18.

2   S. Kelsey, 'Unkingship', in B. Coward (ed.), *A Companion to Stuart England* (Oxford, 2003).

3   A.S.P. Woodhouse (ed.), *Puritanism and Liberty* (1938; 2nd edn, London, 1974), pp. 244–5, 246.

4   Josselin, pp. 227–8.

5   Abbott, III, 5–8, 28–9, 55–66.

6   Abbott, III, 60–1, 64.

7   Richard Baxter, *Reliquiae Baxterianae*, ed. M. Sylvester (1696), I, 70.

8   Josselin, p. 315.

9   Watts, p. 150.

10   Marchamont Nedham, *A True Case of the State of the Commonwealth* (1654).

11   Edmund Ludlow, *Memoirs*, ed. C.H. Firth (2 vols, Oxford, 1894), I, 371; *Thurloe State Papers*, III, 110; *CSPD 1653–4*, pp. 302–4.

12   J.C. Davis, *Oliver Cromwell* (2001), p. 87.

13   B. Coward, *The Cromwellian Protectorate 1653–59* (Manchester, 2002), p. 3.

14   Abbott, III, 434–43.

15   Abbott, III, 511; Josselin, p. 340.

16   B. Worden, 'Oliver Cromwell and the Sin of Achan', in D. Beales and G. Best (eds), *History, Society and the Churches* (Cambridge, 1985); *Thurloe State Papers*, IV, 510.

17   Edward Reynolds, *Joy in the Lord* (1655), sig. A3r.

18   *CSPD 1655*, p. 410.

19   *CSPD 1655*, p. 411.

20   *Thurloe State Papers*, V, 334, 545, 582.

21   *Thurloe State Papers*, V, 241, 434.

22   *Thurloe State Papers*, V, 296, 215, 328, 384.

23   Josselin, p. 377.

24   *The Clarke Papers*, ed. C.H. Firth (Camden Society, new series, 4 vols, 49, 54, 61, 62, 1891–1901), III, 72–3.

25   Abbott, IV, 417.

26   Abbott, IV, 473.

27   Abbott, IV, 732.

28   Richard Gilpin, *The Temple Rebuilt* (1658), p. 33.

29 Abbott, III, 585–6; J. Morrill (ed.), *Oliver Cromwell and the English Revolution* (1990), p. 18.

30 N. McDowell, *The English Radical Imagination* (Oxford, 2003), p. 18.

31 J. Morrill (ed.), *The Impact of English Civil War* (London, 1991), p. 65.

32 J.C. Davis, *Fear, Myth and History* (Cambridge, 1986).

33 Watts, p. 148.

34 Josselin, pp. 350, 380.

35 John Downame's imprimatur to John Collinges, *Vindiciae Ministerii Evangelici* (1651).

36 Richard Baxter, *Autobiography*, ed. J.M. Lloyd Thomas and N. Keeble (London, 1974), p. 84.

37 John Shaw, 'Autobiography', in *Yorkshire Diaries and Autobiographies of the Seventeenth and Eighteenth Centuries* (Surtees Society, 65, 1877), p. 403.

38 Evelyn, III, 80–1.

39 Watts, p. 154.

40 W.A. Shaw, *A History of the English Church during the Civil Wars and under the Commonwealth* (2 vols, London, 1900), II, 102.

41 Watts, p. 154.

42 *The Minute Book of the Wirksworth Classis 1651–1658*, ed. J.C. Cox (Derbyshire Archaeological and Natural History Society, II, 1880), p. 153.

43 Gardiner, p. 416.

44 Abbott, III, 586.

45 B. Worden, 'Toleration and the Cromwellian Protectorate', *SCH*, 21 (1984), 211–12, 217.

46 Josselin, pp. 362–3.

47 D. Hirst, 'The Failure of Godly Rule in the English Republic', *P&P*, 132 (1991), 42.

48 Edward Reynolds, *The Peace of Jerusalem* (1657), p. 33.

49 Baxter, *Autobiography*, p. 135.

50 C.G. Bolam, J. Goring, H.L. Short and R. Thomas, *The English Presbyterians* (London, 1968), p. 50.

51 Heywood, I, 171.

52 R.E. Mayers, *1659: The Crisis of the Commonwealth* (Woodbridge, 2004), ch. 10.

53 *The Letter-Book of John Viscount Mordaunt 1658–60*, ed. M.H. Coates (Camden Society, 3rd series, 69, 1945), p. 179.

54 J.C. Spalding, 'The Demise of English Presbyterianism 1660–1760', *Church History*, 28 (1959), 64; J. Hunter, *The Rise of the Old Dissent Exemplified in the Life of Oliver Heywood* (1842), p. 119.

55 *The Diary of Samuel Pepys*, ed. R.C. Latham and W. Matthews (11 vols, London, 1970–83), I, 158.

56 *The Diurnal of Thomas Rugg 1659–1661*, ed. W.L. Sachse (Camden Society, 3rd series, 91, 1961), pp. 88–90.

CHAPTER 6

Charles II (1660–85)

Determined not to go on his travels again, Charles II concentrated on winning over his former opponents and promoting reconciliation. Thus the King employed more of his old enemies than his old friends in government, cooperated with Parliament, pardoned past crimes, and (with the important exception of church and crown estates) left land in the hands of those who had bought it over the past twenty years. There was only one element in the political settlement of the early 1660s that did not follow this moderate pattern, and that was religion. The conciliatory tone and promises of 1660 were dramatically reversed by the religious settlement embodied in the 1662 Act of Uniformity. The Uniformity Act set out strict terms for those who wished to be clergymen of the Church of England and it outlawed other religious denominations. It rent English Protestantism into two. And its revision was a fundamental political issue until 1689. Thus the politics of Protestantism were to trouble Charles II's reign. But it was the politics of popery that were to destabilise Charles's government and in due course to bring down his successor, James II. After 1660, Roman Catholicism was no longer an external threat, but one that had wormed its way into the very heart of government and the court – the Queen, the royal mistresses, the heir to the throne, even, it was feared, Charles himself, were Roman Catholics. And, as all good Protestants thought they knew, wherever popery went, 'arbitrary government' was sure to follow.

The Church of England and Dissent

Charles II was restored to the throne on the understanding of some sort of 'liberty to tender consciences' in religion. It was recognised that a national

Church of England would be established, but many anticipated that this would be a broad inclusive church that allowed clergy and members a fair degree of freedom in belief and practice. Some also assumed that those who wished to remain outside the national church would be permitted religious freedom. During 1660 the omens for political compromise and a generous religious settlement were generally good. The new bishops had varied backgrounds: one, Reynolds, was a former Presbyterian. In December 1660, the King's Worcester House Declaration sketched a broad-based national church and suggested that the parish minister would have some choice in his use of the liturgy, his dress, his preaching and the exercise of discipline, especially in the vexed matter of which parishioners he admitted to the sacrament of the Lord's Supper. 'Moderate' or 'reduced episcopacy' would be the form of church government: bishops would exercise their powers, such as ordination and excommunication, in consultation with their diocesan clergy. This compromise had much to recommend it to moderate Presbyterians and episcopalians alike. A clerical commission to review the Prayer Book had been promised, as had a synod on the question of ceremonial conformity.

Within a year the situation had changed beyond recognition. The settlement imposed by the Act of Uniformity and the revised Book of Common Prayer was uncompromising and restrictive: all ministers of the national church must have episcopal ordination; there was to be strict uniformity to the Prayer Book; and the religious and political affiliations of the past had to be renounced. Although there is no adequate single explanation for the nature of the religious settlement, the breakdown of negotiations between Presbyterians and episcopalians at the Savoy Conference and the election of a new 'Cavalier' Parliament in the spring of 1661 are important factors.

The first act of the new House of Commons was to order the burning of the Solemn League and Covenant and to require all members to take communion according to the Prayer Book rite. Its subsequent actions were designed either to suppress subversive groups such as the Quakers or to tighten the government's control over political offices. The 1661 Corporation Act, for example, empowered commissioners to purge municipal office-holders by requiring them to abjure the Covenant, swear the oaths of allegiance and non-resistance, and receive the Anglican communion. The Commons made it plain that it would take steps to enforce clerical conformity, but this was more out of a desire to ensure obedience to authority than out of any clear grasp of the theological niceties of the Book of Common Prayer. Indeed, its first demands for conformity were made before the final contents of the Prayer Book had been agreed and many of the requirements of the Act of Uniformity had originally been part of a different bill concerned with sorting out the gentry's rights to ecclesiastical patronage and tithes. Most MPs were more concerned with their own property rights and local influence than with the precise theological complexion of the restored Church of England. They reflected the anxieties and preferences of the nation at large. They feared Quakers and other sects that had abused the 'abundant liberty for religious exercise both in public and private'.[1] They shared the popular enthusiasm for the old familiar church, clergy and Prayer Book. At St Paul's, Covent Garden, for example, the 'affection of this parish to the liturgy of the church' led the minister to daily reading of the Prayer Book, 'and if all his brethren would do the like we should have more devotion and less news'.[2] Many of the gentry were enthusiastic proponents of the church, reminding their tenants and neighbours of its social and spiritual function, and defending its rites and institutions: in one homely simile, the Nottingham Grand Jury were told that the discipline and ceremonies of the church were as necessary to preserve religion in its purity as the skin of an apple was to preserve its fruit.[3] In Parliament, Gilbert Sheldon, Bishop of London and from 1663 Archbishop of Canterbury, with the help of a small group of sympathetic MPs, skilfully played on these sympathies to strengthen the position of the church. Overall, it would be unrealistic to expect the gentry or MPs as a group to weigh the finer points of theology or churchmanship: the Church of England was restored because it was a familiar institution that bolstered their material interests and social vision.

The Act of Uniformity was therefore a blunt instrument by which to define a church. That it was primarily designed to exact conformity is evident from the four requirements made of all clergy. They were to have or obtain ordination from a bishop; earlier Presbyterian ordination would not be recognised. They were to repudiate the Covenant for themselves and declare it illegal for others. They were to give their full assent to the Prayer Book as if every word and ceremony was true and necessary. And they were to subscribe to the Thirty-nine Articles, three of which concerned church government. Many ministers who would *in principle* have continued to serve a national church refused to serve the church under these terms. Refusal often turned on an individual's personal difficulty rather than an issue of general principle. 'I scruple to be reordained,' explained Philip Henry, 'to declare my assent and consent to the liturgy, to renounce the covenant as an oath in itself unlawful, which are the common stumbling stones to me with others.'[4] Yet the Uniformity Act, which came into force on 24 August, St Bartholomew's Day, 1662, made no allowance for 'tender consciences' and so 936 ministers left or, as they preferred to describe it, were 'ejected' from their livings. Almost 700 ministers with uncertain legal claims on their parishes or no relish for national churches had already left. In total, 1,760 English clergy were forced to leave their parishes between 1660 and 1663, along with another 120 clergy in Wales and around 200 lecturers, university dons and schoolmasters. At least 171 of the 1,760 are known to have later conformed to the church.

*

The Church of England once more claimed the allegiance of all the English people. The population were again legally required to attend its parish services, to pay its tithes and solemnise baptisms, marriages and funerals according to its rites. And that is what most of them, either out of apathy or enthusiasm, did. But this did not necessarily mean that they were all Anglican zealots. Conformism was the name of the game, especially for those in the upper ranks of society. Almost everyone of note in Charles II's England was an outwardly conforming member of the Church of England, even if they also frequented Nonconformist conventicles, Roman Catholic masses, or atheist debauches.

It is a mistake to assume that the social and political position of the church was assured or monolithic. The clergy of the Church of England came from a variety of backgrounds. They included self-styled 'sufferers', the royalist clergy who had been sequestered from their livings in the 1640s and had spent much of the interregnum in retirement or exile. These were enthusiastic defenders of the rights of the church and her bishops, of the liturgy, and of the Stuarts, and many of them leaned towards an elevated view of episcopacy and an elaborate ritualism. Many of these divines were already middle-aged in 1660, however, and the next generation was compromised by collaboration with the regimes of the 1640s and 1650s. Some of these younger men were reluctant conformists who in time came to pronounce themselves more satisfied with the church, others like John Tillotson, Edward Fowler, Simon Patrick and Richard Kidder were more enthusiastic converts to the church and, despite being criticised by some as time-servers or 'latitudinarians', eventually rose to bishoprics. Also to be found among the conformists were out-and-out puritans, like Ralph Josselin of Earls Colne or John Angier of Dedham, who by evasion, connivance and good luck managed to retain their livings without using the surplice or Prayer Book. In due course another generation of Anglican clergy emerged: these were the high-flying divines of the later 1670s and the 1680s, a new breed of highly politicised and aggressive churchmen, educated in the Restoration universities, and all too ready to wield their pen in support of the royal prerogative and the indefeasible divine right of hereditary monarchy. Whether they embraced the principles of the Uniformity Act with enthusiasm or marked reluctance was, however, irrelevant: they were all Anglicans.

As an institution the Church of England had regained something very like its pre-1640 position. Ostensibly all members of the community were also members of the Church of England. They were obliged to attend their parish church and to suffer the penalties laid down in various Elizabethan statutes if they failed to attend. The entire population were also liable to pay tithes to the local incumbent and any other fees for marriages, funerals, baptisms and their registration. The church was the only place where people could legally be baptised, married or buried. The state and law upheld these obligations, but so too did the church courts. The ecclesiastical courts had been restored (with a few exceptions such as the prerogative High Commission) in 1661 and continued to operate. Their penalties culminated in excommunication which denied the culprit the sacraments and worship of the church, prevented them pleading at law or acting as executor of a will, excluded them from all offices of authority, and supposedly cut them off from all converse with their neighbours. The ecclesiastical and secular courts tended to reinforce each other's efforts to enforce religious observance and uniformity. The church continued to exert control over education: the two universities were an Anglican monopoly; the bishops licensed schoolmasters; and the young were still catechised by their parish minister. The 1662 Licensing Act returned the task of licensing publications on 'divinity, physic, philosophy or whatsoever science or art' to the university and church authorities. The political influence of the church was visible in Parliament. The twenty-six bishops once again sat in the House of Lords and Archbishop Sheldon ensured that his allies in the Commons were always primed to speak up for the interests of the church. In 1664 Sheldon bound the church's fortunes to Parliament by surrendering the clergy's right to self-taxation in return for a clerical vote in parliamentary elections. Nor should we overlook the informal influence that the church could exert as a corporate landowner and a major patron. There was a natural convergence of interests between the Church of England and the governing elite. The church prided itself on its close association with the monarchy and the Stuart dynasty. Reverence for kingship was part of its scriptural heritage; thanks to the cult of Charles the Martyr, whose memory was kept green every 30 January, the annual day of national humiliation for the regicide, this reverence verged on idolatry. Incongruously, the notion of a sacred monarchy even seemed to apply to Charles II who was an assiduous 'toucher' for the king's evil. The identification of church and monarchy was inescapable. The Anglican liturgy marked the anniversaries of 5 November, 30 January, and 29 May (the restoration of Charles II), when preachers explained the function of divine providence in chastising a wicked nation. These sermons are a repository of the church's political teaching: God punished the disobedient, sometimes directly and sometimes by removing the King and giving the disobedient a taste of anarchy; divine providence was the people's guarantee against royal misrule and they had no right to resist royal authority, other than by passive disobedience and then they must bear the penalties incurred.

Despite all this privilege – legal, political and ideological – the Restoration Church of England felt persecuted and vulnerable. The gentry seemed to value the church only for its social utility and were unprepared to cooperate in the extirpation of Dissent. The people were sunk in vice and impiety, deaf to the appeals of the clergy, whoring after Rome or the 'fanatic' preachers, and critical of the church and its bishops. 'The present clergy will never heartily go down with the generality of the commons of England,' concluded Pepys in 1663. Five years later there was still talk 'about the bad state of the church, and how the clergy are come to be men of no worth – and, as the world doth now generally discourse, they must be reformed'.[5] There was little sign that Charles II reciprocated the loyalty the church had shown him. The truth is that 'Anglican political dominance was surprisingly shaky, nowhere more so than at court, and churchmen, lay and clerical, had to fight hard and long ... to defend it and the integrity of the Church of England.'[6]

*

The 'Dissenters' were those English Protestants who could not accept the Church of England as established by the 1662 Act of Uniformity. The clergymen who left their parishes because they could not conform to the four major requirements of the act were just a small section of Dissent. These ministers were followed by some of their parishioners who as lay people were not directly subject to the act, but presumably valued the spiritual leadership of their pastor and resented the church's liturgy and ceremonies. However, 'Dissent' was far wider than these Nonconformist congregations. The label applied to all those who did not worship in the Church of England. Separatists and sectaries, Quakers, Baptists, Independents and Presbyterians now all fell into the same legal category. Yet they had little else in common: learned, university-educated and conservative

Presbyterian ministers shared nothing with Baptist ex-soldiers or wandering Quaker preachers. Except perhaps for resentment at the category: 'it is a palpable injury to burden us with the various parties with whom we are now herded by our ejection in the general state of dissenters'.[7] The size of the Dissenting community created by the Act of Uniformity was not large. Figures are treacherous, but at a generous estimate Dissenters represented somewhere between 4 and 10 per cent of the population. They tended to be concentrated in particular places, often in large towns or cities, and were increasingly identified with artisans, workers and traders. They were divided between different denominations even in one location: Bristol, for example, was home to a Quaker meeting, one Presbyterian, two Independent and three Baptist congregations. In rural Oxfordshire, however, one meeting place might host several different groups: 'sometimes Quakers, sometimes Presbyterians and Anabaptists' at Adderbury; or even joint meetings, as at Kingston Blount, 'Presbyterians, Independents, Quakers and Sabbatarians mixed'.[8]

The Presbyterians legitimately felt that they had lost most in 1662. St Bartholomew's Day was remembered as 'the killing day for all the Nonconformist ministers', the day of their 'civil death'.[9] A conscious attempt to portray the ejected ministers as 'Bartolomeans', as a group of martyrs, may have begun as early as their 'farewell sermons', preached for the most part on 17 August and published soon after. Some ministers continued to live in their former parishes, others moved to puritan centres such as the huge London parish of St Giles Cripplegate, and others took up chaplaincies with sympathetic gentry. Talk of a mass exodus to New England came to nothing. These ministers found themselves dependent upon the generosity of their followers and patrons, or forced to earn a living as schoolmasters, tutors or physicians: 'though they were sent without staff or scrip, they have lacked nothing', boasted their followers.[10] They came to be venerated for their conscientious stance, respected for their courage (especially those who remained in London during the Great Plague), and courted by those who hoped to modify the religious settlement of 1662. Many were happy to attend the Church of England as laymen. Thus the ejected Presbyterian Thomas Manton went to St Paul's Covent Garden to hear the sermons of his successor, Simon Patrick. Such ministers would lead their followers to the parish church and would advise them to attend prayers and hear the best preachers in the Church of England. However, they might then hold private meetings with their friends and neighbours for Bible study, prayer and impromptu preaching. Their followers managed to keep a foot in both camps: Sir John Gell attended 'divine service and sermon constantly' at the parish church while also holding conventicles at his family home; Sir Edward Harley 'was a favourer of such as dissented from the church for conscience's sake . . . yet he constantly attended the church'.[11] Many lesser folk, like the Lancashire shopkeeper Roger Lowe, supplemented the services and sermons of their parish church with attendance at a meeting led by some godly ejected minister. This grey area of religious allegiance where people might attend parish church and a Nonconformist conventicle was widely recognised: one Anglican minister described such people as 'neutralists between Presbyterians and conformists'.[12]

The Uniformity Act was only one in a series of discriminatory laws known as the 'Clarendon Code'. Together these statutes amounted to a ruthless attempt to keep Dissenters out of power and to suppress them if possible. Dissenters were punished for meeting in conventicles, ministers who preached and prayed at such gatherings were liable to drastic penalties, and civil office, education and other opportunities were denied to those who were not conformists. Each of the acts had a distinct purpose. The Uniformity Act was intended to exact conformity from Anglican clergy; the Corporation Act to ensure that urban government and consequently parliamentary elections were under the control of loyal Anglicans; while the Quaker Act (1661) was designed to suppress that movement, especially by exploiting their refusal to swear oaths. In 1664, in the aftermath of a failed rising in Yorkshire, MPs passed an act against 'seditious sectaries and other disloyal persons'. This Conventicle Act forbade meetings for worship of more than five people other than members of the same household. After expiring in 1668, it was succeeded by the permanent 1670 Conventicle Act which Andrew Marvell described as 'the quintessence of arbitrary malice'. The new act focused attention on the clerical leaders of Nonconformity and sought to encourage prosecution by rewarding informers and penalising negligent local justices. In 1665 the so-called 'Five Mile Act' prohibited Nonconformist clergy from preaching, teaching or even coming within five miles of any corporate town, or any parish in which they had previously served, unless they took an oath of non-resistance.

This legislation was an assertion that England had only one form of religion, the Church of England, and that it was illegal to attend, practise or minister in other forms. Designed to break up the congregations of ejected ministers and other Nonconformists it was of course a tacit acknowledgement of the existence of this separate Protestant community. The first measures were focused on the regime's security. They were

designed to ensure that urban corporations and hence parliamentary elections were under the control of loyal Anglicans. Later legislation reflected
the conviction among churchmen and MPs that the Nonconformist clergy
were the root of the problem. The Five Mile Act, for example, was
designed to cut the links between ejected clergy and their former flocks,
while the 1670 Conventicle Act increased the penalties for ministers and
decreased them for lay conventiclers.

Dissenters suffered various kinds of persecution. They were spied upon
and harassed: in Yorkshire Oliver Heywood's house was watched by
Widow Bancroft and other informers who uttered 'bitter threatening
words' against the congregation.[13] Dissenters were often fined under the
Clarendon Code, and when they refused to pay, the fines would be levied
by distraint – the seizure and sale of their household goods – or they were
imprisoned. Imprisonment, which always carried a risk of illness or even
death from gaol fever, appears to have been almost arbitrary in its imposition: Isaac Pennington, the Quaker leader, suffered six spells in gaol
between 1662 and 1679; Bunyan was imprisoned between 1660 and 1672,
but was allowed out to travel and preach. Nonconformists suffered under
the legislation of Elizabeth and James, as well as that of the 1660s, and
under the penalties of the Church of England: the results could be both
cruel and contradictory. Heywood was told by the churchwarden that he
would be fined for non-attendance at the parish church and ejected as an
excommunicate if he did attend: 'for the law must be executed, both
to keep me away and to punish my absence'.[14] Campaigns of persecution
varied according to place and time and object. Sober Presbyterians were
often left to their own devices for many months or years, while more radical or feared groups would attract repeated attention: the Somerset
Quaker John Whiting counted seven great persecutions of the Quakers,
and the Bristol Baptists counted eight. Persecution waxed and waned
according to political priorities and the zeal of local magistrates. Very few
of the gentry were ready to enforce the harsh penal laws on their neighbours. Archbishop Sheldon lamented that 'there wants power and zeal in
the magistrates and justices to do their duty' in prosecuting conventicles,
while other bishops complained of living 'under a slack magistracy'.
Clergymen reported that Dissenters 'could all be suppressed with a wet
finger' if the JPs would but enforce the laws.[15] The enforcement of the
conventicle acts in many counties rested on just a very few individual JPs,
such as Sir Daniel Fleming in Westmorland and Cumberland, Thoroton
and Whalley in Nottinghamshire in the later 1670s, or the lone campaigner
Sir Roger Bradshaigh in Lancashire. In Newcastle, Coventry and Bristol,

mayors were known to 'wink' at conventicles, while Yarmouth was a notorious safe haven for Independents in the 1660s. Since the lack of prosecutions under the 1664 Conventicle Act was blamed on the unwillingness of JPs and constables to prosecute their neighbours, the next Conventicle Act transferred the initiative for prosecution to informers who for their efforts collected part of the fines imposed on those convicted. Informers encountered popular hostility and reluctance to give evidence: Sir Peter Leicester was 'amazed' in 1668 that 'there is not a man' in the county of Cheshire who had reported these preachers or their meetings 'though there be hundreds that knew it'.[16] The laity also signalled their distaste for such persecution by declining to buy goods distrained from convicted Nonconformists.

The fear as well as the experience of persecution undoubtedly honed the zeal of the different Dissenting denominations, helped them shed the half-hearted, and hardened them to withstand suffering. They readily applied the biblical language of suffering and martyrdom to themselves, and some eagerly embraced the persecution itself, refusing to meet in secret or to protect themselves, since it was their duty to witness to the Lord and present tribulations were 'a manifestation of our predestination to the ease and peace of another world'.[17] Such attitudes of self-sacrifice did not preclude organising and cooperating so as to be able to withstand persecution. Congregations reinforced their sense of spiritual separateness by exercising discipline over their members, regulating their social and moral behaviour as well as their piety. Even the sects began to create hierarchies: the Quaker movement set up its system of Monthly Meetings and began to log the tribulations of its members in the Book of Sufferings, which remains the most detailed account of the effects of Restoration persecution; the Baptists appointed 'messengers' to superintend groups of congregations and held General Assemblies in 1663 and 1668. Bristol's congregations cooperated in lawsuits and eventually met together for prayer; in London the Presbyterians and Independents set up joint lectures, and by the later 1670s there were talks about a union between the two denominations. Yet, however much external forces drove Dissenters towards unity, there were strong pressures in the opposite direction. It was the nature of Dissent to encourage individuals to examine their consciences and to question ecclesiastical authority. Few of the congregational churches avoided internal divisions; they quarrelled about weighty issues like predestination and adult baptism, and about whether singing was permissible during worship or whether Sunday or Saturday was the Sabbath. Presbyterianism was held together by the moral leadership of its ministers, but these ministers had begun to fall out among themselves over questions of policy and theology. Many of the older Presbyterian clergy refused to embrace sectarianism and had become suspicious of traditional Calvinism, but the younger generation were ready to accept that they would never be part of the national church and were surprisingly loyal to Calvinist theology.

Charles II

Charles II was, when he roused himself, an adroit, and sometimes ruthless, politician, but one who rarely revealed his true intentions and feelings to others – especially not to his councillors – and subscribed to few principles or programmes. This was no absolutist ruler, but a King determined to keep his throne, respect the line of succession, and retain as much freedom of political manoeuvre as would accord with his own interests and self-indulgent temperament. Sir John Reresby, who was not the most perceptive commentator, nevertheless had the King about right when he described his 'temper and constitution' as 'not stirring nor ambitious, but easy, [he] loved pleasures, and seemed chiefly to desire quiet and security for his own time'.[18] A worldly man, Charles regarded religious belief as a fundamentally personal and private matter and disliked persecution for the sake of belief. True, during his exile, Charles had acquired a distaste for Scottish Presbyterianism and a sympathy for Roman Catholics and for Catholicism – he was to be received into the Catholic church on his deathbed by Father John Huddlestone, the priest who helped him escape after the battle of Worcester – but he rarely sought to advance the interests of any religious group unless it also gave him a political advantage. In making this prudential calculation, Charles II took a decidedly modern attitude towards religion that put him at odds with many of his subjects.

Royal government in the 1660s fell between two stools. Charles left most matters in the hands of his minister the Earl of Clarendon. But Clarendon was committed to an ideal of government in which a strong monarch directed affairs with the help of a loyal but independent Parliament and in accordance with the laws, liberty and property rights of the subject. Without strong leadership from either man in Council or Parliament, politics descended into factionalism. Clarendon attracted criticism for his manner and wealth, and, less fairly, for the marriage of his daughter Anne to James, Duke of York, the King's brother and heir. He was blamed for the marriage of Charles to a Catholic Portuguese princess, Catherine of Braganza, who failed to produce an heir to the throne and entangled England in the expensive colony of Tangier. The country suffered a series of catastrophes – bubonic plague killed 70,000 in London in 1665 and the Great Fire of September 1666 destroyed 13,000 houses and 87 churches – but other disasters were more obviously man-made. In 1665 Charles had launched a naval war against the Dutch with hopes of commercial gains and dishing out a lesson to these Calvinist republicans. Initial success gave way to a string of defeats that culminated in humiliation when the Dutch entered the Thames in June 1667, seized the English flagship the *Royal Charles*, and burned three other vessels as they lay at anchor. The scapegoat was Clarendon, who was hounded from office and into exile. Now 'our fears are of a standing army, papists and persecution', wrote Josselin.[19]

Charles exhibited no 'British vision' of his three kingdoms: Scotland and Ireland were treated as entities distinct from his English realm. Separate settlements were made in each territory and Charles ruled them in different ways. In Scotland the Act Recissory (1661) turned the legislative clock back to the days before either Charles I or the Covenanters had attempted to make their mark on the country. Charles II worked with his former enemies and the traditional nobility, especially in the Highlands, restoring their feudal rights and local autonomy. In return, Charles acquired sweeping control over political appointments, parliamentary business, revenue, the militia and ecclesiastical government. He exercised this power to restore bishops to Scotland. Superimposed over the existing Presbyterian ministry, the bishops acted as moderators of the local synods. Presbyterian clergy could retain their positions if they acknowledged the bishops, but about a quarter of them refused this offer and were deprived of their livings. Religious tensions found expression in factious mutterings and open-air preaching; combined with grievances about heavy-handed government they gave rise to the 1666 Pentland Rising. Such protests were brutally suppressed by the standing army that Charles maintained in Scotland. He also had the right man in place. From 1669 the Earl of Lauderdale ruled Scotland in the King's name. While always prepared to act firmly, Lauderdale initially suspected that a more conciliatory line would best serve royal interests, and he sought to prevent either the Presbyterians or Episcopalians getting the upper hand in the Scottish church.

In Ireland, Charles employed another effective viceroy in the shape of the Earl of Ormonde, Lord Lieutenant between 1662 and 1669 and again between 1677 and 1684. Other than a little cosmetic restitution of estates, the massive Cromwellian transfer of Irish lands was not reversed. Ireland remained a Roman Catholic country: 80 per cent of the population were Catholics, and were dispossessed of lands and excluded from political power because of their religion; however, by maintaining their political loyalty to the English monarchy, Irish Catholics were able to enjoy effective freedom of religious practice. When Sir William Petty anatomised the state of Ireland in 1672, he estimated the Protestant part of the population at 100,000 Scots Presbyterians and 200,000 'English' of whom less than half were adherents of the Church of Ireland, while the remainder were Quakers, Baptists, Independents and other Nonconformists. It was this last group, the English Nonconformists, who appear to have declined in numbers across the later seventeenth century. The Protestant Church of Ireland evidently and rightly regarded the Roman Catholics as a lost cause, but it did attempt to face up to the mounting challenge from the Presbyterians of Ulster. The Church of Ireland used the anti-conventicle legislation to harass Presbyterian clergy and congregations. In 1666, the church was further strengthened by the Irish Act of Uniformity which imposed the English Prayer Book and required all clergy to have received episcopal ordination. On the other hand, from 1672 Presbyterian ministers were paid the *regium donum*, a royal contribution to their maintenance derived from customs revenues at Belfast, and this technically illegal church was effectively recognised as the majority church of Ulster.

After the fall of Clarendon, Charles took a greater role in government. The notion of a 'Cabal' ministry is a myth: if anyone was in control of policy it was Arlington, but always subject to the wavering attention of the King and the rivalry of other ministers and favourites, most damagingly the Duke of Buckingham. Charles explored his options, privately discussing an alliance with France while also attempting to placate MPs. Religion was a pressing and difficult issue. Public opinion was not in tune with the policy of persecution, especially as in some cases the authorities had overstepped the legal mark and trespassed on sacrosanct property rights. Nonconformists and their sympathisers were producing cogent arguments for liberty of conscience, arguments that appealed as much to self-interest and prudence as they did to ideology. The King was known to favour some relaxation of the Act of Uniformity, but both his methods and purposes aroused anxiety. Late in 1662 he had asked Parliament to consider ways he might exercise his 'inherent' power of dispensing with the Act. Parliament rushed to defend the Act, denying that the King had any such constitutional power and warning that this could be a Trojan horse for popery: as MPs told Charles, if religious liberty is permitted 'in time, some prevalent sect will, at last, contend for an establishment; which, for aught can be foreseen, will end in popery'.[20]

If the religious settlement was to be revised then this should be done through Parliament. A legislated revision might take two forms. The Church of England could relax its terms of clerical membership so that the scrupulous Nonconformist ministers might be readmitted to or 'comprehended' within the church. The other option was to allow an 'indulgence' or 'toleration' of those religious groups who stood outside the Church of England. Comprehension and toleration were raised in Parliament on several occasions in the 1660s and 1670s, often after a hint from the King, but they had little real chance of success. The clergy had severe reservations. Anglican leaders would not swallow a possible dual standard within the clergy, some of whom would have subscribed under the terms of 1662 and others under revised terms. Once Nonconformist ministers had been comprehended they would still find themselves confronted by unpalatable liturgical and disciplinary demands. Nor was it clear that lay Nonconformists would automatically follow their pastors into the parish church and abandon their conventicles. The younger generation of Presbyterian clergy, brought up after 1662, did not dream of a role in a national church but saw their future in terms of an autonomous denomination. The rival attraction of religious toleration was therefore a crucial factor. Comprehension proposals were usually twinned with plans for a toleration. Those, like Presbyterians, who sought comprehension generally welcomed toleration for others, but those who sought toleration feared that a comprehension would simply leave them as an isolated and vulnerable minority. The determination of the Independents or Congregationalists, under the leadership of the redoubtable John Owen, to achieve toleration, repeatedly thwarted the delicate political negotiations for a comprehension. While espousing a tolerant attitude, many politicians were equally wary of the dangers of double standards or unnecessary concessions. Sir John Holland, for example, argued in Parliament that it would be 'very prudent to grant a relaxation of some things the law in force at present exacts and some indulgence to truly tender consciences'. But in practice he restricted these concessions to those who, accepting the Thirty-nine Articles, episcopacy and the Prayer Book, 'differ with us only in things that are indifferent in their own nature and which we so hold though possibly they do not'. In 1668 Pepys expected a toleration of the Presbyterians as 'most of the sober party be for some kind of allowance to be given to them'. But out in the provinces, loyal gentlemen were less enthusiastic: Sir Peter Leicester told the Grand Jury at Knutsford that the Nonconformist clergy 'were the main occasion and drawers on of the late rebellion . . . so that if these men receive a toleration again, every man may easily guess what will follow'.[21]

*

Politics took a sudden new turn in the spring of 1672 when Charles, in alliance with Louis XIV of France, launched a war against the Dutch Republic. In an earlier secret agreement Louis had promised Charles an annual subsidy in return for the involvement of the English fleet. Louis had also promised a subsidy of £150,000 and the aid of troops when Charles announced his conversion to Roman Catholicism and reintroduced that religion to England: the timing of this supposed conversion was left deliberately vague and it is impossible to say just how serious Charles was about the plan. Secret though it was and remained, this was a dangerous skeleton in his cupboard. Charles carefully paved the way for war. He suspended repayments on the government debt. The loyalty of non-Anglicans was bought by a Declaration of Indulgence which suspended 'the execution of all and all manner of penal laws in matters ecclesiastical, against whatsoever sorts of nonconformists or recusants'. Nonconformists were allowed freedom of public worship if their ministers and meeting places were licensed, and Roman Catholics were allowed to worship in private; meanwhile, the Church of England was to be preserved as 'the basis, rule and standard of the general and public worship of God'. Contemporaries were well aware that this was a wartime expedient: ''twas because of a war with Holland that 'twas granted; and as the King said, it kept peace at home'.[22] But the effect was immediate and extensive. Around 1,500 licences were issued and Dissenters began to build their own meeting houses. In a move that suggests they now accepted their status as a church outside the national church, some Presbyterians began to ordain ministers. Yet Dissenters had misgivings: this was another nail in the coffin of comprehension; and for many it was a 'cause of grief that papists and atheists enjoy so much liberty' under the Indulgence.[23] Conformists believed that the Indulgence was 'to the extreme weakening [of] the Church of England'.[24] It 'hath made the church empty', wailed the Rector of Somerford Magna; 'I warn communion and none appears and often times [I] read prayers to the walls.'[25] Many – of all religious persuasions – were perturbed by the unconstitutional way that Charles had unilaterally suspended the execution of a parliamentary statute.

Charles had gambled on a quick military victory, but when the war went badly and the money ran out, he was forced to face Parliament. In

March 1673, after a frosty exchange of messages with his MPs, the King cancelled the Indulgence. It was its unconstitutional nature which most upset parliamentarians, and so 'to let him see that we did not dislike the matter of his declaration but the manner, and did not doubt the prudence, but only the legality of it', MPs drew up a bill 'for the ease of dissenters' which 'passed with little opposition, and as little approbation' before running aground in the Lords. They also underlined the distinction between Protestant Nonconformists and popish idolators by enacting a Test Act, requiring anyone, commoner or peer, who held any office, military or civil, to take the oaths of supremacy and allegiance, to furnish a certificate that they had received the sacrament in the Church of England, and to repudiate the doctrine of transubstantiation. Among the casualties of this legislation were the leading minister Lord Clifford and, most spectacularly, the King's brother and heir, James, Duke of York, who resigned the office of Lord Admiral. This confirmation of the widespread suspicion that he was a Roman Catholic 'gave exceeding grief and scandal to the whole nation', observed Evelyn. 'What the consequences of this will be, God only knows, and wise men dread.'[26] Worse was to come when James married a young Italian Catholic that autumn. On 5 November, Londoners let off fireworks, built bonfires and burned effigies of the 'Whore of Babylon' to demonstrate their displeasure 'at the Duke for altering his religion, and marrying an Italian lady'.[27]

Yet as heir apparent, the Duke of York remained a dominant figure at court. The faction-ridden Parliament was increasingly unmanageable, critical of York, Arlington, Buckingham and Lauderdale, but Charles could not afford to live without a Parliament. One solution came from a rising political star, Thomas Osborne, soon to be created Earl of Danby, who proposed 'to keep up Parliament, to raise the old cavaliers and the church party and to sacrifice papists and Presbyterians'.[28] Lord Treasurer Danby's crude calculation was designed to play on the prejudices of backbench MPs. He signalled his intentions with plans for an elaborate funeral and monument for Charles I and by meeting the bishops at Lambeth Palace. Although the bishops' ambitious call for moral and spiritual reform was watered down to action against papists and the revocation of the licences issued to Nonconformists, this was 'more severity than has of late been expected from the court, against all sorts of recusants'.[29] In 1675 Danby provoked a storm of controversy by proposing that the oath against alteration of government in church and state that had been part of the Clarendon Code should become a general test for all public offices.

These were opportunistic policies based on a strong, but not over-whelming, block of votes in Parliament, which Danby was more careful than earlier ministers to manage, and on an overestimate of the morale and appeal of the Church of England. Although a census of the parishes organised by Bishop Compton in 1676 had demonstrated the numerical preponderance of conformist Anglicans – Nonconformists were usually less than 5 per cent of the population of each diocese, and Roman Catholics less than 1 per cent – this was not the same as a demonstrable enthusiasm for intolerance and persecution. If anything, it was Danby's opponents who imputed extreme ideological motives to him rather than the minister who espoused a conscious policy.

The Earl of Shaftesbury led the opposition to Danby and alleged that the 'high episcopal men and cavaliers' were engaged in a plot to establish absolute government, a standing army and immutable *iure divino* episcop-acy. He saw popery and slavery advancing hand in hand in Scotland under Lauderdale, in Ireland and increasingly in England itself. He took particu-lar exception to the Anglican divines who flattered monarchs and encour-aged their delusions of power: 'I am sure they are the most dangerous sort of men alive to our English government.' The bishops 'neither are nor can be otherwise than creatures to prerogative, for all their promotions, digni-ties, and domination depends upon it'. This line of argument was even applied to the bill offered by the bishops in 1677 that would have tied the hands of a popish monarch in ecclesiastical matters. To their critics, this was an invasion of monarchical powers by 'proud prelates' and persecut-ing priests. They deliberately raised the spectre of Laud and insinuated that the church was soft on popery. In this context of heated and public political argument, 'popery' meant any stance that diminished the civil magistrate's ecclesiastical power by emancipating the church and establishing its auto-nomy. 'Popery' was any threat to the Erastian foundation of English Protestantism, to the Reformation achieved by Parliament and monarch. It could emanate directly from Rome or from ambitious Anglican bishops seeking to seduce gullible princes into absolutism and to claim a status for the church independent of the monarchy.

Andrew Marvell's tract *An Account of the Growth of Popery and Arbitrary Government* (1678) supplied not always consistent or convin-cing chapter and verse for the alleged plot to convert the lawful govern-ment into 'absolute tyranny' and the established religion into 'downright popery'. But in doing so, it placed these twin dangers at the forefront of popular and historical consciousness. Rolled up into this simple slogan about popery and arbitrary government were many other anxieties – about national decline and trade, luxury and effeminacy, the self-indulgence of the monarch and his court, the corruption of the House of Commons and the power of the clergy, and the dangerous direction of foreign policy – and, quite naturally, a strong dose of personal rivalry between politicians.

Crisis and reaction: 1678–85

Three related crises shaped the political turmoil of autumn 1678 to spring 1681. One was the campaign to unseat Danby. The second was the supposed Popish Plot to kill Charles II, place the Duke of York on the throne, and return England to Roman Catholicism. And the third was the struggle between the King and three Parliaments to exclude York from the succession. Together the Popish Plot and Exclusion Crisis were a political melt-down – as many contemporaries recognised – of precisely the nature and scale that had led to civil war in 1641–42. On this occasion armed conflict was avoided and a revolution averted. On the other hand, English society became deeply politicised and the partisan labels of 'Whig' and 'Tory', if not the political parties, emerged from this crisis. This was a religious contest too. Anglican and Nonconformist clergy took sides in print and appeared at the polls. The three Exclusion Parliaments were the first to contain openly Nonconformist MPs. From March 1681 until his death in February 1685, Charles II governed without Parliament, but permitted and even connived at an unprecedented level of religious persecution and political harassment in what has become known as the 'Tory revenge' or 'Tory reaction'.

*

In the late summer of 1678 the King and his Council were badgered by informants peddling a worryingly detailed story of a Jesuit-inspired plot to assassinate the King. The principal informant, a disreputable former clergyman called Titus Oates, also took his accusations outside government. He gave his evidence on oath to Sir Edmund Berry Godfrey, a Middlesex JP, and when, shortly afterwards, that magistrate was found mysteriously murdered the Popish Plot acquired both greater credibility and its first Protestant martyr. Oates's story touched some sensitive nerves. He alleged the involvement of Edward Coleman, former secretary to the Duke of York. When Coleman's papers were seized they were found to contain compromising if vague talk of reintroducing Catholicism to England. Oates appeared before the Commons and gave evidence 'of that nature that it is impossible to be feigned without contradiction'. On 1 November

MPs resolved 'that there hath been and still is a damnable and hellish plot, contrived and carried on by popish recusants' to murder the King, subvert the government and root out Protestantism.[30] Oates's story, based on his fertile invention and fluency, spiced with circumstantial detail, and soon bolstered by the tales of further 'witnesses', exploited the rabid antipopery of the late seventeenth century and expanded at every opportunity. The allegations involved humble artisans and priests but also reached into the royal court, even touching the Queen.

The Duke of York was 'surrounded with difficulties almost inextricable' since, although Oates cleared him of all involvement, he was the obvious beneficiary of such a plot. In the Lords Shaftesbury gingerly raised the issue of the Duke's removal from political influence, but in the Commons MPs talked openly about the succession and one even raised the question of excluding James from the line of succession. On 9 November, Charles assured Parliament that he would accede to some measure to 'pare the nails', or limit the powers, of a Catholic successor, but made it plain that he could not contemplate any interference in the line of succession. He did, however, assent to the new Test Act which excluded Roman Catholics from Parliament. After a hard-fought battle the Duke of York had been exempted from the Act by a majority of just two votes. Charles also promised to enforce the laws against popish recusants and Jesuits.

Danby, too, was in the eye of the storm. Many charges were levelled against him – including a failure to investigate the Plot thoroughly – but the bombshell was the revelation of secret negotiations for a French subsidy, negotiations moreover undertaken at the very time when Danby had been assuring Parliament of the government's intention to ally with the Dutch against France. The country had been sold for six million livres to the French; MPs sniffed 'treason' and saw a link with Coleman's letters in a plot 'to destroy the government and our liberties'.[31] Not only had Danby been acting under the King's orders, but he also had written proof of the fact, so Charles could not permit his minister to go before Parliament and answer his accusers. The King prorogued Parliament – provoking fears of a massacre by papists in the City of London – and then, after much negotiation behind the scenes, he dissolved Parliament on 24 January 1679. 'Honest men' had formerly wanted this corrupt Parliament dissolved, noted Josselin, 'but now its continuance was desired in reference to the discovery of the plot.'[32]

The general election of February and March 1679 was the first since 1661 and was fiercely fought. At the heart of the campaign was recent government policy: for example, the contests in Yorkshire were 'much poisoned' by the suspicion that Danby 'was concerned in the design to bring in popery'.[33] So when Parliament assembled, MPs expected 'reformation', by which they meant measures to safeguard Protestantism and Parliaments such as further investigation of the Popish Plot, some kind of limitations on the powers of any future Catholic monarch, and the encouragement of Protestant unity by a broadening of the Church of England.[34] First, however, they had to bring the Lord Treasurer to book. This was no easy task since the King was determined to protect his minister in order to prevent revelations of his own part in the secret negotiations with France. The fate of Danby was to be the rock upon which the new Parliament ultimately foundered. Initially, Danby had gone into temporary hiding; on his re-emergence he had unsuccessfully proffered a royal pardon as his defence against a parliamentary impeachment; then his case was diverted into a debate over whether bishops were eligible to sit as judges in a capital trial – which Danby's impeachment before the Lords might turn out to be. The King could not risk losing the vote of the bishops in Danby's trial, and 'he told the bishops that they must stick to him, and to his prerogative . . . by this means they were exposed to the popular fury'.[35]

Charles was unable to silence discussion of the succession. Not only was James a threat to the government and religion of the country as the Catholic heir to the throne, but his existence was a standing incitement to every popish assassin to murder Protestant Charles. Several solutions suggested themselves. 'Limitations' could be imposed upon a Catholic monarch, either by statute or, in the most extreme form, by appointing a regent to govern while the Catholic King ruled in name only. Alternatively, a new heir to the throne could be supplied, perhaps by a royal divorce and remarriage or by legitimising the King's illegitimate son the Duke of Monmouth. A third possibility was to 'disable' the Duke of York from succeeding to the throne. This would need a statute to exclude him from the line of succession and to allow the crown to skip a generation and pass to his daughter Princess Mary who had been married to the Dutch prince William of Orange since 1677. None of these were enticing options. Was it feasible to expect a ruler to respect statutes that curbed his powers? Was it constitutional for Parliament to regulate the succession or lay down what a King could or could not do? What would happen in the kingdom of Scotland? Yet the Commons, excited by the evidence its committees were turning up about the Plot, egged on by petitions from the City of London, and stirred up by Danby's enemies, formulated a 'bitter bill' to exclude James from the succession and, fully aware that neither the King nor House of Lords would swallow it, sent it to the upper chamber. Alarmed,

Charles prorogued Parliament on 27 May, claiming that the continuing wrangling over Danby's trial had frustrated business, and he subsequently dissolved this refractory assembly.

In Scotland, meanwhile, a Presbyterian rebellion had broken out. On 3 May Archbishop Sharp of St Andrews was murdered. At the end of the month the Covenant was proclaimed and a rebel force drove off the royal army protecting Glasgow. The task of putting down the rebellion was entrusted to the Duke of Monmouth whose 10,000 men defeated the rebels at Bothwell Bridge on the Clyde on 22 June. He returned a hero, a good Protestant on the grounds of the clemency he displayed towards the rebels, and – in the eyes of some – a potential successor to his father. The rebellion also confirmed the general unease felt about Lauderdale's harsh rule in Scotland. Lauderdale had provoked the rising by using Highland troops to terrorise the south-west and by his intolerance of the Scottish Presbyterians. Such policies were fuel to the incendiary claims of Shaftesbury that the fates of the two kingdoms were intertwined: 'in England, popery was to have brought in slavery; in Scotland, slavery went before, and popery was to follow', he told the Lords on 25 March.[36]

Although no Parliament was sitting, the political temperature in England rose steadily during 1679. The Exclusion Bill had persuaded some that 'there was a wheel within a wheel, a conspiracy within a conspiracy', as the clergyman Francis Turner put it. 'The republican plots and conspiracies to destroy the government were so transparent that as one nail drives out another they had put the danger of popery out of men's heads and scarce left room in our thoughts but how to preserve the monarchy and the church.'[37] Two political groupings were taking shape: one was variously known as the 'court', the 'church', 'loyal' or 'Yorkist' party; and the other was patriotic and Protestant, the 'country' party, in its own eyes, but 'Presbyterian', 'fanatic' or 'republican' to its enemies. These identities and their mutual animosity were deepened during the general election of the summer of 1679. There were 'vast feuds' in the Chilterns, reported Edmund Verney, 'and so 'tis all over England I suppose'.[38] The principal slogan in these polls was 'no courtier', but voters were also aware of how candidates stood on exclusion and of their past voting record. The Parliament did not meet as planned in October, indeed the King repeatedly postponed its meeting for a year until October 1681, but this simply forced Shaftesbury and the 'exclusionists' (as historians call his supporters) to exploit every opportunity to put political pressure on Charles. So Shaftesbury continued to find more 'witnesses' to the Plot, and then to find more plots, including one in Ireland; he presented the King's French

Catholic mistress as a common whore and the Duke of York as a popish recusant to the Middlesex Quarter Sessions; and he orchestrated petitions for the sitting of Parliament. His adversaries replied in kind, manufacturing their own 'Presbyterian Plot' and petitioning against the petitions for the meeting of Parliament. The printing presses produced an avalanche of polemic, all of it now legal since the Licensing Act had expired, and most of it 'very licentious, both against the court and the clergy'. 'The bishops and the clergy, apprehending that a rebellion and with it the pulling the church to pieces were designed, set themselves on the other hand to write against the late times [i.e., the civil wars], and to draw a parallel between the present time and them.'[39] Both sides mobilised the London crowd by means of demonstrations, processions and pope-burnings.

The terms 'Whig' and 'Tory' were not current before 1681, but they helpfully label the two contending parties and their goals in these years. Most Dissenters were Whig sympathisers and most Tories were Anglicans, but it is not true that all Whigs were Dissenters nor that all Anglicans were Tories. It has been shown that Whig propaganda was designed to play on Dissenters' grievances, because the Whigs needed their political support. What is less easily demonstrated is the contention that the religious issue, specifically some easing of the plight of Dissenters, is what united the Whigs, rather than the constitutional issue of exclusion. Meanwhile, each side claimed to be the champion of antipopery: the Whigs saw future popery in the Duke of York and present popery in the church; the church saw the real threat of popery coming from another puritan revolution, since everyone knew that 'the pope would come in on the puritan's back'.

Parliament finally met on 21 October 1680 and within three weeks the Commons had sent a bill to the Lords that provided for the crown to pass as if James was dead to the next in line. The King stood by the fire in the House of Lords while the peers debated and rejected the bill. Thwarted, the 'exclusionists' in Parliament turned to other expedients such as a royal divorce or the 'Association', a bond that could operate as a backdoor form of exclusion. The Popish Plot claimed another victim when the House of Lords voted the elderly Catholic peer Lord Stafford guilty of involvement. Stafford's guilt was widely doubted and his shabby trial and subsequent execution smacked of political expediency. The Commons continued work on a proposal 'for uniting his majesty's Protestant subjects' and eventually produced two bills, one for the comprehension of moderate Nonconformists, the other for an 'indulgence' of the remaining Protestant Dissenters. The appeal of comprehension was limited, even among

Nonconformists. Roger Morrice, a go-between for Presbyterian politicians, recorded that 'all that I have heard of who desire comprehension,
desire indulgence also for others; though multitudes desire indulgence that
most fervently oppose comprehension'.[40] Meanwhile the Commons openly
bargained with the King, proposing to grant taxation in return for guarantees of regular parliaments and the exclusion of the Duke of York.
When this gambit failed, they turned their anger on royal ministers, and
an exasperated Charles dissolved Parliament.

Charles announced that a new Parliament would meet at Oxford in
March. The elections did not produce many new faces, but they did reveal
a resurgence of 'loyalty' towards the Church of England, monarchy and
the Stuarts. The bitter contest at Bristol turned on religion – exclusion was
not even mentioned – and the two loyalists to church and state narrowly
defeated the candidates backed by local Dissenters. Charles II's position
was strengthened by a secret deal agreed with Louis XIV just days before
the opening of Parliament. Charles was to receive £385,000 over three years
provided that he did not help Spain against France or call a Parliament for
that purpose. Accompanied by 700 soldiers, Charles arrived at Oxford,
and took a high tone with his new Parliament: 'I, who will never use
arbitrary government myself, am resolved not to suffer it in others.' He
repeated his 'love' for parliaments and ruled out exclusion, but he did offer
to accept some expedient which would entrust government to Protestant
control during the reign of a Catholic monarch. MPs took no notice. They
pressed on with an exclusion bill and Charles dissolved the Parliament
after it had sat for just one week.

Charles explained his actions in a declaration read from the pulpit
of every parish church. He pinned the blame for the crisis on 'the restless
malice of ill men who are labouring to poison our people, some out of
fondness for their old beloved Commonwealth principles, and some out
of anger at their being disappointed in . . . their own ambition'. And he
made it plain that he intended to call future Parliaments, suppress popery,
redress grievances and rule according to the law.[41] Although this declaration 'in many places was not very pleasing', few had any reason to think
that Charles was about to embark upon a new style of government.[42] It is
only with hindsight that the period between 1681 and 1685, the last four
years of Charles's reign, appears as a distinct era of political and religious
revenge. During these years the loyalist resurgence, based first on a revulsion
against the extreme tactics and rebellious principles of the exclusionists,
then gathering strength as royal policy and propaganda supplied the
opportunities and slogans, extended political partisanship into the urban

corporations and parish vestries, the courts and the bureaucracy, even the streets and churches of the kingdom.

*

The government was determined to pursue its enemies, those 'ill men' whether small fry such as Stephen College, pamphleteer and activist, or Shaftesbury, the biggest fish of all. It was prepared to exploit the law to do so. College was accused of planning to seize the King by force during the Oxford Parliament, but when a London jury threw out the case, it was transferred to Oxford where a more pliant jury duly convicted him. In November a London jury rejected the treason charge against Shaftesbury. Charles complained bitterly that he could not obtain justice in his own courts because the Whigs controlled the offices which selected the juries. Using a procedure called *quo warranto*, Charles investigated the charter under which the City of London was governed and eventually replaced it with one that gave the King control of the City's major offices such as Lord Mayor and Sheriff. The government had already begun to remove its opponents from the Commissions of the Peace. In 1680, 272 JPs were sacked. These were, in the eyes of exclusionists, 'such as were very active against the papists, such as are against arbitrary power and such as approved the bill against the Duke [of York]'.[43] The politicisation of local justice and government continued relentlessly through the early 1680s. 'If anything of Whig or Tory comes in question, it is ruled according to the interest of the party', observed one contemporary.[44] Yet it would be too simplistic to suggest that these were solid ideological groups or to claim that they held undisputed power in any particular place. Government had created circumstances ripe for exploitation by local rivalries and personal animosities. Miller has shown, for example, how the fifty-one new borough charters issued between 1681 and 1685 were generally a response to the requests of local groups, not the initiative of central government. Old scores could be settled and interests advanced by adopting party labels. Yet equally, those on the ground knew that local government would not function if it became the preserve of one faction and so they sought to dominate rather then to monopolise administration and justice.

This is not, of course, to deny that religion remained a crucial marker of political difference. Nonconformists were a particular target: in late 1681 the King ordered the execution of the penal laws against Nonconformists and their removal from the navy and the revenue service; harassment and prosecution of Nonconformist ministers and their conventicles intensified.

In London, Nonconformists were kept on tenterhooks as officials made threatening speeches, redcoats were seen in the streets, and rumours flew about: 'I think few were actually disturbed, but the difficulties upon them are great,' observed Morrice in March 1683.[45] When the storm did arrive, ministers were hauled off to gaol, meeting houses were pulled down and great bonfires made of their furnishings and fittings. 'Tidings of great trouble to ministers and people both at London and elsewhere. How long Lord!' exclaimed Philip Henry in his diary.[46] Prosecutions were often designed to make a point, as at Coventry where 200 Dissenters were presented for not attending church, 19 of them Whig former aldermen. The Quakers, who would not bend before the force of the storm, suffered most: about 400 died in the unsanitary gaols of England between 1681 and 1685. So too did several notable Nonconformist ministers. This was undoubtedly the most intense persecution of Nonconformity during the Restoration period: many congregations shed their fair-weather members and once again took to secret meetings and worship. The experience of the early 1680s convinced many of the hitherto moderate Nonconformists that their religion would never be safe under the Stuarts and the Church of England.

The Church of England meanwhile basked in political favour and apparent popular support. Church attendance seems to have improved – although much of it may have been constrained – and clergymen campaigned for more frequent celebration of the sacrament and reading of the daily prayers in churches. The Ecclesiastical Commission erected in 1681 has been described by Beddard as 'an instrument of Tory reaction'. Led by Archbishop Sancroft and the two Hyde brothers, the Commission restricted clerical preferment to men of known zeal for church and crown. The gloves came off in Anglican pulpits. In October 1681, Ralph Thoresby heard 'a very ordinary mean sermon, full of bitter, malicious reflections upon the Nonconformists, ripping up the wounds of the late unhappy times . . . expressly affirming that, but for the goodness of God and wisdom of our rulers, we had at this day been brought to the same pass again; unworthily reflecting upon the whole Parliament, as though the abatement of a few ceremonies would have been the ruin of both Church and State'.[47] Those churchmen known for their conciliatory attitude towards Dissent were subject to vitriolic attack from their brethren within the church. 'We were mad with loyalty,' observed one clergyman.[48] 'Such of the clergy as would not engage in that fury were cried out on as betrayers of the church, and as secret favourers of the Dissenters,' complained Gilbert Burnet.[49]

Although each side portrayed itself as moderate and its opponents as extreme, the middle ground was an undoubted victim of the heated debate of the 1680s. In politics, the moderates were reviled as 'trimmers' and 'moderate' itself became a dirty word. In religion, the Church of England was increasingly cast as a persecutor while the Nonconformists were impugned as fanatics, tub-preachers and rebels. Mainstream Anglican clergy found themselves caught between those who protested at the persecution and those 'who profess great loyalty and zeal for the church, as loud complaining because we do not proceed violently beyond the rule of law'.[50]

Such caricatures were heightened by the revelation of the Rye House Plot in the summer of 1683. This was a tangle of conspiracies and half-made plans by desperate Whigs, former Cromwellians, Baptists, republicans and other radicals, that encompassed the assassination of Charles and James and a popular rising. Shaftesbury had died in exile in January, but the government's net caught William Lord Russell, Algernon Sidney and the Earl of Essex, as well as many lesser figures such as Rumbold and Walcott. Essex died, apparently by his own hand, in the Tower, but Russell and Sidney were both convicted on rather strained evidence and executed. It was a decisive defeat for radical hopes. Many of those under suspicion went into hiding or fled abroad. Anglican preachers drew appropriate lessons: the planned rebellion was an illustration of 'the sinister practices and opinions of the Jesuits and Presbyterians' said one; while another, preaching in Manchester, remarked that nothing had earned the Church of England's clergy more hatred 'than their frequent preaching up submission to government, and to our government as by law established both in church and state'.[51] The University of Oxford, a Tory Anglican stronghold, issued a decree condemning a string of political opinions drawn from the works of, among others, Milton, Hobbes, John Owen and Richard Baxter, and held a bonfire of their books in the quadrangle of the Bodleian Library.

In the spring of 1684, Charles blithely ignored the Triennial Act which required a sitting of parliament. There was grumbling, but no overt protest. Charles had no immediate need of a parliament since healthy foreign trade was pushing up his income from customs duties and he had both cut back on his own costs and forsworn foreign policy adventures. After the recent instability, perhaps many of Charles's English subjects appreciated his authoritative, occasionally authoritarian, rule, even if religious persecution and Anglican pretensions appealed to few of the laity. Those who looked further afield were more concerned. In France, Louis XIV had effectively made himself head of the Catholic church and had begun to persecute the Huguenots, the French Protestants. Although Louis had accepted a general European peace in 1679, by the early 1680s he was once again menacing territories along France's eastern frontier and fomenting trouble in the Mediterranean, Hungary and Flanders. In Ireland, the government of Ormonde had deliberately marched in step with that of England, persecuting Nonconformists in Ulster, and raising royal revenues wherever possible. But Ormonde was ageing and among the rising stars were members of the Catholic Old English community, such as Richard Talbot who was closely identified with the Duke of York. It was in Scotland, however, that James had established himself most securely. Between 1679 and 1682, James served as the King's Commissioner in Scotland, supplanting Lauderdale, and developing his own powerful circle of allies, such as the Earls of Queensbury and Perth. The presence of James and his attention to Scottish politics paid dividends: the Scottish Parliament ostentatiously recognised James as heir to the throne – no talk of exclusion here. A Test Act imposed a sweeping oath, acknowledging the King as 'the only supreme governor of this realm, over all persons and in all causes as well ecclesiastical as civil'. Among its effects was the exodus of fifty clergy from the Kirk and the flight abroad of the Earl of Argyll. The conciliatory, even consensual, policies of Lauderdale in the 1670s were forgotten as a new generation of politicians, often identified with James, harried Presbyterians and jockeyed with each other for power. By 1685, the governments of Scotland, Ireland and England all showed marked signs of authoritarianism and intolerance; these trends were mitigated as always by inefficiency, factionalism and opportunism, but they were distinct and distinctly out of line with the principles which had underwritten the restoration of the monarchy in 1660. The unexpected death of Charles II in February 1685 brought to the throne a ruler whose instincts were authoritarian and whose Catholic principles were inimical to most of his subjects. Under James II the British were about to find out just how close popery and arbitrary government could be.

Notes

1   J. Hunter, *The Rise of the Old Dissent Exemplified in the Life of Oliver Heywood* (1842), p. 127.

2   *The Diurnal of Thomas Rugg 1659–1661*, ed. W.L. Sachse (Camden Society, 3rd series, 91, 1961), p. 154.

3   Peniston Whalley, *Episcopacy* (1661), pp.10–11.

4   *The Diaries and Letters of Philip Henry*, ed. M.H. Lee (1882), p. 254.

5 *The Diary of Samuel Pepys*, ed. R.C. Latham and W. Matthews (11 vols, London, 1970–83), IX, 72–3; III, 127, 134–5.

6 P. Seaward, *The Restoration, 1660–1688* (Basingstoke, 1991), p. 51.

7 John Corbet, *An Account Given of the Principles and Practices of Several Nonconformists* (1680), p. 27.

8 *Bishop Fell and Nonconformity*, ed. M. Clapinson (Oxfordshire Record Society, 52, 1980), pp. 44, 42.

9 Heywood, I, 198.

10 Hunter, *Rise of Old Dissent*, p. 307.

11 J.T. Cliffe, *The Puritan Gentry Besieged, 1650–1700* (London, 1993), pp. 84, 88.

12 *The Compton Census of 1676: A Critical Edition*, ed. A. Whiteman (London, 1986), p. xxxix.

13 Heywood, I, 192.

14 Heywood, I, 190.

15 Spurr, *RC*, p. 57; *Buckinghamshire Dissent and Parish Life 1669–1712*, ed. J. Broad (Buckinghamshire Record Society, 28, 1993), p. 9.

16 Sir Peter Leicester, *Charges to the Grand Jury*, ed. E. Halcrow (Manchester; Chetham Society, 3rd series, 5, 1953), p. 47.

17 Spurr, *EP*, p. 142.

18 *The Memoirs of Sir John Reresby*, ed. A. Browning, 2nd edn, revised by M.K. Geiter and W.A. Speck (London, 1991), pp. 112–13.

19 Josselin, p. 537.

20 Spurr, *RC*, p. 50.

21 *Diary of John Milward MP*, ed. C. Robbins (Cambridge, 1938), p. 326; Pepys, *Diary*, IX, 31; Leicester, *Charges*, p. 46.

22 CUL, Add. MS 8499, fo. 161.

23 Hunter, *Rise of Old Dissent*, p. 224.

24 Evelyn, III, 328.

25 D.A. Spaeth, *The Church in an Age of Danger: Parsons and Parishioners, 1660–1740* (Cambridge, 2000), p. 174.

26 Evelyn, IV, 7.

27 Evelyn, IV, 26.

28 *Essex Correspondence*, ed. C.E. Pike (Camden Society, 3rd series, 24, 1913), p. 1.

29 J. Spurr, *England in the 1670s: 'This Masquerading Age'* (Oxford, 2000), p. 62.

30 Spurr, *England in the 1670s*, pp. 263–4.

31 Spurr, *England in the 1670s*, p. 269.

32 Josselin, p. 618.

33 Reresby, *Memoirs*, p. 170.

34 Spurr, *England in the 1670s*, p. 274.

35 Gilbert Burnet, *History of My Own Time*, ed. O. Airy (2 vols, Oxford, 1897–1900), II, 220.

36 Spurr, *England in the 1670s*, p. 282.

37 Bodl. L., MS Rawlinson Letters 99, fo. 111.

38 J. Miller, *After the Civil Wars: English Politics and Government in the Reign of Charles II* (Harlow, 2000), p. 259.

39 Burnet, *History of Own Time*, II, 221.

40 DWL, Morrice Entering Book P, p. 288.

41 Spurr, *England in the 1670s*, pp. 299–300.

42 N. Luttrell, *A Brief Historical Relation of State Affairs 1660–1714* (6 vols, Oxford, 1857), I, 77.

43 A. Fletcher, *Reform in the Provinces* (New Haven, Conn., 1986), p. 22.

44 Luttrell, *Historical Relation*, I. 199.

45 DWL, Morrice Entering Book P, p. 362.

46 Henry, *Diaries*, p. 320.

47 *The Diary of Ralph Thoresby*, ed. J. Hunter (1830), pp. 108–9.

48 *The Life of Richard Kidder DD . . . Written by Himself*, ed. A.E. Robinson (Somerset Record Society, 37, 1922), p. 36.

49 Burnet, *History of Own Time*, II, 290.

50 Bodl. L., MS Tanner 35, fo. 170.

51 William Bolton, *Core Redivivus* (1684), p. 2; E. Foreness, *A Sermon Preached at Manchester* (1683), p. 1.

CHAPTER 7

James II, revolution and toleration (1685–89)

James II

James II was a Roman Catholic before he was an autocrat. Unfortunately he managed to persuade his subjects that he was both. That popular conviction played a large part in his downfall. In all likelihood, James had no desire to force the English into Catholicism. He genuinely believed that if they were allowed to hear the Roman Catholic message without impediment or prejudice, they would flock back to the one true church. All that was needed, therefore, was to dismantle the anti-Catholic laws that stood in the way. In pursuing this goal, James was single-minded. If necessary, he trampled on local autonomy or aristocratic privilege, bent the law and threatened cherished property rights. He was even prepared to make common cause with Nonconformists – back in the 1670s it had been noted that James 'made it his business to court the sectaries and the fanatics, hoping thereby to strengthen the popish interest'.[1] A terrifying example of the power and ruthlessness of Catholic rulers was supplied by James's French cousin Louis XIV. In October 1685 Louis tore up the legal guarantees that had protected the French Protestants for decades and offered them the stark choice of conversion or exile. When thousands of Huguenot refugees arrived in England, fleeing 'inhumane' and 'cruel persecution', the consequences of popery and arbitrary government were plain to all.[2] Whatever James's aims, his methods smacked of arbitrary government, and they go a long way to explaining how he alienated his subjects with such startling rapidity.

James succeeded to the throne on a tide of popular support. Anglican preachers claimed that the nation was 'scarce sensible even of a change'. James was full of assurances that he would respect the laws, property and religion of the country. Apparently Parliament believed him. On 27 May the Commons voted that they 'acquiesce, entirely rely, and rest wholly satisfied' in James's promise to defend the Church of England as established by law 'which is dearer to us than our lives'.[3] A further wave of loyal enthusiasm for the rightful monarch and avowals of the principles of divine right and passive obedience were provoked by the rebellions of the Duke of Argyll in Scotland and the Duke of Monmouth in the West Country. Yet beneath the public pronouncements of devotion and the generous grants of taxation there was unease about James and the 'insolence' of Catholics. After defeating the rebels, James did not disband the royal army and when he sought to divert funds to it from the county militias, Parliament reacted badly. In November MPs complained about the eighty or ninety Catholics who, quite illegally, had received commissions as army officers. Edward Seymour and Thomas Clarges stated that a 'standing army' was inconsistent with the safety of the kingdom. The expression of similar views in the House of Lords cost Bishop Compton his seat on the Privy Council. It became clear that this Parliament would not be as submissive as James had initially hoped. It was ominous that the King had antagonised the Tories and the Church of England within the first months of his reign.

The Church of England was a bastion of loyalism, but it was necessarily also on the front line of the conflict with James. Loyalty was part and parcel of the Church of England's Protestantism: William Sherlock told the Commons on 29 May 1685 that to be 'true to our prince, we must be true to our church and to our religion' for 'it would be no act of loyalty to accommodate or compliment away our religion and its legal securities'.[4] Conflict was inescapable. Bishop Compton of London ran foul of James over the question of anti-Catholic sermons. In 1686 the King began to exert pressure on the Church of England not to devote so much of its preaching to rebutting Roman Catholicism. Compton was adamant that the Anglicans must be allowed 'a modest latitude . . . in this point, whilst we are permitted to assert our own religion: because many of our doctrines do necessarily engage us to it'.[5] In July 1686 a new Ecclesiastical Commission was established with wide-ranging powers of visitation and examination, but its first priority was to curb the audacity of the bishops and preachers. By September, Compton had been suspended from the exercise of his episcopal office for refusing to suspend anti-popish preachers such as John Sharp; meanwhile, Archbishop Sancroft, who had refused to serve on the Commission, lost his place on the Privy Council and retired from court. James also weakened the church by leaving the see of York unfilled and promoting the pliant Parker to Oxford and Cartwright to Chester.

If James was to achieve a legislated toleration for Catholics he would need a more amenable parliament than the one he had, but as things stood only Anglicans were eligible to vote. He had to find a way of enfranchising the Nonconformists and Catholics. The first step was to exercise the royal power to *dispense* with the penalties of the laws for certain individuals: this was the principle upheld in a staged legal case between Godden and Hales in June 1686. But only *suspending* the operation and penalties of the laws across the whole kingdom – as Charles II had done in 1672 – would really answer James's political needs. On 4 April 1687 he issued a Declaration of Indulgence suspending all penal laws in matters ecclesiastical, allowing freedom of public worship and removing all civil disabilities from non-Anglicans. This was the most far-reaching attempt at religious freedom proposed in the seventeenth century. James even promised to seek parliamentary approval in due course, which may have drawn the unconstitutional sting of this royal setting aside of the laws of the land. But if the Declaration sounded less arbitrary than the 1672 Indulgence, it was blatantly pro-Catholic: James stated that he could not 'but heartily wish' that all his subjects were members of the Catholic Church.

Both reactions and effects were mixed. Former Cromwellian soldiers in Lincolnshire thanked the King, while tactlessly remarking that they had once 'been driven into arms to obtain that by force which now your majesty hath so mercifully condescended to'.[6] The 'thankful acceptance' of Dissenters was expressed in eighty addresses whose signatories included the Presbyterian ministers Alsop, Read and Burgess. Others would not sign. Bates and Howe, the Presbyterian leaders, Stretton the Congregationalist, and Kiffin the Baptist, refused. So did Richard Baxter, in part because he did not want to offend the conforming clergy of the Church of England. Dissent was torn between taking advantage of this Catholic-inspired generosity or closing ranks with the Protestant Church of England. In May the churches in York, Leeds, Sheffield and elsewhere were reported to be as full as ever 'and the only Dissenters that seem pleased with their toleration are the Quakers and Independents, the number of either not very considerable'.[7] Several months after the Declaration, Oliver Heywood was delighted that 'we have sacraments, solemn ordination of ministers, conferences, and exercises set up on weekdays, discipline, and no disturbance in any thing'. He had heard 'papists and Quakers complain nobody is a gainer by this liberty but Presbyterians'.[8] Public masses were held at York in five different rooms hired for the purpose, 'but it is computed the whole number of that persuasion will not reach sixty of the whole city', and only three of those were converts.[9] Simultaneously there were 'great expectations of several great men declaring themselves papists', noted Evelyn. All government and justice would be given over to Catholics, 'so furiously does the Jesuit drive and even compel princes to violent courses and destruction of an excellent government both in church and state'.[10] Overall, Catholics rejoiced at their religious and civil emancipation, Anglicans were dismayed, and Dissenters agonised over a liberty which also embraced Catholics and the danger that, as the Earl of Halifax warned, they were being used as a stepping stone to the revival of an intolerant popery. One concerned onlooker was the Dutch prince, William of Orange, who was married to James II's eldest daughter and heir, Princess Mary. Since 1672, when the French had invaded the Netherlands, William had assumed the role of chief European opponent to Louis XIV and had become, in the eyes of some, the champion of the international Protestant cause. Watching his father-in-law's self-destructive progress, William intervened judiciously in English affairs from the Hague when it suited his priorities. In 1687 William and Mary made it plain that they supported liberty of conscience for papists and 'an entire liberty for the full exercise' of the Dissenters' religion, but 'cannot agree to the repeal of the Test, or of those other penal laws . . . that tend to the security of the Protestant religion'.[11]

When seen in the wider context of James's Irish and Scottish realms, these developments were even more worrying. In Ireland, Richard Talbot, now the Earl of Tyrconnell, promoted an aggressive policy of catholicisation which enjoyed free rein after his appointment as Lord Deputy in place of Clarendon in January 1687. The Irish army was rapidly turned over to Catholics, as were the judiciary, Privy Council and local government; the Catholic majorities established in urban corporations by the use of *quo warranto* ensured that any future Irish Parliament would be overwhelmingly Catholic. Meanwhile, resources were redistributed from the Church of Ireland to Catholic priests and monks; and, most ambitiously of all, Tyrconnell planned to reverse the Protestant ascendancy created during the course of the seventeenth century by returning estates to Catholic landowners. In Scotland, Catholics had been appointed to civil and military positions in the aftermath of the Argyll rising. James offered the Scottish Parliament 'free trade with England' in return for religious freedom and civil rights for Roman Catholics. When his offer was rejected, the King dissolved Parliament. In February 1687 he proclaimed freedom of private worship for Catholics and Quakers, but not for Presbyterians.

In June he issued a Declaration of Indulgence out of his 'absolute power, which all our subjects are to obey without reserve'. Scottish Roman Catholics were granted complete religious toleration and access to civil offices. The penal laws were relaxed against Presbyterians who could now worship in private. On the ground, in areas like the west of Scotland, this was an effective emancipation of Presbyterianism and a near fatal blow to the pretensions of the episcopalian church.

English privileges and property were under threat from James. He was, for example, determined to break the Protestant monopoly on the universities. After a bitter contest, James eventually succeeded in imposing a Catholic president on Magdalen College, Oxford, but only at the cost of ejecting the entire fellowship of the college and alienating Protestant opinion. It was not simply that he had attempted to force the fellows to vote against their conscience and oaths, but he had stripped them of their property rights. A fellowship was just as much a property right as was the right to appoint someone to a parish living, to collect tithes, or to own former church lands. The Protestant English saw a direct challenge here to their property as well as their religion. Radical critics could plausibly claim that the Magdalen case meant that 'we could no longer be said to have properties or inheritances. But what we possessed was precarious, and held by no other tenure but that of court pleasure and connivance.'[12] The case also set alarm bells ringing about the security of property that had once belonged to the medieval church. Edgy landowners began to ask themselves whether a restored Catholic church might reclaim all those abbeys, priories and lands lost when Henry VIII had dissolved the monasteries.

The King now turned his attention to the Anglican political monopoly. The same intrusive policies that had been so successful in driving Whigs from local office were now turned against the Tories. Borough charters were called in and renewed, municipal officers and JPs were replaced by Catholics, Dissenters and former Whigs: in Norwich the doomed Tory aldermen marched as a body to the cathedral to receive the sacrament so that all would see that they were about to lose office for loyalty to the church. As always, control of local government was seen as the key to parliamentary elections. James also took the precaution of having his agents pose 'Three Questions' to all those who might be elected to Parliament about their attitude towards the repeal of the penal laws and the Test Act. Their replies were not encouraging. The mayor of Lancaster, for instance, answered that 'he was for taking away the penal laws, but as to the test he was doubtful'; in other words, he would not have people prosecuted for their religious beliefs, but equally he would not share power with

Catholics.[13] The third of the Questions asked respondents whether they would live 'friendly' alongside those of other religions, and here the replies seemed to indicate that many people were now ready to accept religious diversity as a fact of life. Sir John Reresby 'believed most men were now convinced that liberty of conscience was a thing of advantage to the nation', provided it gave 'due regard to the rights and privileges of the Church of England'.[14] Another archetypal Tory, the second Earl of Clarendon, could concede religious liberty 'with a very good conscience', but he would not accept the employment in the state of men 'who by their mistaken consciences are bound to destroy the religion I profess'.[15]

Matters came to a head when, disappointed by the initial response, James reissued his Declaration of Indulgence in April 1688 and required the clergy of the Church of England to read it from their pulpits. This was a step too far for the church and its leaders. The leading London clergy met to discuss their options: they canvassed other clergy, including Nonconformists; estimated how many ministers would refuse to read the Declaration; and asked the bishops to petition the King. It was this petition, presented in the name of Archbishop Sancroft and six other bishops to James on 18 May, which became a symbol of the church's resistance to royal policy. The petition itself was at pains to explain that the clergy were neither disobedient to the monarch nor lacking in 'due tenderness to Dissenters, in relation to whom they are willing to come to such a temper as shall be thought fit, when that matter shall be considered and settled in Parliament and Convocation', but they simply understood the dispensing and suspending power to be illegal.[16] Within weeks the seven bishops had been charged with publishing a false, seditious and malicious libel. They cannily outmanoeuvred the King. When he demanded recognisances, they refused and forced him to remand them in custody in the Tower. Here they were visited and fêted by fellow clergy, aristocratic supporters and a Nonconformist deputation. At the bishops' trial on 29 June the prosecution was forced on to the defensive – justifying the royal dispensing power even though it was not the legal point at issue – and the bishops' acquittal was greeted with jubilation throughout the country. This one gesture of civil disobedience over the Declaration had won the bishops and the Church of England far more respect and even popularity than they had enjoyed for many years.

That summer Archbishop Sancroft urged his clergy to greater efforts to win people to the church, to catechising, daily reading of prayers and frequent celebration of the sacrament. Nonconformists should be gently persuaded to comply with the church and disabused of their errors about the 'popish' inclinations of the bishops. He also opened negotiations with Nonconformist leaders and permitted consideration of liturgical revisions that might be needed to placate some of the sober Nonconformists. The clergy involved drew comparisons with the unprepared state of the church in 1660 and argued 'that should another revolution come, we ought to be better provided; and to have duly considered how we might not only improve our own constitution, but bring in the honest and moderate Dissenters, especially of the laity, to join in communion with us'.[17] Simultaneously, the bishops cajoled James to return to the pro-church policies of Charles II's last years. These were all indications that English Protestantism was building a common front to oppose the Catholic threat. And the Catholic threat had suddenly become a great deal more alarming. On 10 June, the Queen gave birth to a healthy son, James Francis Edward. James II now had a Catholic heir and England, Scotland and Ireland faced the prospect of a Catholic dynasty stretching out into the future.

Revolution

The English Revolution of 1688 has been viewed as a palace coup, a dynastic reshuffle or a Dutch invasion. It was all of these things and something more – it was one further political readjustment to the complex legacy of the Reformation.

Events unfolded slowly during 1688. William of Orange, motivated by a diplomatic and military need to draw England into the anti-French camp, kept his options open and exploited every opportunity. This Dutch Calvinist and patriot presented himself as the champion of liberty, law and Protestantism, and tailored his message to suit his audience. 'He speaks constantly with great zeal and affection concerning the sad estate of the Reformed Churches in general,' reported one well-informed observer. And just before setting sail for England he had told 'some serious persons' that 'his predominant and prevalent end was not carnal or selfish, but advancing the glory of God, and the promoting the Protestant religion, together with our laws and liberties, and therein he could appeal to the great God, and [he] desired he might prosper according to the sincerity of his heart'.[18] Of necessity, his propaganda addressed several audiences, including some of his Catholic allies in Europe, and of course the Anglican establishment in England. So he let it be known that his intervention in English politics was intended to deliver King James from his evil advisers, protect Mary's rights as James's heir, defend Protestantism and ensure a free Parliament. He undertook to convene a Parliament to prepare what legislation it saw fit to confirm the Test Act and other laws for the security of the Protestant religion, to establish a 'good agreement' among Protestants, and to secure all who live peaceably – even Roman Catholics – 'from all persecution upon the account of their religion'.[19]

William offered something to everyone, while James II, at almost every stage, offered too little, too late. James had repeatedly spoken of meeting another Parliament – it was mentioned, for example, in the 1688 reissue of the Indulgence – but it was only in late August, with fears of a Dutch invasion growing, that he decided on elections and even these were not to be held until the winter. Late in September, admitting that the Dutch were going to invade 'in good earnest', James announced his readiness to preserve the Church of England and retain the Test Act if he could establish a universal liberty of conscience. By early October he appeared to have accepted the advice of the bishops to return to the policies of the early 1680s: the Ecclesiastical Commission was dissolved and the King entrusted the affairs of Magdalen College to an Anglican bishop. But the King showed little constancy, listening to 'rogues', promoting unsuitable candidates to vacant sees, and pressing on with the Catholic baptism for his heir. Even his younger Protestant daughter, Princess Anne, thought the bishops were wasting their time; 'the King will not hearken to them'.[20]

William had raised a massive force of 20,000 men and 500 ships to invade England. After a false start, he set sail on 1 November and aided by a 'Protestant wind' landed unopposed at Torbay on the auspicious date of 5 November. He and his army gradually moved through the West Country, issuing propaganda and reassuring people wherever possible. The royal army took up position on Salisbury Plain, where James joined it, but his generals were already losing heart or arranging to defect to William. Plagued by nosebleeds and insomnia, James returned to London and despatched commissioners to negotiate a truce with William but, unnerved by anti-popish disorder and rumours, he first sent the Queen and infant prince abroad and then on 11 December he himself fled, only to be stopped by a group of officious fishermen and brought back to the capital five days later. No one had yet raised a hand in the King's defence. There were various explanations for the strange passivity of the people. One view was that he simply had no support. As one godly lady commented, 'thank God there is like to be no fighting, all people being of a mind'.[21] Another is that William's preparations were so thorough, his inducements so seductive, and his army so large, that opposition was pointless. Some of the leading gentry and nobility took effective action to ensure his success. They took control of Nottingham, York, Hull, Scarborough, Ludlow,

Worcester and Norwich. They later bound themselves in an Association to protect the life of the Prince of Orange. 'Some say it is for defence of themselves against the papists, who are armed . . . others declare for defence of the Protestant religion, the laws and liberties which have been invaded, and are yet in danger of being utterly subverted by priests and papists', observed Sir John Bramston. 'How these risings and associations can be justified I see not; but yet it is very apparent, had not the prince come, and these persons thus appeared, our religion had been rooted out.'[22]

The Revolution still rested on a knife-edge. In James's absence a council of peers meeting at Guildhall had taken it upon themselves to invite William to obtain a free Parliament which could secure the laws, liberty and property of the subject and 'the Church of England in particular, with a due liberty to Protestant Dissenters'. No sooner had James returned to London, however, than Bishop Turner, Archbishop Lamplugh and other churchmen waited upon the King at Whitehall 'and he and they gave one another the most full and reciprocal satisfaction, and parted with great complacency'.[23] William was not prepared to allow James to prevaricate like this. On hearing of the meeting with the bishops, William sent troops to London to 'secure' the palace and 'escort' James out of the capital. On 18 December James was taken under armed guard to Rochester. The same day William entered London with his Dutch troops and installed himself at St James's Palace. Three days later Bishop Compton of London, his diocesan clergy and four leading Nonconformists thanked William for the country's deliverance from popery and slavery and promised their assistance. On 23 December, with the connivance of his guards, James II escaped to France.

William was, by now, thinking of taking the throne. He called an assembly of some four hundred commoners, mainly surviving members of Charles II's Parliaments and representatives of the City of London, and this manoeuvre forced the peers at the Guildhall to invite him to summon a Convention and to govern until that assembly could meet. On 28 December, William issued letters authorising elections. Three weeks later, on 22 January 1689, the Convention Parliament assembled at Westminster.

The Commons voted that King James had 'abdicated the government' and the throne of England was 'thereby vacant'. But many were unhappy with this interpretation of recent events. Tories and Anglicans favoured a regency. When John Evelyn dined with the bishops at Lambeth Palace on 15 January 1689, he found that 'they were all for a regency, thereby to salve their oaths, and so all public matters to proceed in his Majesty's name, thereby to facilitate the calling of a parliament according to the laws in being'.[24] This conscientious reluctance to interfere in the divinely appointed succession was not restricted to what one Dissenter called 'the old rotten Tories', 'but of the better sort of the Church of England clergymen even those that were most forward, and without whom the bishops had never refused to read the Declaration, nor made one step towards the recovering of their reputation, nor to the putting of a stop to those papal methods then carrying on'.[25] Political realities carried the day: the majority in the Conventions voted for 'vacancy'; William was determined to be King and his wife Mary – the rightful heir in Tory eyes – would not take the throne without him, and so by February it was established that William and Mary would be joint sovereigns with William having sole responsibility for government.

The Convention Parliament of 1689 devoted itself to the task of tying William to various conditions 'more strictly . . . than other princes had been before'.[26] The resulting Declaration of Rights may have been 'an implied contract' between William and his new subjects. This was certainly what radical Whigs in the Convention Parliament intended. The Declaration spells out James II's misdeeds, asserts the nation's ancient liberties, declares William and Mary King and Queen, and sets forth the immediate succession. But William did not promise to respect these liberties before he was crowned – they were simply read to him and his queen at a curious ceremony in the Banqueting House at Whitehall. Later, the Declaration became a statute, the Bill of Rights, with the additional proviso that the monarch cannot be, nor be married to, a Roman Catholic. The royal assent may have been assumed to be a promise to respect these rights: yet the Act had no provisions to ensure that these rather airy principles were enforced.

*

News from Scotland and Ireland 'gives men apprehension of great difficulties before any settlement can be perfected here', reported John Evelyn.[27] The Scottish Revolution of 1689 was a much more radical affair than England's Revolution. There was no action in Scotland against James until after his flight. Then at the request of Scottish peers and gentlemen William called a Convention of Estates at Edinburgh. On 4 April this Convention resolved that James had forfeited the crown. A few days later the Claim of Right stated that since James had attempted 'the subversion of the Protestant religion, and the violation of the laws and liberties of the kingdom', he had 'forfeited the right to the Crown and the throne is become vacant'. Such a naked assertion of the 'contractarian' principle (that allegiance was only due to rulers while they respected the terms upon which they ruled) was made easier because Scottish Tories and Jacobites had effectively boycotted the Convention. The Claim unequivocally asserted that the Scots could bestow the title of monarch where they wished. In reality, of course, there was little choice. William and Mary formally accepted the Crown of Scotland on 11 May. As in England, the arrangements managed to obscure the precise nature of the arrangement. All the King and Queen did was to swear to maintain the true religion of Jesus Christ and to uphold the laws and constitutions. But the Claim of Right had listed several grievances and some of these were redressed; the Lords of the Articles, the standing committee by which the Scottish Parliament had been managed by the crown, were abolished. Perhaps most significantly, the Claim called for the abolition of prelacy, a 'great and insupportable grievance and trouble to this nation'.

It was widely appreciated that the Scottish Presbyterians were William's most reliable 'friends' north of the border and that the Scottish bishops with their deep residual loyalty to King James had little leverage on the new King. Bishop Rose of Edinburgh visited London to lobby the English bishops and William, but seems to have misplayed his hand disastrously. On being presented to William, Rose told the King that he would 'serve you as far as law, reason, or conscience will allow' upon which William simply walked away without a word.[28] In July, William gave his assent to an act removing 'prelacy and all superiority of any office in the Church in this kingdom above presbyters'. A year later Presbyterian government was restored to the Scottish Kirk. The act of 7 June 1690 established Presbyterianism as it had been under the 1592 'Golden Acts'; no reference was made to the Covenants nor to the divine right of Presbyterianism; provision was made for the purging of 'insufficient, negligent, scandalous and erroneous ministers'; and shortly afterwards lay rights of patronage were abolished and the appointment of ministers was vested in the Kirk sessions. The 1669 Act of Supremacy had been repealed, but William had not abandoned all hope of control over the Scottish Kirk: the convening of a General Assembly of the Clergy still lay in the hands of a royal commissioner, although Presbyterians noisily asserted that ministers 'have a spiritual intrinsic power from Jesus Christ, the only head of his church, to meet in assemblies about the affairs thereof'.[29] William battled against the Presbyterians' intolerance and their ambition to impose the Westminster Confession on the whole country despite the fact that there were many other denominations to be considered, Catholic Highlanders,

Cameronian Presbyterians, and, of course, Episcopalians. In vain he pleaded that 'such as are of the episcopal persuasion [should] have the same indulgence as Dissenters have in England provided they give security to live peaceably under the government and take the oath of allegiance'.[30] There would be no Toleration Act in Scotland until 1712.

William could exert limited control over his northern kingdom and its diverse population. It is doubtful whether he comprehended its complex regional, religious and clan composition. The debate over the country's religious settlement took place against a backdrop of disorder, factionalism and war. The Convention had met in Edinburgh while the city was under the control of armed Cameronians, the radical Presbyterians based in the south-west. Meanwhile, John Graham of Claverhouse, Viscount Dundee, had raised a Highland force of about 2,000 in the name of the deposed King James. In the summer of 1689, Dundee's army destroyed a Williamite force at Killiekrankie, but the loss of their own leader in the battle left the Highlanders purposeless and after their defeat at Dunkeld by the Cameronians, they withdrew into the mountains. Although the Scottish Jacobite forces were now largely contained within the Highlands, over the next few years King William's ministers pursued a policy of bribery and intimidation in order to bring the clans to heel. The most infamous act in this inglorious campaign was the massacre of thirty-six Jacobite MacDonalds at Glencoe in February 1692. These operations, however, were little more than a small-scale guerrilla diversion from the bigger struggles.

Ireland was the arena in which the long-postponed military encounter between James and William would take place. No sooner had James arrived in France than Louis XIV was kitting him out to lead a military campaign in Ireland. James landed in Ireland in March 1689 and with French help, supplies and weapons began to train his large Catholic Irish army. In the first campaigning season, James's army besieged Enniskillen and Londonderry, and skirmished inconclusively with a Williamite expeditionary force led by Schomberg. In June 1690, determined to end this sideshow to the main European military contest, William arrived to take personal command of an army of 37,000 professional soldiers. On 1 July William's army defeated James's troops at the battle of the Boyne. In many ways an unremarkable victory, it was enough to dishearten James. On 4 July he sailed for France and exile, and later that summer Louis XIV recalled his French regiments. The Irish war, however, dragged on for another year, through the bitter sieges of Cork, Kinsale and Limerick, and the bloody defeat of the Catholic army at Aughrim in County Galway on 12 July 1691, before the final capitulation of the Jacobite forces. The

Treaty of Limerick, which was signed on 3 October 1691, can perhaps be seen as the final act in the extended revolution across the three British kingdoms.

*

And what a revolution it was! 'The greatest revolution that ever was known,' in the opinion of Abraham de la Pryme.[31] Morrice admitted that he had never entered Westminster Hall 'without fear' since 1662, but on 4 February 'I walked with true liberty.'[32] 'The whole face of things [had been] changed next to a miracle' in just three months, gushed the Nonconformist Oliver Heywood. 'The management of all things is put into other hands and the scene of things so altered as if it were a new world, and great hopes of further mercy, and gracious dispensations both in church and state and church.'[33] 'Thus the Lord changeth times and seasons, removeth kings and setteth up kings,' hymned the chronicle of one Dissenting congregation, 'he poureth contempt upon princes and causeth them to wander in a wilderness.'[34] 'We were in danger of slavery, and popery, if God had not sent the Prince of Orange,' preached a Suffolk clergyman at Christmas 1688. By the following Easter, he could give praise 'that God hath settled us in a new and wonderful way, by the Prince of Orange's being made King. The government is new, and as a tender plant, I desired that God would send down on it the dew of heaven.'[35] God had raised up the Prince of Orange like another Moses, Joshua or David 'to deliver his people from the most pitiful state and condition'.[36] William was a providential deliverer – this was how his rule could be legitimised – not only to the puritanical but also to the Tory churchmen who increasingly saw him as appointed through divine providence. It was a comfort to accept the dispensations of providence. After all, was not the history of the British church 'a continued series of providential revolutions'?[37] Numerous self-congratulatory sermons and speeches stressed that God had once again saved the English, and probably just as many that pointed out the need to reciprocate: Burnet preached on 'the obligation lying upon the nation, to walk worthy of God's particular and signal deliverances of this nation and church'.[38]

At the heart of the Revolution was the change of ruler. This was the central political fact for contemporaries. With hindsight it is easy to see how much more flowed from this one change – the reorientation of British foreign policy, the consequent changes in taxation, finance and political life – but in 1689 this all lay in the future. At the time, the constitutional changes were discussed in terms of allegiance to the sovereign. How had the change of sovereign been effected? By whose authority? And where did it leave those who had sworn their personal allegiance to James Stuart and his direct descendants? A range of arguments were used so that as many of the English as possible could reconcile themselves to what had occurred. Whigs accepted that there was a right of resistance against tyrants and that James II had broken the contract, enshrined in the coronation oath or the mythic 'ancient constitution', between the sovereign and people. Tories shrank from the right of resistance, preferring to focus upon James's departure, desertion or abdication, or to emphasise the role of divine providence in allowing William to win the throne, or to see William as King 'by conquest' or 'in fact' rather than the King 'by right'. Of all the many immediate consequences of the Revolution, there was only one that contemporaries recognised as even approaching the change of monarch in significance. This was the legislation of a religious toleration.

Toleration

The symbolic impact of the Toleration Act was undeniable. 'Thanks be to God,' wrote Robert Harley, on hearing that it had received the royal assent.[39] 'Now we were freed from the fears of persecution,' wrote one Dissenter.[40] 'Now had the churches and people of God more rest and peace, freedom from those oppressions and persecutions which they had formerly met with from a malignant generation of men.'[41] John Locke reported to a Dutch friend that it was 'not perhaps so wide in scope as might be wished . . . still it is something to have progressed so far' and to have laid the foundations for liberty and peace in the church of Christ.[42] According to Bishop Barlow, the Act gave freedom 'against the express law of God, of nature, and all' to those who had 'ruined church and state, and murdered their king'.[43] The genesis of the Toleration Act deserves to be traced in some detail, as do its real effects.

In the febrile atmosphere of 1688–89 the prospect seemed momentarily to arise of a reconfiguration of English Protestantism. Was it possible, some asked, that the terrible mistake of 1662 could now be rectified? Could the 'moderate' wing of the Church of England cast off the extremists, the 'hierarchists', the 'high churchmen', and be reconciled with the sober 'nonconformable clergy'? Such optimism was encouraged by William's image as a godly ruler. It was prevalent among Presbyterians such as Roger Morrice, whose chronicle of public events, normally a clear-eyed, dispassionate record, becomes quite besotted with William in the winter of 1688–89: 'The Prince's design . . . is to retrieve and promote the Reformed interest and religion here and abroad, and to repress the tyranny of France.'[44] William apparently possessed all the virtues and personal qualities needed to kick-start England's moral regeneration, and his wife was another such paragon. On 2 January 1689 about a hundred Presbyterian and Congregational ministers led by John Howe presented a loyal address to William, who assured them 'that he came purposely for the defence of the Protestant religion, and that it was his own Religion wherein he was born and bred, and the religion of his country and his ancestors; that he was resolved by the grace of God always to adhere to it, and to do his utmost endeavours for the defence of it, and the promoting a firm union amongst all Protestants'.[45] Moreover, there was a willingness to compromise among some Anglicans. Bishop Compton not only took Nonconformists with the Anglican deputation to William on 21 December 1688, but he 'very candidly' drew attention to their presence, and described the Nonconformists as the Church of England's 'brethren who differed from them in some minute matters but nothing substantial'.[46] Archbishop Sancroft, nominal leader of the Church of England and resolute loyalist, remained aloof. When approached by the London clergy, 'the archbishop would not speak out, but said we were wise men and needed not his direction'.[47] He told Bishop Rose of Edinburgh that since matters were 'very dark', the bishops 'knew not well what to do for themselves, and far less what advice to give'.[48] Within weeks, the moment had passed and Morrice reported that 'there is no doubt to be made but that the Prince will preserve episcopacy, and the doctrine of the Church of England, but he will not preserve the tyranny, the persecution, nor the debaucheries of the Church of England . . . and it's likely he will not preserve the oaths and subscriptions that made the divisions amongst Protestants imposed by the Church of England'.[49] In other words, the Church of England would continue, but its privileged political position and its coercive powers might be curtailed.

This broad agenda lay behind the parliamentary discussion of three connected measures – a new oath of allegiance, a 'comprehension' or the reunion of Dissenters with the Church of England, and an 'indulgence' or religious toleration – out of which emerged the Toleration Act of 1689. As so often before, the proposal was for comprehension of the moderates alongside toleration for the recalcitrant minority. Work started early on the Comprehension Bill: on 14 January 1689, while the succession was still under discussion and after Sancroft had refused to become involved, a group of Anglican clergy, Tillotson, Sharp, Patrick, Tenison and Bishop

Lloyd of St Asaph, had met to draft the bill; this was then refined in a series of meetings between Daniel Finch, Earl of Nottingham, and 'the bishops'. Further revised in the Lords during March, this bill made so few concessions to the Dissenters that Morrice did not think that it would 'comprehend' any of them at all.[50] Moreover, its prospects had already been blighted by William's speech in the Lords on 16 March when he urged Parliament to hasten the legislation for the new oaths of allegiance and to provide for 'the admission to public office of all Protestants, that are willing and able to serve'. There was a predictable uproar among the Tory MPs who were determined to preserve the Anglican monopoly of political office.

Perhaps William overplayed his hand. The speech had backing from Whigs and Dissenters and William may simply have asked for what he wanted and misjudged the likely support in Parliament. However, the association he made between the oaths bill and repeal of the Test Act suggests a cannier strategy: Burnet took him to be offering a deal, 'excusing the clergy from the oaths, provided the Dissenters might be excused from the sacrament'.[51] In other words, he was suggesting repeal of the Test Act for Protestants in exchange for a loophole for those Anglican clergy who would find it difficult to go against their sworn allegiance to James II by taking the new oaths of allegiance to William and Mary. Yet William's offer was not pursued. Four weeks later the King took a new tack. Reassuring the Commons that he was 'of the judgement of the Church of England', he suggested that they refer comprehension to Convocation. This they duly did.

The way was now clear for Parliament to proceed with the Toleration Bill and most observers, including many Dissenters, were relieved that the Comprehension Bill had been laid aside. Morrice's reading of the situation was that the Comprehension Bill was useless and the political complexion of Parliament doomed any initiative; 'none but malicious enemies and weak friends to Dissenters would bring in any bill for the uniting, or giving impunity to Dissenters, because all wise men knew [such bills] would be prostituted and made ineffectual to their end'. 'All true friends to the Reformation or to the uniting of Protestants would feign have [the two bills] laid aside at least till a better opportunity.'[52] Morrice's prognosis that the two measures would fall together was wrong. Toleration did succeed. On Friday 24 May King William gave his assent to 'the Bill of Indulgence, Ease or Toleration for Protestant Dissenters, and they have great reason to be thankful for it, for it answers its end, and gives them a due liberty with entire security, and I hope they will make a discreet and serious use of it'. However, continues Morrice, 'I do not understand the mystery of it.' Why the bishops, lords and Tories allowed the measure through was baffling, but it is 'certain they do now heartily repent they have passed it'.[53]

Historically the Act has been portrayed as the long-delayed admission of a prized civil right, when in fact it was a grudging concession born out of deadlock. Its practical significance can be mistaken. The Toleration Act did not repeal the laws against Nonconformity, but exempted from their penalties those who took the Oath of Allegiance and the declarations in the 1678 Test Act. Roman Catholics and non-Christians, such as Jews, gained nothing from the Act. Dissenting clergy were free to exercise their ministry if they additionally subscribed to thirty-six of the Thirty-nine Articles. Dissenters were free to worship in public provided their meeting place was registered with the authorities. The Act took some account of Baptist and Quaker scruples. Protestant Dissenters, however, did not gain full civil rights, a point that was not lost on Dissenters. 'There are several things in it very acceptable, particularly freedom from juries and offices,' wrote Philip Henry to his son. But, continued Henry, slipping into Old Testament mode, 'the quarrel is, will you let my people go, that they may serve me; we will, but let them not go very far away, the men but not the women and children; the women and children but not the cattle. But let not Pharoah deal deceitfully any more: When God judges, he will overcome.' He advised his son, 'when you write to any of our law-makers, acknowledge their kindness and pains in procuring it with all thankfulness, but until the sacramental Test be taken off, our business is not done'.[54] Sir Edward Harley regretted that the Test Act remained as 'a sad profanation of the highest and most awful spiritual mystery of religion'.[55] The Toleration Act spelled the end of moderate Nonconformist hopes of reunion with the Church of England. The sidelining of the Comprehension Bill meant that the Toleration Act applied to perhaps four times more Protestants than had originally been intended. Within a year, 143 permanent and 796 temporary meeting houses had been licensed. Dissent was on its way to becoming institutionalised.

*

Many Dissenters saw the Toleration Act as a parliamentary endorsement of the religious freedom granted by James in 1687, but it was surely not what James had anticipated. The Revolution of 1688-89 confirmed that the Protestant Reformation was irreversible. It also revealed that a transformation had occurred in the religious significance of the ruler. In the 1530s Henry VIII changed the official religion of England and Wales, but in 1688–89 the country changed its ruler rather than surrender Protestantism. In England the Revolution was a defence of the unwritten constitution as well as Protestantism; in Scotland, the Revolution was a defence principally of the Protestant religion; and in Ireland, it cemented the Protestant ascendancy over the Catholic majority. In the Stuart multiple monarchy, the anomalous situation now prevailed of a single ruler presiding over two distinct and antagonistic churches in his two realms. Moreover, the legal toleration of Protestant minorities called into question the sovereign's role as nursing father to a single church of all his people. The Revolution disclosed just how inseparable religion and politics remained in the late seventeenth century.

Notes

1 *The Memoirs of Sir John Reresby*, ed. A. Browning, 2nd edn, revised by M.K. Geiter and W.A. Speck (London, 1991), p. 121.

2 Evelyn, IV, 514–15.

3 Spurr, *RC*, pp. 87–88.

4 T. Harris, *Politics under the Later Stuarts: Party Conflict in a Divided Society 1660–1715* (Harlow, 1993), p. 123.

5 Bodl. L., MS Tanner 31, fo. 268.

6 C. Holmes, *Seventeenth-century Lincolnshire* (Lincoln, 1980), p. 251.

7 Reresby, *Memoirs*, p. 582.

8 J. Hunter, *The Rise of the Old Dissent Exemplified in the Life of Oliver Heywood* (1842), pp. 349–50.

9 Reresby, *Memoirs*, pp. 581–2.

10 Evelyn, IV, 535–6.

11 *A Letter wrote by Mijn Heer Fagel* (1687).

12 H. Nenner, 'Liberty, Law, and Property: The Constitution in Retrospect from 1689', in J.R. Jones (ed.), *Liberty Secured? Britain before and after 1688* (Stanford, 1992), p. 109.

13 M. Mullett, 'Conflict, Politics and Elections in Lancaster, 1660–1688', *Northern History*, 19 (1983).

14 Reresby, *Memoirs*, p. 497.

15 J. Miller, *The Glorious Revolution* (London, 1986), p. 5.

16 See Kenyon, p. 444, for the conflation of 'suspending' and 'dispensing'.

17 R.A. Beddard, 'Observations of a London Clergyman on the Revolution of 1688–9: Being an Excerpt from the Autobiography of Dr William Wake', *Guildhall Miscellany*, 11/9 (1967), 414.

18 DWL, Morrice Entering Book Q, p. 368.

19 E.N. Williams (ed.), *The Eighteenth-century Constitution* (Cambridge, 1960), pp. 10–16.

20 *The Correspondence of Henry Hyde, Earl of Clarendon*, ed. S.W. Singer (2 vols, 1828), II. 194.

21 J.T. Cliffe, *The Puritan Gentry Besieged, 1650–1700* (London, 1993), p. 140.

22 *The Autobiography of Sir John Bramston*, ed. Lord Braybrooke (Camden Society, old series, 32, 1845), p. 338.

23 DWL, Morrice Entering Book Q, p. 381.

24 Evelyn, IV, 614.

25 DWL, Morrice Entering Book Q, p. 379.

26 Reresby, *Memoirs*, p. 546.

27 Evelyn, IV, 629.

28 C. Jackson, *Restoration Scotland, 1660–1690* (Woodbridge, 2003), p. 212; I. Cowan, 'Church and State Reformed? The Revolution of 1688–9 in Scotland', in J. Israel (ed.), *The Anglo-Dutch Moment* (Cambridge, 1991), p. 175.

29 Cowan, 'Church and State Reformed?', pp. 180–1.

30 Cowan, 'Church and State Reformed?', pp. 178–9.

31 *The Diary of Abraham de la Pryme*, ed. C. Jackson (Surtees Society, 54, 1870).

32 DWL, Morrice Entering Book Q, p. 458.

33 Heywood, III, 234–5.

34 *The Axminster Ecclesiastica 1660–1698*, ed. K.W.H. Howard (Sheffield, 1976), p. 141.

35 CUL, Add. MS 8499, p. 213.

36 Edmund Bohun, *Three Charges Delivered at the General Quarter Sessions* (1693), p. 9.

37 T[homas] R[ogers], *Lux Occidentalis* (1689), sig. A2.

38 Evelyn, IV, 623.

39 Cliffe, *Puritan Gentry Besieged*, p. 193.

40 M. Hunter and A. Gregory (eds), *An Astrological Diary of the Seventeenth Century: Samuel Jeake of Rye 1652–1699* (Oxford, 1988), p. 197.

41 *Axminster Ecclesiastica*, ed. Howard, p. 141.

42 *The Correspondence of John Locke*, ed. E.S. De Beer (8 vols, Oxford, 1976–89), III, 633.

43 Bodl. L., Tanner MS 38, fo. 131.

44 DWL, Morrice Entering Book Q, p. 378.

45 DWL, Morrice Entering Book Q, p. 411.

46 DWL, Morrice Entering Book Q, p. 384.

47 Beddard, 'Observations', p. 415.

48 Jackson, *Restoration Scotland*, p. 212.

49 DWL, Morrice Entering Book Q, p. 435.

50 DWL, Morrice Entering Book Q, p. 493.

51 H. Horwitz, *Parliament, Policy and Politics in the Reign of William III* (Manchester, 1977), pp. 21, 23.

52 DWL, Morrice Entering Book Q, pp. 533–4.

53 DWL, Morrice Entering Book Q, p. 558.

54 *The Diaries of Philip Henry*, ed. M.H. Lee (1882), p. 362.

55 Cliffe, *Puritan Gentry Besieged*, p. 193.

CHAPTER 8

William III and Anne (1689–1714)

War and succession

As a consequence of the Revolution of 1688–89, Britain became involved in major European wars for eighteen of the next twenty-three years. William of Orange had intervened in England in order to bring her into his war against Louis, but once he had gained the British thrones William III was forced to defend them against Stuart forces in Scotland and Ireland before he could return to the European battlefield. Thereafter, William spent summer after summer – sixty-two months of his reign in total – campaigning abroad, often with little to show for it. The Nine Years War of 1689 to 1697 was unspectacular, a war of attrition that ended in exhaustion and compromise rather than outright victory. In the Spanish Netherlands William and his allies were bogged down: Namur was lost in 1692 and William was defeated heavily at Landen in 1693, but the French war effort faltered after poor harvests, the allies achieved a crucial victory with the recapture of Namur in 1695, and the combatants eventually came to the peace table at Ryswick in 1697. A land war so wasteful of men and money simply confirmed the English in their entrenched preference for a blue-water strategy, a naval war against French trade, shipping and colonies: although, in reality, the war at sea had also been inconclusive. The English went down to a defeat off Beachy Head in 1690 but scored a notable victory at La Hogue two years later; otherwise the French fleet avoided battle and concentrated on privateering. The second great bout against Louis XIV, the War of the Spanish Succession, coincided with the reign of Queen Anne. John Churchill, Duke of Marlborough, conducted a series of remarkable campaigns and won famous victories at Blenheim, Ramillies and Oudenarde. This was a colossal war fought on both land and sea, in Europe – the Rhineland, Bavaria, Italy, Portugal, and Spain, as well as the Spanish Netherlands – and in the Caribbean and North America. It was brought to an end by the Peace of Utrecht in 1713, just a few months before the deaths of Queen Anne and Louis XIV.

Such unprecedented warfare was not cheap: the war of 1689–97 cost £4.9 million a year, the war of 1702–12, £7.8 million.[1] However, Parliament in 1689 had deliberately kept William short of money. 'If you settle such a revenue as that the King should have no need of a Parliament,' said Paul Foley, 'I think we do not our duty to them that sent us hither.'[2] William's ordinary revenue was less than £1 million a year, whereas James II had £1.5 million. So Parliament had to finance the war with a land tax fixed by an assessment of rental value and rated at two shillings in the pound in peacetime and four shillings in wartime. Accuracy of assessment varied but for most of William and Anne's reigns the land tax was a 20 per cent income tax on those who lived off rents: this was taxation on a twenty-first-century scale. It represented 40 per cent of the government's revenues and brought in £2 million each year. But the war demanded more. The government raised huge sums, some of them directly against parliamentary revenues such as the land tax, others against long-term income, and others simply on public credit or, in other words, on confidence in the government's ability and intention to repay. That confidence was based not only on efficient new taxation, but also on the newly established Bank of England. The government in turn borrowed from the Bank and from concerns like the East India Companies and the South Sea Company which was set up in 1711 as a device to incorporate government creditors and convert the £9 million owed to them into their stock. Investors, who rushed to buy stock in all of these institutions, were generally rewarded with good returns on their money.

It was not only the war that gave the twenty-five years between 1689 and 1714 their historically distinctive character. There were some striking political and social developments. Parliament became increasingly prominent in national life. In 1689 William admitted that 'whilst there was a war he should want a Parliament'.[3] Parliament met regularly – the Triennial Act of 1694 required a general election every three years – it met for longer sessions, and it conducted more business, although the majority of that business was private legislation. In the long term, Parliament's regular sessions and fiscal powers gave it a new constitutional importance. More immediately, the frequent elections – ten in the nineteen years after 1694 – and the feverish politics conducted in the provinces and in Parliament gave new impetus to adversarial and partisan politics, to the contest between Whig and Tory parties.

These political divisions were mirrored by social tensions. Contemporaries perceived English society as divided between the rival 'moneyed' and 'landed interests'. Henry St John claimed in 1709 that 'the whole burden' of twenty years of war had fallen on 'the landed interest', men who have 'neither served in the fleets nor armies, nor meddled in the public funds and management of treasure'. Meanwhile, the new moneyed interest had arisen on the back of 'a sort of property which was not known twenty years ago'.[4] The moneyed interest was thought to 'ruin those that have only land to depend on, to enrich Dutch, Jews, French and other foreigners, scoundrel stock-jobbers and tally-jobbers, who have been sucking our vitals for many years'.[5] In broad terms, this perception of social change was justified. Before 1688 the English were under-taxed and possibly under-governed by an amateur bureaucracy of gentlemen landowners; by the 1700s they paid a swingeing land tax, supported an enormous national debt, and found professional administrators interfering repeatedly in their affairs. A social order dominated by landowners was giving way to a more complex society that included new professional and administrative classes – opportunities were burgeoning for advancement through the army, navy, customs and excise, or diplomatic service, as well as the law and medicine – and a powerful group of moneyed men who saw no reason to abandon commerce and investment as they assumed the lifestyle of country gentlemen. There were, of course, Whig country gentlemen – some of them dyed-in-the-wool Whigs, others post-1688 converts – just as there were Tories who invested in the East India Company and government stocks. Yet for all the variations, the perception of a starkly divided society remained strong. Those who cut a figure in Augustan England were, said Dean Swift, 'a species of men quite different from any that were ever known before the Revolution; consisting either of generals or colonels, or of such whose whole fortunes lie in funds or stocks: so that power, which . . . used to follow land, is now gone over to money'.[6]

Many institutions and practices replicated these political and social divisions. The numerous coffee houses became venues for debate and party meeting rooms. Printing presses, which had now spread beyond London to Bristol, Liverpool, Newcastle, Norwich, Nottingham, Stamford and Warwick, churned out pamphlets, broadsides, sermons and, of course, newspapers – there were twelve a week, selling a total of 44,000 copies, in the capital by 1714. This was the heyday of 'Grub Street', hack and partisan journalism that managed to command the talents of professional writers of the calibre of Defoe, Richardson, Steele and Addison, and of gifted clerics such as Swift, Atterbury and Kennett. Every effort was made to capture popular attention. Never mind that only 4 per cent of the population had the vote, there were processions, bonfires, dinners, religious services, illuminations, toasts and other entertainments laid on – even a riot could be organised. The whole nation was politicised by the frequent general elections: 'there is not a chambermaid, prentice or schoolboy', reported Swift from the 1707 election at Leicester, 'but what is warmly engaged on one side or the other'.[7]

*

War was the primary political issue in the reigns of William and Anne, but it was related to many others. The succession was precarious: William, whose health was far from robust, had no children, and his wife died in 1694, the heir, Princess Anne, James II's younger Protestant daughter, had only one surviving child and he succumbed to smallpox in 1700. In due course, Parliament stipulated that the succession would pass after Anne to an obscure Lutheran dynasty from the north German territory of Hanover. The succession issue was, in turn, linked to the threat from Jacobitism. The cause of James II and his son, the Pretender, was tainted by their French association as much as it was compromised by their religion. There was little reason, bar the opinions of a few alehouse loudmouths, dubious Irishmen and extremist Anglican clergy, to suspect widespread popular support for the Jacobites. So the government feared a popular Jacobite rising in England less than French-backed invasions or assassination plots, which certainly existed and were usually based on hopes of a rising in the Scottish Highlands. In 1708, for example, Louis XIV provided 6,000 troops and thirty ships to take the Pretender to Scotland. Although the fleet never even landed and there were few signs of popular support in Scotland, the expedition provoked a major scare in England and largely determined the outcome of the next election. Highland sympathy for the Jacobite cause was one issue, but the Lowland Scots had their own ways of exploiting the succession question.

After forging its own revolutionary path in 1689, the Scottish Parliament and Kirk had regained a degree of confidence and autonomy. Scottish politicians vociferously asserted the rights and needs of Scotland in a number of fields: one was the economic argument for access to markets in England and her colonies; another was a demand for guarantees for the Presbyterian religion. In 1703 the Scottish Act of Security threw down a challenge to the Westminster government. Without concessions, the Scots would not commit themselves to the Hanoverian succession. This may have been bluff, but it concentrated minds and by 1707 the Union of Scotland and England as 'Great Britain' had been established with little fuss on the English side and a great deal of soul-searching among the Scots. The English had found a solution to the awkward Scottish Parliament and had secured the succession. The Scots won access to a British free trade area; the new British Parliament included 45 MPs and 16 peers from Scotland; and the succession of the British throne was vested in the Hanoverians. Scotland retained its Presbyterian Kirk, its laws and legal system, its universities and its burghs. The Scottish dream of exporting reformation to England had faded. Both nations could take comfort that the Stuart habit of playing the kingdoms against each other, 'making use of each (by turns) to oppress and enslave the other', would be thwarted by the union.[8]

Catholic Ireland was treated rather differently, largely as a result of the Protestant minority's privileged position. Although less than 20 per cent of the population, the Protestants owned nearly 90 per cent of Irish land in 1703. The Protestant ascendancy was shored up by a series of harsh laws in the 1690s and 1700s designed to perpetuate an Irish Catholic underclass through restrictions on property ownership, Catholic education, inter-marriage, and office-holding. Yet the Catholic population grew and main-tained its high level of religious devotion. So, too, did Ireland's Protestant Dissenters, who profited from an influx of Scots co-religionists escaping from a run of failed harvests in Scotland in the 1690s. The Church of Ireland, meanwhile, continued to be no more than the church of a tiny elite of landowners and to draw most of its resources and expertise from England.

War, the succession, national security, and relations with Ireland and Scotland, all seem a world away from the political obsession with the nature of English Protestantism in, say, the reigns of Charles I or James II. Was religion retreating as a political issue? Far from it. Whig and Tory arguments were framed in terms of the political debates of the seventeenth century and, above all, in terms of the Revolution of 1688 and its defence of Protestantism and liberty. Religious slogans and affiliations were prom-inent among the defining characteristics of the rival political parties and gained further momentum from their use as party political weapons. This does not mean that the religious principles contested so fiercely in the decades after 1688 were identical to earlier principles, nor at this distance can we judge the sincerity of religious convictions. But some contem-poraries did. 'That which they call religion seems to me to look no farther than the affairs of this world,' wrote a jaundiced Whig clergyman from

Gloucester in 1710. 'Our disputes are not for the sake of truth, but zeal for parties.'[9]

The rage of party

The Whigs and Tories have mesmerised generations of historians. Political life under William and Anne appears to be a see-saw in which the two parties battled for victory in parliamentary elections, dominance in the Commons and Lords, and influence at the royal court. The parties had distinct and conflicting views of the world, they exerted parliamentary discipline – so that, certainly by Anne's reign, MPs can be seen consistently voting along 'party lines' – and they deployed the patronage system to reward their followers and punish their enemies. Yet appearances can be misleading. The Whigs and Tories were not yet nineteenth- or twentieth-century parties with the level of organisation and procedure that modern parliamentary parties enjoy. They were more nebulous groupings than modern readers might assume and large numbers of MPs were of no party, better described as 'Country' or 'backbenchers'. The 'Country party' outlook was conservative but intrinsically oppositional: it was the job of Country MPs to limit the pretensions of government, keep the state small and cheap, weed 'placemen' from Parliament, and preserve the morality of public life. One foreign observer reported in 1700 that these MPs rarely looked beyond the shores of England and were concerned with four principles – the religion of the country, liberty of the individual, trade and agriculture.[10] Country attitudes owed much to earlier, often godly, ideas about personal duty and civic responsibility, divine providence, antipopery, and the association between piety and prosperity. Periodically, these attitudes reasserted themselves in parliamentary politics and could override Whig and Tory loyalties.

The government's relationship to the parties was a subtle one. Under William and Anne, the 'government' was simply the ministers appointed by the monarch to conduct his or her business. There was no formal mechanism by which the monarch had to appoint ministers whose 'party' was dominant in the Commons. Indeed, most of the ministers, such as Sunderland, Shrewsbury, Godolphin, Marlborough or even Harley, were parliamentary managers, men who stood above party and whose aim was to get the government's business through Parliament. This often required careful attention to the disposition of party forces, and it is undeniable that royal freedom of action in the appointment of ministers was contracting – pressure was growing to choose what one Tory called 'men of one principle and interest'.[11] Administrations were not necessarily homogeneous, but were frequently riven by the self-interest and intense personal rivalry of great ministers, by tensions between ideologues and parliamentary managers, and by the personal agenda of the monarch. Thus the very notion of Tory or Whig ministries in this period is an oversimplification: most administrations blurred party lines and power shifted gradually from one grouping to another.

Whigs and Tories were divided over the Revolution of 1688 and the related issues of the succession, the defence of the Church of England, the conduct of 'King William's war', and the abjuration of James II and his descendants. The Whigs identified themselves with the Revolution and its benefits, such as the Toleration Act and limited monarchy. They accepted that 'resistance' to the monarch had occurred, but justified it as a consequence of James's unconstitutional government. They sympathised with Dissent, but probably attended Anglican services, and did not have any plans to dismantle the Test Acts. Tories were ambiguous about the Revolution. Many retained a residual loyalty to James II, the rightful king, even while they recognised William as the king in fact. Reluctant to justify 'resistance' to any monarch, Tories explained away the events of 1688 as an abdication by James or as the mysterious action of divine providence. Tories resented the Toleration Act, and as the self-proclaimed 'church party', they increasingly feared that the church was in danger from Dissent, atheism and vice. The intensity of political conflict and propaganda in the 1690s and 1700s created caricatures of both parties: Whigs were portrayed as republicans, 'against all revealed religion', and 'for an absolute unlimited toleration', while Tories were represented as 'for the Pretender, for arbitrary power, for repealing toleration, for persecuting good loyal Protestants who agree with the church in fundamentals'.[12] Although a few in each camp probably did hold these extreme positions, it is unwise to place too much weight on partisan polemics. The propagandists knew little restraint and often indulged their overdeveloped sense of history: the Tory candidates at Guildford in the 1710 election were described by their supporters as 'true to the Queen and Church against all managers of Oliver's party and principles, that once murdered their king and thousands of the nation, to reign over us'.[13]

Tories and Whigs relied heavily on their respective religious 'constituencies'. The Anglican clergy, who had had the vote since 1664, would often ride together in a black-coated phalanx to cast their ballots, usually in favour of the Tory candidate. In some counties, such as Suffolk, perhaps four-fifths of the clergy voted Tory in the general elections, while in the Lincolnshire election of 1710 about 150 of the clergy 'marched in a body' to support the Tory candidates. Elsewhere clerical allegiances were more evenly divided; in Yorkshire in 1708 about half of the 146 clerical voters backed the Tory party.[14] In general, however, the parish clergy could be relied upon to preach up the Tory cause: 'the parsons bestow more pains for votes than ever they did for souls', complained one critic.[15] Whig supporters among the Anglican clergy were a minority, but one that included many of the bishops. The prelates, too, rolled up their sleeves and took a hand in the political process: in Wiltshire, Bishop Burnet was said to have recommended candidates 'who lie under great mistrust of favouring Dissenters and making alterations in the church'; Bishop Lloyd of Worcester was denounced by the Commons for his 'malicious, unchristian and arbitrary' threats against any of his diocesan clergy who supported the Tory candidate.[16] Crucially, the Whig bishops formed a powerful block of votes in the House of Lords. Since the Whig party was identified with the Toleration Act, Whigs could count on the support of Nonconformity both in word and deed. Although Nonconformists were banned from public office, the practice of 'occasional conformity', by which individuals received the sacrament once a year in an Anglican church simply to qualify for office, was widespread. Thanks to this device, Presbyterians and some Congregationalists happily served in local government – much to Tory irritation. The partisan control of local offices and the limited nature of the franchise – restricted in some boroughs to the mayor and aldermen – made it simple enough to evade the letter of the law when it came to electing MPs. In some cases, the subversion of the law was blatant. In 1702, to prevent the election of Tory MPs, the Whig mayor of Wilton in Wiltshire quite openly created nineteen new burgesses, all of them Dissenters, which had the desired result of sending two staunch Whigs to Parliament.

*

William III was wary of both political parties from the outset. After a brief moment of unanimity in the winter of 1688–89, Whigs and Tories adopted different lines – many Tories hoped for a regency and were slow, even reluctant, to espouse the new sovereigns. William was not, however, prepared to entrust political power to the Whigs. Indeed, he initially appointed a mixed set of ministers, including Halifax, Danby (now Marquis of Carmarthen) and the Tory Earl of Nottingham. But this neither led to effective government nor reassured the nervous. Through the first years of the new reign, old Tories like Evelyn bemoaned the miserable management of public affairs and alleged a Republican–Dissenter plot to subvert what was left of the English constitution. 'The government seems now to be brought to a kind of anarchy,' observed one Anglican cleric. 'Nothing can long stand upon such a bottom of confusion; we must again tack about to our old constitutions or be lost.' Meanwhile, the Whig John Hampden knew no one who understood the present 'scheme' of government, 'and that which is most melancholy and discouraging is that there seems to be no scheme at all. The only maxim that I see followed is this, secure the church – no bishop, no king.'[17] Satisfying no one and weary of parliamentary obstruction, William was close to throwing in the towel: 'I see that I am not made for this people, nor they for me.'[18]

After a long and generally unhappy flirtation with a mixed ministry of Tories and Whigs, William began to identify himself with a group of Whig aristocrats, Lords Somers, Halifax, Wharton, Orford and Sunderland, known as the Junto. Gradually these ministers came to dominate his counsels in the middle years of the decade. William's own political position was strengthened in February 1696 when a Jacobite plot led by Sir John Fenwick was discovered. 'Though many did formerly pity King James's condition,' commented Evelyn, 'this design of assassination, and bringing over a French army, did much alienate many of his friends and was like to produce a more perfect establishment of King William.'[19] The ramifications of the conspiracy implicated James; hundreds of suspects were arrested, although only a handful of plotters eventually went to the scaffold. The revelation of the plot was further confirmation that God watched over the English: 'oh how many a time have we provoked him,' wailed one diarist, 'how easy a prey would our enemies make of us, if God would but let them loose upon us'.[20] To the Whigs this was a marvellous chance to make Tories squirm. An 'Association' was drawn up by the Commons which acknowledged William 'as rightful and lawful king' and promised to defend him against his enemies. Anyone who refused to sign this supposedly voluntary recognition of William and repudiation of James's claims would be revealed as a Jacobite or fellow-traveller. Eventually more than a hundred MPs and over twenty peers were exposed in this way, and a substantial purge of JPs, deputy lieutenants and other local officials followed.

By 1697 the Junto Whigs had come close to establishing something that looked like a homogeneous administration. These great lords pulled together in formulating plans and were able to coordinate those policies with their supporters in Parliament; but it was a short-lived success. Country MPs continued to snipe from the backbenches at the land tax, the Bank, the influence of William's Dutch favourites, parliamentary corruption, and a host of other targets. In the winter of 1697–98, this opposition scored a significant victory when, in the wake of the Peace of Ryswick, they forced William to accept a peacetime army of 7,000 English-born troops, rather than the much larger number that he claimed was necessary to ensure the nation's safety. King and Country opposition viewed national safety in different lights. Fought out in pamphlets and on the floor of the House, the 'standing army controversy' saw the Country party arguing that any form of permanent army under royal control was inimical to true liberty. Echoes of earlier republicanism were to be heard in some of the more radical tracts and a line of political argument was enunciated which would be advanced in eighteenth-century America. In the later 1690s, tired of the English Parliament's pursuit of party quarrels, unable or unwilling to trust his ministers, who were so clearly losing control of parliamentary business, William offered little leadership: he shuffled ministers, vented his frustrations in a draft abdication speech, and escaped to the Netherlands whenever he could.

In 1700 two dynastic disasters forced the King back to the grind of parliamentary politics. The first was the sudden death of the young Duke of Gloucester, Princess Anne's only child, which threw the English succession into doubt. The other was the long-anticipated demise of Carlos II, King of Spain, who had no direct heir to inherit the huge Spanish territories in Europe and America. A complex series of public and secret treaties had laid down the division of the Spanish possessions between the Austrian Habsburgs and the French Bourbons, but Louis XIV now had other ideas. There could be little doubt that Louis's menacing attitude was a prelude to a new European war. With war looming, William needed to settle the succession after Anne and the preferred, but hardly enthusiastic, choice was James I's Protestant granddaughter Electress Sophia of Hanover and her heirs. Parliament accepted this proposal with barely a murmur, but appended to the 1701 Act of Settlement a catalogue of protest at William's abuse of the conventions of government. The Act imposed a series of statutory limitations on the monarch who henceforth had to be a conforming Anglican; it stipulated that parliamentary consent was necessary for foreign wars and before the sovereign could leave the country; it banned foreign-born subjects from holding crown office, or sitting in Parliament or the Privy Council; and freed the judiciary from royal interference. All of these restrictions would take effect when a Hanoverian monarch ascended the throne, but they were a reproof to William III and represented a clear constitutional shift towards greater parliamentary control over the crown.

In the teeth of fierce parliamentary criticism of his foreign policy, William made his diplomatic and political preparations for war: promoting the Duke of Marlborough to a central military and diplomatic role, dissolving Parliament in the hope that the next would contain more Whigs, and signing an alliance between Britain, Holland and Austria – but he was greatly aided by the death of James II in September 1701 and by Louis XIV's provocative reaction to it. Reneging on the commitment he gave in the Treaty of Ryswick, Louis now recognised James's son as James III and promised him that 'I will subordinate all material and political considerations for the sake of true religion. Remember then that it is your religion that makes you King.'[21] As Hoppit has remarked, the effect was to mobilise in England the same fears of popery, tyranny and universal French Catholic domination that had inspired the Nine Years War. However, before William could launch another great war against his old French adversary, fate intervened in the mundane form of a riding accident and a fatal fever: on 8 March 1702 William III died, little mourned, but generally respected, regarded by some as an able and shrewd politician and general, and by others as a prince raised by divine providence to save the nation from popery and arbitrary government.

Religion and reformation under William III

William had always been adept at playing the religion card. His personal religion may have been tepid, but the image for public consumption was strong and deeply pious. The accession of William and his Anglican wife – 'two good angels', as Tillotson described them – held out the promise of religious and moral reform. William's alleged piety was much discussed by English Protestants: while preparing the invasion 'he used to go to his closet and spend much time in prayer' sometimes in a voice loud enough to be overheard or leaving pools of tears behind him. He would not permit 'atheism, infidelity and the ridiculing of religion' among his entourage.[22] 'The prince and his court do give more discountenance to debaucheries etc. then is known to us, or then we can bear.'[23] The new King wrote to Bishop Compton on the need for 'a general reformation of the lives and manners of all our subjects'. No wonder that Burnet looked forward to 'the completing of our Reformation, especially in the lives and manners of men'.[24] Burnet was one of the principal architects of the 'godly revolution', the publicity campaign that portrayed the 1688–89 Revolution as a work of piety and the Williamite court as a vehicle for national moral and religious renewal. This propaganda effort served to divert the attention of Nonconformists and others who clearly expected William to realign English Protestantism with the Reformed church of Europe, and to reconnect the Church of England with what they saw as its roots in the sixteenth-century Reformation. But the 'godly revolution' was designed to appeal beyond the English godly to a much broader audience where it could soothe anti-Dutch sentiment, smooth relations with Parliament and whip up support for the war. Few, after all, would or could quarrel with a call for more piety and morality. Queen Mary also helped to establish the regime's godly credentials. A pious Anglican while living in the Netherlands, Mary was also inclined to the godly practices of afternoon sermons and Bible-reading and was a keen supporter of initiatives against immorality. She exerted a beneficial influence on church appointments – with the help of Nottingham she handled the delicate task of replacing Archbishop Sancroft with John Tillotson – and managed to endear herself to both Anglicans and moderate Dissenters. Her death in December 1694 was 'lamented by all true sons of the Church of England, since while alive she was such a nursing mother to it', wrote one divine.[25] But presentation, however pious, could not mask the practical implications of the Revolution and the Toleration Act for English religion.

*

The Church of England was the great loser from the Revolution of 1688. Its morale and unity were badly dented by a succession of knocks. First came the Toleration Act, a body blow to the church's claim to be the national church. Then came the abolition of episcopacy in Scotland and Presbyterian harassment of the Scottish episcopalian clergy. King William now presided over two different churches in his two kingdoms. Further damage was done to the Church of England by the secession of the Nonjurors, a small but eminent and vocal minority of clergy who refused to swear allegiance to the new monarchs. Perversely, even the new bishops appointed in the wake of the Revolution – men like Tillotson, Stillingfleet, Tenison, Fowler, Patrick and Burnet – did more to divide than unite the church: 'we see among the new-made bishops those who were formerly fanatical preachers; and those who, of all our number, are least zealous for the church, and most latitudinarian, for a comprehension of Dissenters, and a dispensation with our liturgy and discipline', alleged a Tory in 1694.[26] A rift had opened up between the bishops and the majority of the lower clergy.

Beyond the personal hurt and accusations of betrayal and self-seeking spawned by 1688–89, this clerical rift reflected divergent views about what the Revolution represented and the direction that the church should take in a new era of religious toleration. The bishops and their supporters were essentially Whig in outlook. These Low Churchmen accepted that the Revolution had been a breach of political loyalty but laid the blame on the Catholic James II. They accepted the permanence of the Toleration Act, and they were realistic about the consequences for the Church of England. The church must now be ready, they conceded, to allow a degree of diversity within its ranks, to cooperate with laymen and even Dissenters in fields such as charity and religious education. They were prepared to contemplate ways around the civil disabilities borne by Dissenters. They could see that Dissenters, barred from the two universities, should be permitted to set up schools and academies even though no provision had been made for it in the Toleration Act. Some Low Churchmen could even collude with the practice of occasional conformity. However, the majority of the Anglican clergy, including many of those in the universities, took a very different line. These High Church clergy were Tory in politics. They yearned for a lost and mythical partnership between church and state, which would exact strict conformity from the Anglican clergy and laity and would limit the Dissenters to the precise letter of the Toleration Act. They saw the Whig bishops as a 'latitudinarian gang', betrayers of the church and its principles, and fellow-travellers with Dissent. 'The church in danger' was their slogan. In 'sermons preached at visitations, and the constant ordinary discourses of the clergy,' reported one Whig clergyman in 1696, 'the Church of England is always represented, as at this time, in greater danger than ever it was'.[27]

The High Church clergy drew strength from the example and arguments of the Nonjurors. Archbishop Sancroft, seven other bishops, and about four hundred (less than 4 per cent) of the Anglican clergy had refused to swear allegiance. The difficulty for many was a simple one of conflicting oaths. Having sworn solemn allegiance to James II, they feared the sin of perjury or false swearing if they now swore allegiance to another ruler. Perhaps a majority of Nonjurors were motivated by this scruple of conscience and their belief in the divine right of monarchy, rather than by an underlying Jacobitism or devotion to the person of James II. Indeed, five of the Nonjuring bishops (Sancroft, Turner, Ken, White and Lake) had been among the seven bishops who had defied James over the reading of the Declaration of Indulgence. At first, William had stayed his hand. For more than a year the Nonjuring bishops were allowed to draw their revenues and retain their palaces. There was talk of a compromise solution: perhaps the oath could be sworn in a 'lower' sense as recognition of *de facto* rather than *de jure* authority of the new monarchs. The discovery late in 1690 of an incriminating letter from Bishop Turner to James II exhausted William's patience. In April 1691 Tillotson was nominated as Sancroft's successor and William began to replace the deprived bishops. This brought a new issue to the fore. Did the civil magistrate have the right to remove bishops?

In the face of the exercise of naked political power, the Nonjurors denied that monarch or Parliament possessed such authority. In their eyes the Church of England had broken with its rightful pastors and was in schism. The exasperated John Evelyn believed that the 'stout demeanour of the few bishops who refused to take the oaths to King William, animated a great party to forsake the churches, so as to threaten a schism'. But there was no theological issue here in his eyes. 'The truth is, the whole clergy had till now stretched the duty of passive obedience, so that the proceedings against these bishops gave no little occasion of exceptions': the clergy were victims of their own stubborn adherence to the Stuarts and to the doctrine of passive obedience.[28] Evelyn's irritation betrays just what damage the Nonjurors' arguments were doing to the Church of England's cohesion and its political allegiance.

The Nonjurors saw themselves as the true Church of England. But they did not all draw the same conclusions from that claim. Some, for example, Ken and Frampton, retired but remained in communion with the church as laymen; others, such as Dodwell and Cherry's circle at Shottesbrooke, argued that the church's schism would cease with the death of the deprived bishops. The more extreme Nonjurors not only separated but took steps to perpetuate their own ministry. In 1691 Sancroft conveyed his archiepiscopal powers to William Lloyd, deprived bishop of Norwich, and in 1693, with James II's approval, Lloyd consecrated George Hickes, deprived Dean of Worcester, as suffragan Bishop of Thetford, and Thomas Wagstaff as Bishop of Ipswich. Later, with the help of Scottish bishops, Hickes consecrated more Nonjuring bishops. But the Nonjurors had quite rapidly become a political irrelevance. Some drifted back to the Church of England, others into outright Jacobitism. Internal dissension took its toll. Their historical significance came to lie in their intellectual distinction as displayed in the works of theologians of the stature of Dodwell and Charles Leslie, devotional writers such as Kettlewell and Law, and liturgical scholars such as Johnson, Nelson and Brett.

The clergy, and the High Churchmen in particular, saw themselves as guardians of theological orthodoxy. They confronted 'an universal conspiracy among a sort of men under the style of Deists, Socinians, latitudinarians, deniers of mysteries, and pretending explainers of them, to undermine and overthrow the Catholic faith'.[29] This roll-call of errors deliberately conflates different strands of argument, but then this was a period of intellectual ferment. Challenging ideas were being thrown up by the new science, by biblical criticism, and by the radical thought of Hobbes, Spinoza, Locke and others, and thanks to the expiry of the Licensing Act in 1695, the press was free to disseminate these sceptical views without the restraint of censorship. Such ideas emanated from so many different sources, some impeccably orthodox, others simply mischievous, that they defy easy generalisation, but they did all share a tendency to make reason the benchmark of religion. In this they represented a challenge to revealed religion and foreshadowed Enlightenment thought.

One intense debate of the 1690s concerned the Trinity – God the Father, Son and Holy Ghost – a crucial Christian doctrine which has no basis in scripture. Anglican defences of the doctrine in reply to antitrinitarian writers opened a can of worms. One after another the theologians confused themselves and their readers and were then denounced by their own side for straying into errors such as Arianism (a denial of the Trinity which retains the notion that Jesus is in some sense divine and can atone for human sins) or Socinianism (the denial of the divinity of Jesus and the doctrine of atonement). The doctrine of the Trinity unravelled as it was debated and eminent thinkers such as the Cambridge mathematician William Whiston and the London preacher Samuel Clarke arrived at Arian conclusions. A more openly sceptical attack on Christianity was mounted by those known as 'freethinkers'. Two leading freethinkers, Charles Blount and John Toland, propounded Deism, a dilute form of religious belief that accepted only that there is a creator, but saw no need for a divine revelation or personal redeemer. For the Deist, the true religion is the 'natural religion' that all human beings can attain through the use of their senses and reason. Freethinkers debunked miracles and superstition, railed against the 'priestcraft' by which the clergy hoodwinked the laity, and argued for 'civil religion', a religion defined and judged by its utility to society in promoting desirable virtues and conduct.

The Church of England took on the forces of scepticism and doubt. The clergy constantly preached of the dangers of impiety and atheism, especially of the sort retailed in the taverns and coffee houses among the addled-brained followers of Hobbes, Toland or Spinoza. They argued at greater length in defence of Christianity in the Boyle Lectures, an annual lecture series established in 1692 under the will of the scientist Robert Boyle, and in many other venues. Such defences could sail perilously close to the rationalism of their opponents and were on occasion exploited by High Churchmen eager to discomfit their Low Church brethren. It was no coincidence that the learned Trinitarian controversies of the 1690s also allowed the High Churchmen to berate Whig bishops like Fowler, Tillotson and Tenison. The suppression of heterodox ideas through legislation (the 1698 Blasphemy Act banned antitrinitarian teaching), book-burning and victimisation (Whiston was expelled from Cambridge and Samuel Clarke was coerced into silence) created an atmosphere of intellectual intolerance and did little to silence the questions of doubters. Seventeenth-century Protestants did not, however, see themselves as simply combating false ideas, but as tackling the evil lives built upon those erroneous ideas and the social consequences of those vicious lives. Humphrey Prideaux found the 'republicans' of Norwich 'openly sedulous to promote atheism, to which end they spread themselves in coffee houses and talk violently for it, and . . . confute the account the scriptures give us of the creation of the world' and books were dispersed to the same end: 'You see where licentiousness and confusion at last end'.[30] The nation's problems were due, claimed John Evelyn, to 'men's vices, and they, for want of stable Christian and moral principles, an universal, atheistical or sceptical humour over-spreading the nation'.[31] In Scotland, an even more robust approach was adopted. One of the first pronouncements of the re-established General Assembly in 1690 had been against the 'dreadful atheistical boldness' of the age. This was followed up by legislation against blasphemy and heterodoxy, a crackdown on the bookshops, and in 1697 the execution of Thomas Aikenhead, an Edinburgh law student convicted of blasphemy.[32] The situation in Ireland was different again. The 1712 Convocation of the Church of Ireland regarded atheism and deism as minor challenges by comparison with the dangers posed by Catholicism and Dissent.

*

The Church of England remained the nominal church of the overwhelming majority of the English. Very few people belonged to the minority Protestant denominations and even fewer to Roman Catholicism, but the political and social significance of both groups was far greater than their numerical strength. Protestant Nonconformity, which was made up of the Presbyterians, Congregationalists (earlier known as the Independents), the Quakers, and the General and Particular Baptists, had at last attained freedom of worship, but it had now to create the financial and institutional structures which would perpetuate each denomination. Meeting houses had to be built and furnished, academies set up and staffed, statements of faith drawn up, pastors trained, and regional and national meetings established. Several thousand licences were taken out for meeting places in the first twenty years of toleration, but many of these were for temporary locations and the size of congregations could vary dramatically. The traveller Celia Fiennes found 'the largest chapel and the greatest number of people I have ever seen of the Presbyterian way' at Coventry in 1697. In Amersham there were 'dissenters of all kinds, chiefly Anabaptists and Quakers,' Bishop Wake was told in 1709: 'one third part of the parish are Dissenters'.[33] But elsewhere in rural Buckinghamshire, the reports spoke of a family of Quakers here, another of Baptists there, or a small knot of Presbyterians who met in one another's homes. Dissent was becoming concentrated in towns and cities, above all in Norwich, Birmingham, Bristol, Exeter and London, and among a distinct social stratum, that of the small-scale merchant, retailer or artisan, rather than the gentry or the poor; furthermore, women made up the majority in many of its congregations. There were advantages of many sorts to the concentration of Dissent in certain towns. Occasional conformity permitted Dissenters to seize control of municipal government in some places: Coventry was 'esteemed a fanatic town', reported Fiennes. In one notorious episode, Sir Humphrey Edwin, Nonconformist Lord Mayor of the City of London, proceeded to Mead's meeting house with the City sword carried before him: 'this has given great offence, even to the most considerate Dissenters, who look upon it as a very imprudent act'.[34]

Dissent had been a creation of the Clarendon Code. A motley crew had all been forced into one boat by persecution, but now that the external threat had been lifted the different denominations were in a quandary. Practical needs dictated that they should cooperate, but alliances were fraught: the Presbyterian–Congregationalist union of the early 1690s soon collapsed, although associations which had a more explicitly political focus, such as the Committee of Three Denominations set up in 1702, tended to have a longer life. Even within a single denomination, organisation and centralisation bred quarrels and secessions: the General Baptists split in two in 1696. And Dissenters were just as vulnerable to the intellectual and spiritual trends of the age as the rest of the population. They read Locke, Whiston and Clarke, they began to retreat from sixteenth-century Calvinism, and they were divided by the Trinitarian controversy. The debate at Salter's Hall, London, in 1719, on the nature of the subscription required to Trinitarian doctrine split Dissent down the middle and hastened the process by which eighteenth-century Presbyterianism became a Unitarian (or non-Trinitarian) faith.

In the 1690s and 1700s, there are some signs of a loss of vitality and commitment within the Dissenting movement. Meetings were becoming

'routinised', membership was stagnating, and some congregations opted
for a quiet life. More church books survive from this period than earlier in
the century and they reveal congregations that sometimes struggled to
exert discipline over errant members. These were humdrum little problems
about fair dealing in trade, alcohol, swearing, non-attendance, marrying
outside the denomination, or marital relationships, but they, along with
the theological wrangling of the pastors and others, paint a depressing picture of life within Dissent. It would be uncharitable to allow such sources
to dictate our view of the Dissenters. The experience and aspirations of
Dudley Ryder, a young London Presbyterian and law student, was rather
different: his friends were argumentative, confident and ebullient; in 1716
they considered taking 'an account of the numbers and strength and riches
of the Dissenters in all the counties of England; that by that means they
might know how far their interest went and of what service they might
be'.[35] Ryder was conscious of the potential of his community and of the
disabilities under which they laboured. The Whigs were often prejudiced
against Dissenters. 'There are indeed too many of the churchmen who are
not Tories nor for downright persecuting them [the Dissenters] and yet
think they have no right to have any thing to do with the government. Even
the Whigs themselves that are churchmen have not all got over their prejudice. They look upon themselves as persons in a higher rank, of a superior
degree and therefore grudge them all the privileges that they have.'[36]

Roman Catholics were another minority with a mixed experience of the
Revolution and the Toleration Act. The Revolution reversed the Catholic
gains of James II's reign – Catholics surrendered benefices and offices, many
retired into private life, a considerable number followed James into exile
– but it was not especially vindictive towards Catholics. That was not
William's style, nor would it have pleased his European Catholic allies, so
Catholic religious practices probably continued much as before, unobtru-
sive and largely undisturbed. Bishop Burnet claimed that the 'papists have
enjoyed the real effects' of the Toleration Act even though it gave them
no legal protection. The claim is confirmed by accounts of gentry households in which a priest or congregation found shelter, and of plebeian
Catholicism in several towns. Defoe found Durham 'full of Roman
Catholics, who live peaceably and disturb no body, and no body them; for
we being there on a holiday, saw them going as publicly to mass as the
Dissenters did on other days to their meeting houses'.[37] On the other hand,
Catholics continued to pay for their faith: the Stonor family in Oxfordshire
spent £240 a year on recusancy fines.[38] Catholics were subject to double
land tax, were excluded from the legal profession, and were vulnerable to

whatever occasional gesture – such as the 1700 Act against popery – emerged from Parliament. The protection that they enjoyed from the great Catholic peers was also beginning to diminish as the Catholic peerage died out. In broad terms, English Catholics remained politically suspect as potential Jacobites, and a prey to the recurrent bouts of antipopery that would convulse the country in the eighteenth century.

*

It was common knowledge that England was awash with immorality and crime in the 1690s. Preachers, magistrates and moralists agreed that the nation was being engulfed by profanity – a term which covered everything from petty theft to sodomy – and that divine punishment would surely follow. This anxiety (and the phenomena which lay behind it) was a complex matter and one not unrelated to earlier moral panics and campaigns for the reformation of national manners. It can be traced in part to the self-conscious godliness of William and Mary: one of the first measures they took was to order national fasts and issue proclamations for the suppression of vice. Such stern moralism, laced with a healthy dose of providentialism, suited the grim war years of the 1690s. 'What dreadful judgments may we not fear, if we continue unreformed? But if this blessed work of reformation (as we have great hopes) prospers, what blessings may we not expect?'[39] Another cause of the moral panic lay in the determination of urban magistrates, especially in London, to stamp down on the crimes and vices of the poor. Many also attributed the perceived growth in profanity to the Toleration Act. The Act will 'turn half the nation into downright atheism', complained one minister in 1692. 'The mischief is, a liberty now being granted, more lay hold of it to separate from all manner of worship [and] to perfect irreligion' than to go to conventicles. 'Although the Act allows no such liberty, the people will understand it so, and, say what the judges can at assizes, or the justices of the peace at their sessions, or we at our visitations, no constable or churchwarden will present any for not going to church, though they go nowhere else but the alehouse, for this liberty they will have.'[40] Complaints about the abuse of the Toleration Act by those without any religion were to echo down through the eighteenth century.

The Societies for the Reformation of Manners emerged to tackle this moral degeneracy. These societies were composed of laymen intent on prosecuting drunkards, whores, swearers, profaners of the Sabbath, and other offenders in the criminal courts. The societies began in London and soon spread to the provinces: the Bristol Society, founded by the mayor of

Bristol in 1699, met regularly until 1705 to discuss how private citizens and city and parish officials could enforce the laws concerning drunkenness, swearing and Sabbath observance. By 1701 London had about twenty such societies, Edinburgh over a dozen and there were several in Dublin. The London societies distributed blank printed warrants for sympathetic JPs to sign and published long lists of those who had been successfully prosecuted for moral offences: they claimed responsibility for more than one hundred thousand prosecutions over forty-four years. At the same time the societies spread edifying literature about the stews and slums of the city in an attempt to wean the people from vice. The censorious reform societies were complemented by pious groups like the Society for the Propagation of Christian Knowledge, established in 1698, whose aim was to educate the English into religion rather than prosecute them until pure, and the Society for the Propagation of the Gospel which worked overseas. As is often the case with voluntary movements of this sort, the fortunes of the reform societies depended heavily on the enthusiasm of their members and on the local political context. In most cases they attracted more support from Whigs, Low Churchmen and Dissenters than from High Church Tories who resented the cross-denominational nature of the societies and the invasion of what they took to be the church's province of moral regulation. In some towns, the societies were thwarted by High Church hostility, elsewhere the SPCK usurped some of their functions. In 1700 a Chester correspondent of the SPCK reported that 'vice is very rife and public and the Lord's Day sadly neglected'. Although the bishop and aldermen had set up a society to punish immorality, the local magistrates would not act upon information from private individuals. Until the 'ecclesiastical laws are in force,' he concluded, 'all the effect of their punishment would be to drive people to the Dissenters, who . . . are grown very insolent'.[41]

A Church of England Queen

On 25 May 1702, the new Queen assured Parliament that 'I shall be very careful to preserve and maintain the Act of Toleration, and to set the minds of all my people at quiet. My own principles must always keep me entirely firm to the interests and religion of the Church of England, and will incline me to countenance those who have the truest zeal to support it.'[42] Raised as a staunch Anglican under the eye of Bishop Compton, Anne had little time for Dissent and less for popery. She modelled herself on Queen Elizabeth and chose Isaiah 49: 23, on monarchs as the 'nursing fathers' and 'nursing mothers' of the church, as the text for her coronation sermon. For all her limited abilities, poor health, and dependence upon ministers and favourites, Anne did make notable improvements to the Church of England. In 1704 the fund known as Queen Anne's Bounty was established: the crown surrendered its revenues from 'first fruits' – a tax exacted on clerical incomes – so that they could be redistributed to poor clergy. The Fifty New Churches Act of 1711 was designed to tackle the shortage of church space for congregations in London, but had the incidental advantage of paying for some of Nicholas Hawksmoor's finest city churches. These were uncontroversial initiatives by comparison with the aspirations of the more ardent Tory and High Church politicians. To them, the accession of an Anglican queen was an opportunity to launch a campaign against the abuse of the Toleration Act and the actions of Dissenters.

Tory politicians had coerced William III into the recall of Convocation in 1701. Much to Archbishop Tenison's irritation, the Lower House, dominated by the High Church party, gave itself over to the pleasure of debating the theological errors of works like Bishop Burnet's *Exposition of the Thirty-nine Articles* or the outright heresy of Toland's *Christianity Not Mysterious*. Convocation served as a weapon with which Tory politicians could attack the Whig episcopate or Whig parliamentarians, but it also had real potential as a vehicle for a programme of church reform. Tory MPs and High Church divines like Dr Henry Aldrich, prolocutor of the Lower House, now began to coordinate their efforts. Their first target was the hypocritical practice of occasional conformity. In 1702 Henry Sacheverell, an Oxford cleric, preached the first of a series of intemperate and highly publicised sermons on the danger from Dissent and 'these crafty, faithless and insidious persons, who can creep to our altars, and partake of our sacraments' simply to qualify themselves for office. He called on all true churchmen to oppose 'a party which is an open and avowed enemy to our communion' and 'to hang out the bloody flag and banner of defiance'.[43] Such preaching, in tandem with the disturbing case of the nineteen new Dissenting burgesses created at Wilton, provided the impetus behind the 1702 Bill against occasional conformity. This legislation would have swept all occasional conformists from any municipal office or position: some 'thought that this was such a breaking in upon the Toleration as would undermine it, and that it would have a great effect on corporations; as indeed the intent of it was believed to be the modelling elections, and by consequence of the House of Commons'. One moderate Whig concluded that most of the Bill's supporters were most interested in influencing the choice of MPs and 'they are the least concerned about religion'.[44] Whig opposition, and especially the decisive majority of Whigs and bishops in the House of Lords, thwarted this Bill and its successor of 1703. One Anglican clergyman was 'ashamed to think that fourteen bishops should be thought to vote against the apparent interest of the Church of England'.[45] Such obstruction drove the High Church extremists in the Commons to attempt to 'tack' a third Bill to the land tax in 1704. But this expedient was far too controversial to command support even among Tory MPs. Its defeat spelt the end of the Bill and drove a wedge between moderate and High Church Tories.

The following year High Church Tories pressed on with the campaign by proposing a motion that 'the church was in danger'. Sir John Packington argued that danger came from pamphlet attacks on the church and the clergy, the growth of Dissent and Dissenting academies, occasional conformity, and the Kirk (which teaches that episcopacy is against the word of God 'and yet this is the church our princes must now swear to preserve and maintain'). His blustering speech was full of threat: Dissenters abuse the Toleration Act by libelling the church, 'and perhaps it may become this House to let them understand 'tis not to be endured, and to put them in mind that an ill use of liberty is a just cause of abridging it, and when still abused after admonition a just cause of taking it quite away'.[46] Convocation reinforced the campaign with assertions that the church was being betrayed from within by lukewarm bishops, corrupt officials and occasional conformists. In December 1705 the 'church in danger' motion was decisively voted down in Parliament, and the Lords passed a counter-motion that the church had been 'rescued' by William and preserved by Anne so that it 'is now in a most glorious and flourishing condition' and that 'whoever insinuates or suggests that the church is in danger . . . is an enemy to her Majesty, the church and the kingdom'.[47]

Yet the volatile politics of the period and the frequent elections meant that the issue was unlikely to fade. One never knew which party might suddenly gain the upper hand. Or what the consequences might be. Even High Church Tories admitted that some Dissenters 'talk of persecution, they foresee its approaches, and their liberty of conscience they expect will be taken from them'.[48] The Tories naturally claimed that they were aiming only to outlaw occasional conformity, but Dissenters' fears were real enough. So, too, were the concerns of Tories and churchmen that the Whigs were prepared to repeal the Test Act and to open public office to all Protestants. This seemed a real possibility when the Whigs, benefiting from the invasion scare, won a decisive majority in the 1708 general election. Although repeal was not attempted, the Whigs' tolerant tendencies were evident in the 1709 General Naturalisation Act, designed to help the 'poor

Palatines', Protestant refugees from Germany. The Act permitted all foreign immigrants to become naturalised subjects of the Queen if they swore the required oaths and received the sacrament in a Protestant, not necessarily an Anglican, church.

Mutual fear, the provocative views of the extremists on each side, and the turmoil of party politics eventually found an outlet in the Sacheverell affair. In 1709 Henry Sacheverell used a 5 November sermon before the Corporation of London in St Paul's Cathedral to attack the Revolution, the Toleration Act, occasional conformity, and the growth of heresy and schism. This turbulent preacher blamed 'false brethren' for the introduction of every kind of error: 'atheism, deism, tritheism, socinianism, with all the hellish principles of fanaticism, regicide, and anarchy, are openly professed and taught'. Dissenters were 'miscreants begat in rebellion, born in sedition, and nursed in faction'; he vilified ministers and bishops by insinuation. Once printed, the sermon sold like hotcakes. In the Commons, MPs queued to support and to denounce Sacheverell. Mobs cheered him in the streets and crowds flocked to hear him preach. The Whig government decided to make an example of Sacheverell and organised a show trial by impeaching him for his 'wicked, malicious and seditious intention' in aspersing Queen Anne's government, King William's memory, and 'the late happy Revolution'. This was the chance to discredit the myth that 'the church was in danger'. The trial was a huge public event – even the Queen attended incognito – and although Sacheverell was convicted by a majority of seventeen, the mild punishment imposed, and the rapturous welcome he received wherever he went, suggested that the Whigs had lost this round of the battle. Popular feeling had been inflamed: in London 'the mob is up, and have pulled down eight conventicles or meeting houses', reported one diarist; in Devon, a magistrate found 'the country in a ferment'.[49] And for what? From a Whig perspective, Sacheverell was crying up the 'damnable doctrine' of passive obedience and 'whatever cloak the assertors of the danger of the church may put upon their expressions' if they were forced to speak plainly they would be revealed as opponents of the Hanoverian succession or even Jacobites.[50] The High Churchmen, on the other hand, saw their opponents' principles as equally subversive. They complained that Sacheverell's Whig adversary, Benjamin Hoadly, rector of St Peter-le-Poor, 'has raised a great ferment in the nation by his antimonarchical and rebellious principles, which he has preached and published and maintains; he is much applauded and supported by persons of his own way'.[51] While MPs wanted to reward Hoadly, a pro-Sacheverell crowd burned his books in the cathedral close at Exeter. The nation could hardly have been more polarised than it was in the spring of 1710: Tory and Whig, High Churchmen and Low Churchmen represented diametrically opposed views of the country, its religion and its future. 'This damned priest has made all people declare themselves of a party.'[52]

The last of the Stuarts

During 1710, the Queen, advised by Robert Harley, carefully began to reshape the administration. By September, when a general election was announced, Godolphin and many of his allies had stepped down, and the Queen had entrusted the government to Harley and his 'moderate' colleagues. Anne and Harley wanted to secure peace and repair the damage that the war had done to public finances. For this, a more amenable Parliament would be necessary. But all year, Tory politicians had been using the popular response to the Sacheverell trial to precipitate an election: addresses to the crown streamed in from the shires; Sacheverell made a seven-week summer progress around the country; and in October the election swept the Tories to dominance in the Commons. These Tories were a disorderly bunch who espoused diverse and often rather extreme views. They were keen defenders of the Church of England and ready to take the Dissenters down a peg; they wanted an honourable peace and an end to high taxation; some of the more belligerent intended to drive every Whig from public office. And not a few were Jacobites. Neither Harley nor the Queen fully shared the enthusiasms of the new intake of Tory MPs, but the combination of a Tory majority and the new ministry promised that the last years of Anne's reign would see a distinctly Tory tone to government.

The maelstrom of politics in these years owed much to the personalities involved, the quest for a peace, anxiety about the succession, and the contentions within the Tory party. Political life was destabilised by the power struggle between Harley, ennobled in 1711 as the Earl of Oxford, and his lieutenant Henry St John, created Viscount Bolingbroke in 1712. Oxford was the scion of an old puritan family, but it was as much his temperament as his background that made him reluctant to pander to the religious prejudices of the current crop of Tories. However, Bolingbroke, who had few religious convictions and ended up as a Deist, was quite ready to exploit these intolerant High Church Tories to advance his own interest.

Harley and the Queen were determined for the nation's sake to secure a peace, even at the price of some duplicity and the betrayal of Britain's allies, including Hanover. While Marlborough's army menaced Paris, they brought

Louis to the negotiating table and in September 1711 secret peace pre-liminaries were signed between France and Great Britain. The Whiggish House of Lords would not contemplate such a dubious peace and so political deals were done to thwart it: disaffected Tories voted with the Whigs against Harley's peace terms; in return Whig peers helped Nottingham and the Tories finally pass an Occasional Conformity Act which required that conformists took Anglican communion at least three times a year. To help force the peace terms through Parliament the Queen created twelve new peers. Meanwhile Marlborough was replaced as commander-in-chief, the army was told to avoid battle, and formal peace negotiations were opened at Utrecht.

The question of the succession loomed over the peace negotiations as it did over domestic politics. Louis XIV agreed to banish the Pretender from French territory and to recognise the Hanoverian succession. But as that succession came nearer, English Jacobitism seemed to gain in strength. The Tories were divided between Hanoverian and Jacobite groups. Both Oxford and Bolingbroke maintained secret connections with the Pretender's court. Oxford was pragmatically keeping all options open, but Bolingbroke was genuinely inclined towards Jacobitism. When Anne became seriously ill in the new year of 1714, both ministers urged the Pretender to convert to the Church of England. As the Queen's health declined in 1714, there were few who could confidently predict whether the Act of Settlement would be respected.

What of the 'church in danger' and the Tory ambition to bring Dissent to heel? In the intervals between diplomacy and power politics, measures were passed to curb Dissent. In 1712 the General Naturalisation Act of 1709 was repealed and a measure enacted to give Scottish episcopalians a degree of toleration. The 1711 Occasional Conformity Act was reinforced by the Schism Act of 1714, which banned the Dissenting academies. Yet neither of these acts had much real impetus behind them: one was the result of a shabby deal, and the other was promoted by Bolingbroke as a means to unsettle his rival Oxford. The Occasional Conformity Act did lead to the ousting of Nonconformists from municipal government in Bristol and Coventry. Elsewhere Nonconformist aldermen became more discreet about their religious practices. Due to come into force on the day that Queen Anne died, the Schism Act was effectively null and void. Although Convocation met again in 1711 after a three-year hiatus, it was not allowed to become a mouthpiece for a High Church programme. Nor were the leading lights of the High Church party, such as Sacheverell and Swift, appointed to high office in the church; instead a succession of politically moderate men were promoted. The four years of Tory dominance under Harley and Queen Anne were a grave disappointment to the High Church party.

*

God 'has now saved us by a train of wonders', rejoiced the Whig Bishop Burnet on the accession of George I. 'We were, God knows, upon the point of at least confusions, if not of utter ruin, and are now delivered and rendered as safe as any human constitution can be.'[53] George himself was hardly a wonder – fifty-four years old, unable to speak English, honest but dull, preoccupied with the affairs of Hanover and of his dreary entourage. The tone and the image of the monarchy had changed dramatically over the preceding twenty-five years. Party politics would now follow suit. King George had made it plain that he had little time for Tories: a Whiggish ministry was formed; Bolingbroke fled to the Pretender in France; and in the summer of 1715 the Highlands rebelled in expectation of the Pretender and of a reciprocal English Jacobite rebellion. The Pretender arrived late, and the English rising not at all: the Fifteen was undermined by lack of unity and leadership. But the abortive rebellion led to a purge of the Tories from political life. The way was being prepared for single-party government. In 1716 the Septennial Act prolonged the existing Whig parliament for another four years and extended the maximum life of future parliaments to seven years. Between 1718 and 1719 the Occasional Conformity and Schism Acts were repealed and an attempt was made to ensure a permanent Whig majority in the House of Lords. A political world made safe for Whig oligarchy was also a world in which both the Toleration Act and the Church of England would be secure. In Hanoverian Britain religion was no longer to be the combustible political issue that it had been in the seventeenth century.

Notes

1 J. Hoppit, *A Land of Liberty? England 1689–1727* (Oxford, 2000), p. 124.

2 J. Miller, *The Glorious Revolution* (London, 1983), p. 42.

3 H. Horwitz, *Parliament, Policy and Politics in the Reign of William III* (Manchester, 1977), p. 94.

4 G. Holmes and W.A. Speck (eds), *The Divided Society: Party Conflict in England 1694–1716* (London, 1967), p. 135.

5 G. Holmes (ed.), *Britain after the Glorious Revolution, 1689–1714* (London, 1969), p. 137.

6 Hoppit, *Land of Liberty?* p. 129.

7 Holmes and Speck (eds), *Divided Society*, p. 48.

8 C. Kidd, 'Religious Realignment between the Restoration and Union', in J. Robertson (ed.), *A Union for Empire* (Cambridge, 1995), pp. 160–1; C. Kidd, 'Protestantism, Constitutionalism and British Identity under the later Stuarts', in B. Bradshaw and P. Roberts (eds), *British Consciousness and Identity* (Cambridge, 1998), p. 340.

9 G. Holmes, *British Politics in the Age of Anne* (1967; 2nd edn, London, 1987), p. 29.

10 Holmes and Speck (eds), *Divided Society*, p. 19.

11 C. Rose, *England in 1690s: Revolution, Religion and War* (Oxford, 1999), p. 84.

12 Holmes, *British Politics*, p. 57.

13 Holmes, *British Politics*, p. 96.

14 For the split clerical vote in Yorkshire see R. Hall and S. Richardson, *The Anglican Clergy and Yorkshire Politics in the Eighteenth Century* (Borthwick Papers, 94, York, 1998), p. 15.

15 Rose, *England in 1690s*, p. 77.

16 *Diary of Thomas Naish*, ed. D. Slatter (Wiltshire Archaeological Society, 20, Devizes, 1965), p. 46; Holmes, *British Politics*, p. 29.

17 Evelyn, IV, 646; *Letters of Humphrey Prideaux*, ed. E.M. Thompson (Camden Society, new series, 15, 1875), p. 163; Rose, *England in 1690s*, p. 78.

18 Hoppit, *Land of Liberty?* p. 144.

19 Evelyn, V, 233.

20 Rose, *England in 1690s*, p. 52.

21 Hoppit, *Land of Liberty?* p. 110.

22 DWL, Morrice Entering Book Q, p. 367.

23 DWL, Morrice Entering Book Q, p. 364.

24 Gilbert Burnet, *Discourse of Pastoral Care* (1692), sig. A3r.

25 Rose, *England in 1690s*, p. 43

26 T. Harris, *Politics under the Later Stuarts: Party Conflict in a Divided Society 1660–1715* (London, 1993), pp. 156.

27 Harris, *Politics under the Later Stuarts*, p. 153.

28 Evelyn, V, 59.

29 [Francis Atterbury], *Letter to a Convocation Man* (1697), p. 6.

30 Prideaux, *Letters*, pp. 162–3.

31 Evelyn, V, 23.

32 M. Hunter, ' "Aikenhead the Atheist": The Context and Consequences of Articulate Irreligion in the Late Seventeenth Century', in M. Hunter and D. Wootton (eds), *Atheism from the Reformation to the Enlightenment* (Oxford, 1992).

33 *Buckinghamshire Dissent and Parish Life 1669–1712*, ed. J. Broad (Buckinghamshire Record Society, 28, 1993), p. 99.

34 *CSPD 1697*, p. 467.

35 *The Diary of Dudley Ryder 1715–1716*, ed. W. Matthews (1939), p. 233.

36 Ryder, *Diary*, p. 65.

37 Daniel Defoe, *A Tour Through the Whole Island of Britain*, ed. P.N. Furbank and W.R. Owens (New Haven, Conn., 1991), p. 281.

38 S. Jordan, 'Gentry Catholicism in the Thames Valley, 1660–1780', *Recusant History*, 27 (2004), 229.

39 *Proposals for a National Reformation of Manners* (1694), p. 29.

40 Prideaux, *Letters*, p. 154.

41 W.O.B. Allen and E. McClure (eds), *Two Hundred Years: The History of the SPCK 1698–1898* (1898), p. 65.

42 Holmes and Speck (eds), *Divided Society*, p. 26.

43 G. Holmes, *The Trial of Dr Sacheverell* (London, 1973), pp. 51–5.

44 Holmes and Speck (eds), *Divided Society*, p. 119; Holmes, *British Politics*, p. 101.

45 Holmes, *Trial of Dr Sacheverell*, p. 40.

46 W.A. Speck, 'An Anonymous Parliamentary Diary 1705–6', *Camden Miscellany XXIII* (Camden Society, 4th series, 7, 1969), pp. 83–4.

47 *The London Diaries of William Nicholson, Bishop of Carlisle, 1702–1718*, ed. C. Jones and G. Holmes (Oxford, 1985), pp. 324–5.

48 Holmes, *British Politics*, p. 99.

49 Naish, *Diary*, p. 67; *Charges to the Grand Jury 1689–1803*, ed. G. Lamoine (Camden Society, 4th series, 43, 1992), p. 78.

50 *Charges to Grand Jury*, ed. Lamoine, pp. 78–9.

51 Naish, *Diary*, p. 67.

52 *The Correspondence of Sir James Clavering*, ed. H.T. Dickinson (Surtees Society, 178, 1967), p. 73.

53 Holmes and Speck (eds), *Divided Society*, p. 113.

PART TWO

Religion and society

Introduction

The second part of this book describes the social and cultural place of religion in the stormy seventeenth century. Although it is primarily concerned with the 'ordinary people' in the pews and with what religion might have meant to them, it is not simply a portrait of routine practice. As the preceding narrative has amply demonstrated, religious beliefs and fears were a cause of conflict and crisis. So, even as we concentrate upon listening to the undemonstrative majority, the voices of the radicals and dissidents, the zealous conformists, the cantankerous puritans, and the ecstatic sectaries, will keep breaking in – just as they do in the historical sources – and the distracting hubbub of political argument and events will remind us that neither categories such as 'orthodoxy' nor labels such as 'Presbyterian' or 'Arminian' have a fixed meaning, but were and still are subject to debate and redefinition. Above all, we will encounter the sheer diversity of religious experience in the seventeenth century.

The following chapters discuss many themes. They describe the nature and creation of the surviving evidence for seventeenth-century religious practice. They draw attention to the close involvement of the church and the community, to what people actually did in church and to the religious exercises that occupied them outside the church. They describe the dissemination of religious values and doctrines and the institutional structures of the Church of England. The discussion is framed in rather Anglo-centric terms: most of my examples are drawn from England and Wales. Although the different forms taken by social and religious life in Scotland and Ireland should never be overlooked, there are difficulties in synthesising these diverse experiences with the English material within the confines of a fairly short account of this kind.

The nature and the social and cultural roles of religion varied markedly across the territories of the Stuarts. Wales was most closely assimilated to the English model. The Welsh were predominantly adherents of the Church of England, albeit with the one major difference that in Wales the church spoke in the Welsh tongue. The minority tradition of Welsh Protestant Nonconformity preserved a strain of itinerant evanglicalism and a powerful heartfelt piety that would burst forth dramatically in the revival of the 1730s. Irish religious life, on the other hand, was over-whelmingly Roman Catholic. Although some Irish Catholics were more receptive than others to the values and ideals of the Counter-Reformation, the Catholic church provided the rites of passage and sacramental life for the mass of the population. Irish Protestantism took several forms: the English-speaking Church of Ireland was small in numbers and concen-trated in particular areas; Ulster Presbyterianism, mainly of a Scottish origin, had plausible pretensions to operate as the established church in its own heartland. The flow of influences and practices – the Calvinist hue of the Church of Ireland early in the century, the spiritual revivals in Ulster in the 1620s and 1690s, the tensions between the different versions of Presbyterianism, the part played by landowners and immigrants, and the overall context of a colonial society linguistically, religiously, and cultur-ally at odds with the native population – created a rich tapestry of religious life. Lowland Scotland, by contrast, presented a picture of pronounced religious uniformity. Where Presbyterianism held sway, there was little variety in theology, worship or the social role of the Kirk, its ministers and elders. But it was a very different story in the Gaelic-speaking Highlands and Islands. A Gaelic Calvinism did exist, but so, too, did a powerful Celtic version of Roman Catholicism, which was not always to the taste of the Franciscan and other missionaries sent to these remote areas. For all the undoubted interaction between some of these religious communities, most of them developed at their own pace and in response to local, often unique, factors. Few if any of these different forms of piety and religious association can readily be subsumed under the English model. So in view of the political predominance of England within the 'British Isles', the institutionalised and closely observed religious practice of the country, and the sheer wealth of surviving evidence, an investigation focused primarily on English religion is the obvious starting point. And, as we have already noted, seventeenth-century England did not lack for religious experi-mentation, controversy or conflict. It is true that the world depicted in the following pages is largely lost to us, but its clamorous insistence on religious diversity may still speak to the twenty-first century.

CHAPTER 9

The evidence of religion

This chapter introduces readers to the surviving evidence of seventeenth-century religion. As a central activity and belief in most people's lives, religion generated an inordinate amount of heterogeneous material that has found its way into the historical record. Thus historians of religion can explore institutional records at parish and diocesan level, the church books of separatist congregations, architecture and church furnishings, autobiographical memoirs, letters, devotional material, printed sermons and books, and much more besides. Sometimes there is a direct relationship between evidence and belief: personal meditations or private diaries allow us to get close to the significance of religion for specific individuals. More often, what has survived is only indirect evidence of belief. What we can trace is cultural and social behaviour, the evidence of religion as one of the ways of interacting with family, neighbours and officialdom, and we must interpret such material with caution. We always need to take account of the circumstances that produced our evidence. So the second half of this chapter describes the structure and institutions of the Church of England. Understanding the church is the key to understanding the place of religion in early modern England. It was the church's institutions that bound together religion and society, clergy and laity, prescription and practice. The same institutions created the principal records, especially the serial records of visitation returns and ecclesiastical prosecutions, upon which we rely when we investigate popular religion in the seventeenth century.

The evidence of belief and practice

The most intimate and vivid glimpses of religious belief and practice in seventeenth-century Britain are to be obtained from personal writings.

Diaries, autobiographies, letters, and scrapbooks of prayers and devotions survive in large numbers, both in manuscript and printed form, and some of them have become justly famous. Nehemiah Wallington, a melancholic Puritan woodturner from Eastcheap in London, left behind over 2,600 pages of prayers, letters, autobiography, political news, and 'God's judgements upon Sabbath breakers, drunkards, and other vile livers'. And this is only the small surviving proportion of his efforts, just six of the fifty notebooks that he filled in night after night of self-absorbed writing between 1618 and 1654.[1] Yet another, equally astounding, literary feat, Samuel Pepy's diary offers us only a conventional and rather tepid religious life. And who is to say whether Wallington or Pepys speaks for his contemporaries? Such personal revelations are by their nature unusual, even atypical; they depend upon the chance survival of such writings and the exceptional nature of their authors in having the leisure, ability and drive to record their experiences and aspirations.

Diaries and autobiographical writing were new and distinctive features of life in seventeenth-century Britain. Prominent among the possible causes for this development was the Protestant emphasis on introspection. 'Keep always a watch over your precious soul,' one puritan lady advised her son, 'tie yourself to daily self-examination.'[2] The devout Protestant was encouraged to monitor the state of his or her soul for signs of faith and grace, for backsliding towards sin, and for instances of God's mercies and judgment. Sarah Henry wanted to keep 'something in the nature of a diary . . . that I may thereby be furthered in a godly life'.[3] Although this was primarily private work, it was not long before examples of the genre appeared in print. Some were closely allied to the puritan godly biography, others, such as Bunyan's *Grace Abounding to the Chief of Sinners* (1666), were more in the vein of a 'conversion narrative', a long and often psychologically tortured account of how God extended the mercy of saving faith to an unworthy sinner. From the middle of the century the published conversion narrative became more closely identified with the sects: several compilations were published of the 'spiritual testimonies' offered by those joining Baptist or Independent congregations; Quakers published accounts of their own personal spiritual journeys; and radical prophets such as Anna Trapnel, Arise Evans, Abiezer Coppe and John Rogers committed their own struggles and visions to print. Of course, most diaries and autobiographies were not published and they vary according to the personality and preoccupations of their authors. Clergymen were inclined to record their lives in this manner. Some, such as William Laud, Richard Baxter or Philip Henry, were important national figures, others, such as Ralph

Josselin, minister of Earls Colne, Essex, were unremarkable, except for the fact that they left behind them these revealing documents: Josselin's diary covers his whole adult life, and between 1644 and 1664 he made almost daily entries about every conceivable subject – his health, family, dreams, preaching, income, crops, the weather, politics, and any possible sign of divine pleasure or wrath at his own and the nation's progress. The laity, too, recorded their lives. Gentlemen like John Winthrop and Sir Archibald Johnston left autobiographical accounts, as did those on their way up in the world, such as William Stout, a Lancaster Quaker, and Dudley Ryder, a Dissenting law student. Personal accounts by more humble folk, such as the tailor John Dane, the apprentice shopkeeper Roger Lowe, and the Bedfordshire Baptist Agnes Beaumont, have also survived. Nor should we regard this as simply a godly obsession: devout Anglicans such as Alice Thornton and John Evelyn committed the details of their lives and hearts to paper, as did Roman Catholics such as Lucy Knatchbull and Nicholas Blundell. Whether we exploit these writings for their uniquely personal revelations or we read across the genre on the lookout for common assumptions and concepts, for theological, psychological or linguistic patterns, we deepen our understanding of seventeenth-century Christianity.

Yet historians also need to generalise and this is difficult to do on the basis of individual cases. There are several ways in which to take a broader perspective. Traditionally, when historians have sought to assess the nature and depth of popular religious conviction, they have laid much weight on the clergy's views of their flocks. Most ministers were only too willing to offer an opinion of lay piety, and often a rather negative one. Josselin divided his Essex parishioners into those that 'seldom hear' his preaching, 'my sleepy hearers', and 'our society', a small, self-selecting group of the committed godly. Some of his brethren discerned more subtle gradations of religious commitment. Eamon Duffy has drawn attention to Richard Baxter's characterisation of his own parishioners in the Kidderminster of the 1650s.[4] In his tract *Confirmation and Restoration* (1658), Baxter described twelve different categories of parishioners. In this large parish there were 3,000 or 4,000 people (in 800 households), of whom 1,800 were old enough to be communicants. About 500 of these were, in Baxter's words, 'serious professors of religion . . . such as the vulgar call precise'. Another hundred were sincere, knowledgeable Christians of blameless lives. A third group were willing and tractable but 'seem to be ignorant of the very essentials of Christianity': when examined these turn out to be true Christians who are merely 'weak in the faith'. The parish also included sincere Christians whom Baxter could not win over because they remained committed to the banned Church of England. The fifth category was the 'secret heathens' who, while outwardly respectable and orthodox, privately mocked religion. Sixth were those who 'have tolerable knowledge' of Christianity, but live in drunkenness or whoredom or other vices. Seventh were those ignorant of the most basic doctrines, the sort who, although they learned the catechism, were addicted to superstitious errors and relied upon the merit of good works for their salvation. Such as would accept no teaching from Baxter formed the next group who wed 'heathenish ignorance and wicked obstinacy together'. The ninth category were those of tolerable knowledge but vain lives, who opposed Baxter's attempts to restrict access to the communion to the strict professors of religion. The parish also included some 'antinomians' who, misunderstanding the doctrine of predestination, believed that everything is predestined by God and that they could do nothing to effect their own salvation. Category eleven comprised a number of Anabaptists. A handful of papists made up Baxter's final category of parishioners.

Such impressions, however finely graded, are the view of just one individual and not a very dispassionate individual at that. The Protestant clergy as a whole were prone to impose their own values, to focus on failure, on the persistence of apathy, vice, ignorance or even the old ways. In the winter of 1681 on the moors above Wakefield, Oliver Heywood fell in step with the ten-year-old illiterate orphan Thomas Brooks who 'could talk of any worldly things skilfully enough' but knew nothing of Jesus Christ, the Trinity, heaven or hell, or the eternal life, 'nor for what end he came into the world, nor what condition he was born in'.[5] For godly ministers, there had never been enough reformation. In the 1650s, Baxter was still complaining that the 'profane, ungodly, presumptuous multitude are as zealous for crosses and surplices, processions and perambulations, reading of a gospel at a cross way, the observation of holidays and fasting days, the repeating of the Litany or the like forms in the Common Prayer, the bowing at the name of . . . Jesus . . . with a multitude of things which are only the traditions of their fathers'.[6] The congregations seemed incapable of hearing the clergy's message, or, even worse, to be resisting it: 'report to them an human history, tell them some strange news; or a tale for their worldly profit or corporal health; and they will keep it well enough and at any time in any company will relate it very readily: but teach them a mystery of salvation, instruct them in virtue to God or man, they forget it as soon as they have heard it'.[7] In 1655 a Wiltshire cleric complained that the majority of those who bring their children to him for baptism 'hate instruction and are as ignorant of Christianity, I mean of the plainest principles (which they have heard of me I believe a hundred times) as if they had never heard them . . . they seem to be afraid of knowledge lest it should force them upon holiness'.[8]

It is, of course, possible to approach the issue from the opposite direction, to consider the laity's understanding of religion. One route into this terrain is via folklore. 'Unofficial' beliefs about witchcraft, magic, prophecy or astrology, 'folk' practices of healers and charmers, cunning men and witches, and local rituals, celebrations and calendar customs, have been used by scholars, alongside the observations of the 'elite' and the teachings of the church and clergy, to recreate the mental world of the British peasantry and to argue that Protestantism was adapted as it was absorbed.[9] Recently, the cheap printed material of the seventeenth century has also been used to explore popular belief. This genre of 'penny godlies', ballads and broadsides featured pious deathbed scenes, calls to conversion, warnings against sin, and marvellous prodigies and omens, often enlivened with a crude woodcut illustration. This was ephemeral material, pasted on to alehouse walls, passed from hand to hand before fetching up in the privy. But it sold well and consistently across the century; and this commercial success surely indicates that it caught and created popular tastes. Various soundings have been taken: Jenkins mapped the Welsh language materials, Spufford investigated Pepys's collection of ballads and chapbooks, Watt analysed the cheap print trade, and Walsham took a different tack to explore the full range of printed works dealing with the theme of divine providence. In the most ambitious study yet of print and Protestantism, Green has constructed a sample of 727 best and steady sellers (defined as those going through five editions in a thirty-year period) between the 1530s and 1730s.[10] This is an eclectic list of lurid cautionary tales, aids to scripture study, manuals of devotion and edification, dialogues on faith and repentance, and much else. Despite differences in their detailed findings, these scholars have offered some broad conclusions. One is that these truly popular works deal in simple moral lessons about doing good, repenting one's sins, or preparing for a 'good death'. They exhibit some distinctly traditional piety, even some interest in Catholic themes, alongside a formulaic understanding of basic Protestant doctrines such as justification through faith. There is less sign, predictably, of complex theological doctrines such as predestination. Indeed, Calvinism is the only discernible theological emphasis in Green's sample and then only for the period between 1590 and 1640. The Bible was a powerful influence and one that tended to reinforce the common elements of belief rather than inspire unorthodox individual interpretation. Popular religious literature also has to be seen against the background of the cheap print dealing with prodigies and astrology, witches and murders, romance and adventure, gallows speeches and antipopery. In other words, the popular religious beliefs of the seventeenth century were probably a heady combination of the Bible, official teaching, sensationalism and good old-fashioned prejudice. Two changes are particularly evident in religious publishing. One is that the commercial impulses of the booksellers came to replace the ideological zeal of the clergy as the driving force behind the expansion of the market. The other is that religious publishing increasingly concentrated upon providing material suited to the needs of the humbler Christian, the less educated, less wealthy and less spiritually ambitious reader. Inevitably the message reached different strata of the population and different regions at different times. It was only in the later seventeenth century, for example, argues Jenkins, 'that the central doctrines of the Reformation were disseminated intensively in print, in intelligible and popular forms, for the first time in Wales'.[11]

The effect this material had upon its readers is, of course, a separate question. From what was on offer to the laity, Green suggests three broad categories of Protestantism: the orthodox message of the church – albeit with more devotional content than is normally recognised; a subtly different and generally more optimistic version which lays more weight on human abilities and works; and a pretty vacuous version which pays lip service to the Bible and God, but reduces religion to social duty, belief to conduct, and the gospel to a series of threats and warnings. Where we can track the reading of individuals, the picture becomes confusing. Just like modern students, people in the past rarely read what they should have read or in the right order. We know that puritans were reading Catholic works, that Nonconformists had a soft spot for the Anglican poet Herbert, and that many individuals in the later seventeenth century were still reading Elizabethan authors. Richard Baxter began his pious reading with Bunny and Sibbes, one a Protestantised version of a Catholic meditation manual and the other an affecting 1620s preacher, but he moved on. Others never did. Many went no further than the penny godlies and their simple moral messages. The religious attitudes of John Taylor, waterman and hack poet, have been reconstructed from his popular works by Bernard Capp. Taylor saw himself as a good Protestant. The Bible was central to his piety, but he liked the Prayer Book. He admired Calvin and Beza, acknowledged the principle of 'election', and dismissed an Arminian as a 'mongrel papist'; but he believed that people were free to reject saving grace and that good works were inseparable from faith. He hated popery and mocked Catholic doctrines, but believed that the prayers of the faithful could help speed a sinner's soul to heaven.[12]

Fascinating as it is, the evidence from printed material remains suggestive rather than conclusive. Nowadays we yearn for scientific precision. Modern record-keeping and statistics allow us to quantify contemporary religious activity: we can count those who go to church or enrol in various congregations; we can estimate the physical capacity of church buildings, the number of voluntary religious societies, the value of donations, and the number of missions at home and abroad; and we can take polls about religious convictions.[13] In its own fashion, the seventeenth century attempted to do the same.

*

Seventeenth-century religious belief and behaviour can be quantified, if only in a fairly rough-and-ready manner, from several sources. The churchwardens of each parish kept accounts of money received and spent on the church and its activities. These accounts survive in abundance: there may be as many as 750 sets in existence around England and Wales, although they are more likely to be the accounts of a fairly wealthy urban parish than of a rural backwater. Wales contained 7 per cent of the English and Welsh parishes, but the surviving Welsh churchwardens' accounts represent less than 1 per cent of those known to have survived.[14] Occasionally, these accounts of parish life can be supplemented by a report on the condition of the local churches drawn up at the behest of the bishop or the archdeacon. Some of these reports were undertaken on the orders of the archbishop, but more often they were the personal and local initiative of a particular official. They tended to concentrate upon the practicalities: the physical state of the church buildings, the finances of the parish, responsibility for various local duties, whether the 'terrier' – a survey of the glebe or lands attached to the clergyman's position – was up to date, and so on. In 1602 Archbishop Whitgift ordered a survey of the fabric of the churches and this may have inspired a boom in repairing and beautifying churches. Similar surveys were conducted in various dioceses later in the century, sometimes in association with visitations and sometimes as a free-standing venture: the inspections conducted by clergymen in the archdeaconry of Lewes in 1686 did not follow preordained questions but simply listed defects.[15] A more standardised procedure was adopted in the early eighteenth century when Bishop Wake of Lincoln began to issue questionnaires to his clergy on the state of the churches and parish life. Administratively more efficient than relying upon the churchwardens and the machinery of visitation (which is described later in this chapter), this practice spread widely across the dioceses and resulted in a series of bishops' *Notitiae* or *Specula* – detailed reports of the state of the parishes covering everything from endowments and almshouses to resident gentry and numbers of Easter communicants.

Surprisingly, perhaps, the established church took national surveys of religious commitment from time to time. In the summer of 1603 the parish clergy were asked to provide their bishops with 'the certain number of those that do receive the communion in every several parish', and the numbers of male and female non-communicants and recusants. Astonishingly, the returns suggested that there were only 8,600 'recusants' as against 2.3 million communicants: the whole exercise was probably vitiated by poor data and the tendency of diocesan officials to confuse recusants and non-communicants.[16] Where they are most trustworthy, the figures suggest that 2 per cent or less of potential communicants were dissidents from the Church of England. The situation over the following decades is obscure. John Morrill has made a shrewd guess that even in the 1640s the number of those who went somewhere other than their parish church was less than 5 per cent. Of course, the religion on offer in the parish church of the 1640s could have been very different from that of the Church of England. But it need not have been. Two-thirds of parish clergy were not disturbed in their ministry between 1640 and 1660. After the Restoration the Anglican hierarchy took great pains to ascertain the precise size of the Catholic and Nonconformist communities, launching statistical enquiries in 1665, in 1669 when the information gained was probably used to argue for the Conventicle Act, and most comprehensively in 1676. The so-called Compton Census of 1676 has been reconstructed by Anne Whiteman who, while regarding it as a genuine attempt to gain accurate information, was wary of many of the figures it threw up. Based on the earlier enquiries, the Compton Census asked each incumbent for (1) the number of inhabitants in the parish, (2) the number of popish recusants, known or suspected, in the parish, and (3) the number of 'other Dissenters . . . (of what sect soever) which either obstinately refuse or wholly absent themselves from the communion of the Church of England at such times as by law they are required'. The returns suggest that the proportion of non-Anglicans in the national population was around 4 per cent. The diocesan returns of Catholics vary between 0.1 per cent and 1.67 per cent of the diocese's population. The proportion of Dissenters in each diocese varies between 0.8 per cent and 10.6 per cent of the diocesan population, but is below 5 per cent in most dioceses.

The Compton Census nicely illustrates the difficulty of defining meaningful categories in such surveys. What, after all, was a 'Dissenter' in this context? In some cases it was obvious. Carlson has shown how local records can pinpoint the individuals behind the Compton Census figures: Great Abington, Cambridgeshire, returned a figure of six Dissenters and diocesan court records identify these as Thomas Amye, his wife Mary and daughter Margaret, the Quaker widow Mary Smith and her son Robert, and Joan Barker.[17] But many ministers were unsure who to include and were confused by the third question of the census. 'If by this last expression be meant joining in the public worship with the congregation in hearing the prayers of the church in the parish church on the Lord's Day' then there was not above fifty of the 1,200 adult parishioners of St Lawrence in Thanet who 'wholly absent themselves from the church but if by communion be meant the holy sacrament of the Lord's Supper then our answer is that there are not two hundred that receive the holy sacrament once in a year and not one hundred persons that receive thrice in a year as is so commanded by the Canons. For though the most part of the said 1,200 come constantly to the church to prayers and sermon yet few of them will be induced to receive the communion by any arguments or persuasions.'[18] As Whiteman and others have observed, the 'partial conformity' that was so prevalent in the Restoration period, with many going to church on Sunday morning and to the conventicle in the afternoon, undermines the apparent clarity of the census's finding that 4.2 per cent of the population were Dissenters. In the later seventeenth century census statistics can be supplemented by other data from the hearth tax or the licences issued under the 1672 Indulgence Act or the 1689 Toleration Act. A study of Warwickshire in the 1680s finds that out of a population of 37,000, 6 per cent or 2,200 were Catholics and between 11 and 13 per cent (4,000 to 5,000) were Dissenters, these can be further broken down into 500 Baptists, 900 Quakers and between 2,600 and 3,500 Presbyterians and Independents.[19] When early-eighteenth-century bishops made enquiries, the returns were more impressionistic: in 1706 the parish of Buckingham contained 800 families, and 'some few Dissenters, who are Presbyterian and have a meeting house within the parish', and 'four reputed Papists'.[20] The most exhaustive count of Nonconformist congregations was made by the Nonconformists themselves between 1715 and 1718. It established the existence of 1,845 congregations and this in turn implies a total of 338,000 Dissenters out of a national population of 5.4 million.[21] At this date the Roman Catholic community is put at about 60,000, but that figure obscures some difficulties of definition.

Measuring the numbers of non-Anglicans was only one problem. Things were not much easier when it came to assessing the level of commitment among conformists to the Church of England. One measure, as the Compton Census suggests, might be the number of eligible parishioners who received the sacrament. Yet the evidence about the sacrament is patchy and inconclusive. Churchwardens' accounts often record the money spent on bread and wine for communions and sometimes detail the volume of wine purchased or the different seasons of the year at which communions were celebrated. From some urban parishes, there survive documents called variously Easter Books, Rate Books, Tithe Books and Token Books, which sometimes record the names or numbers of communicants. Churchwardens distributed tokens to parishioners in return for a fee or 'communion due' (which seems to have been about six pence in the early seventeenth century): the tokens were then handed back at the Easter communion table so that the churchwardens would know whether those who attended the communion had paid their dues. Since in city parishes the Easter communion often took the form of a staggered series of services to allow space and time for all of the communicants to receive, the token system allowed the churchwardens to chase up those who were dragging their feet over making their communion.[22]

Church court records are far more abundant than Easter Books and have been used to calculate rates of regular attendance at church and even rates of reception of the sacrament. Clarke suggested an attendance rate of 80 per cent in late-sixteenth-century Kent, while some Chester parishes had attendance rates of between 60 and 80 per cent in the late sixteenth century and only 50 per cent in the late 1630s. Calculations of this kind are based on the number of parishioners reported to the church courts for not attending weekly services or not receiving the sacrament. But these figures are not always straightforward. Between 1570 and 1600 the churchwardens of Terling in Essex reported thirty-one parishioners for failure to receive communion, and in the first three decades of the seventeenth century there was an even larger number of prosecutions from the parish for failure to attend church. As Wrightson and Levine stress, these prosecutions were the work of a group of parish zealots under the leadership of two puritan ministers. Something similar lay behind the 114 presentations for not receiving which were made from the Kent town of Cranbrook between 1560 and 1607.[23] The Laudians, too, used the church courts to harry those who failed to attend their parish church or to take communion. All that we can be certain of is that those who absented themselves were at odds with the version of religion they were being offered by these particular activists. To establish a norm against which to measure them we would need a vast survey of the number of presentations for non-attendance and non-reception from a large sample of parishes: this has not yet been done, but Marchant's fundamental work on the diocese of York suggests that Terling and Cranbrook are far from typical.[24] Even then, the figures would only tell us about the number of prosecutions made by church-wardens. Such figures cannot indicate the scale of residual antipathy or apathy towards the church or religion among early modern English people.

The institutions of the Church of England

The Church of England was the only institution with a presence in every English and Welsh community in the seventeenth century: it offered a national service that embraced the entire population from the cradle to the grave. Yet, as we shall see, it was a far from uniform organisation. As the church had evolved over several centuries, it developed regional diversities and acquired anomalous and idiosyncratic structures. One important explanation for these irregularities was the church's close involvement in secular life. As a political and administrative machine the church was exploited and distorted by the demands of royal, noble and civic author-ities. The church offered career opportunities to bureaucrats, lawyers, scholars and those skilled in property management, as well as individuals with a calling to the religious life. The church was one of the kingdom's largest landholders. Bishops, deans, cathedral chapters, university colleges or churches owned estates, buildings and moveable goods, and were inevitably sucked into close relations with the property-owning laity. In the seventeenth century individuals high and low exercised property rights over church lands and buildings or even had a stake in the appointment of a particular clergyman or in the tithe income that he drew from his parish-ioners. As a consequence of this and other factors, such as local bureau-cratic tradition, the Church of England's institutional arrangements were of baffling complexity and are still only partially recorded and understood. Geographically, its units of government were irrational: parishes and dioceses varied widely in size and wealth; and there was a strange patch-work of anomalous jurisdictions – known as 'peculiars' or 'liberties' – which were outside the authority of the local bishop. Such matters fascinate historians whose challenge it is to master the peculiar details of a particu-lar diocese or cathedral, but here our need is to present a clear set of definitions, to lay bare the bones of the church's institutional arrangements without explaining every discrepancy and exception.

The primary unit of the church in the seventeenth century was the parish. The reality of seventeenth-century parishes is the subject of the next chapter, but a good rule of thumb is that few parishes match our expectations. Some did neatly coincide with the natural boundaries of the local community, but others were sprawling areas that embraced several villages, each with its own chapel, while at the other extreme, in the big cities like Norwich and London, a parish might comprise just a few alleyways and tenements. Each parish was under the spiritual care of a clergyman who was known as the incumbent. A parish was also referred to as a clergyman's 'living' or 'benefice'. Parishioners paid 'tithes' to support their parish minister. Clergymen were known by several titles: theologically they were 'priests', but that term was shunned because of its Roman Catholic overtones, so they were popularly known as 'ministers', 'divines' or even 'pastors'; technically, they were the 'rector' of a parish if they received all of the tithes or other revenues paid by that parish. In the seventeenth century a rector was also called a 'parson' (although nowadays 'parson' simply means a member of the clergy). The title of 'vicar' had a more restricted meaning. It arose from the medieval practice of 'appropriating' parish churches to institutions such as monasteries which received the parish tithes. In return the monastery sent one of its monks to perform the duties of the rector; in Latin this substitute for the rector was 'vicarius', hence vicar. One-third of the tithes was set aside to support the vicar – these were the vicarial or small tithes – while the rest of the tithes, the rectorial or great tithes, were reserved for the monastery. The great tithes were usually corn, hay and wool, while the small tithes were composed of all other produce. When Henry VIII dissolved the monasteries, the rectors' tithes were granted to laymen. These laymen were said to have 'impropriated' the tithes, so they were described as 'lay impropriators' or 'lay rectors'. The rector's tithes were far more valuable than the vicar's or small tithes, indeed, in most seventeenth-century parishes, the small tithes were not a living wage. Thus the struggle for control of the tithe income of a parish living was often a serious business with vital financial consequences for both clergy and laity.[25]

As a parish minister, the clergyman who was a vicar had exactly the same spiritual status as the clergyman who was a rector. Legally, the rector or vicar held the freehold of the church, the churchyard, the vicarage house and the glebe (the parcel of farmland attached to the vicarage). In this period, the title 'curate' was used of clergymen without their own benefice who were appointed to assist or to stand in for a vicar or rector. This was usually because the incumbent was a pluralist. 'Pluralism' was the practice of allowing a clergyman to hold two or more benefices, provided that the parishes were no more than thirty miles apart, and he supplied a curate to perform his duties in the parish where he did not reside. Pluralism was often necessary where the income from a single parish was insufficient to support a clergyman: it was a recurrent grievance. Critics complained of Welsh clergy 'pinched with poverty and forced to officiate in three or four parishes and therefore cannot pretend to do well in either' so that the children go uncatechised and the congregation lacks sermons.[26] An 'advowson' was the right of patronage, that is, the right to present or appoint a clergyman to a benefice. This right of presentation was treated as a piece of property in the seventeenth century and was often owned by laymen or institutions. A gentleman might value this as a way of ensuring the preferment of his second or third son to a comfortable parish living, or a college in one of the universities could use this as a means to reward a member of the college who wished to marry or leave the academic life.

Parishes were grouped into dioceses under the authority of a bishop. Bishops had oversight of the clergy, parishes and parishioners in their dioceses. The office of bishop was a special calling as bishops alone exercised two significant spiritual powers: they had the power to 'ordain' or confer 'holy orders', that is, to make someone a deacon and then a full priest; and they had the authority to excommunicate sinners, that is, to exclude them from participation in the sacraments and the life of the church. There were nineteen medieval dioceses in England and four more – Llandaff, St David's, Bangor and St Asaph – in Wales. Henry VIII had created the additional dioceses of Bristol, Peterborough, Gloucester, Oxford and Chester. The dioceses (also known as sees) differed in size, wealth and prestige. The see of Durham was a virtual principality, Lincoln covered a huge swathe of England from London up to the Humber, while Bristol and Gloucester were small and impecunious, and the impoverished Welsh dioceses were regarded as little better than a poisoned chalice by those unlucky enough to be nominated to them by the King. The most ambitious hoped to work their way up from a small see to one of the plum jobs. All of the bishops had a seat in the House of Lords and could expect political service to earn them further recognition. Although the church was divided into the northern and southern provinces, each led by its archbishop or 'metropolitan' and each with its own clerical convocation or parliament, the Archbishop of York acknowledged the primacy of the Archbishop of Canterbury.

The size of these dioceses was an impediment to the bishop's pastoral oversight. The diocese of York, for example, contained 903 parishes and chapelries, served at the end of the century by more than 700 clergy. Sixteenth-century reformers had campaigned for smaller dioceses in which real supervision would be possible: Knox suggested that there should be ten times the number of bishops and a similar proposal was made in the Elizabethan Parliament. But such radical – and expensive – reform was not pursued. Bishops remained rather too obviously 'princes of the church' along medieval lines and their critics jeered at them as 'prelates'. Bishops relied upon their archdeacons to help them supervise their dioceses. Most dioceses were divided into several archdeaconries. Lincoln contained seven archdeaconries, although Ely diocese was just one. York was divided into the four archdeaconries of York, Cleveland, the East Riding and Nottingham, and each of these was further divided into three or four deaneries. Ecclesiastical boundaries had no relation to any other units. Chichester diocese was unusual in being coterminous with a county: the diocese was divided between two archdeaconries and these were subdivided into four rural deaneries. Each of these units covered a number of parishes: the archdeaconry of St Albans in the diocese of London, for example, contained twenty-six parishes. As we will see, dioceses were governed by a system of reporting up from the parish level to the dean or archdeacon and thence up the chain to the bishop.

There were many complications and exceptions to this general picture. It often seems that every diocese or archdeaconry contained small enclaves, often no more than a few parishes, where a different bishop or archdeacon exercised jurisdiction. There were other pockets of territory that were exempt from the authority of the local bishop. These were the 'peculiars', those parishes subject to other jurisdictions for historical or technical reasons. In Wiltshire, for example, there were forty-five parishes within ecclesiastical peculiars. Most of these were under the jurisdiction of the dean of Salisbury whose authority extended over a total of seventy parishes in four counties.[27] Some peculiars were previously associated with monasteries which had, since the Reformation, become the responsibility of cathedrals or minster churches. The jurisdiction of Southwell Minster, for example, covered twenty-four neighbouring parishes that were all therefore exempt from the bishop's authority. The nature of cathedrals and other 'collegiate churches' needs a word of explanation.

Cathedrals were independent institutions, governed under their own statutes by a dean and chapter of canons or prebendaries, and often wary of the claims of the local bishop who usually had his seat in the same church. There were twenty-two such institutions in the seventeenth century and they varied in size, structure and wealth. Some, such as

St Paul's in London, Salisbury, Exeter and Lincoln, were governed according to their medieval statutes, others, such as Canterbury, Winchester and Durham, had housed monastic communities and were refounded by Henry VIII, while elsewhere Henry established cathedrals in newly created dioceses. The staff of a cathedral included the dean and a number of prebendaries (clergymen who received an income from an endowment attached to their seat or 'stall' but who often lived elsewhere as parish ministers), residential and non-residential canons, singing men, choristers, organists, vergers and other functionaries. In many ways the cathedrals were a remnant of the medieval church, a reminder of the monasteries and other churches that had existed to offer up masses and prayer, which now had to adapt to the new post-Reformation conditions and to a new function as centres for preaching and as beacons of Protestantism. Unsurprisingly, some of them were slow to adjust and, while adopting the Prayer Book, they preserved a richer liturgical practice than was to be found in most parish churches; MacCulloch has referred to them as a 'liturgical fifth column within the Elizabethan church'. Westminster Abbey was a particularly important example, given its metropolitan location and the long protection it enjoyed from reforming zeal, thanks to the Cecil family and its conservative dean, William Goodman; later both Lancelot Andrewes and Richard Neile served as the Abbey's dean, and in this way a tradition of ceremonialism was kept alive and passed on to the Laudians.[28] Other cathedrals, such as Durham and Norwich, also played a significant part in preserving the traditions of ceremony, beauty and sacred music that were generally so alien to the worship of the parish churches. The gorgeous vestments, luxurious fabric, thunderous organs, and melodious choirs – Norwich had a minimum of five basses, five tenors and five countertenors – presented a ravishing spectacle: some were alarmed by the 'cringing' and 'fawning', the apparent superstition and idolatry on display; others, like the dean and chapter of Chester, were simply concerned that 'when full services and anthems are sung few of those who are either not skilled in music or have not copies' can participate in worship and be edified – their solution was to order 'verse services' and 'hymns . . . sung in the ordinary chanting tune which all who frequent cathedrals may easily learn a part in'.[29]

Given their ostentation and their religious functions, cathedrals might easily serve as the butt of popular ridicule or animosity. There were, no doubt, many obscure episodes like the New Year Day 'profaned' at Ely when the citizens 'made a great noise and disturbance . . . by the roasting of a cat tied to a spit' on the cathedral green.[30] More is usually known about the perennial conflicts between cathedral dignitaries and civic authorities. As the Jacobean mayor of Exeter put it, the problem was simply that of 'two masters in one house'.[31] Touchy cathedral clergy took umbrage at invasions of the sanctity of the cathedral close; there were countless squabbles over the symbols of authority, from civic authorities carrying maces and erect swords within the cathedral, to the collection of taxes or the arrest of clergymen within the precincts. Clearly much of this was to do with asserting status and defending political or legal privileges, but it is often impossible to separate religious motives from such quarrels: a long-running dispute in Jacobean Chester about the city sergeant's sword was at least in part a result of the bishop's suspicion of the puritanism of many of the citizens. Disputes about precedence in processions or seating were a feature of the entire century, and it is not unrealistic to see them as being fomented by both clerical and civic sides as part of broader campaigns to assert or deny particular views of the proper religious life of the community or the authority of the clergy. Yet cathedrals remained important places of public resort and display: citizens would saunter in the aisles on a Sunday or holy day; and after death the more substantial of them would be commemorated in those same aisles by ever more elaborate brasses, plaques, effigies or monuments.

*

A visitation was an enquiry into the state of the church and the morals and manners of the laity and clergy. A medieval practice that was reinvigorated by the Elizabethan bishops and enshrined in the 1604 canons, visitation was the routine form of government of the Church of England in the seventeenth century. The churchwardens were obliged to 'present' or report offenders and offences in their parish. They were supplied with a book of 'visitation articles' specifying the faults that were to be reported and they could themselves be prosecuted if they neglected their duty. The churchwardens were to present those suspected of 'adultery, whoredom, incest, drunkenness, swearing, ribaldry, usury and any other uncleanness and wickedness of life'; those who did not receive the holy communion, who behaved indecently or disorderly in church, and schismatics (those who had separated from the communion of the church). Parish ministers were charged with reporting 'recusants'. The churchwardens were required to report on the officials of the church from the minister down to the clerk and sexton, on the schoolmaster, the midwives and the parishioners, on the fabric and furnishings of the church, and occasionally on such issues as the patron and the value of the benefice. Although visitation articles tended to follow a predictable pattern, they might be varied to suit circumstances or preoccupations: in 1613 Archdeacon Johnson of Leicester issued articles which were obsessed with 'the infection of recusancy being the very fruit and badge of antichristian irreligion' and a national danger.[32]

The churchwardens made their reports twice a year – in some dioceses four times a year – to the archdeacon. The churchwardens attended in person at a specified church and took their oath. Their verbal responses to the articles were noted down by the archdeacon's officials. Visitations by the bishop were more infrequent. A bishop visited the whole diocese on his appointment and was then expected to visit the diocese every third year when he was also supposed to confirm those who had been prepared to receive the communion. The reality varied with the commitments and diligence of individuals. Some seventeenth-century bishops delegated the task, a few were negligent, but not even the most dynamic, such as Bishop Compton of London, could visit every parish church every three years. Compton was, however, an exemplary and thorough visitor by any standard: his visit to Tottenham parish church on 20 July 1685 led to the order that 'a third lock be put on the chest and the register books to be kept in it. A new Bible and new common prayers, books of articles, canons, and book to register strange preachers to be bought. The covering of the steeple to be repaired; the communion table to be railed in.'[33] The printed visitation articles issued by individual bishops were regarded as significant in setting the tone and priorities of their episcopate. They could announce a particular ecclesiastical policy and have been used by historians to track anti-puritan, Arminian, ceremonialist and other initiatives. The presentments made in response to such articles often revealed the scale of the task confronting the bishop or the success of his policy.

Episcopal and archidiaconal visitations were the backbone of church government in the seventeenth century: although official concerns changed over time, and the system was in abeyance during the 1640s and 1650s, the machinery creaked on. Admittedly, this was an imperfect machine. It depended, as did all government, on a host of imponderables, the right people turning up, finding the keys to the church, the weather and the roads. It relied upon the churchwardens who were notorious for replying *omnia bene* – all is well – for fear of the disruption that might be caused by reporting their neighbours' offences or faults in the parish church. To judge from the many defects and failings that were reported, the system did not attain its goals, but it was perhaps the best that could be managed. To historians, the system has bequeathed a wonderful fund of evidence. Where full returns survive, they afford a vivid picture of ordinary life. The parishes of the archdeaconry of Chichester, for example, were troubled by drunks, illegitimate children, errant neighbours, negligent ministers: the presentments reveal 'a popish schoolmaster who is also suspected to baptise and do other offices of a priest' in Midhurst; John Sanders the sidesman of Arundel who was 'most shamefully drunk and most swinishly vomiting in the midst of the town'; and little personal tragedies such as John Wood's wife who 'is distempered in her brains and almost lunatic' and so no longer comes to church as she did 'before she fell into this grief'. From a parish in Ely diocese we learn of David Scott 'making it his common practice to sleep in time of divine service and sermon'.[34] He was not alone in this habit.

Most of this was, of course, also evidence in the legal sense. Presentments were the first step in bringing offenders and offences before the church courts.[35] These courts were a familiar part of everyday life. The archdeacon's court sat regularly, perhaps every few weeks, as did the bishop's court, also known as the Consistory Court, which had jurisdiction over the diocese. Above the bishop's court were the provincial courts of Canterbury and York and above these were the Courts of Arches and Audience and, ultimately, the Court of Delegates, a royal tribunal that effectively filled the void left by Henry VIII's ban on taking appeals to the pope. Archdeacons' and bishops' courts were often presided over by lay 'chancellors', 'principals' or 'surrogates' and were staffed by various lay personnel – registrars, clerks and apparitors or messengers. The lawyers who appeared before these courts were known as proctors. The church courts followed the principles of canon law – a quite distinct system from that of the secular law – and their procedure produced a distinctive legal experience. Cases were decided by the judge and progressed through a series of stages in which most of the evidence was written. This was a lawyer-friendly system and an expensive one since fees were attached to most of a case's many stages. While cases heard in the secular courts of the Quarter Sessions and Assizes were dispatched in an hour or two and recorded in terse formulae, cases before the church courts had many hearings and generated a mass of paperwork in both Latin and English, which, although technically complex, difficult to decipher and often physically dispersed, remains a treasure trove of historical evidence.

The church courts were not concerned with matters that would now be considered criminal and their sanctions did not extend to life, limb or property. Their business fell into three broad categories. The first was the essential but purely administrative matters of granting probate on wills and issuing marriage licences. The second was made up of 'instance' cases:

these were brought by one party against another, generally about such matters as defamation, matrimony and tithes, and they were generally dealt with by the full or 'plenary' procedure. Plenary procedure had several stages: the case was set out in a 'libel'; depositions or responses were required to each of the allegations; each party could pose 'interrogatories' to witnesses, and then further 'exceptions' and 'informations'; finally, a judgment was reached by the court, a penalty imposed, costs fixed, and time allowed for any appeal. Not all cases progressed through these stages. It is likely that the length and expense of the system was an incentive to early settlement. The third category of business was the 'office' cases. These were cases 'for the reformation of morals and the soul's benefit' brought against individuals by the court, often on evidence supplied by the churchwardens' presentments or the clergy. They tended to be 'disciplinary' or 'correction' cases involving the drunkards and sleepers in church, the unmarried mothers and wayward fathers, and the absentees from church, although they might also touch on the provision of services by the minister or the use of vestments. The procedure was often summary. The presentment was read to the defendant and the response noted. There were no witnesses and not much written record, but a decision was reached speedily and a penalty issued.

The church courts had a limited range of penalties. The culprit could be admonished to behave better or a penance could be imposed. A public penance required the penitent to appear in the parish church, barefoot and dressed in a white sheet, holding a candle or a white wand, and to acknowledge their fault, ask God's forgiveness, and request the prayers of the congregation. A private penance required the same acknowledgement to be made but in the presence of the minister and the churchwardens rather than the whole congregation. Performance of a penance had to be certified by the minister and reported to the court. It was often possible to commute a penance to a money payment. The most serious penalty that a church court could impose was excommunication. Theoretically, this deprived the individual of the sacraments of the church, access to the law, and all social dealings with his or her neighbours. Yet excommunication was imposed widely and – as many thought – inappropriately by lay officials in trivial cases. A significant proportion of the population was excommunicate at any one time: there were 377 excommunicates in the archdeaconry of Stowe in 1664; one authority estimated that 5 per cent of the population could be excommunicate. Although most probably did make their peace with the church, there were some who, out of stubbornness or religious principle, did not submit. Some refused to accept their exclusion and would turn up at church anyway and disrupt the service. In 1625 the wardens of Coldwaltham had reached the end of their tether with Richard Hale who had repeatedly been returned as an excommunicate: we 'know not what course to take; therefore we pray you to take a course with him'. Keeping track of who was excommunicated and who absolved was a headache for officials. In 1608 George Chapman was reported for saying in the church in time of service that he 'would the churchwardens had kissed his arse for coming to him to know whether he had his absolution whither [so that] he might come to church'.[36] In the second half of the century the church sought to improve the efficacy of excommunication by restricting its use, but by then the rise of Nonconformity had also undermined the penalty: as one MP observed, it 'was of no force at all with some men, especially those that did willingly absent themselves from the church'.[37]

Only a fraction of the material produced by the church courts during the seventeenth century has survived, and only a part of that fraction has been explored by historians, but it has proved to be of immense value. Each successive generation of historians has used these records to illuminate a different aspect of the past. Initially the church courts were studied as a way of assessing the efficiency of the church's administration. They were also used to explore the church's treatment of dissident puritans and Nonconformists. Several scholars echoed the puritan perception of the ecclesiastical courts as oppressive, vexatious and unpopular. However social historians came to a different conclusion. Exploiting the court records for their evidence of popular religion, sexual morality and gender relations, which were prominent themes in, for example, matrimonial and defamation suits, they saw the courts working 'with the grain' of the community. They stressed that for many in the seventeenth century the church courts were a usable, accessible, local means of reconciling quarrels, bringing errant spouses and neighbours to heel, or resolving property disputes. In time this picture too will be refined as more studies demonstrate that the church courts appealed to some social groups more than others and chart the changing nature of business in the courts across the century. It is clear that the enforcement of religious conformity declined in the courts in the second half of the century – partly because it was pursued in the secular courts under the Clarendon Code and partly as a result of greater religious freedom – but in the York courts there was an increase in defamation suits. In the courts of Durham and York, the correction cases against adultery dwindled away, again in part because alternative mechanisms now existed to deal with adulterers.[38] As the seventeenth century progressed the focus of the church courts' activities changed, and their ability to enforce their decisions and buttress the national church declined, but they did not lose their relevance to society.

*

The parish minister must be taken into account both as a powerful influence on much of the evidence of early modern religion and as the obvious representative of the institutional church in most communities. The minister made his own returns to the archdeacon and no doubt shaped those of the churchwardens. Clerical correspondence and publications often epitomise the religion of the flock and the success or otherwise of the individual's ministry. The minister was the point of contact between the national institution of the church and the grass-roots community: it was his function to reconcile the imperatives of the bishops and monarchs with the interests and expectations of villagers and townspeople. It was usually a balancing act. The clergyman was a member of a specific social group, marked out in the community by his distinctive dress and behaviour, his educational background, his clerical network, his income and, of course, his pastoral and preaching duties. On the one hand, he was set apart from the community by his sacred function and yet, on the other, if he was to be effective and popular he needed to be well integrated with his neighbours. He had much in common with his neighbours. Many clergymen were married, with children and dependents, and many were part-time farmers of their glebe or had a vested interest in local agriculture because it underpinned their tithe income.

The anomalous position of the parish clergy was built into their pastoral duties. Although preaching was vital, other duties were just as important. The good pastor was an adviser and counsellor, a catechist and conciliator. He taught by his personal example and through fireside chats. Contemporary discussions of the effective pastor stress this all-round communal role. Some of the most eloquent tributes come from the parishioners who had enjoyed such a ministry. In 1605 the Lincolnshire minister John Maltby received a glowing testimonial as 'a great friend to the poor and very charitable to all: a painful peacemaker amongst all men: civil and sober in his conversation, wise in government, of a very honest life and carriage'. He eked out his 'small stipend' to buy books so that he was 'not inferior to many in his calling'. 'We receive great comfort daily from him . . . in comforting the sick both poor and rich very painful: doing always what good he can to all: hurting none, worthy to be beloved, and is in our town and country very well beloved.'[39] In 1662 a Cambridgeshire minister was given a clean bill of health by his parish: he 'baptises and catechises as is commanded, advises them that are troubled in conscience to look out for comfort; goes the perambulations yearly and abstains from mechanical trades'.[40]

The clergy of the Church of England enjoyed some of the attributes of a modern profession. The ministry was a largely graduate-entry career with a single career ladder and a national job market.[41] But the modern parallel will only stretch so far. If he was a rector the minister owned his benefice. He was not paid a salary nor did he depend upon fees for services rendered. His parishioners were legally obliged to contribute to his upkeep through their tithes. This both ensured his independence – it was often alleged that those sectarian ministers who were supported by the voluntary contributions were in thrall to the whims of their congregations – and guaranteed the animosity of those parishioners who were either dissatisfied with his performance or members of some other denomination. Urban clergy, however, were less independent since tithes had often been converted to a fixed cash payment. The clergy had a strong corporate identity. Since all graduate clergy had been trained at the universities of Oxford or Cambridge, they were able to exploit the networks created through colleges and their extensive patronage systems. In some cases, a group of ministers trained in one college might gravitate to one county. Other routes to preferment were opened by service to bishops, nobles and gentry. Familial ties were probably the most important factor. Frequently described as the 'tribe of Levi', many of the clergy were the sons and grandsons of clergymen. Clerical dynasties spread across society. William Coe, a minor Suffolk gentleman in the late seventeenth century, provides just one example: he was great-grandson of the Archdeacon of Norfolk, grandson to the registrar of the Archdeacon of Sudbury; two of his aunts married Suffolk clergymen, and a third married an ejected Presbyterian minister, and his sister married the rector of Tuddenham. In this most concrete sense, the clergy of seventeenth-century England were fully integrated into contemporary society.

Notes

1 P. Seaver, *Wallington's World: A Puritan Artisan in Seventeenth-century London* (Stanford, Calif., 1985).

2 *Letters of Lady Brilliana Harley*, ed. T.T. Lewis (Camden Society, old series, 68, 1854), p. 69.

3 P. Crawford, *Women and Religion in England 1500–1720* (London, 1993), p. 93.

4 E. Duffy, 'The Godly and the Multitude in Stuart England', *17C*, 1 (1986).

5 Heywood, IV, 24.

6 E. Duffy, *The Stripping of the Altars* (New Haven, Conn., 1992), p. 578.

7 K. Wrightson, 'The Puritan Reformation of Manners with Special Reference to the Counties of Lancashire and Essex 1640–1660' (Cambridge University PhD thesis, 1973), p. 113.

8 *Calendar of the Correspondence of Richard Baxter*, ed. N.H. Keeble and G.F. Nuttall (2 vols, Oxford, 1991), I, 166.

9 See K.V. Thomas, *Religion and the Decline of Magic* (London, 1971); R. Hutton, *The Rise and Fall of Merry England* (Oxford, 1994); R. Hutton, 'The English Reformation and the Evidence of Folklore', *P&P*, 148 (1995).

10 I. Green, *Print and Protestantism in Early Modern England* (Oxford, 2000).

11 G.H. Jenkins, *Literature, Religion and Society in Wales 1660–1730* (Cardiff, 1978), p. 54.

12 B. Capp, *The World of John Taylor the Water Poet* (Oxford, 1995), pp. 133–5.

13 R. Currie, A. Gilbert and L. Horsley (eds), *Churches and Churchgoers: Patterns of Church Growth in the British Isles since 1700* (Oxford, 1977).

14 Hutton, *Rise and Fall*, appendix; A. Foster, 'Churchwardens' Accounts of Early Modern England and Wales', in K.L. French, G.G. Gibbs and B. Kumin (eds), *The Parish in English Life 1400–1600* (Manchester, 1999).

15 *Chichester Diocesan Surveys 1686 and 1724*, ed. W.K. Ford (Sussex Record Society, 78, 1992), pp. 34–54.

16 *The State of the Church in the Reigns of Elizabeth and James I*, ed. C.W. Foster (Lincoln Record Society, 23, 1926), p. 248; M. Spufford, 'Can We Count the "Godly" and the "Conformable" in the Seventeenth Century?' *JEH*, 36 (1985).

17 E. Carlson, 'The Origins, Function, and Status of Churchwardens', in M. Spufford (ed.), *The World of Rural Dissenters 1550–1725* (Cambridge, 1995), p. 178.

18 *The Compton Census of 1676: A Critical Edition*, ed. A. Whiteman (London, 1986), p. xxxix.

19 J. Hurwich, 'Dissent and Catholicism in English Society: A Study of Warwickshire, 1660–1720', *JBS*, 16 (1976).

20 *Buckinghamshire Dissent and Parish Life 1669–1712*, ed. J. Broad (Buckinghamshire Record Society, 28, 1993), p. 77.

21 See Watts, pp. 267–89, 491–510.

22 J.P. Boulton, 'The Limits of Formal Religion: The Administration of Holy Communion in late Elizabethan and Early Stuart London', *London Journal*, 10 (1984); S.J. Wright, 'Easter Books and Parish Rate Books: A New Source for the Urban Historian', *Urban History Yearbook* (London, 1985).

23 K. Wrightson and D. Levine, *Poverty and Piety in an English Village: Terling 1525–1700* (1979; rev. edn, Oxford, 1995), pp. 155–6; P. Collinson, *Godly People* (London, 1983), p. 410.

24 R.A. Marchant, *The Church under the Law 1560–1640* (Cambridge, 1969), ch. 6 and table 32.

25 L. Brace, *The Idea of Property in Seventeenth-century England: Tithes and the Individual* (Manchester, 1998).

26 Jones of Llanddowror, 1715, quoted in Jenkins, *Literature, Religion and Society*, p. 7.

27 D.A. Spaeth, *The Church in an Age of Danger: Parsons and Parishioners, 1660–1740* (Cambridge, 2000), p. 206.

28 D. MacCulloch, 'The Myth of the English Reformation', *JBS*, 30 (1991), 8; J.F. Merritt, 'The Cradle of Laudianism? Westminster Abbey, 1558–1630', *HJ*, 52 (2001); C.S. Knighton and R. Mortimer (eds), *Westminster Abbey Reformed, 1540–1640* (Aldershot, 2003).

29 S.E. Lehmberg, *Cathedrals under Siege: Cathedrals in English Society, 1600–1700* (Exeter, 1996), p. 189. There are numerous histories of individual cathedrals available: P. Collinson, N. Ramsay and M. Sparks (eds), *A History of Canterbury Cathedral* (Oxford, 1995); M. Hobbs (ed.), *Chichester Cathedral: An Historical Survey* (Chichester, 1994); P. Meadows and N. Ramsay (eds), *A History of Ely Cathedral* (Woodbridge, 2003); G. Aylmer and G. Tiller (eds), *Hereford Cathedral: A History* (London, 2000); I. Atherton, E. Fernie, C. Harper-Bill and H. Smith (eds), *Norwich Cathedral: Church, City and Diocese, 1096–1996* (London, 1996).

30 Meadows and Ramsay (eds), *History of Ely Cathedral*, p. 188.

31 C.F. Patterson, 'Corporations, Cathedrals and the Crown: Local Dispute and Royal Interest in Early Stuart England', *History*, 85 (2000), 546; Lehmberg, *Cathedrals under Siege*, ch. 8; R.A. Beddard, 'The Privileges of Christchurch, Canterbury: Archbishop Sheldon's Enquiries of 1671', *Archaeologia Cantiana*, 87 (1972).

32 *Visitation Articles and Injunctions of the Early Stuart Church*, ed. K. Fincham (Church of England Record Society, 1, 1994), I, 122–9, esp. 124.

33 E. Carpenter, *The Protestant Bishop* (London, 1956), p. 218.

34 Sussex, pp. 12, 57, 37; *Episcopal Visitation Returns for Cambridgeshire*, ed. W.M. Palmer (Cambridge, 1930), p. 50.

35 The best guides to the courts and their procedure are M. Ingram, *Church Courts, Sex and Marriage in England, 1570–1640* (Cambridge, 1987) and Marchant, *Church under the Law*.

36 Sussex, p. 105; C. Marsh, 'Sacred Space in England, 1560–1640: The View from the Pew', *JEH*, 53 (2002), 305.

37 *The Diary of John Milward MP*, ed. C. Robbins (Cambridge, 1938), p. 240.

38 See B.D. Till, 'The Ecclesiastical Courts of York 1660–1883: A Study in Decline' (unpublished typescript, Borthwick Institute, York, 1963); J. Bailey, *Unquiet Lives: Marriage and Marriage Breakdown in England, 1660–1800* (Cambridge, 2003), p. 141; Spurr, *RC*, pp. 209–19; T. Meldrum, 'A Women's Court in London: Defamation at the Bishop of London's Consistory Court, 1700–1745', *London Journal*, 19 (1994).

39 C. Holmes, *Seventeenth-century Lincolnshire* (Lincoln, 1980), p. 61.

40 *Visitation Returns for Cambridgeshire*, ed. Palmer, p. 99.

41 Our understanding of the subject will soon be transformed: see A. Burns, K. Fincham and S. Taylor, 'Reconstructing Clerical Careers: The Experience of the Clergy of the Church of England Database', *JEH*, 55 (2004).

CHAPTER 10

Church and community

The parish in the seventeenth century was a religious, civil and social unit: it was at the same time a legal abstraction and a real place made up of fields, woods, hills, streams, farms, houses and people. The parish defined the community and vice versa. According to one contemporary authority, 'a parish, collectively taken, may be defined to be a body of people living within a certain district, to which belongs a parish church, with a right of burial, and of having the holy sacraments duly administered there, with a right of tithes, and other church dues, and of making parish rates, and choosing their own parish officers, etc. which officers with the incumbent, by order of the vestry, have the direction and management of all the parish affairs and business'.[1] To many, the parish seemed as natural, as organic as other parts of the social and political community: in the words of one preacher, 'a kingdom is but a collection of families and parishes'.[2] Ideally, the parish, village and manor were all compact and coterminous; the parish of a middling size, small enough to be served by a single parish church with a resident minister and to be governed by a resident squire, and yet large enough for the village elite to supply the parish offices. Among the nine thousand parishes of England and Wales there were such communities, mainly but not exclusively in the arable areas where villages were 'nucleated', that is, bunched together around the church and manor house and surrounded by their fields. The ideal middle-sized parish could also be found in towns such as Doncaster or even in communities like Myddle in Shropshire which was a dispersed rural settlement. Elsewhere, parishes took different forms. The large Yorkshire parish of Halifax had over 18,000 inhabitants in the 1660s and was broken down into three administrative districts and then into twelve further chapelries each with its own churchwardens and overseers of the poor. Other parishes were too small to be viable. In the countryside, depopulation might leave too few parishioners to fill the parish offices and to pay the tithes to support a resident minister: as a result church buildings fell into decay or were put to profane uses. In cities, such as Chester, Norwich, York, Bristol and London, the large number of surviving medieval churches could not always be sustained by the small populations of their neighbourhoods, while the populous new suburbs lacked sufficient parish churches. From time to time, new parishes were created and old ones amalgamated: the system responded but in a sclerotic fashion.

A sense of belonging to a community mattered as much as parish boundaries. Many individuals felt an allegiance to more than one parish. They remembered several parishes in their wills. Nearly 50 per cent of Chester benefactors left money to the poor of their home parish and 30 per cent made monetary bequests to the city's poor, but 19 per cent left money to two specific Chester parishes and 10 per cent to the poor of a parish outside the city – probably their birthplace. Social and geographical mobility naturally led individuals to other parishes. Many town-dwellers in the course of a lifetime moved from one parish to another within the town, but retained links with their previous parish: after all, their parents, spouse or children might be buried there, or they might hold a residual right to a pew or to a say in the vestry meeting.[3] Other allegiances existed besides those to people and place. Principles, often expressed through slogans about such issues as the gospel, hierarchy and order, or the authority of the church, had a powerful effect on parish life and communal identity. Parishes could be torn in two by quarrels over religious practices, local office, communal property or national politics. This chapter describes the place of the parish in communal life and the tensions and conflicts that brewed up within many parishes; a subsequent chapter discusses what happened when people went outside the parish for religious sustenance.

Church and parish

Let us begin with the physical reality of the parish church. Sitting there at the very heart of the parish and giving the community a sense of itself, its heritage and its duties, the church building was a unique local structure and is a major historical source. There were very few villages that possessed any building larger than the parish church. And the church was the only building intended to accommodate the entire community, the only building, as Richard Hooker put it, designated as a 'place of public

resort'.[4] The church was a communal resource and a communal responsibility. To gauge its significance, we must, in our imagination, subtract
from the village scene all the later buildings which are as substantial as the
church, all the village halls, all the schools, all the Methodist chapels: we
must blot out the noise of anything louder than the church bells, the single
bell that called parishioners to church every Sunday, the peal of bells
that rang out in honour of victories and great anniversaries, such as
5 November, and the passing bell which was tolled for all parishioners on
their deathbed. Nor should we picture the churchyard as a trim modern
lawn, but as a community resource, which afforded space for the festivities
of the parish, which produced trees and grass to be managed and sold, and
which was the final resting place of the entire village.

The church we enter is unheated and unlit: during the hours of daylight
the plain glass windows permit barely adequate illumination, although
here and there a splash of coloured light reveals the survival of some
medieval stained glass. Aesthetic considerations come second to practical
needs. In 1662 the churchwardens of Morsley, Buckinghamshire, sought
and received permission from the archdeacon to brick up the great west
window of their church 'with stone so high that it may be out of the boys'
reaching, who do continually break it'.[5] Perhaps we have stumbled into a
church which still has rushes strewn about the earth floor, although many
parishes began paving their churches during the course of the century.
There are stools and benches at the back of the building, some of them
marked in red letters 'for the poor', but the body of the church is taken up
with pews. These are of different sizes and shapes, some are rough forms,
others are 'box pews', built in squares with seats on all four sides; some of
these pews have doors with locks, most of them have painted numbers.
These pews may occupy the chancel too: in some churches there are even
benches under the east window, much to the disgust of the official visitors.
There is perhaps nothing more than a step and an arch to demarcate the
nave from the chancel: the medieval rood screen is long gone and its
Victorian replacement as yet undreamt of. Although the font, the pulpit
and the reading desk were where one would expect them to be today, the
communion table was often kept in the chancel, with its shorter ends
aligned to the east and west: as the seventeenth century progressed, more
and more churches placed the communion table altar-wise against the east
wall and railed it off.[6] Perhaps most striking to modern eyes are the edifying texts painted on the whitewashed walls: the churchwardens of Hungry
Hatley, Cambridgeshire, reported that 'the Ten Commandments are set up
in our parish church where the people may read them, and other chosen

sentences are written upon the walls of our said church in places convenient.'[7] In 1635, 'J. Percevall the painter' was paid thirty-eight shillings
'for writing the Ten Commandments, the Lord's Prayer, the creed and
flourishing the King and Queen's arms in the church' of St Edmund at
Salisbury; in one Essex church in 1651, six pence was paid for erasing the
royal coat of arms and ten shillings for painting that of the new Commonwealth.[8] By the second half of the century, it was common for churches
to have the commandments and the Lord's Prayer on panels at either
side of the communion table, and for the royal arms to be displayed
above the arch leading into the chancel.

We are only able to imagine what the seventeenth-century parish church
looked like, stripped of its eighteenth-century tombs and nineteenth-
century 'improvements', but that we can even imagine it is largely due
to the survival of the churchwardens' accounts.[9] In these accounts, the
community left a record of its guardianship of the parish church. The
church building was part of the vicar's freehold, so legally speaking it was
his property and his responsibility. However, a convention had grown up
that the parish took care of the nave, the part of the church they used,
while the minister cared for the chancel. As churchwardens' accounts
demonstrate, the upkeep of the church building was a constant drain on
communal finances and energy. They detail the time and money spent on
maintaining the windows, the graves, the churchyard, the churchyard wall
and so on. And yet there was always more to do – as the visitations conducted by ecclesiastical officials revealed. Their returns are full of leaking
roofs, doors standing open, broken windows, falling ceilings, damp walls,
weed-choked churchyards and decaying parsonages. One Cambridgeshire
church was 'thatched, dilapidated, very nasty', according to the visitor;
another suffered 'a very dangerous crack in the steeple'.[10] In the 1660s the
steeple of Budbrooke church collapsed, and the parish struggled financially
to rebuild it, only then to find that an aisle was also likely to subside and
the chancel was in danger.[11] Elsewhere, of course, the situation was different as the community or its leading members lavished money on adorning
their parish church: a spate of church improvements occurred in the
Jacobean era, and other better-known efforts were made by the Laudians
and in post-Great Fire London.

Since the contents of the church were communal property, churchwardens drew up inventories of the church's goods. They catalogued
the prayer books, Bibles, surplices, altar cloths, and the church plate, the
chalice or communion cup, the plate for the bread, and the candlesticks. In
1618, St Christopher le Stocks, London, possessed a Bible, two new and

one old prayer books, copies of Jewel's *Apology*, and Erasmus's *Paraphrase of the New Testament*, a green pulpit pillow, and a communion table carpet, pulpit pillow and pulpit cloth, all of purple velvet with gold embroidery and silk fringe (the gift of Sir Samuel Tryon). In the 1680s, Basildon parish church owned a Bible, two prayer books, a surplice, a green carpet, a flagon and a silver cup and chalice. Churches often contained other mundane items – buckets and ladders for fire-fighting, chests for special documents or money, tables of consanguinity, register books – but they were sparsely equipped by modern standards: for all that many communities and individuals spent on their parish church, there were none of the vestments, little of the plate, few of the ornaments, that we might expect today. There may have been a few books, a Bible and a copy of the Homilies, or a folio of Foxe's *Book of Martyrs*, probably chained to a reading desk. In some towns, the parish church boasted a small library, usually bequeathed by a clergyman or local dignitary: in 1598 books to the value of £100 were left to St Wulfram's church in Grantham to be kept chained in a chamber over the south porch; in the 1630s a Bury man left 600 books for the use of the parish, the local ministers, schoolmasters, 'and others that seek for learning and knowledge'.[12] In this manner benefactors seeded various parish libraries, sometimes with books in English specifically aimed at the humble parishioners, but it was only at the beginning of the eighteenth century that the efforts of Thomas Bray and an offshoot of the SPCK led to a concerted drive to establish parish libraries.

Parish churches were intended to accommodate the entire community when it came together for worship, yet not all of them could do so. Some churches could not physically hold the number of people, others could not provide them all with sufficient space or seating. Churchwardens' accounts are littered with references to the need for and construction of further seating: in 1622, at St Edmund, Salisbury, the seats were made narrower in order to squeeze more people in, 'flap seats' were installed against the pew doors, and in 1637, portable seats in the aisles were instituted to accommodate the youths of the parish. In Sussex wardens presented 'boys and servants for striving and rustling and pinching one another for want of seats in Ferring church, to the offence of the congregation and disturbance of divine service'.[13] Elsewhere precarious galleries were built to house the overflowing congregation. Significantly, it was a matter of pride in Jacobean Great Yarmouth that the parish church could hold the entire population of 6,000. Plymouth, whose population grew from 4,000 in 1550 to over 13,000 by 1740, had only one parish church until a second was built in the 1640s. In the 1750s the parishioners of St Michael's Bristol argued that their church needed rebuilding: it would hold only 550 people out of a population of 2,000. Excluding 200 Dissenters and 500 who had a good excuse for non-attendance, this left 750 souls without a place, individuals who were liable to use the argument that the church was full 'to stay at home or wander to other parishes'.[14] London was, of course, uniquely underequipped with churches, a situation exacerbated by the destruction of eighty-nine churches in the Great Fire of 1666. The provision of accommodation in parish churches almost certainly lagged behind the shifts of population. Across the seventeenth century and into the eighteenth century, there were marked changes in the concentration of population as people moved to London, and to regions such as the Pennines, the West Midlands and the Black Country, places where the parish boundaries had been drawn long before and where there were often fewer parish churches.

The ability of a parish church to accommodate the parishioners is not the end of the story, for once people arrived at church they were faced with the important question of where to sit. Historians have only recently begun to explore the revealing subject of church seating. Seats or pews had gradually become more common in parish churches in the later Middle Ages. New pews were constructed in many Elizabethan and Jacobean churches to replace old, rotten benches or to seat the people who were having to stand in aisles 'and in such corners thereof as they could press into'.[15] But these were not seats for all comers. Seating arrangements are a key to the structure of the community, a sort of social map of the parish with the well-to-do in the best front pews, the respectable behind them, and the servants, youths and poor at the back of the church. The traditional practice in many rural churches was to assign seats to different 'tenements', meaning farms or houses. This was the custom in Myddle, Shropshire, and that is why Richard Gough wrote his seventeenth-century history of the parish and its inhabitants according to the seating plan of the church. In Myddle church there was a rough correlation between status and seating: the seats assigned to the bigger farms tended to be towards the front of the church. Although in most seventeenth-century churches there was a mixture of seating available, some allocated, some held by a private inherited right, and some open to the young or unattached, it does appear that during the century the allocation of seats in church on the basis of custom, with each seat assigned to a tenement, was giving way to an allocation based on personal wealth and tax contribution. Underdown has described the haphazard nature of this process, stressed its urban and its pre-Reformation origin, and showed how natural changes in the social composition of the parish required the reallocation of seats; but he also argues that in the West Country at least the early seventeenth century was the turning point in the transition from church seating based on custom and residence to seating based on the ability to pay.[16]

Despite parishioners' use of the language of ownership, their pews were never their legal property; at best they enjoyed a title to the seat that arose from their contribution to the costs of constructing and maintaining pews. It was the churchwardens' duty to allocate seats, but they knew better than to antagonise their betters: in Salisbury the wardens were not allowed to reassign any pew used by members of the select vestry or their wives without the vestry's consent. It was common for women to sit apart from their menfolk in church: mixed sitting was 'not decent and seemly', in the view of one Oxford cobbler, who had lived in many towns and 'never knew but that the custom in all the said churches was always for men to sit there in seats by themselves apart from the women, and the women likewise by themselves'.[17] In some parishes, such as Tewkesbury, segregated seating was a recent arrival in 1600. It is possible that the practice of separate seating declined across the century, but there were certainly parishes where the sexes continued to sit apart throughout the century.[18] Since the older men might sit at the front and younger men at the back, and since married brothers would each have their own pew, going to church could fragment the family and rearrange the individuals who made up the community in an artificial way. In other parishes it was only the wealthier sort who sat apart from their wives: since this meant paying for two pews, perhaps this was a way of displaying one's affluence. The potential for trouble was endless. Ostentatious pews, like bulky tombs, obscured access and sightlines for the congregation. There never seemed to be enough seats and sometimes people took matters into their own hands. The outraged churchwardens of Sherston Magna complained of 'a row of seats or boards unseemly set up, wherein the meanest of the parish have for some time sat, and divers more substantial men . . . do want seats'.[19]

The church building was not the only parochial space. The churchyard was a vital communal amenity. Most obviously it housed the parish's dead, generation upon generation of them interred in the same small patch of consecrated ground, generally without any permanent marker or memorial, although there was a growing fashion in the seventeenth century for the erection of tombstones. It was also the location for games and sports, for fairs and markets, for recreation and meetings, especially during the summer months. We might count within the churchyard space the church porch, which was used by the parish school, or for vestry meetings, or to store parochial equipment. Many parishes built a 'church-house', a separate building within the precincts of the churchyard that served as a form of parish hall. John Aubrey recalled that 'every parish' in seventeenth-century Wiltshire had a church-house where neighbours 'met and were merry and gave their charity', while outside in the church-yard the young people danced, bowled, practised archery, and were watched by 'the ancients sitting gravely by, looking on'.[20] All of these facilities had to be maintained: the buildings repaired, grass cut, trees felled, fences and hedges tended; and all the behaviour within this sacred and communal space had to be watched and policed.

Parish administration

The parish church clearly needed management. As a religious institution, it required officers to administer its affairs. In the civil sphere a parish was defined as a place for which a poor rate was made and overseers of the poor were appointed. This social duty was first laid on JPs and the parishes by a statute of 1572, but reached definitive form in 1601. The vestry was the governing body of the parish. It ordered the day-to-day running of the church and administered the poor rates and any legacies to the parish, the poor or the church. The vestry was composed of the incumbent and the churchwardens with a number of lay parishioners. There were two types of vestry: the 'open' or 'general' vestry, which was attended by all of the adult male parishioners, or those who paid local rates, or substantial householders; the second type of vestry was the 'select' vestry, a self-perpetuating com-mittee of perhaps twelve or twenty-four who ran all of the parish's affairs. Some parishes appear to have been administered by a cross between the two types of vestry.

The churchwardens were the guardians or keepers of the parish church. There were usually two wardens each year, 'chosen by the joint consent of the minister and the parishioners,' said the canons, 'but if they cannot agree then the minister shall choose one, and the parishioners another'. It was, however, quite common for the office to be held by rotation accord-ing to a list of local houses or farms. It was a post actively sought by those 'that affected to be accounted somebody in this parish' and just as actively avoided by others.[21] As we have seen, the wardens were responsible to the bishop and his officials. Guided by the visitation articles, the wardens had to report anything amiss or irregular in the parish, the church or the clergy. But the churchwardens were also members of their own community, and it is likely that their first loyalty was to their parish and their neighbours. The oath of office at Pulverbatch, Shropshire, in 1661 ran, 'you shall duly administer the office of a churchwarden for the best benefit of the church and the good government of the parishioners, and take care especially yet the church be sufficiently repaired in buildings, as likewise well provided with ornaments and preserve the church goods and deliver them up with a just account at the end of your office to the next churchwardens and parishioners'.[22] As the principal officers of the parish, the wardens' duties were myriad. They kept the peace at meetings of the congregation, prevented any profane usage of the church, saw that all parishioners attended services regularly, and policed the pubs in time of divine service. They were responsible for the day-to-day receipts and disbursements, for paying the parish clerk, for repairs of the church; they organised the church-ale or collected the church rate, they let fields belonging to the church, they managed the parish flock. All of this work was carefully recorded in their annual accounts. Other, civil duties were laid upon the churchwardens either by the parish or by statute. The warden took a part in relieving the poor, and in some parishes, service as churchwarden was followed by a year as overseer of the poor. Churchwardens were concerned in the control of vermin, swearing, tippling, vagrancy, apprenticeships and other issues of good order.

The parish clerk was chosen by the minister. 'His duty is to assist the minister and make responses in reading prayers, baptizing, marrying, burying, and the other divine offices, setting the Psalms, etc. Though his office be but a lay-office.'[23] The clerk, who was supposed to be literate and musical, might also keep the parish register. His was a paid office: at Houghton-le-Spring in Durham, he received 'yearly at Easter time' nine pence from each plough, four pence from each cottager; and 'for a marriage, 4d; for asking the banns, 2d; for a christening, 1d; and for a burial, 4d; which duties are paid for entering the same in the register book'.[24] Not all clerks measured up to the job description: in 1623 Richard Blake, the clerk of Barnham, Sussex, was reported for neglecting his duties, and described as 'unlearned' and 'an aged man'.[25] Some clerks doubled up as sexton, although in general this was the preserve of some village ne'er-do-well or local character; the sexton was the grave-digger, church-sweeper, dog-whipper, and bell-ringer: he kept the spades and the shovels, and was paid by a mixture of yearly contributions, fees for graves dug and 'upon good will each householder to give him buns at Christmas and eggs at Easter yearly'.[26] Many church records include references to negligent, drunken or inadequate sextons: the sexton of St Thomas, Salisbury, was deprived of his wages for a quarter for not obeying the rules about ringing knells for the dying and for failing to ring the church bell at 6.0 a.m. and 8.0 p.m.[27]

*

Money loomed large in parish life. The funds needed to maintain the church came from several different sources: from fund-raising drives and events; from the income of church lands or other property; and from a church rate or parish tax. In the early seventeenth century many parishes were still raising money through a system of voluntary contributions, but by the end of the century a system of rates levied by the churchwardens was near universal. Sometimes a note of panic intrudes in the records – the archidiaconal visitation of Thurrock in 1685 instructed that 'the church-wardens must make a rate very speedily for the repair of the steeple'.[28] Some parishes treated the communion bread and wine as a separate item, and either raised a special rate or took a specific collection to pay for them. There were charges for almost all of the services provided by the church: if someone was to be buried in the church there was a special fee to be paid: at Houghton-le-Spring it was '3s 4d for a man or woman, and 20d for a child; with the which money the harm done either to the pavement or seats by making the grave is within fourteen days after to be repaired, and the rubbish remaining to be clean carried forth of the church'.[29] Fees were charged for bells at weddings and funerals, for the registration of baptisms and marriages, even for seats in the church: at Houghton-le-Spring it cost four pence to renew each seat in a pew at the death or exchange of the owner of the seat, and twelve pence for altering or erecting new pews.

Vestries were always keen to regularise the parish finances, and if possible to establish greater economy. One of the best known of these reforms was the introduction of the church rate, a parish tax, in place of the traditional ways of raising money for the maintenance of the church. Among the traditional methods was the 'church-ale', a village feast with dancing and sports, at which money was donated to the needs of the church. The food and the ingredients needed to brew the beer were usually donated and all the profits were collected by the churchwardens. At Ashton Keynes, Wiltshire, in 1602, the churchwardens presented their pre-decessors for 'ill husbanding of their ale'. The three-week-long festivity had produced no profit, so the retiring wardens had to pay the minstrels out of their own pocket. It is clear that the church-ale was not an efficient way of raising funds, but a common objection to it was a moral one. The church-ale was an occasion of drunkenness, profanity, sexual licence and disorder in the eyes of its opponents. The replacement of the church-ale by the rate was not always a smooth or uncontested process. At Thatcham in Berkshire, the ale led to disorder and a reprimand from the Assizes in 1598; the parish sold its maypole and went over to rating, but in 1617 the Whitsun ale was revived and only in 1621 was rating permanently established. At Bere Regis ales were held until 1614, but when a rate was adopted it produced less than half the amount normally raised by a church-ale, and it took a decade before the rate was bringing in more than the church-ales had done.[30] The decline of church-ales was inexorable: only one parish has been identified as holding an ale after 1662.[31]

Poor relief was a separate issue but no less contentious in most parish vestries. There were hard battles over setting a rate, the assessment of individuals, and the audit of payments: in severe cases an appeal could be made to the local justices. The mechanics of poor relief easily spilled over into the parish's religious life: at Whitstable, William Cole refused to contribute to the collection and 'abused the churchwardens and the rest of the parishioners'; in one Cambridgeshire village, the collector of poor relief went round the congregation during service making 'such a noise that the minister could not be heard'.[32]

*

The parish was a strong and resilient unit of administration. On the evidence of the neat and orderly entries in the many hundreds of surviving vestry minute books and churchwardens' accounts, we can conclude that parish administration continued year by year in a steady course, attending to the community's needs, both civil and spiritual, whatever the external challenges and disruptions. It weathered the storms of the Civil War and Interregnum as both a religious and administrative entity. Since the Church of England and its system of visitations had been abolished, there was no one to supervise the work of the churchwardens above the level of the parish, so the Justices of the Peace stepped into the breach. Throughout the 1650s, the JPs of Sussex, Warwickshire, Durham and other counties seem to have taken it upon themselves to supervise parochial appointments of clerks and elections of churchwardens and to intervene in disputes over churchwardens' accounts or levies for church repairs.

Parish administration grew steadily in the seventeenth century. In the parish of St Mary's, Chester, for instance, there were by 1630 two churchwardens, two overseers of the poor, two sidesmen, four collectors for the poor, and ten assessors for the poor. Alldridge suggests that there may be a connection between the burgeoning lay officialdom of this parish and the succession of conflicts between the parish and the parson. The parishioners asserted their sole right to appoint churchwardens, they chose and paid a parish clerk to read services, they hired a preacher, they refused the parson and his curate a rise in stipend, and they stopped the parson enclosing pews in the choir of the church. Perhaps not surprisingly, the parson eventually became a non-resident. This increase in the number of offices was a heavy burden on the community. There were six offices to be filled each year in the Chester parish of St Oswald's from a pool of just one hundred eligible candidates.[33]

The century witnessed a trend towards the creation of oligarchical vestries. The annual Easter meeting of the open vestry, usually comprising all of the adult male parishioners or householders, began to vote in favour of handing over parish affairs to a select vestry, a sort of committee, who usually appear in the records as the 'ancients', the 'elders', the 'four and twenty', the 'masters and governors of the parish', and suchlike. It seems that the consent of the majority of the parish was always required for this change, but many select vestries also took the precaution of obtaining a faculty or licence from their bishop – even though the bishop's legal authority in the matter was uncertain. Thirty faculties were issued in the diocese of London for the creation of select vestries between 1611 and 1637 and another eleven between 1660 and 1662. A common formula was that 'the general admittance of the parish into the vestry' had produced 'great disquietness and hindrance to the good proceedings'.[34] Although the transfer of parochial power to a small group made for efficiency, it also meant that a clique could dominate the parish and its religious and civil life. In the 1640s there was a 'democratic' backlash, and many London parishes, for instance, reverted to the open or general vestry; but by the 1650s the tendency towards a select vestry was already reasserting itself: as one petition put it, 'when decency and order were cast . . . aside, the whole parish assumed a power to themselves to convene in a public vestry to determine all things belonging to the said church and parish, according to their own several fancies and opinions, which hath caused so much division and distraction amongst the said parishioners as tends to the obstructing of the business in the hand, and the good and well government of the said church and parish'.[35] The Restoration authorities were well disposed towards select vestries that were loyal and Anglican, but feared those which harboured Nonconformists or their sympathisers. As a result, the 1663 Select Vestries Act demanded that members of select vestries take oaths of political and religious loyalty. There were further legislative attempts to reform select vestries in the 1690s and 1710s.

Parish politics

Politics is not an activity confined to monarchs, nobles, courtiers, bishops and gentlemen. If we take the word to mean the process of negotiation and decision-making by which people exerted a degree of meaningful control over their own lives, then there was scope for quite humble folk to engage in politics, especially within their neighbourhood and through such institutions as the vestry and the parish.

The parishes of seventeenth-century Britain were face-to-face communities in which everyone knew each other's business and few were prepared to tolerate disruptive or even anomalous behaviour. The power of communal expectations was formidable: 'common fame' or well-founded public knowledge was often sufficient to accuse individuals of drunkenness, immorality, sexual deviance or a host of other anti-social offences. Those who led disordered lives, who were bad neighbours or who lived apart from their husband or wife, were all subject to intense social pressure. Only the tip of this iceberg of moral control is revealed in formal presentments by the churchwardens' or constables' reports to the JPs. Beneath the surface of parish life, much social control was exerted by quiet chats with the minister or the warden, disapproving glances in church or the vestry, reprimands from fathers and masters, and the ceaseless gossip of one's neighbours. The imposition of standards of behaviour upon members of the community was a powerful and largely invisible form of political authority. In 1621 the wardens of West Itchenor presented 'Thomas Stryant to be a malicious, contentious, and uncharitable person, one that seeks the unjust vexation of his neighbours, a common swearer and such a one as is not fit to be harboured in any parish'. The Sussex parish of Westhampnet was outraged by Robert Taylor, 'an open contender' who sued his neighbours for small sums 'to our great hurt and hindrances, and will not reconcile himself, though it has been sought by some of the parish'; so they prosecuted him as a barrator (a troublemaker) in the secular courts and presented their minister for admitting this uncharitable man to the sacrament of the communion.[36]

Some forms of untoward behaviour had consequences for the whole community. Sex before marriage, especially when it led to illegitimate children (whose upkeep might fall on the community), excessive drinking, idleness, vagrancy and begging, were all forms of behaviour which might be deemed injurious as well as immoral. Churchwardens' presentments reported suspected sexual liaisons, unmarried mothers, drunkards, and sowers of discord, even though church authorities had few real sanctions against these offenders. The parish, or at least the ruling vestry, could deploy various means of discipline against the errant: they could use the machinery of the church, the legal procedures of the constables and the JPs, or even the system of poor relief to make people better neighbours and Christians. One reason for having special benches for the poor in some parish churches was to ensure their dutiful attendance. At least one Warwickshire man was required to turn up at church to be paid his pension; others were threatened with a reduction or even an end to their pension for behaving 'very rudely and irreligiously in the church'. In 1682 Middlesex JPs ordered that 'such poor people as shall go to any meeting house and not to their parish church shall have no benefit of the parish collection'.[37]

*

Moral concern easily degenerates into a moral panic. Periodically, seventeenth-century English communities gave themselves over to crusades for 'the reformation of manners'. These intense local campaigns of public regulation and punishment were aimed at moral and social offences, at personal behaviour such as swearing, drunkenness, railing and scolding, tippling or alehouse-haunting, idleness, 'night-walking', absence from church, and joining in the dancing, football, sports and other pastimes on a Sunday afternoon. The reformers took a dim view of most forms of communal recreation, of feasting, wakes, church-ales, maypoles, strolling players, fiddlers, minstrels and puppeteers. They were preoccupied with the sexuality of young people, with sex before marriage, promiscuity and adultery, and the breakdown of public order and discipline. The offenders were more often than not the poor, the young, the rootless and the marginal. 'Manners' was clearly an elastic term. It covered transgressions with direct social consequences, such as the bastard children who were a financial burden on the parish, and popular pastimes, such as football on the village green, which had no immediate communal repercussions. The reformers offered several kinds of justification for prosecuting and suppressing these disorderly occasions and this immoral behaviour. Some were practical: it was, for instance, wasteful and inefficient to raise parish funds through the church-ales or wakes. Others were purely moral, such as the crackdown on swearing or the presentment of married couples for having begun sexual relations before their marriage. But practicality and morality converged with religion. As one preacher for the reformation of manners observed, 'the great end of human laws for reformation of offences against the moral law is to apply the law of God and set it home by punishment upon the conscience'.[38]

In the late Elizabethan and Jacobean period there were some notable victories in the war to reform English manners. Reformation was successful in several little 'Genevas' or 'Zions', in towns like Rye or Northampton or Dorchester, where a persuasive minister and local political support combined to repress immorality and enforce sobriety. Richard Blackerby at Castle Hedington created a prayer group of 'gracious Christians' from a gang who met to 'dance and frolic in their youthful sports, sins and vanities', and Thomas Hooker transformed Chelmsford: 'the Sabbath came to be very visibly sanctified among the people'.[39] Godly or puritan religion clearly played a significant role in some places. In the small Essex village of Terling the local elite could identify wholeheartedly with puritan religion. Here was a creed which not only explained their own good fortune, but also legitimised their efforts to discipline the poor, to curb their drunken, promiscuous ways and to instill in them respect for sobriety, property, hard work and regular attendance at church. In other communities, however, similar social strains did not find expression in puritanism or the reformation of manners. At Keevil in Wiltshire economic pressures led to a harsher community line against bastardy and bridal pregnancy, but there was no campaign to enforce religious observance or ban games and celebrations.[40] The religious convictions that in some places made moral reformation a success also alienated many of the community. There were numerous points of friction between those who sought to impose order, decorum and responsibility and those who rejoiced in opportunities for good fellowship and neighbourliness. Conflict occurred over daily routines and habits, especially drinking and the sociability of the alehouse; over the weekly challenge to the sanctity of Sunday from dancing or football or, in London, commercial entertainments; and over the highlights of the festive year such as May Day or Christmas. The reformers did not doubt that their opponents were the profane and godless, just as their opponents dismissed the reformers as hypocrites and puritans. These critics mocked Zeal-of-the-Land Busy for seeing idolatry in a puppet show and asked if there are to be 'no more cakes and ale because you are virtuous?'

When the godly achieved political power in the late 1640s and 1650s, 'the work of reformation began to appear'. At last they were able to initiate the cultural revolution of which they had long dreamed: the Rump's Adultery Act of 1650 laid down the death penalty for adultery and a three-month gaol sentence for fornication; draconian legislation was enacted against breaches of the Sabbath, drunkenness, swearing and the like. But the zealots at Westminster and their acolytes in the counties had limited success. Magistrates were generally reluctant to prosecute and juries unwilling to convict. As we have already seen, the New Model Army and its Major Generals were charged with promoting the work, but although the troopers could ensure that alehouses were closed down and the ban on Christmas festivities, cockfights and horse races was observed, they could not make people behave better. 'If it be objected that reformation is obstructed,' commented one preacher, 'I answer, No marvel. It was never otherways.'[41]

Local initiative was more to the fore in the reformation movements of the 1690s. In 1691 the churchwardens, constables, and inhabitants of Tower Hamlets, considering how 'we might glorify God, demonstrate our loyalty to the King, and do good to our neighbours', decided to suppress the numerous brothels in their parish.[42] The Bristol Society was set up 'out of a sense of the duty we owe to Almighty God, and of that due regard we ought to have to that holy religion we profess, and the prosperous and flourishing estate of the city wherein we live' and to the royal proclamations encouraging reformation. The society therefore sought to regulate disorder, tippling, and vagrancy, apprenticeships, Sabbath trade and travel, as well as promoting sermons and charity schools: 'the growth of vice and debauchery be greatly owing to the gross ignorance of the principles of the Christian religion especially among the poorer sort and also . . . Christian virtue can grow from no other root than Christian principles'. Arthur Bedford, a clergyman and leading light of the Bristol Society, was concerned to prevent boys from playing in the streets 'and men from spending their time idly on the exchange, in the fields or elsewhere during divine service'; he distributed tracts on Sabbath observance and family worship and works refuting Quaker principles; and he organised collections to fund the charity schools. But he could not win the backing of the local bishop or the Anglican establishment for his efforts.[43]

It is tempting sometimes to elevate the slogan of 'reformation of manners' into a coherent movement peculiar to early modern England. But the regulation of behaviour and manners is a perennial issue in most communities. The manorial courts of late medieval England were preoccupied with nuisances and disorders of a similar kind, as were eighteenth- and nineteenth-century Assizes and borough magistrates. In Scotland the Kirk sessions provided a rigorous and highly effective local system of moral surveillance and punishment from the sixteenth into the nineteenth century. Early modern Europe has been portrayed as in the grip of a campaign of moral and cultural repression, memorably described as the triumph of Lent over Carnival.[44] What is noticeable in the case of seventeenth-century England is the importance of local involvement. If these disorders were to be effectively prosecuted and manners to be reformed, then neither government nor the church could succeed without community backing: as Fletcher remarks, 'the story in the end has to be told from below'.[45] In England, the cause of the reformation of manners acquired a puritan tang that it could never shake off and that alienated some potential supporters. The evolution of the reform campaigns also underlines the declining role of the church courts in the policing of morality and behaviour. Although the reformation of manners had always involved the full range of secular courts, from borough and manorial courts up to the Assizes, alongside the ecclesiastical court system, there was a discernibly greater reliance on secular courts as the century progressed. This was presumably a reflection of the church courts' weakness and the lay people's initiative. The Toleration Act allowed 'every man liberty to spit in the face of the church, and has taken [away] all the means of correcting strife and envyings in the church'.[46] In 1709 one clergyman admitted the wonderful effects of 'the spirit of reformation now moving upon the hearts of many excellent lay Christians, and quickening the execution of the laws of the land' against the disorderly and impious. Yet he could not help but regret 'the lamentable relaxation and decay of discipline' exercised by the church.[47]

*

After the Restoration admission to and control of the parish vestry became a bone of contention in many communities. Some vestries were infiltrated by those who sympathised with the plight of the Dissenters: the huge London parish of St Giles Cripplegate, home to many thousands of Dissenters, was rocked by scandal in the early 1680s when Tories and Whigs, encouraged by the rector, Edward Fowler, fought for dominance in the vestry.[48] In other parishes the ideological motives were less clear than the expectations of the community that those with sufficient wealth and status should take their turn in the honours and duties of local government. In Terling between 1662 and 1688, eleven Nonconformists served as churchwardens, eight as overseers of the poor, and four as vestrymen.[49] In 1682 the clergyman of Aston Rowant, Oxfordshire, found the local Baptists were playing 'one of their old games' by nominating as churchwarden a man who had never received the sacrament and seldom came to church. He rejected the nominee, but 'the ring-leading Dissenter came to me and insolently asked what my reason was to oppose the parish'.[50] One influential study has argued that Dissenters shouldered the burdens of parochial office because the local demands of good neighbourliness and status far outweighed denominational distinctions.[51] Apart from the small sample of cases that have been studied, the major difficulties in either accepting or refuting broad claims about the integration of religious dissidents within the parish community are that these groups were rarely as clear-cut as they appear and that integration was not a single permanent state. Communities in which Dissenters and Anglicans had worked alongside each other in parish government for many years were not immune to sudden eruptions of denominational animosity. In Halifax a dispute about the choice of a parish lecturer in 1689 provoked some very positive assertions that all residents of the parish had a right to vote and, from the other side, that wives, children, servants and apprentices, 'poor and indigent people that were and are maintained by the charity and contribution of the town', as well as Dissenters and 'frequenters of conventicles', had no such right.[52]

Every parish quarrel was unique, but as historians have investigated increasing numbers of such disputes from different angles and sources, the sheer intensity of seventeenth-century parish politics has become apparent. A legal case may illuminate the power relations in a community, or a pamphlet about some outlandish event, such as a Shropshire axe murder, may reveal the local manoeuvring of clerical groups.[53] A micro-study, such as Beaver's of Tewkesbury and surrounding villages, can reveal the effects of the mid-century turmoil on the parish's spiritual authority.[54] In many cases, the struggle was over control of a local institution – a lectureship in Great Yarmouth or Halifax, or a position at Monmouth school – but these parochial contests easily mushroomed into provincial or even national disputes thanks to the intervention of external patrons, the involvement of the law courts, or an appeal to the political authorities.[55] When an alliance of aldermen and clergy formed up over the control of pulpits in Great Yarmouth, the ensuing discord brought the town to the brink of political crisis. Eventually Charles I pronounced in Privy Council that the affair had been promoted 'by the refractory spirits of some persons who have the chief places of government in the town' and that he was determined to uphold 'ecclesiastical authority and discipline' as well as 'civil order and government'.[56] These local quarrels often demand to be put into a provincial or national context. It is a recurrent theme of this century that local factions were able to appropriate national political slogans and agendas and in doing so to modify them. In some instances religion was undoubtedly a cloak for personal and factional motives, but in most cases it was impossible for participants themselves, never mind for modern historians, to make that sharp distinction between their spiritual concerns and more worldly ambitions.

A kingdom of parishes

The kingdom was a collection of families and parishes. Every parish was unique and knew itself to be so. Without romanticising the English parish – and no reader of Richard Gough's *History of Myddle* could easily succumb to that temptation – these were communities with a sharp sense of their own identity. The old practice of walking the parish boundaries on Plough Monday, the Monday before Ascension Day, was an assertion of community. The minister and parishioners 'beat the bounds' of the parish in what Keith Thomas described as 'the corporate manifestation of the village community, an occasion for eating and drinking and the reconciliation of disputes'. It was also, one must admit, frequently an excuse for brawls between the young men of neighbouring parishes. A Dutch traveller described the serious business of establishing the bounds of a London parish, when all the young people of the parish armed with sticks formed a procession, 'and when a marker is put up or renewed . . . they make a loud noise all together . . . This is done to impress on the young memories of the children the extent of the parish, so that they may preserve it in the future without loss, and everyone gets a loaf of white bread from the minister.'[57] The ritual was not without disorder, nor was it uncontested – some critics believed it to be superstitious, others regarded it as more symbolic than practical – but Hutton has shown that it persisted as a vital social practice throughout the century.[58] In other words, parishes demonstrated their individuality in the common manner. Seventeenth-century parishes were marked by other national trends: they were increasingly undergoing social polarisation; they felt the tensions between the lay people and the clerical profession; and they experienced the reality of religious pluralism.

Although it did not happen overnight, there was a growing polarisation in seventeenth-century English society: the rich were getting richer, the poor poorer, and those between were a dwindling band. The demise of the class of small landowners and the emergence of an agrarian social structure based upon a large body of landless labourers, or 'the poor' (perhaps 85 per cent of the population), and an elite of craftsmen, artisans and tenant farmers, had occurred in parts of Essex and Cambridgeshire by 1600, but probably only effected other areas, such as Shropshire, a century later. This socio-economic differentiation might plausibly be associated with the tendency of the parish notables, the well-to-do yeomanry and gentry, to take the reins of parish power into their hands, to monopolise parochial offices and perpetuate oligarchical vestries. Hindle has identified a series of concerns around the treatment of the parish poor in the early seventeenth century which also seem to suggest that these local notables increasingly saw and spoke of themselves as 'the parish' and promoted a narrower definition of the parish community, based on residence, contribution to the local rates, and full participation in the life and rituals of the parish church, than had been common earlier.[59] Wrightson and Levine's study suggested that the economic and social polarisation of the Essex village of Terling was accompanied by a significant differentiation of attitudes, behaviour, culture and religion. The wealthy of the parish commandeered local offices, proclaimed themselves 'the godly' and the morally responsible, and identified the poor as the profane, ungodly multitude. Self-interest, social duty and puritan religion thus came together to validate the privilege and wealth of these individuals and to justify their efforts to discipline and reform the parish poor. This pattern, however, was not repeated elsewhere. Wrightson has recently argued that there was a convergence between the broad movement for reformation in seventeenth-century England and the rise of government. The process of 'state formation', particularly the involvement of quite humble residents with administering the poor laws, petty sessions, militia and taxation, and the Post-Reformation effort to instruct and counsel the parishioners of the Protestant church, both had their greatest impact at the level of the parish.[60]

Whatever the question marks over social trends and the parish, there is no doubt that parishes felt the forces of clericalism and anticlericalism. These are mutually dependent tendencies: one provokes the other. As Haigh has remarked, 'if it was clericalism which begat anticlericalism, we shall find the latter in the Elizabethan church: the post-Reformation ministry with its university education and professional cohesion, was more clericalist than the pre-Reformation priesthood'.[61] It is not difficult to see the self-righteous puritan minister, the Laudian ceremonialist or the Restoration Anglican divine as representatives of different brands of 'clericalism', but to concentrate upon different clerical styles is probably to overlook the daily reality for most parish clergymen of casual slights, calculated insults and outright defiance from lay people who refused to respect the dignity of the ministry. In 1622 Francis Heap, minister of Binsted, Sussex, presented his own churchwarden who turned up drunk to the making of the accounts in the church. When Heap reproved him, he replied 'with opprobrious words, and dared me to present him, which is too usual an order with him'.[62] Many clergy recorded such confrontations with parishioners who mocked them to their faces: Isaac Archer suffered humiliation over his stammer. One man was presented for defaming his minister as 'an hypocrite and a devil', and 'a spiteful priest and bad and the

turd in his teeth'; another 'cared not a fart' for his pastor.[63] Other parishioners, appreciating the clergyman's duty to warn and admonish them,
were concerned to protect their minister from such affronts. Richard
Knowles was presented in 1623 for his 'unreverent speeches' against the
minister, 'his function and doctrine', particularly for his 'openly in our
hearing in the church before the greater number of the parish saying that
his sermon was of nothing but a dead hog, to the great discouraging of our
minister to discharge his duties'.[64] In such a complaint, perhaps, one can
hear the horror of the community combined with the outrage of the
insulted clergyman. Elsewhere it was the minister who overstepped the
mark. The negligent Mr Robinson of Lancing 'does pray very humour-
somely, urging much at the congregation, and as it may seem against some
more particularly'.[65]

The disposition of power between a clergyman and his parishioners
was infinitely variable and depended upon much more than views of the
clerical vocation. For every minister humiliated at the hands of the laity,
there was a parishioner forced to bow before the will of the clergy. Clergymen had extensive networks of friends and patrons and most would have
been able to mobilise influence in their locality. Hindle has described how
Margaret Knowsley, a servant of the minister of Nantwich, was brought
low and whipped in 1627 when she dared to accuse her employer of sexual
advances – despite the strong likelihood that she was telling the truth.[66] For
all the clergy's role in reconciling disputes, it is unlikely that they were ever
seen as utterly impartial. They were part of the local hierarchy and commonly
worked alongside other parochial authority figures. One Durham parish
had an intricate system of communal arbitration in which the parson,
knights, gentleman and the vestry formed a committee to which all quarrels were to be referred on pain of a fine. The partnership of minister and
magistrate was a powerful ideal throughout the century, as strong in puritan
as in Anglican minds. In Wales the shared language of the clergy and their
parishioners was an important common bond: it was valued as a chief means
by which they 'support the tongue, and retain the customs and traditions
and principles, and proverbs of their ancestors'. When, towards the end
of the century, a new generation of clergy began to preach more often
in English, in part to pander to the pretensions of the English-speaking
gentry, the reaction was often sharp. In 1688 the parishioners of Llandaff
and Whitchurch – 'not one in ten understanding English' – petitioned for
the removal of their minister because he was a 'stranger to the Welsh
tongue'. Bishops too were alarmed at the pastoral consequences of a clergy
that could not or would not preach in the vernacular.[67]

The clergy's professional authority must have been affected by the widening choice of religious association, as must allegiance to the parish. Yet it would be rash to suggest that the seventeenth century witnessed a simple development of religious freedom and a consequent erosion of the parish community. There had, after all, long been plenty of religious activity outside the parish. Collinson has warned us against mistaking the voluntary and quasi-separatist religious behaviour of seventeenth-century puritans for something new: it may, he suggests, be merely 'the pursuit of religious and social instincts which had always existed both within and beyond the parish'.[68] Medieval Christians were offered a host of religious associations besides that of the parish church: they could ally themselves with guilds and fraternities, chapels and hospitals, cathedrals and monasteries, and their loyalty to these institutions did not compete with, but supplemented, their loyalty to their parish. Although the Reformation inevitably curtailed some of these opportunities for extra-parochial piety, its effect should not be overestimated. Chapter 12 will describe the penumbra of voluntary religious associations and practices in the Post-Reformation. What made the seventeenth century remarkable, however, was the emergence by the 1640s of alternatives to the parish church and the establishment of toleration by 1689. Religious choice on this scale was new. It also had a dramatic effect on the *significance* of voluntary religious exercises undertaken outside the parish. What had been a supplement to the worship of the parish church now threatened to become a rival. 'Though we have very few indeed that wilfully and constantly absent themselves from the offices of the church,' complained the parson of Adderbury in 1682, 'yet they many of them will straggle one part of the day [to the Presbyterian conventicle outside the town], when they duly attend the public worship of God in the other, and they seem to be like the borderers betwixt two kingdoms[,] one can't tell what prince they are subject to.'[69] One does not have to swallow the parson's pessimistic insinuation that his parishioners could not tell church and conventicle apart, to take his broader point. Yet for all the challenges faced by the seventeenth-century parish, it remained an obdurate social reality. 'It was the parish which mattered most,' concluded Palliser, 'both in ecclesiastical and secular terms, to the majority of the population from the tenth or eleventh century to the eighteenth or nineteenth.'[70]

Notes

1 J. Shaw, *Parish Law* (1733), p. 7.

2 J. Hoppit, *A Land of Liberty? England 1689–1727* (Oxford, 2000), p. 77.

3 N. Alldridge, 'Loyalty and Identity in Chester Parishes, 1540–1640', in S.J. Wright (ed.), *Parish, Church and People* (London, 1988), pp. 113–15.

4 D. Palliser, 'Introduction' in Wright (ed.), *Parish, Church and People*, p. 8.

5 *Episcopal Visitation Book from the Archdeaconry of Buckinghamshire, 1662*, ed. E.R.C. Brinkworth (Buckinghamshire Record Society, 7, 1947), p. 55.

6 The forthcoming study of altars by Ken Fincham and Nicholas Tyacke will document this trend.

7 *Episcopal Visitation Returns for Cambridgeshire*, ed. W.M. Palmer (Cambridge, 1930), p. 80.

8 *Churchwardens' Accounts of S. Edmund and S. Thomas, Sarum, 1443–1702*, ed. H.J.F. Swayne (Wiltshire Record Society, Salisbury, 1896), p. 202.

9 There are fine photographs of surviving eighteenth- and seventeenth-century interiors in M. Chatfield, *Churches the Victorians Forgot* (Ashbourne, 1979).

10 BL, Egerton MS 2655, fos. 18v, 20v.

11 *Inspections of Churches and Parsonage Houses in the Diocese of Worcester in 1674, 1676, 1684 and 1687*, ed. P. Morgan (Worcestershire Historical Society, new series, 12, 1986), pp. 48, 53.

12 N. Ker and M. Perkin (eds), *A Directory of the Parochial Libraries* (London, 2004), p. 163.

13 Sussex, p. 101.

14 J. Barry, 'The Parish in Civic Life: Bristol and its Churches, 1640–1750', in Wright (ed.), *Parish, Church and People*, p. 153.

15 C. Marsh, 'Sacred Space in England, 1560–1640: The View from the Pew', *JEH*, 53 (2002), 292.

16 D. Underdown, *Revel, Riot and Rebellion: Popular Politics and Culture in England 1603–1660* (Oxford, 1985), p. 30.

17 K. Dillow, 'The Social and Ecclesiastical Significance of Church Seating Arrangements and Pew Disputes, 1500–1740' (unpublished Oxford University D.Phil. thesis, 1991), p. 131.

18 *Tewkesbury Churchwardens' Accounts 1563–1624*, ed. C.J. Litzenberger (Gloucestershire Record Society, 7, 1994), pp. xiii, 76; Durham, pp. 119, 239, 249.

19 Underdown, *Revel, Riot and Rebellion*, p. 31.

20 D. Dymond, 'God's Disputed Acre', *JEH*, 50 (1999), 482.

21 Richard Gough, *The History of Myddle*, ed. D. Hey (Harmondsworth, 1981), p. 239. The best account of the office is E.J. Carlson, 'The Origins, Function and Status of Churchwardens', in M. Spufford (ed.), *The World of Rural Dissenters 1520–1725* (Cambridge, 1995).

22 W.E. Tate, *The Parish Chest* (3rd edn, London, 1969), p. 96.

23 Shaw, *Parish Law*, p. 43.

24 Durham, p. 314.

25 Sussex, p. 65.

26 Durham, p. 314.

27 *Churchwardens' Accounts . . . Sarum*, ed. Swayne, p. 320.

28 'Visitations held in the Archdeaconry of Essex', ed. E. Pressey, *Transactions of Essex Archaeological Society* XXI (1933–4), 105.

29 Durham, pp. 310–11.

30 Underdown, *Revel, Riot and Rebellion*, pp. 60, 91; J. Bennett, 'Conviviality and Charity in Medieval and Early Modern England', *P&P*, 134 (1992).

31 R. Hutton, *The Rise and Fall of Merry England* (Oxford, 1994), p. 229.

32 S. Hindle, *On the Parish? The Micro-politics of Poor Relief in Rural England c.1550–1750* (Oxford, 2004), pp. 370–1.

33 Alldridge, 'Loyalty and Identity in Chester', pp. 104–5.

34 S. Hindle, 'A Sense of Place?', in A. Shephard and P. Withington (eds), *Communities in Early Modern England* (Manchester, 2000), pp. 102–3; C. Hill, 'The Secularization of the Parish', in Hill, *Society and Puritanism in Pre-revolutionary England* (London, 1964; 1969 edn), p. 420.

35 P. Seaward, 'Gilbert Sheldon, the London Vestries and the Defence of the Church', in T. Harris, P. Seaward and M. Goldie (eds), *The Politics of Religion in Restoration England* (Oxford, 1990), p. 54.

36 Sussex, pp. 18, 116.

37 S. Hindle, *On the Parish?* pp. 380–1.

38 Alsop (1695) in A.G. Craig, 'The Movement for the Reformation of Manners, 1688–1715' (Edinburgh University PhD, 1980), p. 184.

39 W. Hunt, *The Puritan Moment: The Coming of Revolution in an English County* (Cambridge, Mass., 1983), pp. 140–1, 42.

40 K. Wrightson and D. Levine, *Poverty and Piety in an English Village* (London, 1979; rev. edn, Oxford, 1995); M. Ingram, 'Religion, Communities and Moral Discipline in Late Sixteenth- and Early Seventeenth-Century England: Case Studies', in K. von Greyerz (ed.), *Religion and Society in Early Modern Europe* (London, 1984).

41 A. Hughes, 'Godly Reformation and its Opponents in Warwickshire, 1640–1662' (Dugdale Society Occasional Papers, 35, 1993), pp. 16, 17.

42 *Antimoixeia* (1691).

43 *Reformation and Revival in Eighteenth-century Bristol*, ed. J. Barry and
    K. Morgan (Bristol Record Society, 44, 1994), pp. 15, 19, 26; W.O.B. Allen
    and E. McClure (eds), *Two Hundred Years: The History of the SPCK* (1898),
    pp. 78–80.

44 P. Burke, *Popular Culture in Early Modern Europe* (London, 1978), ch 8.

45 A. Fletcher, *Reform in the Provinces* (New Haven, Conn., 1986), p. 277.

46 C. Rose, *England in the 1690s* (Oxford, 1999), p. 172.

47 E. Duffy, 'Primitive Christianity Revived: Religious Renewal in Augustan
    England', *SCH*, 14 (1977), 296.

48 M. Goldie and J. Spurr, 'Politics and the Restoration Parish: Edward Fowler
    and the Struggle for St Giles Cripplegate', *English Historical Review*,
    CIX (1994).

49 Wrightson and Levine, *Poverty and Piety*, p. 168.

50 *Bishop Fell and Nonconformity*, ed. M. Clapinson (Oxfordshire Record
    Society, 52, 1980) pp. 2–3.

51 Bill Stevenson, 'The Social Integration of Post-Restoration Dissenters,
    1660–1725', in Spufford (ed.), *The World of Rural Dissenters*.

52 S.S. Thomas, 'Religious Community in Revolutionary Halifax', *Northern
    History*, XL (2003), 89.

53 P. Lake, 'Puritanism, Arminianism and a Shropshire Axe Murder', *Midland
    History*, 15 (1990).

54 D.C. Beaver, *Parish Communities and Religious Conflict in the Vale of
    Gloucester 1590–1690* (Cambridge, Mass., 1998).

55 See R. Cust, 'Anti-Puritanism and Urban Politics: Charles I and Great
    Yarmouth', *HJ*, 35 (1992); Thomas, 'Religious Community'; N. Key and
    J. Ward, 'Divided into Parties: Exclusion Crisis Origins in Monmouth',
    English Historical Review, CXV (2000).

56 Cust, 'Anti-Puritanism and Urban Politics', 2–3.

57 *The Journal of William Schellinks' Travels in England 1661–1663*, trans.
    and ed. M. Exwood and H.L. Lehmann (Camden Society, 5th series, 1, 1993),
    p. 85.

58 K.V. Thomas, *Religion and the Decline of Magic* (Harmondsworth, 1971:
    1978 edn), p. 74; Hutton, *Rise and Fall*, pp. 142–3, 175–6, 217–18, 247–8.

59 Hindle, 'Sense of Belonging'.

60 K. Wrightson, 'The Politics of the Parish in Early Modern England', in
    P. Griffiths, A. Fox and S. Hindle (eds), *The Experience of Authority in Early
    Modern England* (Basingstoke, 1996), pp. 26–7.

61 C. Haigh, 'Anticlericalism' in Haigh (ed.), *The English Reformation Revised* (Cambridge, 1987), pp. 73–4.

62 Sussex, p. 34.

63 Sussex, pp. 102, 118.

64 Sussex, p. 64.

65 Sussex, p. 93.

66 S. Hindle, 'The Shaming of Margaret Knowsley: Gossip, Gender and the Experience of Authority in Early Modern England', *Continuity and Change*, 9 (1994).

67 G.H. Jenkins, *Literature, Religion and Society in Wales 1660–1730* (Cardiff, 1978), pp. 9–11.

68 P. Collinson, *The Religion of Protestants* (Oxford, 1982), p. 282.

69 *Bishop Fell and Nonconformity*, ed. Clapinson, p. 2.

70 Palliser, 'Introduction', in Wright (ed.), *Parish, Church and People*, p. 23.

CHAPTER 11

Churchgoing

What did people do when they went to their parish church in the seventeenth-century? Apart from the legal obligation, what made them go to church? These questions are not easily answered. True, there are plenty of complaints from the clergy that their parishioners grasped little of the preaching, prayer or sacraments, that they arrived late and left early, they slept and chattered: 'they gaze about the church as if they should be asked that question when they come home what went you to church to see, and not what to hear'; these country folk were 'blocks that go to church as dogs do, only for company'.[1] Protestant congregations in Dublin were accused of 'whispering, sleeping or gazing about on everyone that come in'.[2] 'How many thousands are there,' asked a Yorkshire preacher, 'that only of mere custom and not out of any conscience of duty towards God come to the communion?'[3] Churchwardens' presentments reveal that the churchgoers did not always behave with due decorum in the House of God: individuals made it their common practice to sleep in time of divine service and sermon; they 'made water' in church in time of divine service, indeed one could almost categorise these offenders according to whether they 'pissed' against the pillar, in their seat, in their neighbour's hat, or in one memorable and possibly significant case, against the pulpit during the sermon; members of the congregation spewed, farted, smoked, snored, spat, sang, knitted, told jokes, laughed and fought during time of divine service. That these offences were reported may show just how intolerable other parishioners found such disturbance of their worship. But neither presentments nor clerical complaints tell the whole story. Things may have looked different from the pews. What one did at church out of personal conviction or a sense of custom and community has a claim to be considered just as much a part of seventeenth-century religion as the liturgy or sermon. This chapter describes what went on in and around the parish church, and in doing so it attempts to imagine the laity's experience of churchgoing.

Worship

Although many pious works tell us what the clergy hoped for from their congregations, we know less about what went on in the parish churches. What form, for instance, did the Sunday services normally take and how did the laity participate? The usual Sunday morning service comprised the Morning Prayer, then the Litany, followed by the Communion Service – with a sermon – up to and including the prayer for the Church Militant. The Elizabethan Injunctions of 1559 allowed for psalms or hymns to be sung before or after service, but they were often sung before or after the sermon, or between the litany and the ante-communion, or in some churches after the second lesson.[4] Although shorter, Evening Prayer on Sundays and holy days also included the instruction and examination of children in the catechism, or a second sermon which was often described as a 'catechetical lecture'. The Prayer Book service was probably read about two hundred times a year in a typical parish; on each occasion the Lord's Prayer and the Creeds were recited several times, and several passages of scripture were read: the liturgy was potentially a wonderful vehicle for sustained instruction. Among some clergy there was an enthusiasm for daily reading of the prayers. In 1673 one eager new incumbent planned 'every day in the week in summer time they shall have morning prayers in the church, in the winter time, only on Litany days and festivals, on Sunday morning a sermon and the Church catechism explained to the children and concluded with a practical meditation for those of riper years in the afternoon'.[5] However, for all the good resolutions of some ministers and the constant exhortations of the hierarchy, a daily sacrifice of prayer and thanksgiving was uncommon in the nation's churches: the rector of Clayworth in Nottinghamshire thought himself conspicuously pious when he resolved to read prayers on Wednesdays and Fridays during Lent.

It was the clergy's view that, in public, the minister 'prays as the common mouth of the congregation'. The congregation said the confession and the Lord's Prayer after the minister, they recited alternate petitions in the service and the Litany, and 'the custom is, more or less in most places' for the people to 'recite the Psalms and other godly hymns with the minister by way of answering in turns'.[6] In fact it was more often the parish clerk who made the responses. It was the clerk's function to lead the congregation in their part of the liturgy and in their singing. Unlike modern churches with their great racks of Prayer Books and hymn books, the early modern parish church was lucky to possess two clean copies of the Book of Common Prayer, one for the minister and one for the clerk. In 1674 the woefully delapidated parish of Budbrooke, Worcestershire, had 'but one Book of Common Prayer, and if they had two there could be no person procured in the parish to be clerk that could read, the person that has served that office for these twenty years being illiterate'.[7] Unless literate parishioners brought their own copy of the Prayer Book to church – and it was mainly the upper and middling ranks that possessed Prayer Books – they would have to rely upon their memory and follow the clerk as best they could. The result was that the laity's contribution 'is in a manner lost to some of the congregation, since in the confused murmur of so many voices nothing can be distinctly heard'.[8]

The clergy rushed to the defence of their liturgy 'by which means the ignorant do not only learn diverse of the Psalms and usual prayers by heart, but also such as can read, do pray together with him [the minister]: so that the whole congregation at one instant do pour out their petitions unto the living God'.[9] This, the view of an Elizabethan minister, was still being maintained a century or more later. 'As for those that cannot' read, explained William Claggett, 'I must needs say, that it is not so hard as is pretended for them also to take those verses which are uttered by those that are near them, if they will carefully attend. And I have been credibly informed, that some devout people that could never read, have attained to an ability of reciting most of the Psalms without book, by often hearing them in those churches where they are alternately recited; which shows that the murmur is not so confused, but that the words may be heard distinctly enough to be understood, if one has a mind to it. And then they that cannot read may by this means be more quickened, than otherwise they would be, to learn to read; however to attend, and to learn the Psalms without book, that they also may bear their part vocally with the congregation in God's praises.'[10]

Congregational psalm-singing was a distinct part of the services. The popularity of the metrical psalms in the sixteenth-century translation by Sternhold and Hopkins was a major cultural phenomenon of early modern England. Their use within Sunday worship was just a small, but significant, aspect of their role in popular religion. The congregation may have seen the psalm-singing as their own contribution to the service: the parish clerk normally chose the psalm or tune to be sung; he 'lined out' the psalm, reading each line before it was repeated by the unaccompanied and untutored congregation, so that the singing often slowed down; and many singers prized the volume and duration above any other element of the performance. 'Some roar, some whine, some creak like wheels of carts,' complained sophisticated critics. Alexander Pope pictured the 'silenced preacher' standing by while 'the blessing thrills thro' all the labouring throng, / And heaven is won by violence of song'. Most clergymen do seem to have disassociated themselves from the singing and some even left the body of the church while it was going on.[11]

Parishioners, or rather churchwardens, did complain if the prayers were not read properly. 'Our minister doth say and sing the service, but as we think he doth sometimes omit part thereof as the litany and Ten Commandments; and, as we take it, at unseasonable times and hours, for he doth hold the parish as we verily think until one of the clock many times,' complained the wardens of Lancing in 1624. 'And we further say that we have not had any service at all upon some one Sabbath day and often we miss upon the holy days and very seldom any upon Wednesdays, Fridays, and Saturdays; and he hath been very forgetful in bidding the holy days and fasting days.'[12] In 1677 the vicar of St Martin's, Leicester, was taken to task for not reading his prayers 'audibly and distinctly', while a few years later the vicar of Lockington was alleged to 'mumble [the prayers] over and read them in such a mumbling and low tone of speech and irreverent manner, that few or none of the parishioners then assembled to hear divine service would or could understand what he read'.[13] Elsewhere parishioners were possessed by a genuine anxiety that the Prayer Book was tainted with popery or superstition.

The evidence seems to point in several directions. The ideal of the Common Prayer was to forge a devotional community. The liturgy's set forms and scriptural language would edify the congregation, their reverent gestures would express and promote invisible devotion, and their common confession would bind them together: as George Herbert enjoined them, 'pray with the most: for where most pray, is heaven'. Contrary to our perceptions of Protestantism as a religion of introspective individualism, this was, observes Targoff, an explicitly collective enterprise. Thus Richard Hooker's assertion that 'one man's contempt of the common prayer of the Church of God may be and oftentimes is most hurtful unto many' might explain the animosity that parishioners felt towards those who disrupted worship.[14] Prayer Book worship, some have suggested, contributed to the creation of a 'Protestant consciousness' almost by an osmotic process; the liturgy 'had earthed itself into the Englishman's consciousness and had sunk deep roots into popular culture'.[15] Yet familiarity with and even affection for the Prayer Book is not quite the same issue as participation in its worship. The common idiom of the day was to describe the laity 'hearing' the divine service and the clergy as 'reading' it. From the perspective of musical engagement, Temperley paints a grim picture of growing 'alienation' in the later century as the congregation increasingly became 'mere spectators to a performance by the minister, assisted by the parish clerk'.[16] So it is quite possible that many parishioners regarded the performance of public prayers as an essential communal activity, but one at which they were witnesses rather than full participants. Inattentively mumbling the occasional response or prayer, they bided their time until the real business of the day, the sermon.

*

In the seventeenth century the sermon was the centrepiece of parish worship. In most parishes, each Sunday morning the minister would ascend the steps of the pulpit, turn the hourglass, identify his text and then preach, often from quite sparse notes, for an hour or more on the doctrine, its uses and applications, and he would expect his auditors to follow his arguments and scriptural citations, to note his main points, and to spend much of the day mulling over and discussing his exposition of God's Word. It was, of course, an exercise in ministerial expertise, showmanship and stamina. Toby Matthew, Jacobean Archbishop of York, preached 1,992 sermons over a period of forty years. John Cotton, the puritan minister of Boston, gave a two-hour sermon each Sunday, followed by several hours of catechism instruction, a lecture on Thursday afternoon, and informal sermons on Wednesdays, Thursdays and Saturday afternoons. Most preachers, whether godly or not, expected only a little less of themselves and their parishioners. North of the Border, the Scottish Kirk organised the life of the community around sermons and Bible-reading. Attendance at the several Sabbath sermons was compulsory and was the basis of systematic indoctrination and testing.[17] Preaching and hearing sermons was a strenuous business in the seventeenth century, and it was popular.

The English were renowned as sermon addicts: they 'generally place their religion in the pulpit, as the papists do theirs upon the altar'; 'we make the pulpit our ark and chain all religion to it'.[18] In the cities, gentlemen and others dropped in to sermons as if to judge the performance. Parishioners set great store by regular preaching. The rector of Gumley, Leicestershire, was denounced by gentlemen from a neighbouring parish as 'a dumb dog, as well as the rest of the ministers about you, who do not preach twice every Sunday or Lord's day as our rector doth'.[19] In Restoration Suffolk, Isaac Archer's congregation did not protest when he curtailed some of the Prayer Book service and used the time saved to preach, 'which they liked better'.[20] Archer's Sunday afternoon sermons drew large congregations and made him unpopular with neighbouring ministers who did not preach twice on Sundays. In some places parishioners expressed their disappointment not to have midweek sermons.

Complaints were heard that all this attention to preaching was detracting from the other religious duties, that 'to place all or most of our religion in hearing a sermon' undermined respect for prayer and the sacrament of the Lord's Supper.[21] In 1602 the Vice Chancellor of Oxford University preached an attack on those who thought that sermons were the be-all and end-all of religion: 'I complain not that our churches are auditories, but that they are not oratories: not that you come to sermons, but that you refuse or neglect common prayer.'[22] 'In these last and worst times some crafty men . . . undervalue the administration of prayers and thanksgivings, which is the duty of the advocate or priest. Hence sermons or prophesyings are extolled to the skies, sacraments and prayers are neglected.'[23] Many parishes contained people like the Sussex couple 'Thomas Searle and his wife [who] never come to their parish church until the common prayers be ended and come only to the preaching'.[24] Visitation articles routinely enquired: 'are there any among you that come only to the preaching, and not to the common prayers of the church?' The community should beware, advised a Cheshire magistrate, of 'the sort of people disaffected to the Book of Common Prayer, which frequently stand without the churches, till the common service be read; and then at the singing of the Psalm, when the minister goes into the pulpit, then they come into the church and not before'.[25] The suspicion was that these were puritans – critics of specific parts of the Prayer Book and opponents of set forms of prayer – or just plain schismatics. But popular ignorance and negligence was another explanation of such behaviour. In 1686 John Gaskarth found that his new flock at Chevening simply required instruction: ''tis only the common insensibility of most part of country people in the prayers of the church and the duty of saying their prayers in a joint assembly that they labour under, which I hope to work of in some time . . . by recommending our liturgy, which I intend to do at large, I shall bring them to a true sense of their coming to church, that is to say their prayers together and not hear a sermon only, and so be more frequent there'.[26]

*

The third component of worship was the Holy Communion or Lord's Supper. It was, as the church's catechism put it, a sacrament 'generally necessary to salvation': the minister invited his congregation to 'the most comfortable sacrament of the body and blood of Christ; to be by them received in remembrance of his meritorious cross and passion; whereby alone we obtain remission of our sins, and are made partakers of the kingdom of heaven'. This was a spiritual rite with a strong communal overtone. 'This sacrament signified not only our union with Christ our head by faith, but also our communion with the members by love.'[27] Yet for all this, the Lord's Supper was neither celebrated nor received frequently in the seventeenth century.

Most parish churches celebrated the sacrament three or four times a year, generally at Christmas, Whitsun and Easter. Although this matched the Prayer Book's expectation that all parishioners over sixteen should receive the sacrament three times a year, in reality most lay Christians actually received just once a year, at Easter, when a series of sacraments were celebrated to accommodate the whole parish. This is evident from contemporary comment and from the many churchwardens' accounts that detail expenditure on bread and wine for communions: in 1634–35 the typical urban parish of St Oswald in Durham spent between four and six shillings on bread and wine for each of the communions celebrated on 11 January, 1 June, 24 August, 19 October, and 23 November, but twenty-seven shillings on the Easter communion. So although there were six communions a year at St Oswald's, judging by the amount spent on bread and wine, over five times as many people received the sacrament at Easter as did at any other time of the year. At Clayworth, Nottinghamshire, in 1679, 18 parishioners received at Whitsun and 21 at Christmas, but there were 204 communicants at Easter. At Llanboidy, Carmarthenshire, in the early eighteenth century, 300 received at the Easter communion, but only 40 attended the other communions.[28] The more comprehensive information available for the early eighteenth century demonstrates that most rural parishes celebrated communion three or four times a year at the great church festivals. In Scotland, by comparison, there was an annual spring sacrament, held over several Sundays, at which all parishioners were obliged to receive.[29]

The patterns of lay reception in England have yet to be established. There are some striking individual cases: at Great Yarmouth over a thousand potential communicants absented themselves from the 1633 Easter communion, while at Cogenhoe in Essex or Godnestone in Kent half the number of those eligible made their Easter communion, and 200 of the 236 eligible received communion at Clayworth in 1676. The circumstances of all such reports demand careful assessment.[30] In April 1686 a Suffolk

gentleman 'had the blessed satisfaction of seeing three score of the inhabitants of that parish receive [communion] at one time; having scarce ever
seen twenty, at any one time, before'. This new-found devotion was due,
he thought, to a circular letter issued by the Bishop of Norwich and to the
efforts of the minister 'who is a good man and a good preacher, and very
much beloved by his people'.[31] Much also depended upon location. There
was a marked difference between some rural and urban or metropolitan
parishes. Boulton used the Easter token books from the large suburban
parish of St Saviour's, Southwark, to calculate that between the 1570s
and the Civil War 80–98 per cent of potential communicants in the
parish made an annual communion. However, in the London parish of
St Botolph, Aldgate, attendance at the ordinary monthly communions in
1598 was about 50 while the nineteen Easter communion services saw
1,758 receive communion out of about 4,500 potential communicants.[32]
In rural Wiltshire at the beginning of the eighteenth century, reception
rates were low. In Pewsey only one in five adults took the communion at
either Christmas Day 1709 or Easter 1710; forty years earlier the rector
had alleged that half of the parish never received.[33] The evidence from
Bedfordshire is striking. At Milton Bryant 'seldom more than nineteen
receive' out of 104 eligible parishioners; at Clapham, 'about ten receive,
out of fifty'; but at Dunton 'not above twelve receive' out of 160 communicants, while at Astwick the communicants were 'but two or three
besides the clerk. Sometimes none at all.'[34] Time and time again the parish
clergy reported that a large number of their parishioners 'seldom or never'
received. It is difficult to avoid the conclusion that the sacrament, even at
Easter, was a minority interest in most seventeenth-century English and
Welsh parishes.

Ministers urged their congregations to receive the sacrament but also
insisted that they be properly prepared. It was the clergy's duty to warn the
congregation of an imminent communion and to exhort them to preparation: as one minister noted in his diary, 'I gave my parish notice a month
before and expounded on Lord's days; and privately instructed the
younger sort, finding them very serious, so that I hope my pains will not be
in vain.'[35] In 1630 John Randall observed that 'ordinary people commonly
do make some kind of preparation, according to their manner, when they
come to receive the sacrament of the Lord's Supper'.[36] Whether such
preparation measured up to the clergy's expectations is doubtful. There
were many manuals to help the laity in the task: some, such as Christopher
Sutton's *Godly Meditations upon the Most Holy Sacrament* (1601),
Jeremiah Dyke's *A Worthy Communicant* (1635) or John Tillotson's

Persuasive to Frequent Communion (1683), became best-sellers; and as the century progressed a formidable catalogue of such handbooks was built up to suit all pockets and tastes.[37] But we cannot measure the effect of this literature. Many of the minority of the population who received the sacrament probably did so out of convention and after the most rudimentary spiritual preparation. In Scotland, by contrast, the system of admission to the sacrament by a token, received only after personal examination and the performance of other duties, went a long way towards ensuring a prepared congregation.[38]

An undeniable tension existed between the exhortations to receive the sacrament and the preparation demanded. The clergy were aghast when their prescriptions for a 'worthy reception' were thrown back in their faces as justifications for non-reception, as in the case of those parishioners of Imber, Wiltshire, who told their minister they would not receive 'till they are better and fitter prepared'.[39] Communicants were also required to be in a state of perfect love and Christian charity with their neighbours. This could pose genuine dilemmas: one regular Suffolk communicant did not receive the sacrament at Whitsun 1709 because he had accused James Clift, a neighbour, of fathering an illegitimate baby 'which caused Clift and I to have words so that I could not think my self in charity with him, or he with me'.[40] Other cases, such as the Wiltshire man who excused his failure to receive for three years by alleging that he was 'perplexed with law suits', are more difficult to interpret.[41] Yet some attitudes were unambiguous. In 1635 a Durham man refused to make up his quarrel with a neighbour so that he could receive the sacrament and insolently asserted of the minister, 'I care not three-halfpence for his communion.'[42] Parishioners were quick to take offence if a notorious evil liver, who was judged to be beyond the social pale of the community, was allowed to receive the sacrament alongside the respectable. Equally, parishioners became concerned when their minister seemed morally unsuited or unfit to administer the sacrament: for instance, the vicar of Charlton made himself 'ridiculous' by conducting the service while drunk.[43]

The Prayer Book required the minister to distribute the consecrated bread and wine 'to the people in their hands kneeling'. In some quarters there was a deep-rooted hostility to kneeling because it supposedly implied the adoration of the sacrament and aroused memories of the Catholic doctrine of transubstantiation. The churchwardens and parishioners of Fenny Drayton would not make their Easter communion in 1607 'because they refuse to take the same kneeling'.[44] Recalcitrant clergymen were reported for refusing to give the sacrament to those who did not kneel or for taking the bread and wine to seated communicants. It is not clear just how many ministers insisted upon a kneeling reception before the Laudian campaign for greater reverence. In Scotland there was a ferocious reaction to the 1618 Articles of Perth which replaced 'Christ's gesture of sitting' with 'the Antichrist's gesture of kneeling', but then in the Kirk the annual communion was distributed to the congregation while they sat at a series of tables erected in the nave of the church.[45] In England, kneeling probably prevailed as the century progressed, but it was a gradual and incomplete process. The upheaval of the mid-century threw practice and convention into confusion, as can be seen by three examples dating from the 1660s. At Impington, Cambridgeshire, 'some (who can conveniently place themselves), do receive the sacrament in the chancel the rest do receive in their seats, all receive reverently and kneeling'.[46] In London, Richard Kidder found that many of his parishioners 'kneeled not at the communion, but were otherwise very devout and regular', so he humoured them rather than drive them into the arms of Nonconformity. At Exeter the Presbyterian George Trosse attended his parish church and admired the preaching, but for all the clergy's persuasion he would not receive communion there because he refused to kneel, although he would not condemn those who did so.[47]

Strangely, in view of the general lack of enthusiasm for the sacrament, there was often a swift and adverse reaction from parishioners when a minister attempted to limit admission to the Lord's Supper. It was as if the sacrament was seen as a service which should be available to all in the community if they wanted it. Occasionally a brave clergyman would deny the sacrament to the negligent or ignorant, to those 'who could say none of the Ten Commandments', presumably in the hope that the refusal would prompt their amendment, but such ministers were usually forced to back down.[48] On the other hand, the godly lived in fear of the 'promiscuous' communions of the national church, of receiving the sacrament side by side with notorious evil livers, who because they were unworthy to eat at the Lord's Supper, were eating to damnation (I Corinthians 11: 29). One or two puritan ministers, such as Samuel Fairclough of Suffolk and John White of Dorchester, did succeed, with the help of lay allies, in excluding the 'visibly profane' from the parish sacrament in the years before the Civil War, but it was the advent of Presbyterianism which raised the real prospect of imposing 'discipline'. In 1647 London's Presbyterian ministers decided 'to engage all persons of an unblameable life, of competent age, before they come unto the Lord's Table to give an account of their faith before the parochial presbytery'. This personal examination before the lay elders as well as the clergy was reminiscent of the practice of the Scottish Kirk, but while in Scotland the people were obliged to attend, in the England of the 1640s there was no such compulsion. The very prospect of such examination drove people away from the sacrament. This may well have been the intention. In 1651 Ralph Josselin decided to celebrate communion in his Essex parish for the first time in nearly nine years. Many of his parishioners indicated that they wished to receive the sacrament, but Josselin was concerned that he could not 'comfortably join with' many of them and he made it clear that most of them were unfit to receive: eventually only thirty-four parishioners remained to receive the sacrament.[49]

The experience of the 1640s and 1650s is revealing. Parishes generally kept up communions during the Civil War years, but from the later 1640s the sacrament fell into neglect; there were fewer celebrations of the communion and more people stayed away from the communion. There was wide variation in practice. At St Oswald's, Durham, there were no communions celebrated between 1645 and 1662, although there were private communions for the sick at home. The churchwardens' accounts of Cratfield, Suffolk, show a sudden decline by 80 per cent in the expenditure on communions around 1646. At Chippenham it was noted in 1663 there had been no sacrament 'for about twenty years last past' and the newly appointed vicar realised ''twas expected now'.[50] During the 1640s and 1650s there was a demand for the sacrament from certain sections of the laity: the pious at Lichfield requested a celebration; the vestry of St Bartholomew Exchange, London, asked their minister to administer the sacrament 'to all his parish to beget love with one another'. These communions ought to have followed the rite of the Directory of Public Worship, but services were conducted in some parishes according to the Prayer Book or something approximating it.[51] Although there was evident popular interest in the revived Common Prayer sacrament at the Restoration, the second half of the century was no better than the first when it came to the frequent celebration and reception of the Lord's Supper. The country slipped back into the routine of three or four celebrations a year, with one supposedly universal reception at Easter. But now at least the clergy could attribute the neglect to 'the late distracted times' when the sacrament had been laid aside 'for near twenty years together'.[52]

In general, the seventeenth-century laity's attitude towards the sacrament was low-key, lukewarm, almost apathetic, with only a small proportion of those eligible, perhaps a fifth in many parishes, taking a real interest. This pious minority nevertheless merit attention both as a group and as individuals. We know that there were clerical enthusiasts for more frequent celebration of the sacrament and their influence has been detected in several towns, cities and cathedrals in both the early and later seventeenth century.[53] No doubt they attracted the pious minority to their monthly communions, either by sponsoring an upwelling of devotion at parish level or by drawing communicants from other parishes. The lay people who used or sought out such sacraments have often been rather disparagingly dismissed as overwrought spinsters or old ladies. But the testimony of individuals reveals that a regard for the sacrament was not the preserve of any one sex, social group or denomination. Puritans were keen participants in the sacrament and careful to prepare themselves: in the 1620s, Symond D'Ewes devoted a whole day to preparation for 'the glorious feast' of the sacrament; before his first communion in 1647 Philip Henry 'set myself, in the strength of divine grace, about the great work of self-examination in order to repentance; and then I repented; that is, solemnly and seriously, with some poor meltings of soul'. Nehemiah Wallington resolved to receive the sacrament monthly. So did stout supporters of the Church of England such as Viscount Scudamore and John Evelyn. The apothecary Thomas Mowsley was assiduous in preparing and 'taking notice how his soul was affected' by the sacrament. The Suffolk gentleman William Coe generally received at Easter, Christmas and Whitsun and prepared himself by self-examination and fasting. Coe used the sacrament as the watch-spring of his spiritual life: on Whitsunday 1694, 'I received the blessed sacrament and renewed my covenant again with almighty God in my saviour's blood. Lord give me grace to amend my life for the future and to spend every day as if it were to be my last.'[54]

Rites of passage

Rites of passage are those corporate ritual activities that mark the individual's progress through the stages of life. Personal milestones, they also recognise the assumption of new responsibilities and the forging of new connections within the community. They take many different forms in different cultures, but here we are concerned only with the three principal rites that took place within the orbit of the parish church in the seventeenth century: baptism, marriage and burial. These were not the only contemporary rites which had both spiritual and social dimensions – others, such as the 'churching' of women after childbirth or the 'confirmation' of young people before their first communion, have recently been explored by scholars – but they were the most significant.[55]

The Church of England retained just two of the medieval sacraments, baptism and the Lord's Supper. Baptism is the outward badge of Christianity, the public sign of membership of the Christian community. According to the church's catechism, baptism makes the individual a child of grace, it incorporates the child into the body of Christ: repentance and faith are required, but this is promised for the baby by his or her adult sureties, the godparents. In the view of many historians, it was the institution of godparents that gave the ecclesiastical rite its social dimension. Godparents were a way of associating the child with others besides its birth kin. These new 'spiritual kin' could aid and protect the child; the new bonds were cemented by the public ritual, by the exchange of gifts and names, and by feasting. Yet for all these positive aspects, baptism was a bone of contention, its rituals 'sensitive and complex', its scriptural justification and theological implications confused and troubling.[56]

The Prayer Book's baptism service worried some Protestants. It required the minister to mark the child with the sign of the cross and it suggested that the infant was 'regenerate' or saved. To the puritanical this smacked of popish superstition and of the notion that God had distributed his saving grace indiscriminately to all men rather than simply to the elect. Puritan clergy repeatedly asked, at the Hampton Court and Savoy conferences, for these errors to be remedied. Learned exchanges ensued about signs of the cross made in the air or on the forehead, about the 'sprinkling' with water, and the justification for fonts rather than simple basins. Another objection to the baptism rite was that it allowed private baptism by lay people in emergencies. This was eminently sensible given the dangers that attended the first hours of life: if the baby was unlikely to survive, the midwife or family could baptise it. This led to the occasional embarrassment for those who did thrive: in 1738 Thomas Messenger of Hanwell in Middlesex was baptised by the midwife in a dreadful panic, 'but [then] proved [to be] a girl'.[57] The provision for emergency baptism clearly implied that baptism was necessary, that in some way it attributed an identity or contributed to salvation, perhaps by conferring 'saving grace'.

These may seem largely theoretical issues until one imagines them within the context of infant mortality and parental anguish. Eliza Franklin was the third wife of the publican who kept the King's Arms in Oxford. After 'escaping death at three several travails in child-bed, [Eliza] died together with the fourth' child in 1622 at the age of thirty-five. She is commemorated in a brass memorial in the south aisle of the church of St Cross, Oxford. The brass depicts Eliza on her deathbed with her dead children all about her; all four infants are described as now 'in the kingdom of heaven', but only one is portrayed with a face, the one who had been baptised before death; the three unbaptised babies are in their shrouds, dark and faceless. Other issues are raised by the agonised diary entry of a clergyman who had omitted to baptise one of his children before it died: 'I know God is a God of the faithful, and their seed, and baptism is a sign of it; and I no more question that child's happiness (whatever St Augustine thought) then that of the Jewish children who died before the eighth day. I take God to witness I do not, did not despise the sacrament; but now 'tis fallen out so, not through the fault of the infant, or our wilful neglect, but through an unavoidable necessity, because of God's hand in Will's sickness, and my not knowing 'twas ill and I comfort my self with hopes that God, who is not tied to means, has washed its soul in Christ's blood!'[58] Such examples reveal the theological confusion surrounding the fate of the unbaptised and hint at the common assumption that all were Christians by inheritance. By implication, they also disclose what comfort the sacrament offered to those whose children were baptised.

Baptism's powerful grip on the popular imagination is evident in several ways. Paradoxically, one is the outrage caused by the Baptists, a mid-century sect which grew to become a significant if theologically divided force within English Nonconformity. The Baptists rejected the practice of infant baptism. Believing that only adults could make the promises required of a Christian, they practised adult or 'believer's baptism'. The Baptists were by definition, therefore, gathered or independent congregations, and for most followers this shared spiritual fellowship was the essential characteristic of their movement. Outsiders, however, found their denial of the public rite of infant baptism profoundly shocking – perhaps as much for its social as its sacramental message. To take another angle, the ban on the Prayer Book in the 1640s seems to have had an effect on the practice of baptism. Slowly, even reluctantly, parishes bought copies of the Directory, but we rarely know whether or how they used them: Coster points out that one Shropshire village first used the Directory in 1647, but it was another decade before a child was baptised there 'after the new Presbyterian way, according to the Directory, in a basin of water by the pulpit'.[59] How then, one wonders, were local children baptised before 1657? Demographers have suggested a 10 per cent fall in the national level of public baptism in the period between 1645 and 1653 and one explanation may lie in a rise in the number of private baptisms. These are likely to have been Prayer Book services since we know, from sources such as diaries, that many such baptisms took place in the 1640s and 1650s. Before the Civil War, puritans had exploited the provision for private baptism to have their children baptised without the superstitious trappings of the surplice, the sign of the cross, or godparents. Such evasion was evidently still a concern later in the century since clergy insisted upon a proper regulation of the practice for fear that 'those who were captious and wayward to the laws of the church . . . would use private baptism upon every occasion' to avoid those ceremonies.[60] Baptism at home was also becoming increasingly fashionable in the upper reaches of society. One final consideration concerns the rise of Nonconformity. The majority of Nonconformists would not bring their children to be baptised at church, but there were exceptions such as the four Presbyterian families of Ravensden, Bedfordshire, 'who all baptise, marry and bury according to the Church of England', and even more tangled tales such as that of John Jesson who had a son baptised by a Nonconformist minister in 1689 because the local curate 'would not baptise it (though in health) without godfathers and a godmother' and despite having his other children 'baptised according to the way of the Church of England'.[61] All of these were exceptions that prove the powerful social rule that baptism in the parish church was a fundamental, near universal, rite of passage.

The rite of marriage was also the gateway to another condition, in this case, the holy state of matrimony. The purpose of matrimony, according to the church, was to raise children, avoid fornication, and provide 'mutual help, society and comfort': for the 80 per cent of the population who married, it meant embarking upon new responsibilities as husbands and wives, householders and, in time, parents. Most individuals married first in their mid to late twenties but a sizeable number of these would have subsequent marriages after the death of the first partner. Weddings were therefore a common occurrence in the seventeenth century. They set the church's seal on what was a long process of courtship, family negotiation, and betrothal. The church required that the impending wedding be announced to the community by the reading of the banns in the parish church on three separate occasions. The wedding involved a day or more of merry-making, a round of music, gifts, feasts, drinking and such folk rituals as flinging the bride's stocking; money was spent on fiddlers and ribbons, flowers and bell-ringers, and fees to the parish clerk and the minister. The solemn wedding service at the centre of the festivity was a hybrid, part communal witness of the couple's pledges to each other before God and their neighbours and part ecclesiastical creation of a marriage: theologically, nothing of great significance occurred at a wedding, yet, as Cressy remarks, most onlookers believed that priestly action had married the couple.[62]

Not all weddings were so public. If a couple wanted a quiet or speedy marriage – perhaps they were still 'in service' as single people, or one was promised to another party, or their families disapproved, or the bride was pregnant – then a special licence could be purchased from the bishop to allow a wedding in a parish other than their own or during the prohibited seasons of Lent and Advent. These licences were expensive at five shillings or more and so were probably used more by the fairly prosperous; some London churches made a fashionable speciality of weddings by licence. Poorer couples might instead resort to one of the notorious ministers or remote churches where no questions were asked of them. These irregular or 'clandestine' marriages were of constant concern to the church authorities.

The fact that weddings had little theological weight did not prevent them from becoming controversial. The godly disliked the use of the 'superstitious' or 'popish' wedding ring and many ministers may well have dispensed with it if couples objected. Laudian bishops used this ministerial willingess to marry couples without the ring as a convenient way of identifying those clergy who were likely to be ceremonial nonconformists. The church's wedding service seems to have remained popular even after it had been officially banned in the 1640s. Couples ignored the Directory in preference for the Prayer Book. When the Nominated Assembly of 1653 instituted civil marriage by a Justice of the Peace, there was a rush to marry before the legislation came into force and widespread evasion once it had.[63] There is anecdotal evidence of couples insisting upon a religious (and often a Prayer Book) marriage to supplement the civil ceremony. This may well have been true of Samuel Pepys, who was married at St Margaret's Westminster by a Justice on 1 December 1655, but who celebrated his wedding anniversary on 10 October, suggesting perhaps that a secret religious ceremony took place some weeks before the civil marriage.

The final rite of passage was the funeral. Although there is now a vast scholarly literature about death and its rituals, emotions and institutions, and despite the clergy's intimate role in many of them, such as advising the dying, writing their wills, comforting their relatives or preaching their funeral sermons, we can only focus here upon the church and its role in burial. This is not, of course, to deny the deep involvement of the community in the process. In some places the passing bell, or 'soul peal', was tolled for all parishioners as they lay dying (occasionally, hearing the bell would inspire a recovery), and it brought neighbours rushing to the deathbed. When the puritan regime forbade the passing bell at All Saints,

Newcastle, the church's income suffered so badly that ringing had to be reinstated.[64] The seventeenth century insisted on a decent burial. The funeral gifts, the gloves, ribbons and rings, the feast of baked meats, cakes, ale and wine, attest to the social importance of this last farewell. The community was expected to turn out for all funerals: in 1617, anxious that the custom was declining, the Moot of Liverpool ordered that one representative from every house in the street where the deceased had lived should accompany the body to church on pain of a sixpence fine.[65] If religion was ever to help people through this vale of tears, surely it was now, in the face of death? For, although 'the end of funeral duties is first to show that love towards the party deceased that nature requires,' explained Hooker, 'the greatest thing of all other about this duty of Christian burial is an outward testification of the hope we have touching the resurrection of the dead'.[66] The burial service included a lesson from I Corinthians 15: 55, *death, where is thy sting?*; and the minister committed the body to the ground 'in sure and certain hope of resurrection to eternal life, through our Lord Jesus Christ'. Family, friends and neighbours could say farewell in the confident expectation of a literal bodily resurrection.

Unfortunately, death was not quite that simple. The ascetic impulse within Protestantism and the compulsion to repudiate every last hint of Roman Catholic superstition prompted some to order funerals of brutal simplicity. In his will of 1616, Samuel Hurlstone, a Kent rector, stipulated that 'I will have my body to be buried within the churchyard of Ickham aforesaid, by my wife and faithful lover, and that without any delay after my death, without popish pomp, vain compliments and ringing.'[67] There was little room here for communal grief, although the widow would have her moment. There was a theological rationale to this puritan disdain for the corpse and suspicion of the Prayer Book's cadences. The doctrine of predestination, the ineluctable division of mankind into the saved and the damned, led godly clergymen to baulk at using the phrase about 'sure and certain hope of resurrection' over the bodies of parishioners whom they knew to have lived and died in sin. Puritans and Nonconformists repeatedly questioned the assumption behind this phrase, and demanded that it be rewritten along the lines of 'we commit his body [etc.] believing a Resurrection of the just and unjust, some to joy, and some to punishment'.[68] Yet the evidence suggests that these severe demands fell on deaf ears: the Prayer Book service continued to be read, individuals and communities continued to spend money on funerals, and increasingly on tombstones, individual coffins, and pious mementoes. Theology could not be allowed to intrude upon grief and commemoration.

Rites of passage belonged to the church and the community. They were under strain in the seventeenth century as communities experienced religious separatism or social differentiation. But the vast majority of parishioners continued to rush to church with the newborn, dance their way there with the wedding party, and trudge to the churchyard behind the shrouded corpse.

Beyond the church door

On Sunday, 21 October 1711, William Coe 'was at church twice but spent the rest of the day idly, talking of worldly business coming home from church forenoon and afternoon'. On another occasion, he confided to his diary, 'I talked with Robert Rolfe as soon as we came out of church about . . . changing some seed barley, which I ought to have put off till another day.'[69] The difficulty of drawing a boundary between religious activities and the worldly business of work, community or pleasure, was a familiar problem in the seventeenth century. Even a man like Coe, who was no puritan, felt the tug of the Sabbath, the pang of conscience when he played cards or talked business on the Lord's Day. But free time was so short, social interactions were so few and precious, it was inevitable that religious duties would have to reach some kind of accommodation with people's need for recreation and social life.

Much of what we know about people's activities outside the church on a Sunday, and by extension on the holy days which were their only other free time, comes from the contest between those who wanted to pursue their recreations and those who wished to suppress them in the name of devotion or reformation. For example, Parliament's 1644 ban on Sunday activities extended to 'any wrestlings, shooting, bowling, ringing of bells for pleasure or pastime, mask, wake, otherwise called feasts, church-ale, dancings, games, sport or pastime whatsoever'. A few years later William Cavendish penned some advice on government for the future Charles II. He suggested that 'after Evening Prayer every Sunday and holiday, the country people with their fresher lasses [should] . . . trip on the town green about the maypole to the louder bagpipe, there to be refreshed with their ales and cake'. When Charles regains his throne, he ought to revive and encourage country recreations, such as May Games, Morris dances, the Lord and Lady of the May, the hobby horse, the thrashing of hens at Shrovetide, and carols and wassails at Christmas, with good plum porridge and pies, all of 'which now are forbidden as profane, ungodly things'.[70] As Cavendish pointed out, James I had appreciated the value of such pastoral diversions. In the 1618 Declaration of Sports, James had commanded 'that after the end of divine service our good people be not disturbed, letted, or discouraged from any lawful recreation; such as dancing, either men or women, archery for men, leaping, vaulting, or any other such harmless recreation, nor from having of May-games, Whitsun ales and morris-dances, and the setting up of May-poles and other sports therewith used, so as the same be had in due and convenient time, without impediment or neglect of divine service'.[71] This was a vision of the marriage of mirth and virtue, of recreation and religion, rather than their competition.

Dancing on a Sunday was a common way of adding a little fun to life. In Richard Baxter's Shropshire village, once the Common Prayer had been read, the rest of Sunday was 'spent in dancing under a maypole and a great tree'. Most of our knowledge of these dancers comes from complaints against them. William Witcher, a Sussex fiddler, was alleged to bring up to forty dancers to Yapton where they spent the whole Sabbath dancing. In 1624 five young men of the village of Keevil in Wiltshire were presented for drunkenness, haunting the alehouse, leaving church during the sermon, and for dancing. The last charge they readily admitted. They had danced 'in the company of divers men and women of Keevil in a bower in the midst of the town at a dancing match'. They explained that 'there is usually dancing in Keevil upon the Sabbath days after . . . evening prayer, which is no otherwise then is allowed'.[72] These exchanges doubtless grew out of local tussles between puritans and their antagonists. The dancers frequently appealed to the law, citing the Declaration of Sports of 1618, or its reissue of 1633, or asserted their traditional right to Sunday recreations so long as they did not trespass upon the time of divine service. When a Mrs Grundien of Eccles was presented in 1611 for 'having ales on the Sabbath day and thereby drawing people from church', she confirmed that her ale had taken place *after* evening service, and the charge was dropped.[73] Those who were children during the 1680s later recorded the familiar youthful activities: 'dancing took much with the young people of our town . . . the dancing master was a fiddler and a juggler and after we broke up school every night he went to play his tricks. I did not learn many dances before it became an exceeding trouble to my soul and spirit . . . after some time my playfellows would entice me to feasts where young men and women went to be merry . . . and such like was I invited to under a pretence to improve our dancing.'[74]

Dancing was not the only pastime for the young. A Cambridgeshire man reminisced that 'as a young man [this would be in the 1630s] I was greatly addicted to football playing and as the custom was in our parish and in many others, the young men, as soon as church was over, took a football and went to play'.[75] The churchwardens of the Sussex parish of Boxgrove presented a group of young men in 1622 'for playing at cricket in the churchyard on Sunday, the fifth of May, after sufficient warning given to the contrary, for three special reasons: first, for that it is contrary to the seventh article [presumably one of the archdeacon's visitation articles]; secondly, for that they use to break the church-windows with the ball; and thirdly, for that a little child had like to have her brains beaten out with a cricket bat'. They also presented the 'old churchwardens . . . for defending and maintaining them in it'.[76] The Nonconformist Heywood complained that on Easter Sunday 1681 'as my hearers went from us through Halifax there was hundreds of people at Clark brig, in the church yard, on the green, and all along the town of young people and others playing at stool-ball [a predecessor of cricket], and other recreations, without any control'.[77] None of these pastimes was entirely independent of the parish church. The games were played in or around the churchyard or close to times of the services. Other activities, such as the growing interest in change ringing on church bells or the formation of parish bands, encroached upon the church itself.

The other great Sunday pastime was drinking. Although drinking did not necessarily conflict with religious duties, drunkenness did. In 1627 a Suffolk man came out of church grumbling at the sermon's criticism of drunkenness and promising that 'he would drink for all that, till his knees or legs did buckle'.[78] Presumably he crossed the street to the local alehouse and proceeded to spend the afternoon fulfilling his promise. There was nothing untoward in going to the alehouse after church, but it was an offence to 'tipple' in alehouses during time of divine service. Churchwardens were sent out to track down the tipplers. This was a practice which long outlived the seventeenth century. On the afternoon of Sunday, 25 April 1756, Thomas Turner, churchwarden of Lewes, went to church, 'and as soon as the prayers was ended, Mr French and I went out and searched the public houses: to wit, John Jones's, where we found no one person but John Jones, from whence we went to Fran Turner's where we found a man and his wife who came in overnight. They seemed to be very sober sort of people and not a-drinking so that we did not meddle with them. We came back just as the people came out of church. Mr French went to Jones's and had a dram, and I a pint of beer.'[79] Pillars of the church that they were, French and Turner obviously saw nothing wrong with stopping off for a pint on the way home from church.

Then as now, nostalgia easily casts a rosy glow over these Sundays spent in church and on the village green. They always represented a world that had just been lost – the good old days of Queen Bess or Merry England – and when mirth and religion had been broken asunder, it was only to be expected that people would grumble. In Cromwell's day, when the authorities struggled to impose a strict regime of Sabbath observance, laments were heard: at Maldon, Essex, William Barnes was accused of having said, while working in the harvest field, 'in former times when the Book of Common Prayer was read the people did usually go out of the church to play at football and to the alehouse and there continued till they were drunk and it were no matter if they were hanged'.[80] A few years later, after the restoration of the Prayer Book, Sunday was alleged to be once again 'the sport, and pleasure day of the general rout of people'.[81]

The recreations of the weekly day of rest were closely associated with the celebrations of other holidays. These were literally 'holy days' as the communal calendar was derived in large part from the ecclesiastical calendar. The year was marked by the great church festivals of Easter and Christmas, and much of the mundane business of paying rents and settling bills was pegged to dates such as Lady Day, All Saints', Lambas and Candlemas; fairs, processions, feasts, ales and dances were commonly held on St George's, St Luke's or St Bartholomew's Day, Shrove Tuesday, Whitsun and Ascension Day. Many of these occasions were originally pre-Christian: the eve of St John the Baptist was also Midsummer Eve (23 June), and some were merely seasonal, such as May Day. Grafted on to this calendar were the Protestant anniversaries such as 5 November or the accession day of Queen Elizabeth or the reigning monarch. James I had the nation observe the anniversary of the Gowrie Plot, and after 1660 holidays were ordered on 30 January, the anniversary of the regicide, and 29 May, the anniversary of the Restoration. These were days with special church services, sermons, civic processions and banquets. The late-seventeenth-century Church of England celebrated over forty feast days, fasts and special anniversaries each year.[82]

Although the church was not at the heart of all early modern festivities – May Day, for example, had no religious significance – it was central to many communal celebrations. The perambulation of the parish on 'Plough Monday' has already been described as a significant expression of communal identity. It was not always harmonious – several perambulations led to brawls and some clergy resented the demands of local custom – but it persisted through the century. Christmas, too, brought church and community together in celebration. In pre-Civil War Myddle, 'upon

Christmas day in the afternoon after divine service and when the minister had gone out of Church, the clerk would sing a Christmas carol in church'. John Aubrey noted that at Danby, Yorkshire, it was customary after receiving the sacrament on Christmas day for the congregation to go to the alehouse and drink together as a testimony of their friendship and charity.

Attitudes towards Christmas and holidays more generally could be a litmus test of religious outlook. Since Christmas was a medieval holiday, an occasion for excess of all kinds, and without any scriptural justification, the godly shunned it rather ostentatiously. In Bristol in the 1630s, Widow Kelly opened her shop on Christmas day 'as a witness for God'; in the 1640s, Parliament abolished Christmas and provoked riots in Ipswich and Canterbury: the multitude kept up Christmas both as a religious festival and a celebration despite the puritans.[83] In 1647 Parliament suggested that in place of Christmas and all the other abolished holidays, the nation should take the second Monday of every month as a secular holiday. A Bristol schoolmaster tried to persuade his pupils to replace 'the popish holidays (as they call them, holy)' with the first Wednesday of each month.[84] These high-minded appeals fell on deaf ears. After 1660, Christmas once again became a joyous public festivity – perhaps too joyous. In 1675 Josselin, a puritan at heart, preached on Christmas Day 'with affection, a small company present; all shops open; trade goes; religion sad'.[85] Was this a puritan who would now prefer to see the shops shut on 25 December if people would come to church?

*

In the last resort perhaps it is not possible to say what made people go to church or what it meant to them: the questions are too broad, too badly framed, and encompass too many individuals. As one authority has suggested, it is impossible to distinguish between the apathetic church-goer and the committed conformist, largely because the evidence is weighted towards outward conformity.[86] As we have seen, there were tensions running through religious practice, tensions between the demands of prayers and sermons, clerical hopes and lay performance, passivity and enthusiasm, communalism and individualism. Ultimately, for many, practical considerations dictated their religious practice. Many needed or preferred to work on the Sabbath despite the fact that this was an offence under the Elizabethan Injunctions of 1559 and was banned except for 'works of necessity' (milking and the like) by a statute of 1676. Wiltshire villagers were in the habit of attending only one of the two Sunday services, choosing whichever fitted in best with the work they were doing that day. Very few of them attended church on the special festivals, other than at Christmas and Easter; nor did they abstain from work as they should have done. In 1623 the churchwardens of Findon, Sussex, reported 'that two of the menservants of Richard Grevet of Worthing ploughed on St Thomas Day last in our parish; whose names we know not.' The wardens of Ogbourne St Andrew, Wiltshire, confessed in 1628 that the whole parish failed to observe holy days: in some places, fairs or markets were held on holy days, inevitably bringing the parish into conflict with the church's rules. One man thought he could mow 'without offence' on St Bartholomew's Day, 'because he saw others . . . were a-mowing likewise'; and another, hired to thresh for the rector of Pewsey, protested when forbidden to work on a holy day: 'let the bishop and church order what they please, I will work upon all week days as well as other folk'.[87]

Parishioners could often insist, then, on an accommodation between religious duties and secular activities. There had to be room for work and play as well as for worship: religious activity was not compartmentalised; it was not protected from contact with the rest of life. One manifestation of this was the prevalence of local 'custom' in matters that touched upon the church. These might be about who sat where in church, who sang, and who wore a hat or kerchief, or about the conduct of parish celebrations. In 1623, for instance, the wardens of Storrington in Sussex reported that 'our parishioners claim of our parson by ancient custom to have bread and cheese and a barrel of beer in the church on Easter day immediately after evening prayer; which custom in regard of the place and day our parson admonished them to be unlawful, yet delivered the accustomed on Easter Monday; and most of the parishioners had into the churchyard without either our approbation or consent'.[88] Religion had to bend before the practicalities of seventeenth-century life. One minister justified his breaking of a cake over the bride's head at a wedding as 'a custom which had long prevailed in his parish and which he thought might be inoffensive, in itself neither good not bad, as many received customs were'.[89]

As this chapter has shown, the vast majority of the population were churchgoers and their religion was of a rather tepid kind, well integrated with their own needs and interests, but undemanding. At its worst, their attitude might be epitomised by the Sussex man who missed services and 'doth unreverently behave himself in time of divine service by leaning upon an elbow or his hand and the other in his pocket and sleeping'.[90] Yet lay people also complained about such behaviour, took an interest in the sermons and the proper conduct of prayers, and resented inadequate or negligent clergymen. One obvious explanation for this confusing state of affairs is that the laity fell into two groups, the worldly and the pious: the worldly came to church for form's sake but their minds were on other things such as football and the alehouse, while the devout and godly, a minority to be sure, were assiduously noting the sermons and examining their souls. A second explanation is that lay ideas of what constituted adequate religious application did not match those of the clergy or the church. These are not alternative explanations, but complementary aspects of the same truth. Most individuals were a mixture of the worldly and godly, and only too aware of their failings. 'I am very much concerned to find in myself such a strong disinclination to these external duties of religion, as prayer, meditation, receiving the sacrament of the Lord's Supper,' Dudley Ryder confided to his diary. 'It proceeds I believe chiefly from the want of due and lively sense of spiritual things and the vast importance of them. They don't affect me as they ought to do.'[91]

Notes

1 B. Reay, 'Popular Religion', in Reay (ed.), *Popular Culture in Seventeenth-century England* (London, 1985), p. 97.

2 R. Gillespie, *Devoted People: Belief and Religion in Early Modern Ireland* (Manchester, 1997), p. 23.

3 A. Hunt, 'The Lord's Supper in Early Modern England', *P&P*, 161 (1998), 81.

4 N. Temperley, *The Music of the English Parish Church: Volume 1* (Cambridge, 1979), pp. 92, 124.

5 Bodl. L., Carte MS 77, fo. 538.

6 Spurr, *RC*, pp. 355–7.

7 *Inspections of Churches and Parsonage Houses in the Diocese of Worcester in 1674, 1676, 1684 and 1687*, ed. P. Morgan (Worcester Historical Society, new series, 12, 1986), pp. 6–7, 19–20, 48, 70.

8 I. Green, *Print and Protestantism in Early Modern England* (Oxford, 2000), pp. 247–50; Spurr, *RC*, pp. 355–7.

9 M.S. Byford, 'The Price of Protestantism: Assessing the Impact of Religious Change in Elizabethan Essex: The Cases of Heydon and Colchester, 1558–94' (Oxford University D.Phil. thesis, 1988), p. 39.

10 William Claggett in *A Collection of Cases and Other Discourses Written to Recover Dissenters* (1694), p. 291.

11 Green, *Print and Protestantism*, pp. 547–8, 506, 551, and ch. 9 passim; Temperley, *Music of Parish Church*, pp. 91–2, 87–8 and passim.

12 Sussex, p. 93

13 J.H. Pruett, *The Parish Clergy under the Later Stuarts: The Leicestershire Experience* (Urbana, Ill., 1978), p. 125.

14 R. Targoff, *Common Prayer: The Language of Public Devotion in Early Modern England* (Chicago, 2001), p. 54.

15 P. Collinson, 'The Church and the New Religion', in C. Haigh (ed.), *The Reign of Elizabeth I* (Basingstoke, 1984), p. 179; J. Morrill, 'The Church in England, 1642–9', in Morrill (ed.), *Reactions to the English Civil War* (Basingstoke, 1982), p. 113.

16 Temperley, *Music of Parish Church*, p. 86.

17 M. Todd, *The Culture of Protestantism in Early Modern Scotland* (New Haven, Conn., 2002), ch. 1.

18 Spurr, *RC*, pp. 332–3.

19 Pruett, *Parish Clergy*, p. 125.

20 CUL, Add. MS 8499, p. 94.

21 Spurr, *RC*, p. 368.

22 C. Dent, *Protestant Reformers in Elizabethan Oxford* (Oxford, 1983), p. 212.

23 *The Diary and Autobiography of Edmund Bohun*, ed. S.W. Rix (Beccles, 1853), p. 32.

24 Sussex, p. 131.

25 Sir Peter Leicester, *Charges to the Grand Jury*, ed. E. Halcrow (Chetham Society, 3rd series, V, 1953), p. 47.

26 Bodl. L., Tanner MS 31, fo. 296.

27 Hunt, 'Lord's Supper', 62.

28 Durham, pp. 187–8; *The Rector's Book, Clayworth*, ed. H. Gill and E.L. Guilford (Nottingham, 1910), p. 43; G.H. Jenkins, *Literature, Religion and Society in Wales 1660–1730* (Cardiff, 1978), p. 71.

29 Todd, *Culture of Protestantism in Early Modern Scotland*, pp. 85–6.

30 P. Laslett, *The World We Have Lost* (London, 1971 edn), pp. 74–6; J.P. Boulton, 'The Limits of Formal Religion: The Administration of Holy Communion in late Elizabethan and Early Stuart London', *London Journal*, 10 (1984), 138; *Rector's Book, Clayworth*, pp. 18–19; J.Gregory, *Restoration, Reformation and Reform, 1660–1828* (Oxford, 2000), pp. 269–70.

31 Bohun, *Autobiography*, pp. 74–5; for other examples see Spurr, *RC*, pp. 365–6.

32 Boulton, 'Limits of Formal Religion'.

33 D.A. Spaeth, *The Church in an Age of Danger: Parsons and Parishioners, 1660–1740* (Cambridge, 2000), pp. 182, 179–80.

34 *Episcopal Visitations in Bedfordshire 1706–1720*, ed. P. Bell (Bedfordshire Historical Record Society, 81, 2002), pp. 65, 25, 32, 8.

35 CUL, Add. MS 8499, p. 208.

36 Hunt, 'Lord's Supper', 45.

37 Green, *Print and Protestantism*, pp. 288–303; Spurr, *RC*, pp. 341–53.

38 Todd, *Culture of Protestantism in Early Modern Scotland*, pp. 91–2 and ch. 3 passim,

39 Spurr, *RC*, pp. 351–2; Spaeth, *Church in Age of Danger*, p. 183

40 *Two East Anglian Diaries*, ed. M. Storey (Suffolk Records Society, 36, 1994), p. 228; cf. Bohun, *Diary*, pp. 52–3.

41 Spaeth, *Church in Age of Danger*, p. 177.

42 C. Haigh, 'Communion and Community: Exclusion from Communion in Post-Reformation England', *JEH*, 51 (2000), 732.

43 Spaeth, *Church in Age of Danger*, pp. 173–6.

44 *The State of the Church in the Reigns of Elizabeth and James I*, ed. C.W. Foster (Lincolnshire Record Society, 23, 1926), p. lxxix.

45 Todd, *Culture of Protestantism in Early Modern Scotland*, p. 103.

46 *The Life of Richard Kidder*, ed. A.E. Robinson (Somerset Record Society, 37, 1922), pp. 19–20.

47 J.H., *The Life of the Reverend Mr George Trosse* (1714), p. 89.

48 Sussex, p. 34; also see Hunt, 'Lord's Supper', 65; Haigh, 'Communion', 732–3.

49 Josselin, pp. 235–6; Spurr, *EP*, p. 31.

50 CUL, Add. MS 8499, p. 81

51 Spurr, *RC*, pp. 17–18; Hutton has traced the celebrations at Easter, Whitsun and Christmas, *The Rise and Fall of Merry England: The Ritual Year 1400–1700* (Oxford, 1994), pp. 213–14.

52 Spurr, *RC*, p. 351.

53 Hunt, 'Lord's Supper', 53; Spurr, *RC*, pp. 364–6; I. Atherton, E. Fernie, C. Harper-Bill and H. Smith (eds), *Norwich Cathedral: Church, City and Diocese, 1096–1996* (1996), p. 545; Gillespie, *Devoted People*, p. 97.

54 *The Diary of Sir Simonds D'Ewes (1622–1624)*, ed. E. Bourcier, pp. 72–4, 96, 107, 110, 130, 188–9; Spurr, *EP*, pp. 178–80; *Two East Anglian Diaries*, ed. Storey, p. 208.

55 See D. Cressy, *Birth, Marriage and Death* (Oxford, 1997), ch. 9; S.J. Wright, 'Catechism, Confirmation and Communion', in Wright (ed.), *Parish, Church and People* (1988).

56 Cressy, *Birth, Marriage and Death*, p. 173.

57 C. Gittings, *Death, Burial and the Individual in Early Modern England* (London, 1984), p. 83.

58 CUL, Add. MS 8499, p. 175.

59 W. Coster, *Baptism and Spiritual Kinship in Early Modern England* (Aldershot, 2002), p. 62.

60 *Rector's Book, Clayworth*, p. 35.

61 Cressy, *Birth, Marriage and Death*, p. 183; *Episcopal Visitations in Bedfordshire*, ed. Bell, p. 72; Coster, *Baptism and Spiritual Kinship*, p. 54.

62 Cressy, *Birth, Marriage and Death*, pp. 340–1.

63 C. Durston, 'The Failure of Cultural Revolution', in C. Durston and J. Eales (eds), *The Culture of English Puritanism, 1560–1700* (Basingstoke, 1996), pp. 228–9.

64 Gittings, *Death*, p. 133.

65 Gittings, *Death*, p. 64.

66 Gittings, *Death*, pp. 47–8.

67 Gittings, *Death*, p. 50.

68 Richard Baxter, *Reliquiae Baxterianae*, ed. M. Sylvester (1696), III, 33.

69 *Two East Anglian Diaries*, ed. Storey, pp. 231, 249.

70 *A Catalogue of Letters and Other Historical Documents Exhibited in the Library at Welbeck*, ed. S.A. Strong (1903), p. 227.

71 *Constitutional Documents of the Reign of James I*, ed. J.R. Tanner (Cambridge, 1952), pp. 54–6.

72 M. Ingram, *Church Courts, Sex and Marriage, 1570–1640* (Cambridge, 1987), p. 117.

73 K.L. Parker, *The English Sabbath* (Cambridge, 1988), p. 146.

74 M. Spufford, *Small Books and Pleasant Histories* (Cambridge, 1981), pp. 176–7.

75 M. Spufford, *Contrasting Communities* (Cambridge, 1974), pp. 231–2.

76 Sussex, p.27

77 Heywood, II, 279.

78 D. Dymond, 'God's Disputed Acre', *JEH*, 50 (1999), 489.

79 *The Diary of Thomas Turner 1754–1765*, ed. D. Vaisey (Oxford, 1984), p. 43.

80 R.W. Malcolmson, *Popular Recreation in English Society, 1700–1850* (Cambridge, 1979), p. 12.

81 Josselin, p. 509.

82 Spaeth, *Church in Age of Danger*, p. 188; J. Maltby, *Prayer Book and People in Elizabethan and Early Stuart England* (Cambridge, 1998), p. 39.

83 *The Records of a Church of Christ in Bristol 1640–87*, ed. R. Hayden (Bristol Record Society, 27, 1974), p. 85; Durston, 'Failure of Cultural Revolution', p. 224; Hutton, *Rise and Fall of Merry England*, pp. 178–80, 210–11, 214–17.

84 *Records of a Church of Christ Meeting in Broadmead Bristol*, ed. E.B. Underhill (1847), pp. 66–7.

85 Josselin, p. 588.

86 Spufford, *Small Books*, pp. 194–5; M. Spufford, 'Can We Count the "Godly" and the "Conformable" in the Seventeenth Century?' *JEH*, 36 (1985).

87 Ingram, *Church Courts, Sex and Marriage*, p. 99.

88 Sussex, p. 68.

89 Durston, 'Failure of Cultural Revolution', p. 210.

90 Sussex, p. 121.

91 *The Diary of Dudley Ryder, 1715–1716*, ed. W. Matthews (1939), p. 369.

CHAPTER 12

Religion outside
the church

This chapter is concerned with those who took religion more
seriously than did their neighbours. They were the self-defined
pious minority spread across many rival religious groups. A catalogue
of all these different denominations and sects, of Catholics and Quakers,
High Churchmen and Nonconformists, puritans and prophets, might
make dreary reading. It could also obscure the relative significance of each
group. So, instead, it may be helpful to think of the myriad forms of
individual and group religious activity in the seventeenth century simply
as religion 'outside the church'. This formulation recognises that much
religious activity was defined by its relationship to the standards of the
national church. Some of it was designed to complement and strengthen
the work of the church, to cultivate the faith of individuals and to reform
the nation; other religious exercises were more detached from the agenda
of the church, or even critical of it, and intended to remedy the church's
defects and to complete the long-delayed Reformation. A third type of this
'religion outside the church' was constituted by those sects and churches
that regarded themselves as superior alternatives to the national church.
Such groups often presented this as a choice between their truth and the
church's error, the path of righteousness and that of idolatry and persecution. Individuals who ruthlessly pursued their own spiritual insights and
vision wherever they led them also fall into this category. To organise our
material in this way has several advantages. It reveals the continuum of
religious exercises and shows that much depends upon perception: one
person's pious Bible-study group was another's seditious conventicle. It
illuminates the structures of religious activity and suggests that they were
often replicated from one denomination to another even when the theological content varied: for example, a regime of preparation for the Lord's

Supper was common among pious Nonconformists, Roman Catholics and Anglicans, none of whom shared the same theological understanding of the sacrament.

The identification of common structures of religious activity arises from the evidence. The sources for religious activity outside the church are predominantly biographical and autobiographical. They are diaries, conversion narratives, correspondence and 'godly lives', supplemented by some evidence from opponents and prosecutions, and, for the second half of the century, a few registers of Baptist and Quaker congregations. These biographical and personal writings circulated at the time as part of the religious life of the pious. So they are not simply evidence of belief and behaviour, they were part of the process by which that belief and behaviour was constructed and disseminated. The devout read the exemplary 'lives' of contemporaries and predecessors and attempted to live up to their example: Josselin found Mrs Elliston's diary 'full of spiritual observation and sweetness'; and, on reading the Countess of Warwick's funeral sermon, Ralph Thoresby 'was mightily taken with her pious diary, religious life, heavenly meditations'.[1] The martyrology of John Foxe or the collection of godly biographies by Samuel Clarke created an ancestry for later Protestants, just as John Wilson's *English Martyrology* (1608) did for Roman Catholics or Charles Doe's *Collection of Experience of the Work of Grace* (1700) did for Baptists. From this literature emerge a series of stock types and circumstances – the pious mother or master, the misspent youth, the sobering escape from death, the epiphany prompted by a book, preacher or divine providence – which are no less real for being part of the stage scenery of a devout life. Even the language and the emotions followed a pattern. A notable example of this is afforded by the sad tale of Francis Spira, a sixteenth-century Italian Calvinist who fell into terminal despair after temporarily recanting his faith. Spira's conviction of his own damnation shaped seventeenth-century understandings of the psychology of conversion. Unsure of his own salvation and 'full of horror', John Crook came upon Spira's book 'but I could not read it over, I thought it so to resemble my present condition'; while for Bunyan, it was 'a book that was to my troubled soul as salt when rubbed into a fresh wound'.[2] Thus we can see the most intimate moment between the individual's soul and God being constructed – both at the time and in the retelling – in accordance with wider social and cultural conventions.

A concentration on the stereotyped social forms and structures of religious activity, however convenient as a tool of analysis, should not obscure the differences between groups nor the changes that occurred across the century. Some religious activities were virtually unique to one particular denomination – adult believer's baptism, for example, or visiting holy wells and shrines – and some groups had cast off institutions such as a priesthood or clergy altogether. Although the familiar socio-logical distinction between 'churches' and 'sects', the former aspiring to embrace the whole population, the latter a selective group with specific tests for admission, is theoretically helpful, it does not quite capture the seventeenth-century realities where even 'churches' like the Presbyterians and Catholics had to behave as if they were 'sects' competing for adher-ents. Competition was a product of the growth of religious choice during the century. From at least the 1640s, the determined and brave had real choice of religious expression. Only a minority pursued their aspirations into this dangerous territory, and they often did so in a hesitant or confused manner. This chapter describes what they did and explains why.

The Christian life

The life of a pious Christian, referred to by contemporaries variously as 'godliness', 'holy living', or 'the devout life', was a widespread ideal, but only a minority of all denominations made strenuous efforts to live the Christian life. It was a demanding lifestyle of personal commitment. Good Christians prayed in their 'closet' and with their family, read the Bible and edifying works, examined themselves and recorded their spiritual progress in diaries and confession. They chose education and employment with an eye to religion, spent their money on charity and pious works, mixed with similarly devout Christians, and devoted themselves to the worship and service of God. The level of personal commitment was determined by factors such as an individual's education, the leisure and resources available, and the prevailing political and ecclesiastical circumstances. Some pious Pro-testants found it perfectly possible to pursue their religious aspirations within the Church of England. They could hear sermons, attend prayers assiduously, and receive the sacrament at every celebration. These were the sort who paid for communion plate or endowed sermons: people like the fifty-two Norwich parishioners who subscribed £31 for daily prayers in St Peter Mancroft; or the York man who bequeathed £6 for his minister to preach a dozen sermons on the third chapter of Proverbs. They often sought to edge the church in a particular direction: witness the Maidstone merchant who paid for a copy of 'Mr Calvin's Institutions in English of the fairest and plainest letter' to be chained to a desk in his parish church 'for the better instruction of the poor and simple'; or the fourteen puritan works that William Bladon contributed to the parish at Repton, Derbyshire, in 1622, to constitute what may have been the earliest English lending library.[3] Of course others, especially sectaries or Roman Catholics, were not always able to exercise their religion unimpeded by suspicious neighbours or hostile authorities. So religion was pursued beyond the walls and control of the national church in various ways: by Catholics congregating outside Wisbech castle to hear the sermons of imprisoned priests; or Jacobean puritans gathered for a private day of prayer and fasting in an Essex farmhouse; or Ulster Presbyterians assembling for huge corporate communions lasting several days; or devout Anglicans closeted away in preparation for a worthy reception of the Lord's Supper in some splendid City church; or Quaker brethren meeting to seek the Lord in Bristol, Leeds or Gainsborough. As the choices and opportunities proliferated, so, for some, did the dangers. However pious, their purposes were easily mistaken by the authorities or misrepresented by their opponents.

*

On Sunday, 6 March 1664, Roger Lowe, an apprentice shopkeeper from Lancashire, 'was very pensive and sad all day, and I betook myself to solitariness, for I walked down to town heath and presented my supplication to the Lord. I prayed to God and showed him all my trouble and I hope the Lord heard for I was abundantly comforted in my spirit.'[4] This direct personal communication with God was at the heart of religious life. It was a principal religious duty required of lay people and it brought them comfort: Anne Bathurst 'went to my closet where all my devotions this day have been full of incomparable sweetness'.[5] Prayer could bring tangible benefits: 'toward night God answered prayer in rain', noted Josselin on one occasion; while Lady Anne Clifford was certain that her mother's 'fervent prayers' had been returned 'with blessings'.[6] Ann Fowkes, a Kilkenny Baptist, found that prayer 'became not only familiar but delightful . . . I have been so carried out at the sacrament and private prayer that I have ardently wished for wings as a dove that I might fly away and be at rest'.[7] Prayer was offered up in the open air and in chambers, in families and groups: 'my wife and I spent some time in prayer in my study', recorded Oliver Heywood; 'oh it was a sweet melting duty, seldom hath my heart been in such a frame, in pleading for the King, the nation, church, congregations, my relations, my children, God will hear'.[8] Robert Bolton prayed 'six times daily, twice with his wife, twice with his family, and twice alone by himself'.[9] It was a natural activity, practiced unselfconsciously, and in all manner of groups. Josselin recorded that 'our women met in prayer, I with them, spoke from Proverbs 31: 30, that the fear of God is the best ornament, and the greatest mercy, the Lord make me to walk accordingly'.[10]

Mental prayers will always be mysterious, and what was said in vocal prayer is generally now lost to us, although its tenor can be discerned in the 'pious ejaculations', the praises and pleading, woven into the fabric of devotional journals: this was the language of affections 'stirred', hearts 'enlarged' and 'melted', and souls 'refreshed'. Some lay people have also left behind written prayers, although these tend to be more formal compositions based on clerical or scriptural models. In private some Christians presumably read or recited parts of the Book of Common Prayer, or of the many available prayer manuals, or adapted such material to their needs. Some found the Prayer Book too dry; but how many shared this opinion and how far it was due to lingering suspicion about the 'popish' origins of the liturgy is unclear. Another factor was distaste for all written or 'set' forms of prayer. 'To imprison and confine by force, into a pinfold of set words, those two most unimprisonable things, our prayers and that divine spirit of utterance that moves them, is a tyranny,' asserted Milton.[11] As a child Lawrence Clarkson was forced to read over the prayers of the Prayer Book and *The Practice of Piety* 'which I have done, till they have fallen asleep and myself, this was our devotion in those days'. After 'long book prayers' it was liberating for Jane Turner, a Baptist, to pray without a book even if only 'in a poor broken manner'. [12]

The practice of extemporised prayer led some to fluency. On 'a private day for seeking the Lord in prayer,' recalls Heywood, 'I was put on duty first, and continued about three hours pouring out my soul before the Lord'. When worshipping with his congregation, he liked to spend an hour 'in confession and prayer' and another 'in the great and sweet duty of thanksgiving, wherein the Lord hath wonderfully enlarged my heart far beyond my expectations'.[13] This was emotionally taxing work. 'As Angier was much in prayer, so he was mighty in prayer, fervent as well as frequent, he wept and made supplication . . . he was by some called Weeping Angier; for as he seldom rose off his knees without tears, so some have observed, tears at some seasons trickle down to his band [collar] in great abundance.'[14] Lay people also prayed spontaneously in congregations: they knew the joys when prayer flowed easily and the despair when they were 'barren', and they took the duty seriously. Roger Lowe visited Peter Lealand's house 'where they were singing Psalms. I went in and Peter would have me pray, but I was unfit at that time, and so desired excuse.'[15] As John Gifford, the Bedford Baptist pastor, remarked, not every brother has been gifted, and in prayer 'all self-affected expressions' and 'vain repetitions' should be avoided.[16] While the godly were comfortable with extemporary prayer, conformist clergy were generally wary of this disorderly and presumptuous practice and encouraged the people to follow trusted models rather than risk offering offensive prayers to God.

Prayer and other religious exercises naturally occurred in the context of the family and the home. A generation of English Reformers had attempted to 'spiritualise' the family and household through sermons and conduct books: the family was a little church and the primary unit of reformation; 'sound professors of the gospel' must 'begin this most necessary discipline in reforming their own households'.[17] These exhortations matched the unthinking condescension of many husbands and fathers towards the women in their families. It was the male prerogative to guide the religion of these 'weaker vessels'. Archibald Johnston of Wariston liked to test his wife's religious knowledge in bed: 'Remember, O soul, how oft God has made thee speak to her of God and godliness in thy bed and to pass over all the principals of religion, making her repeat the Lord's Prayer, the Command[ment]s, and the Belief unto thee; and, having posed her upon some questions therein, she answered thee so perfectly as thou kissed her, blessed God, and rejoiced in thy heart.'[18] Other men imagined a rather confined intellectual and religious role for their womenfolk. 'Good sweetheart, be not so covetous,' wrote Sir Ralph Verney to a god-daughter who wanted to learn the classics, 'believe me a Bible (with the Common Prayer) and a good plain catechism in your mother tongue being well read and practised, is worth all the rest and much more suitable to your sex.'[19]

It would be unwise to conclude from the prescriptive literature and examples of male condescension that women had a circumscribed religious life in the seventeenth century. Several notable individuals refused to be cowed by husbands, fathers, authority and convention: they insisted upon gaining an education and exercising their own religious beliefs, even to the point of suffering. Behind these exceptional women were many more who exercised their piety in private devotion – women like Lady Anne Halkett who set aside five hours a day for devotion. As mothers, wives, and mistresses of households, these women passed on their religious values. Many a spiritual autobiography paid tribute to a 'sweet and gracious woman' who first kindled the spark of piety in the writer. George Boddington fondly remembered his mother who 'was of an excellent spirit and an early riser, a great reader and worker, and took all opportunities to instruct and instil good principles of religion and morals into us her children and would often take us singly to her apartment and pray with us and for us'.[20]

Elizabeth Walker, the wife of a clergyman, was a paragon of piety and ran a model household. She awoke at 4.0 a.m. 'darting up prayers and praises' to God, spent two hours in devotion, and then heard her maids and the day labourers read from the Bible. Her husband recalled that 'about five she retired to her private devotions, and, they finished, came to me, and brought the children with her . . . to be seriously exhorted and counselled'. At night she undressed while her maid read the Bible, and 'then committing herself to God, she went to bed, and after ejaculatory prayers for the mercies of the day, and petitions for protection from the sins, temptations and dangers of the night, she betook herself to sleep'.[21]

This ideal of a well-ordered household can be seen again and again across the century and across the different denominations. It is evident in the description of the Catholic Babthorpe family's life at Osgodby, Yorkshire, in the 1620s: 'on the Sundays we locked the doors and all came to Mass, had our sermons, catechisms and spiritual lessons every Sunday and Holyday. On the workdays we had for the most part two Masses . . . one for the servants at six o'clock in the morning, at which the gentlemen . . . and the ladies if they were not sick would, even in the midst of winter, of their own accord be present; and the other we had at eight o'clock for those who were absent from the first.'[22] A similar regime prevailed in Protestant households. At 8.00 a.m. each Sunday, 'after private devotions in their closets', John Angier's household at Denton gathered to hear a chapter of the Bible and sing a psalm, and at 9.00 a.m. they proceeded to chapel. They had returned and dined by noon, when Angier repeated the morning sermon. Afternoon chapel was followed at home by supper and the repetition of the afternoon sermon, preceded and followed by a psalm and prayers, before they retired to their rooms. On Monday evenings the family repeated the Sunday morning sermon and on Saturday evening they repeated the Sunday afternoon sermon. On Friday nights the family 'said their catechisms', some from the Westminster Assembly's Short Catechism and some from the Long version, 'some also repeating the proofs memoriter', in other words, reciting from memory the scripture texts supporting each doctrine.[23]

The household was the meeting ground between private and public life. The recusant Babthorpes had to lock their door for fear of discovery in the 1620s, and the definition of an illegal conventicle under the penal laws of the 1660s was 'five persons or more assembled together, over and above those of the same household'. The sermon repetition that we have just encountered in Angier's household was just one of the devout activities that connected family duties to public meetings, whether at the church or conventicle. Obviously, repeating the 'heads' or main points of a sermon from memory or notes and considering the relevant scriptural passages, the doctrine of the sermon, and its uses, could be done in private, in one's bed or closet or while writing out a summary of the sermon: Lady Hoby, who was an assiduous sermon-noter, 'walked in the garden meditating of the points of the sermon and praying'.[24] Yet repetition was essentially a group activity: children would be tested; youths and women would benefit from further explication; the mature would gain in scriptural knowledge. Many Elizabethan and early Stuart ministers regarded repetition as an integral part of the observances of a good Protestant. But there was always room for misunderstanding. In 1615, about sixty people remained after service in the chancel of St John's, Beverley, to sing psalms and to 'repeat' the sermon they had just heard. They told an inquisitive clergyman not to interfere and were clearly demonstrating godly or puritan leanings in a confrontational manner.[25] Predictably, the practice attracted some hostility from the Laudian church. In 1634 Thomas Tyler of Calne found himself presented to the church courts for repeating sermons with his neighbours in the church after evening prayers. Tyler claimed that far from initiating a conventicle, he had been given permission by the parish minister to read over his notes of the Tuesday lecture and Sunday sermon and this had been requested by many of the congregation 'for their memories' sake'.[26] The Directory recommended repetition as suitable for the Sabbath. After the Restoration, repetition became doubly suspect, as a tainted practice of the old puritans and as an activity perilously close to an illegal meeting or conventicle. Adam Martindale heard the sermons of his successor and then repeated them in the evening 'to an houseful of parishioners of the devoutest sort, adding a discourse of mine own, and praying for a blessing upon all'. Roger Lowe records that 'after evening prayer there was a few went to Mr Woods to spend the remaining part of the day, I repeated sermon and stayed [for] prayer, and then came our way'.[27]

Lowe also participated in another of the seventeenth century's more popular religious activities, a religious youth group. 'We being some young people that sometimes associated together', Lowe and other apprentices met 'to the edification of one another'.[28] Such fellowships had 'been the practice of serious young men in all ages, and among all the various denominations of Christians', according to one clerical enthusiast.[29] In the 1630s, London apprentices, including John Lilburne and William Kiffin, met an hour before service 'to spend it in prayer and in communicating to each other what experiences we had received from the Lord; or else to repeat some sermon which we had heard before'.[30] Heywood recalled

how 'when I was about fourteen years of age I was entertained into the
society of some godly Christians, we were above twenty young men and
others who joined together by the instigation of an ancient godly widow
woman and propounded necessary questions and held conference every
fortnight and prayed our course about'.[31] Such groups came and went,
often leaving little trace. At Lincoln in the 1650s, Gervase Disney and
his pals 'kept hours, nay often whole afternoons, in religious exercises
by themselves . . . and usually discoursed of some text of scripture'.[32]
In upland areas prayer groups were a natural solution to the difficulties
of travel: Oliver Heywood sponsored a variety of different prayer groups,
'conferences' and 'meetings' among his hearers and followers. Heywood
rejoiced to learn in 1692 that 'God had set the faces of some young men
of my hearers and neighbours heavenwards, and that they met together
frequently in the night to pray'. He called them to his house and six young
men 'prayed very understandingly, experimentally, affectionately, I stood
amazed to hear their gifts, many of them were the children of carnal
parents'.[33]

There were godly youth groups among conformist Anglicans as well as
those on the fringes of Nonconformity. In 1681 the 'devout young men' of
St Martin-in-the-Fields, London, created an association that was restricted
to those who attended the church and received the sacrament. They met
every third Sunday of the month, read 'some prayer as shall be useful for
our purpose' and a chapter from the Bible, repeated the heads of a sermon,
and took a collection for the poor.[34] In London during the 1680s there
were religious clubs of 'young persons' meeting in Ave Mary Lane, St
Clement's Dane, St Lawrence Jewry and elsewhere; by 1694 there were
fourteen such societies with a total of 298 members, and five years later
there were thirty-nine clubs. By the following century, they extended well
beyond London to many provincial towns and some rural districts, such as
Kent and Lincolnshire. Most of these societies made great play of their
devotion to the liturgy and services of the Church of England and in some
cases this was a politically coded assertion of their Tory identity. They also
combined their spiritual purposes with good works such as charity schools
and apprenticeships. In time societies often came to resemble civic or guild
associations more than religious youth groups. The role of the clergy in
such societies was intriguing. If the tenor of the group was 'godly', if it
inclined towards a 'puritan' outlook in the 1630s, or could be suspected
of a leniency towards Dissent in the early 1680s, then it was unwise of a
clergyman to take a prominent role for fear of accusations that he was
leading a conventicle. Yet in other cases, a charismatic cleric could inspire
a real religious fervour among the young of his neighbourhood. If the line

between a pious voluntary meeting of lay Christians and the beginnings of a separate congregation was sometimes obscure to observers, it was generally clear enough to participants.

Separate churches, separatism and sectarianism

A 'separate' church can be defined for our purposes simply as a religious congregation that maintains a distinct identity and existence and usually possesses its own teachings, ministry and sacraments. Despite the Church of England's claim to be the sole and all-inclusive national church, separate churches existed in England throughout the seventeenth century.

*

The most obvious separate communion was the Roman Catholic church. Although the universal Church of Rome was evidently a 'church-type' institution, Roman Catholics had come to accept sectarian status in England. 'If because of unbelievers, we cannot go to the church, but the wicked occupy the place, thou must flee from that place, because it was profaned by them,' wrote Richard Broughton, quoting St Clement, and then proceeded to cite Matthew 18: 20 *where two or three are gathered together in my name, there am I.*[35] The English Catholic community had struggled to find a place in Post-Reformation England. The community had been divided by the competing clerical visions – of an underground missionary church or an attenuated 'shadow' national church – on offer in the Elizabethan and Jacobean eras. The eventual compromise was an untidy and incoherent arrangement. Until 1631 a vicar apostolic was in charge of the Catholic clergy, but thereafter an over-elaborate clerical chapter exercised what authority it could over the three or four hundred secular priests active in the kingdom until the restoration of the vicars apostolic in the reign of James II. The 150 Jesuits active in the country at any one time belonged to the Society's English Province that had first been erected in 1623. Catholic priests in seventeenth-century England and Wales were loosely organised: some were attached as chaplains to gentry and noble families, others lived together in 'houses' or 'colleges'; and many travelled the country celebrating mass or hearing confession. They were Englishmen or Irishmen who had been trained and ordained abroad. They sought to blend into the background since it was still a capital offence to be a Catholic priest and at several periods during the century priests went in danger of their lives. At other times, of course, priests were welcome at court and were familiar figures in the capital.

The Jacobean Oath of Allegiance controversy had highlighted the political dilemmas of English Catholics. Although Questier and others have urged us to give more weight to the political ambitions of Elizabethan and Jacobean Catholics, the present state of our knowledge of mid- and later-seventeenth-century Catholicism suggests that their hopes, repeatedly raised by Stuart rulers, amounted to little more than a lifting of the penal laws and freedom of religious practice. Persecution of the Catholic laity fluctuated, but was generally less ferocious than that of their priests, and even popular hostility and violence seems to have been a sporadic and occasionally manufactured phenomenon. Some historians have written of 'confident' Catholicism under Charles I, and for much of the later seventeenth century, English lay Catholics could, with due caution, live fairly openly as Catholics.

The prevailing characterisation of seventeenth-century English Catholicism as introspective, conservative and increasingly irrelevant to national life is a caricature. Catholicism was rooted in gentry households and remote regions such as Lancashire and the Welsh borders, but there were also Catholic gentry families in the Thames valley, East Anglia, the West Midlands and elsewhere. These communities were part of the local landscape and were often so well integrated, or so powerful, that the incumbent and churchwardens were unsure how to report them: Lady Yates's family at Harvington were not 'heretics' or 'schismatics', according to the churchwardens, but simply 'some that do not hold communion with us at the church, reputed to be papists'.[36] Numerically the majority of Catholics were humble folk, yeoman and labourers, the sort of people who might have met for a secret mass behind the shop of a Newcastle widow where 'hosts in great number in a painted box, books, paternosters or beads' were discovered in 1615 among the salt fish, red herrings and ropes.[37] It was a resilient community too. The churchwardens consistently reported the recusant community at Midhurst, Sussex, in the 1620s – its members were named, its schoolmaster and its priest were identified – yet it was still there in 1664.[38] Even if, as seems likely, recusants amounted to a mere 2 per cent of the population, the Catholic community could still muster impressive popular displays, turning up in crowds to hear mass in the Fylde or a preacher in a Blackfriars tenement.

Historians have begun to suspect that two previously overlooked factors may have shaped the seventeenth-century Catholic community. The first was that Catholicism won converts. It was a more evangelical faith than has often been recognised. The sixteen Jesuits who operated in the eastern counties, thanks to the College of the Holy Apostles funded by

Lord Petre, claimed to be 'reconciling' nearly forty Protestants a year. It has been estimated that the volume of Catholic printed works was second only to that of Church of England publications, and critics complained of the 'infection' of 'popish primers, catechisms, manuals and a multitude of such Romish trash and trumpery' among the young.[39] Research into recusancy has suggested that many of those convicted were not from a Catholic household or family. In other words, they had not inherited their faith but had adopted it. The second factor concerns the distinction between recusants and church papists, those who attended the parish church but remained Roman Catholics in their hearts and in private. It is possible that more individuals than we had realised moved between recusancy and church papistry, perhaps in response to persecution, poverty, or their familial and communal responsibilities. This suggests that the real Catholic community was far wider than the recusants. The 2 per cent of the population who were recusants may not have been the *same* 2 per cent each year. It *may* also say something about the extent of residual Catholicism among the population, or even, as Walsham suggests, offer an explanation of why some parishioners were drawn to the ceremony and liturgy of the Laudian Church of England.[40] The term 'church papist' was a creation of polemic and was used in the sixteenth and early seventeenth centuries by eager Protestants to abuse and stigmatise those they suspected of a lingering affection for popery. That polemical context was overtaken by events in the 1640s and the term of abuse seems to have become irrelevant or extinct. We do not, however, know whether the practice of Roman Catholics attending their parish churches had also died out.

*

Roman Catholicism was not the only alternative to the national church. The seventeenth century saw an irreversible growth in separate churches. What had been no more than a handful of unstable, clandestine congregations at the beginning of the century became a sizeable national presence. Some of these congregations were inherently separatist. The Family of Love, a secretive group who espoused notions of inner 'illumination', human 'perfection' and mutual tolerance, had existed in Cambridgeshire and elsewhere since the 1550s. They disguised their presence but never surrendered their principles. They were last heard of when they addressed James II in 1687 and described themselves as 'a sort of refined Quakers' numbering less than sixty and based in the Isle of Ely.[41] On the other hand, some religious groups were horrified to be forced into a separate existence. Presbyterians had expected to become part of some broad national church at the Restoration and were dismayed to find themselves redefined as part of Nonconformity in 1662. They were slow to realise that comprehension was a lost cause and to grasp their future as a separate denomination. The Nonjurors regarded themselves as the true remnant of the Church of England after 1689 and believed that they had been ejected from the national church which was now schismatic and in the hands of Erastian bishops.

Most of the congregations of the early seventeenth century were obscure. Occasionally they surface in the local records. For example, Ingram has noticed a little group of Brownists active in the Salisbury parish of Slaughterford and a Salisbury Baptist, Mrs Joan Slowe, who spread the word in neighbouring villages.[42] Now, 'Brownist' was a convenient and pejorative label to describe any group that associated itself with the doctrine of congregational autonomy that Robert Browne had advanced in 1582. But this group may have had some association with other like-minded separatists, as might Mrs Slowe. In 1612 Thomas Helwys, a Nottinghamshire gentleman and Baptist, had established a Baptist congregation at Spitalfields, London, which fostered links with other sectarians. Often inspired or led by disaffected former clergy, such fringe groups experimented with forms of church organisation and explored heterodox doctrines. One powerful motive was the creation of a pure fellowship. At Southwark in 1616 the veteran separatist and clergymen Henry Jacob established 'a free congregation of saints, viz., of visible holy Christians', which generated further congregations in London.[43] In other cases, heterodox teachers acquired a following without creating a separate church. In the 1620s, a number of London preachers moved beyond dominant Calvinist theology, largely because of the personal and pastoral difficulties inherent in its account of salvation, and seemed to be teaching antinomianism and Socinianism. Eight or nine such ministers, including John Eaton and Peter Shaw, have been identified, as has a lay 'sect-master', John Etherington, who also had links to the Family of Love. These antinomian ideas may also have owed something to the preaching of Roger Brerely, the Jacobean curate of Grindleton in the West Riding. The significance of all this activity only really became apparent in the 1640s when these undercurrents produced a surge of gathered churches and sects.[44]

Earlier chapters have described the London churches of the 1640s and the spread of such congregations in the wake of the Civil Wars. The radicalism, both religious and social, of many of these tiny groups guaranteed the attention of outraged contemporaries and later historians: some, like the Diggers or Ranters, were short-lived – 'mushroom sects' in the dismissive phrase of their critics – but their members probably found an eventual spiritual home within the Quaker movement. The separatist churches that put down roots in this period were not to be eradicated by persecution after 1660. After 1662 there was a clear legal demarcation between the Church of England and the proscribed 'fanatics' of Nonconformity, blurred only by those ejected Presbyterian ministers who still made themselves available to their former flocks. Meanwhile, the Quakers and Baptists began to organise themselves as denominations, with regular meetings, committees and regional and national bodies. There were even some faltering steps towards cross-denominational cooperation. But the tradition of congregational debate and acrimonious secession also made itself felt: the Quakers, General Baptists and Congregationalists all suffered damaging splits before the end of the century.

*

Separatists followed the scriptural command 'to come out from among them and be ye separate' (II Corinthians 6: 17). Jane Turner, a Baptist, described her own fellowship as 'we that are, according to the gospel, joined to the Lord, and his church, by which we hold out to the world a visible profession of his name, and a separation from all false ways of worship'.[45] Such congregations were autonomous. They appointed their own pastor and elders, they disciplined the brethren, and approved new members. Their practices and worship were simple, indeed austere, and consciously scriptural or 'apostolic': in the 1650s the Bristol Baptists 'met in houses, divers times in the weekdays, for the church meeting, for to exercise the gifts of the church, by way of conference, or for prayer in preparation to the Lord's Supper, once a month, or for prayer on other special or emergent occasions'.[46] They took a pride in their distinctiveness and their distance from the 'profane' world around them: in 1680 the Quakers of York attempted to restrict hasty second marriages among their brethren so 'that the righteousness thereof in our practice may exceed the world's'.[47] Inevitably the pastor was closely involved with his flock, who had after all voluntarily placed themselves under his spiritual leadership and who normally contributed to his income. Many such congregations had an inner core of full members, who received the sacraments, and an outer circle of 'hearers', those who attended occasionally or who were 'on trial' to see if they were worthy of admission as full members. Although congregations were responsible for their own affairs, they naturally sought advice and support from sister churches, especially when it came to the recommendation of a new pastor or the pursuit of an errant member.

A separate church could be formed in several ways. Some groups coalesced within a parish. They were churches formed from the parochial congregation, often on a clerical initiative. This might be no more than an informal circle of godly parishioners as developed at Terling in the 1620s or Earls Colne and Kidderminster in the 1650s. Or it might involve a formal agreement, a 'covenant'. John Vicars, the Jacobean minister of Stamford, Lincolnshire, denounced his parishioners as depraved sinners, drunkards, swearers, sensualists who feasted riotously at Christmas and kept company with 'painted Jezebels, wanton Imaheb, and whorish Dalilas'. Yet a handful had avoided contamination, and these he called his 'family' and his 'children' and they covenanted together 'to do whatsoever God commands'. At Boston, John Cotton withdrew his ministry from his parishioners and restricted it to those with whom he had covenanted 'to follow after the Lord in the purity of his worship'.[48] When the Lancashire minister Oliver Heywood placed his parish church under a covenant in 1655, over a hundred subscribed. Under the 1672 Indulgence, Heywood took out a licence as a Presbyterian teacher and a hundred or more of his former parishioners entered into a church covenant with him. Other separate churches were 'gathered' from a wider community than the parish and owed much to lay initiatives. In 1660, fearing 'a flood of trouble and persecution', the Axminster Independents 'were embodied and constituted a church of Christ' by 'solemnly covenanting and engaging to walk together in a due and faithful attendance upon the Lord Jesus Christ in all his ordinances'.[49]

Admission as a member of a separatist church required a testimony of one's belief and spiritual experience. Applicants to Henry Jacob's church 'made some confession or profession of their faith or repentance' and then subscribed a church covenant 'to walk in all God's ways'. The Baptists meeting at Taunton in 1654 laid down that no one should be admitted 'without a declaration of an experimental work of the spirit upon the heart . . . being attended with evident tokens of conversion, to the satisfaction of the . . . church'.[50] Those who joined the Bristol Broadmead church made 'a declaration of the work of grace upon [his or] her heart': for example, in 1672 Richard Towne 'gave an account of the change upon his soul, and how he came to be convinced of the damnable principles of the Quakers, having been one of them many years'.[51] Some churches required an account of the applicant's conversion, others were satisfied with 'signs of grace'; some demanded that the applicant address the whole meeting, others allowed the pastor or elders to report on the applicant. The degree of doctrinal knowledge required of new members clearly varied. The

Independent church gathered by Gifford at Bedford in the 1650s 'entered into fellowship one with another' on the principle of 'faith in Christ and holiness of life, without respect to this or that circumstance or opinion in outward and circumstantial things'.[52] At Bristol Edward Terrill was troubled about the validity of his infant baptism: 'I was so wavering that I could not join with the church in the Lord's Supper, although they would have admitted me; as their manner is to receive persons if they conceive the Lord hath wrought a work of grace in them, and not for opinion's sake.'[53] In later life the Quaker John Crook reminisced about his spiritual experience within a separatist church: 'we had many refreshings together, while we were kept watchful and tender, with our minds inwardly retired, and our words few and savoury, which frame of spirit we were preserved in, by communicating our experiences each to other; as how our hearts had been kept towards the Lord all the week, with an account of most day's passages between God and our own souls'.[54]

*

How did individuals move towards separatism? Those who had separated tended to portray their movement as a spiritual journey and were usually writing from their final destination. They did not disguise how arduous the journey had been: 'those which walk openly in this way shall be despised, pointed at, hated of the world', warned John Winthrop. The Quaker John Gratton described how as a youth in the 1650s he followed 'the Presbyterians and the hireling priests', then the Church of England, and the Independent meeting at Chesterfield, before a phase of 'walking alone . . . like one that had no mate or companion', sustained only by the belief that 'God had a people somewhere, but I knew not who they were, and was now afraid to join with any, lest they should not worship God aright, and then I might be guilty of idolatry.'[55] What seems clear is that these individuals recognised their new spiritual home when they reached it. They often write of finding true fellowship among like-minded people. 'No sooner had I sat down, and beheld the people, but these words darted into my breast, *this is the way, walk in it*, with such joy in my soul, that I could almost have wept for joy', wrote Edward Terrill on encountering the godly of Bristol. Terrill believed the phrase was 'an answer from God to me' because he did not know 'those words were written in scripture'; six weeks later he discovered that this was a passage from Isaiah, and 'found I was more confirmed that it was of God, because it was scripture, as the spirit of God doth usually work according to the written word'.[56]

This inner conviction, this sense of fellowship, tempered by the discipline of scriptural study, was characteristic of individuals who separated from the parish or national church in search of a more fulfilling spiritual life among 'experienced' Christians. Their quest often began while wrestling with doubt or despair about their own salvation and might progress through Bible study and lay preaching. Most individuals remained within a broad Protestant tradition: some of the separatist groups, such as the Particular Baptists, were predestinarian Calvinists, while others were moving towards Arminianism. Some, repudiating theological labels, saw themselves as no more than 'seekers' after the truth. Separatism was inevitably influenced by the more mystical aspects of Protestantism, by the interest in the transforming power of the Holy Spirit, the rapturous identification with the sufferings of Christ, the sense of millenarian expectation, or the tradition of prophecy. A significant number of seventeenth-century Christians sought and experienced a mystical union with God, a direct and sensual contact which could often only be described in physical terms. Thomas Wynne of Flintshire, who became a Quaker and a leading figure in Pennsylvania, described the 'working of the heavenly power' upon him: 'it wounded as a sword, it smote like a hammer at the whole body of sin, and in my bowels it burned like fire', it made him roar, tremble and quake.[57] The Quaker movement attracted many of those who felt that they had a direct apprehension of divine power.

Some individuals, however, were convinced that their visions and raptures were evidence of their unique communication with God. In the 1630s the Welsh tailor Rhys Evans believed that he had been given a special mission from God and adopted the name of 'Arise' Evans: 'having so many visions upon visions to confirm the certainty of the judgment, I could not contain my knowledge, but was forced to declare [it] to all'.[58] Self-proclaimed prophets and visionaries were a feature of seventeenth-century life, from 'Frantic Hacket' in the 1590s through to the French Prophets who gathered several hundred followers in Queen Anne's London and attracted huge crowds to witness the (unsuccessful) raising of a man from the dead. The undoubted heyday of prophets was the period between 1640 and 1660, when numerous and now largely forgotten individuals pronounced their visions, revelations and warnings of the imminent end of the world. Since prophecy tended to be the preserve of the humble and the uneducated, it was a form of religious expression particularly associated with women. It gave them a voice. In 1654 the young Anna Trapnel of Poplar went into a twelve-day prophetic trance. She was convinced that 'what the Lord utters in me I must speak', but her prophesying simply earned her a spell in the Bridewell.[59] There were perhaps three hundred other female visionaries active in these decades.

Awkward and inspired individuals tested the patience of even separatist churches. In 1653 the Fenstanton Baptists expelled one member who announced: 'God speaks unto men by his spirit . . . he spake unto prophets formerly, and now he speaks unto me.'[60] Other such individuals were repudiated by the separatists and the sects. Yet, according to their critics, such radicalism was the inevitable consequence of separatism. The Presbyterian Thomas Edwards warned that separation from the parish church was the first step on a slippery slope. Clement Wrighter, for instance, was reported to have 'fallen off from the communion' of the Presbyterians 'to Independency and Brownism . . . from that he fell to anabaptism and Arminianism, and to mortalism, holding the soul mortal and after that he fell to be a seeker and is now an anti-scripturist, a questionist, and a sceptic, and I fear an atheist'.[61] Oliver Heywood shook his head over one errant member of his congregation who had been 'a great professor in the antinomian way, then a Quaker married two wives at one time, but is now fallen off to drunkenness and horrible debauchery'.[62] The minister of Chalfont St Giles reported in the 1660s that the parish had as many 'practical atheists' as Nonconformists: 'they have passed on through such variety of persuasions in matters of religion that now at length they are come I fear to be of no religion at all' and spend the Sabbath 'sauntering about in the streets and fields'.[63] Who knew what irreligious or heretical positions had been reached by those who had run the gamut of the sects.

*

Whereas the shadowy pre-1640 congregations have to be reconstructed from fragmentary and later sources, the groups that emerged during the Civil Wars proclaimed their existence in the streets and the press, and by the second half of the century these congregations had acquired formal coherence – their existence and identity given a perverse recognition by the legal category of 'Dissenter'. Organised Protestant denominations had emerged. We can read some of their 'church books', the registers of their meetings, disputes and sufferings, alongside the jaundiced accounts of local JPs and clergymen, and using such sources we can test some of the generalisations about the appeal of Dissent to contemporaries.

Observers reported on the variety and distribution of the denominations. In 1669 the chapel at Colebrook, Buckinghamshire, had a meeting every Wednesday of 'no less than one or two hundred persons and sometimes many more'. There were 'thirteen who preach there by turns as very formal lecturers. These go under the name of Presbyterian.' They included several ejected ministers, some of them coming from London, and took large collections. Elsewhere in the parish there was a meeting of thirty Quakers. Nearby Olney had forty Quakers and two hundred Baptists who had met since the 1650s in a rented malthouse. They 'are of the lower and poor rank, most of them women and maids that get their living by making of bonelace. The men that frequent them are but a few and they likewise but of little esteem and name in the town.'[64] Early-eighteenth-century Luton had a population of 4,000 of whom 500 were Presbyterians, Quakers, but mainly Baptists 'of which there are two sorts' each with a meeting house; meanwhile no more than 140 of the town's parishioners were communicants.[65] Yet Dissenters were a minority in each parish and in the nation. Most parishes reported few or no Dissenters. The geographical distribution of Dissent can be tracked by the licences issued in 1672, ecclesiastical surveys of 1669 and 1676, and the Evans list of 1715–17. Dissenters tended to be concentrated in towns, in for example Taunton, Norwich, Sheffield and Chester: they may have been 20 per cent of Bristol's population. But they were also to be found in rural areas such as Devon and Somerset, South Wales and East Anglia.[66] They were repeatedly dismissed by Anglicans as 'of the meaner sort, for the most part women, and young fellows'.[67] This was not true of congregations in, say, Bristol or London. Evidence from Bedfordshire, Huntingdonshire and Cambridgeshire indicates that Dissent drew members from all social ranks and tends to undermine earlier suggestions that the Quakers were a movement of the middling sort.[68]

In line with patriarchal assumptions and ideals of household piety, the church asked local clergymen to report the number of Dissenting *families* rather than individuals. But was Dissent a family affair? Occasional clerical reports suggest otherwise: there were 140 families in Cardington in 1712, 'of these eighty entirely conformable, thirty-two entirely Dissenters, the rest mixed'; at South Malling there were 'two farmers who are Dissenters, with their wives and several of their servants, and one woman more'.[69] While some denominations such as the Quakers exerted control over members' marriages and the Baptists frowned on 'a marrying out of the Lord or out of the Church', others clearly did not recruit husbands and wives or entire family units. Sheils's study of the Coley Presbyterian congregation reveals the membership of many individual women.[70]

Research into such issues as Dissenters' social status or family structures is often designed to test assumptions about the social functions of religion. Most recent work has tended to undermine suggestions that Dissent was associated with particular social groups or economic functions. The inevitable conclusion is that Dissenters, and indeed other religious minorities, were motivated by *religion*. This does not, however, mean that their religious identities and values were precisely those one would expect. Anglican clergy were frequently mystified by the denominational identities and boundaries of Dissent. They were baffled by Dissenting denominations that shared meeting places or heard each other's ministers. They reported some as followers of specific preachers, as 'Antinomians' or 'free willers', or simply replied, 'the rest do not know what to call themselves'. Many labourers at Bedford 'resort to the Independents' meeting house, but know little more of religion than that they do not like the Church of England, but think they edify more at a conventicle'.[71] The insinuation of ignorance was common. But for lay Dissenters, spiritual edification and fellowship may have been a more important aspect of their faith than doctrinal knowledge. If Dissenters did not always achieve the level of theological knowledge expected of them by their own and Anglican ministers, neither did they always live up to the high standards of morality and piety expected by their profession. Lay Dissenters drank and quarrelled, cheated and fell in love with unsuitable partners, and even strayed into their parish churches from time to time. Even the most fiercely separatist congregations had to battle to keep their members on the straight and narrow and free from pollution by the world.[72] They were sinners like everyone else, but with God's help and the fellowship of their brethren they could glimpse glory. As the all-too-human Roger Lowe noted in his diary after a night of prayer with the godly, 'O how comfortable is the communion of saints!'[73]

*

All the varied forms of voluntary religious activity in the seventeenth century will never be reduced to a few neat categories. Yet by concentrating on some of their similarities and structures this chapter may have shown that meaningful religious expression – the comforts of community and prayer – were at least as important to contemporaries as theological and ecclesiastical issues. This is not, of course, to imply that the seventeenth-century laity failed to understand doctrine, but simply to assert the inevitable connections of theology and psychology. To echo Marsh's formula about the circular relationship, 'faith was *felt*, but to some extent it was also *learnt*'.[74] Likewise, we will never conclusively know whether religious diversity did or did not fragment communities. Those who withdrew spiritually from their neighbours may have found it easier to deal with them socially, just as those who hoped to reform the world while living within it could severely disrupt local life. Reflecting on the activities of the devout minorities sketched in this chapter raises another issue. Could it be that, although they did not know it, these pious Christians of different persuasions had more in common with each other than with the worldly majority? To that extent, their quarrels and competition may bear out the cliché that animosities are never so deep as where the true differences are slight.

Notes

1 Josselin, p. 396; *The Diary of Ralph Thoresby*, ed. J. Hunter (1830); T. Webster, 'Writing to Redundancy: Approaches to Spiritual Journals and Early Modern Spirituality', *HJ*, 39 (1996); E. Findlay, 'Ralph Thoresby the Diarist: The Late Seventeenth-century Pious Diary and its Demise', *The Seventeenth Century*, XVII (2002).

2 John Bunyan, *Grace Abounding with other Spiritual Autobiographies*, ed. J. Stachniewski (Oxford, 1998), pp. 163, 45; M. MacDonald, 'The Fearfull Estate of Francis Spira*: Narrative, Identity, and Emotion in Early Modern England', *JBS*, 31 (1992).

3 W.M. Jacob, *Lay People and Religion in the Early Eighteenth Century* (Cambridge, 1996), p. 61; C. Cross, 'The Genesis of a Godly Community: Two York Parishes, 1590–1640', *SCH*, 23 (1986), p. 220; N. Ker and M. Perkin (eds), *A Directory of Parochial Libraries* (London, 2004), pp. 277, 329.

4 *The Diary of Roger Lowe*, ed. W.L. Sachse (London, 1938), p. 53.

5 P. Crawford, *Women and Religion in England 1500–1720* (1993), p. 82.

6 Josselin, p. 277; *The Diaries of Lady Anne Clifford*, ed. D.J.H. Clifford (Stroud, 1996), p. 115.

7 R. Gillespie, '"Into Another Intensity": Prayer in Irish Nonconformity, 1650–1700', in K. Herlihy (ed.), *The Religion of Irish Dissent 1650–1800* (Dublin, 1996), p. 41.

8 Heywood, I, 250.

9 P. Seaver, *Wallington's World* (Stanford, Calif., 1985), pp. 39–40.

10 Josselin, p. 377.

11 R. Targoff, *Common Prayer: The Language of Public Devotion in Early Modern England* (Chicago, 2001), p. 36.

12 *Grace Abounding*, ed. Stachniewski, p. 174; Jane Turner, *Choice Experiences* (1653), p. 12.

13 Heywood, I, 189–90.

14 *Oliver Heywood's Life of John Angier of Denton*, ed. E. Axon (Chetham Society, new series 97, 1937), p. 73.

15 Lowe, *Diary*, p. 44.

16 *The Minutes of the First Independent Church (now Bunyan Meeting) at Bedford 1656–1766*, ed. H.G. Tibbutt (Bedfordshire Historical Society, 55, 1976), p. 20.

17 John Dod and Robert Cleaver, *A Godlie Form of Household Government* (1612), sigs A2v–A3.

18 D. Booy (ed.), *Personal Disclosures: An Anthology of Self-Writings* (Aldershot, 2002), p. 66.

19 *Memoirs of the Verney Family in the Seventeenth Century*, ed. F.P. and M.M. Verney (2 vols, London, 1925), I, 501.

20 Guildhall Library, London, MS 10823, fo. 36.

21 Booy (ed.), *Personal Disclosures*, pp. 79–81.

22 J. Bossy, *The English Catholic Community 1570–1850* (London, 1975), p. 128.

23 *Heywood's Life of Angier*, pp. 85–6.

24 *The Diary of Lady Margaret Hoby, 1599–1605*, ed. D.M. Meads (London, 1930), p. 66.

25 D. Lamburn, 'Politics and Religion in Early Modern Beverley', in P. Collinson and J. Craig, *The Reformation in English Towns, 1500–1640* (Basingstoke, 1998), p. 68.

26 M. Ingram, *Church Courts, Sex and Marriage in England 1570–1640* (Cambridge, 1987), p. 94.

27 *The Life of Adam Martindale*, ed. R. Parkinson (Chetham Society, IV, 1845), pp. 173–4; Lowe, *Diary*, p. 16.

28 Lowe, *Diary*, p. 49.

29 Josiah Woodward, *An Account of the Rise and Progress of the Religious Societies* (2nd edn, 1698), p. 30.

30 William Kiffin, *Remarkable Passages*, ed. W. Orme (1823), pp. 11–12.

31 Heywood, I, 156.

32 *Some Remarkable Passages in the Holy Life and Death of Gervase Disney* (1692), p. 19.

33 Heywood, IV, 146–7.

34 BL, Add. MS 38693, fo. 137; Spurr, 'The Church, the Societies and the Moral Revolution of 1688', in J. Walsh, C. Haydon and S. Taylor (eds), *The Church of England c.1689–c.1833* (Cambridge, 1993).

35 Broughton, *A New Manual of Old Christian Catholic Meditations* (1617), quoted in L. McClain, 'Without Church, Cathedral, or Shrine: The Search for Religious Space among Catholics in England, 1559–1625', *Sixteenth Century Journal*, 33 (2002), 383.

36 M. Hodgetts, 'The Yates of Harvington, 1631–1696', *Recusant History*, XXII (1994), 170–1.

37 Crawford, *Women and Religion*, p. 60.

38 Sussex, pp. 48, 54, 73–4, 142.

39 F.E. Dolan, *Whores of Babylon* (Ithaca, 1999), p. 30.

40 A. Walsham, 'The Parochial Roots of Laudianism Revisited: Catholics, Anti-Calvinists and "Parish Anglicans" in Early Stuart England', *JEH*, 49 (1998).

41 Evelyn, IV, 554; C. Marsh, *The Family of Love in English Society 1550–1630* (Cambridge, 1994).

42 M. Ingram, 'Puritans and the Church Courts', in C. Durston and J. Eales (eds), *The Culture of English Puritanism 1560–1700* (Basingstoke, 1996), p. 84.

43 Spurr, *EP*, p. 64.

44 T.D. Bozeman, 'The Glory of the Third Time: John Eaton as Contra-Puritan', *JEH*, 47 (1996); D. Como and P. Lake, 'Puritans, Antinomians and Laudians in Caroline London: The Strange Case of Peter Shaw and its Context', *JEH*, 50 (1999).

45 Turner, *Choice Experiences*, pp. 98–9.

46 *Records of a Church of Christ Meeting at Broadmead Bristol, 1640–87*, ed. E.B. Underhill (1847), p. 57.

47 D. Scott, *Quakerism in York, 1650–1720* (Borthwick Paper 80, York, 1991), p. 16.

48 C. Holmes, *Seventeenth-Century Lincolnshire* (Lincoln, 1980), pp. 42–3.

49 *The Axminster Ecclesiastica 1660–1698*, ed. K.W.H. Howard (Sheffield, 1976), pp. 8–10.

50 Watts, p. 172.

51 *Broadmead*, ed. Underhill, pp. 188, 165.

52 *Minutes of Independent Church at Bedford*, p. 17.

53 *Broadmead*, ed. Underhill, p. 65.

54 *Grace Abounding*, ed. Stachniewski, pp. 165–6.

55 *A Journal of the Life of the Ancient Servant of Christ John Gratton* (1720), p. 16.

56 *Broadmead*, ed. Underhill, pp. 60–1.

57 G.H. Jenkins, *Protestant Dissenters in Wales, 1639–89* (Cardiff, 1992), p. 89.

58 Booy (ed.), *Personal Disclosures*, pp. 314–17.

59 Booy (ed.), *Personal Disclosures*, p. 345. Also see D.R. Como, 'Women, Prophecy and Authority in Early Stuart Puritanism', *HLQ*, 61 (2001).

60 *Records of the Churches of Fenstanton*, ed. E.B. Underhill (1854), p. 49.

61 Watts, p. 115.

62 Heywood, III, 116.

63 *Buckinghamshire Dissent and Parish Life, 1669–1712*, ed. J. Broad (Buckinghamshire Record Society, 28, 1993), p. 9.

64 *Buckinghamshire Dissent*, ed. Broad, pp. 2–3, 54–5, 210.

65 *Episcopal Visitations in Bedfordshire, 1706–1720*, ed. P. Bell (Bedfordshire Historical Record Society, 81, 2002), pp. 69–70.

66 See Watts, pp. 267–89, appendix; *Reformation and Revival in Eighteenth-century Bristol*, ed. J. Barry and K. Morgan (Bristol Record Society, 44, 1994), pp. 65–73; *Chichester Diocesan Surveys 1686 and 1724*, ed. W.K. Ford (Sussex Record Society, 78, 1992), appendix iv.

67 *Buckinghamshire Dissent*, ed. Broad, p. 40.

68 Bill Stevenson, 'Social Integration of Post-Restoration Dissenters, 1660–1725', in M. Spufford (ed.), *The World of Rural Dissenters 1520–1725* (Cambridge, 1995).

69 *Episcopal Visitations in Bedfordshire*, ed. Bell, p. 22; *Chichester Diocesan Surveys*, ed. Ford, p. 229.

70 W.J. Sheils, 'Oliver Heywood and his Congregation', *SCH*, 23 (1986).

71 *Episcopal Visitations in Bedfordshire*, ed. Bell, pp. 76, 51, 21, 77, 11.

72 See *Minute Book of the Men's Meeting of the Society of Friends in Bristol 1667–1686*, ed. R. Mortimer (Bristol Record Society, XXVI, 1971).

73 Lowe, *Diary*, p. 107.

74 Marsh, *Family of Love*, p. 253.

Conclusion: Post-Reformation Britain

This book began by introducing the idea of the Post-Reformation. It suggested that the term describes a distinct phase of British history that coincides with the seventeenth century. The Post-Reformation was the process of coming to terms with the unsettling effects of the Protestant Reformation on the religious, political and social life of the British Isles. So the Post-Reformation is a consequence of the Reformation, but there is also a real distinction to be drawn between the two. The sixteenth-century Reformation was an act of state and a coherent evangelical campaign. It sought national and personal conversion to a Protestant faith with a distinct theology, piety, worship and church structure. Although the seventeenth-century Post-Reformation was much concerned with the meaning and legacy of 'reformation', although it witnessed a contest about completing, redefining or reversing the Reformation, there was a different issue at stake. That issue was religious diversity.

The Post-Reformation was a struggle between different versions of religion. Rival churches, denominations and sects differed over fundamental questions of belief, practice and organisation. Each group sought its own liberty, but contemporaries were well aware that those who pursued freedom often also aspired to dominance: Oliver Cromwell had warned that every sect wanted liberty but would not extend the same right to its rivals; the philosopher of toleration, John Locke, observed that every church is orthodox in its own eyes, but heretical in the eyes of its rivals. Fragmentation seems to be a trait of Protestantism. It has often been suggested that the Reformation opened Pandora's box by allowing every individual to follow his or her own conscience in matters of religion. It was claimed in the seventeenth century that the pursuit of individual conscience would eventually dissolve all external authority and leave every individual a 'church of one': as Henry Parker remarked, with pardonable exaggeration, in 1641, 'it may be said here (as it was in Constantine's day) there are almost as many religions as opinions and as many opinions as men.'[1] There may be more than a grain of truth in this reading of Protestantism's long-term implications, but, as we have noticed, seventeenth-century religious experience was often communal and familial, with an emphasis on fellowship, and similar forms of piety tended to recur across different religious denominations. Few contemporaries could readily envisage religion as a purely personal activity or choice; it was fundamentally about belonging to a community of some sort. Religious diversity had not yet become a highway to spiritual individualism.

If the Post-Reformation was a contest between churches, how was it settled? How and when did the Post-Reformation come to an end? Religious toleration would appear to provide a very obvious conclusion to the Post-Reformation. According to this scenario, the freedom of worship achieved in England in 1689 resolved a century or more of religious strife. The suggestion seems plausible when we contemplate Augustan England. In Preston, Lancashire, in 1714, there were five or six houses where 'papists' met and where 'they have chapels decked with all the popish trinkets. They go publicly to their meetings as we go to church, and on Sabbath days they go by our bells.' According to the local Anglican minister, Catholics held the best estates in the county, 'their priests swarm . . . and the Romish party is of late, very upish'.[2] Meanwhile, in London, Dudley Ryder could choose among different Protestant churches and meeting houses. He told his friends that he 'looked upon the several churches according to the English establishment in the same light with those of the Dissenters, only as congregations of Christians met together to worship God without any regard at all to their being established'.[3] But this freedom was hedged about with restrictions and insecurities. Non-Anglicans were excluded from large areas of civil life or forced into shabby compromises such as occasional conformity. Antipopery was as virulent in the eighteenth century as it has been in the seventeenth. And if one looks beyond England, the scene is rather different. In Scotland, many regarded the creation of a Presbyterian national church in 1690 as the final act in the Reformation that Knox and his supporters had begun a hundred and thirty years earlier. The predominance of the Calvinist Kirk allowed non-Presbyterians only limited room for manoeuvre: in 1712 it was the Tory British Parliament that legislated freedom for Scottish Episcopalians, the revival of lay patronage, and a measure of protection against legal enforcement of Kirk censures. The grip of the Kirk on Scottish life would loosen over the eighteenth century, but as much from its own internal dissensions as external opposition. In Ireland, the Reformation was never completed. Instead, a colonial Protestant ascendancy was established and the Catholic underclass consoled itself with religion and, in due course, nationalism.

So perhaps it is simply too neat to tie the end of the Post-Reformation to a specific piece of legislation or the accession of a Hanoverian monarch. It may be more realistic to recognise that the seventeenth century's quarrels gradually began to subside, or to mutate into other forms, as politics and religion began to drift apart as distinct domains of human activity. To risk a simile, it was as if the turbulence of the sixteenth century had mixed politics and religion together like oil and vinegar. For a century or more they had formed an emulsion that simply would not allow contemporaries to distinguish between them. This phenomenon has frequently been encountered by scholars when attempting to pinpoint an ultimate motivation in some specific seventeenth-century episode: for example, in the words of Peter Lake's account of Cheshire politics in the early 1640s, 'different styles of divinity and positions on church government shaded into other more "political" debates about "representation", "order", and the nature and locus of authority throughout the polity'.[4] Slowly, however, the oil and vinegar did begin to separate. The process was unpredictable but discernible. It can be detected in the use of partisan language and labels. Casual constructions such as 'the godly' and the more intricate and pejorative labels such as 'papist' and 'puritan' gave way to sharply defined terms such as Presbyterian, Whig or Tory. By the end of the century some commentators admitted that recent conflicts 'have not at all been upon the account of religion, though indeed that has all along been made use of to amuse and deceive the people', but were at bottom fuelled by purely political ambition.[5] The separation of religion and politics was evident too in the growing distrust of religion and the clerical profession. Denigration of the clergy became ever more insistent across the mid and later century and it began to undermine confidence in religion: in 1699 an Ely preacher protested at those who 'call all religion only priestcraft, a trade whereby we get our living'.[6] Meanwhile, religion was openly and unselfconsciously employed as a social tool: the Societies for the Reformation of Manners and the SPCK stressed the communal and commercial benefits that would flow from Christian education and conduct.

Contemporary discussions of religious toleration were often conducted in terms of unshakeable personal conviction or preference. 'Liberty of conscience, God's word and spirit is their pretended authority,' reported a Buckinghamshire vicar of his Baptist neighbours in 1669.[7] 'They are an unaccountable people,' said an Oxfordshire incumbent of the local sectaries, 'making conscience wholly . . . their refuge.'[8] More sophisticated advocates tended to voice pragmatic arguments that trade and national interest were best served by religious tolerance; or they observed the dangers of persecution, especially ineffective persecution: "tis not the having several parties in religion under a state that is in itself dangerous, but 'tis the persecuting of them that makes them so' – an argument advanced by Charles II in 1672 and James II in 1687.[9] The solution proffered by Locke was for the state to extricate itself from the private religious business of its citizens. This was not something that the Post-Reformation British state would willingly do. It grudgingly lifted penalties, permitted religious exercises, but it did not recognise any rights or even any real distinction between 'private' and 'public' when it came to religion. The strict separation of church and state, religion and politics, was, and still is, a long way from achievement.

How useful, finally, are labels such as 'Reformation' and 'Post-Reformation' in describing the reality of individual religious lives? I believe they capture something of the high ambition of the enthusiasts and of their disappointments. These terms certainly indicate the inexorable narrowing of the Reformation. The Reformation was the work of committed activists. The reformers set up unrealistically high spiritual expectations, their descendants forced the political pace during the seventeenth century, and it was their zeal which energised the sects and separatists: 'it has been a long time [before] our Reformation can be thoroughly polished and perfected as it were to be wished and desired; for there is nothing so perfect, here, but is capable of more perfection.'[10] For such zealots the Reformation would never be over. The Post-Reformation was their story. But it was also the tale of the slow, uncoordinated reassertion of a different mindset. This was an outlook characteristic of those who settled back in their pew each Sunday to hear a good sermon, who lived as best they could and shunned the puritan and the papist, the 'fanatic' and the 'evil liver'. Such people, too, left a record of their intimate spiritual hopes and beliefs. 'I have made now a serious resolution and promise to God that I will make it my duty to obey his laws.' 'May God grant that I may duly perform my vows.' 'At the sacrament I confessed my miscarriage and promised reformation, which God grant!' The imperative was to turn away from sin before it was too late: 'Lord give me grace to amend my life for the future and spend every day as if it was my last.'[11] But the sorry truth was that most Christians would stray from the paths of righteousness again and again. For such people reform would never be over, but the Reformation had already taken place.

Notes

1 [Henry Parker], *A Discourse Concerning Puritans* (1641), p. 6.

2 C. Haydon, 'Samuel Peploe and Catholicism in Preston, 1714', *Recusant History*, 20 (1990), 78–9.

3 *The Diary of Dudley Ryder 1715–1716*, ed. W. Matthews (London, 1939), p. 362.

4 P. Lake, 'Puritans, Popularity and Petitions' in T. Cogswell, R. Cust and P. Lake (eds), *Politics, Religion and Popularity in Early Stuart Britain* (Cambridge, 2002), p. 287.

5 M. Knights, *Representation and Misrepresentation in Later Stuart Britain: Partisanship and Political Culture* (Oxford, 2005), pp. 182–3, 291.

6 Benjamin Laney, *Five Sermons* (1668), p. 15; Charles Lidgould, *A Sermon Preach'd in the Cathedral Church at Ely* (1699), p. 4.

7 *Buckinghamshire Dissent and Parish Life, 1669–1712*, ed. J. Broad (Buckinghamshire Record Society, 28, 1993), p. 39.

8 *Bishop Fell and Nonconformity*, ed. M. Clapinson (Oxfordshire Record Society, 52, 1980), pp. 25, 30–31.

9 Charles Wolseley, *Liberty of Conscience* (1668), p. 25.

10 Cornelius Burges, *Two Sermons Preached to the Honourable House of Commons . . . 17 November 1640* (1641), first sermon, p. 54.

11 Ryder, *Diary*, p. 75; *The Diary and Autobiography of Edmund Bohun*, ed. S.W. Rix (Beccles, 1853), p. 38; CUL, MS 8499, p. 177; *Two East Anglian Diaries*, ed. M. Storey (Suffolk Record Society, 36, 1994), p. 208.

Select bibliography

This bibliography lists the primary printed sources cited in the text and
a few of the more accessible primary sources for the religious life of
the seventeenth century. It also includes a larger selection of relevant
modern secondary works. All books were published in London
unless stated otherwise. This bibliography also includes unpublished
dissertations: I am grateful to their authors for allowing researchers
to consult their work. Although the bibliography does not include
manuscript sources, where such materials have been directly quoted
they are acknowledged in the notes.

The scale of the secondary literature on seventeenth-century Britain
precludes any comprehensive listing in print, but it is now easily
searched through the free online Royal Historical Society
bibliography (http://www.rhs.ac.uk/bibwel.asp). Sources of various
kinds are increasingly available online: one of the premier sites is
British History Online (http://www.british-history.ac.uk/), and
two fine sources are the records of the village of Earls Colne
(http://linux02.lib.cam.ac.uk/earlscolne//contents.htm) and the Old
Bailey Proceedings 1674–1831 (http://www.oldbaileyonline.org/).
The Clergy of the Church of England database
(http://www.theclergydatabase.org.uk) will rapidly become an
indispensable source for any serious study of the clergy. Valuable
online resources that require subscription include Early English
Books Online (http://eebo.chadwyck.com/home), Literature Online
(http://lion.chadwyck.co.uk/) and the Oxford Dictionary of National
Biography (http://www.oxforddnb.com/).

Primary sources

Abbott, W.C. (ed.), *The Writings and Speeches of Oliver Cromwell*
(4 vols, Cambridge, Mass., 1937–47; reprinted Oxford, 1988)

Allen, W.O.B., and McClure, E. (eds), *Two Hundred Years: The History of the SPCK* (1898)

The Axminster Ecclesiastica 1660–1698, ed. K.W.H. Howard (Sheffield, 1976)

Antimoixeia (1691)

Barrington Family Letters 1628–1632, ed. A. Searle (Camden Society, 28, 1983)

[Atterbury, Francis], *Letter to a Convocation Man* (1697)

The Autobiography of Richard Baxter, abridged by J.M. Lloyd Thomas and edited by N.H. Keeble (1974)

Calendar of the Correspondence of Richard Baxter, ed. N.H. Keeble and G.F. Nuttall (2 vols, Oxford, 1991)

Richard Baxter, *Reliquiae Baxterianae*, ed. M. Sylvester (1696)

Bishop Fell and Nonconformity, ed. M. Clapinson (Oxfordshire Record Society, 52, 1980)

Bohun, Edmund, *Three Charges Delivered at the General Quarter Sessions* (1693)

The Diary and Autobiography of Edmund Bohun, ed. S.W. Rix (Beccles, 1853)

Bolton, William, *Core Redivivus* (1684)

Booy, D. (ed.), *Personal Disclosures: An Anthology of Self-Writings* (Aldershot, 2002)

Bramhall, John, *The Works of John Bramhall* (5 vols, Oxford, 1842–5)

The Autobiography of Sir John Bramston, ed. Lord Braybrooke (Camden Society, 32, 1845)

Bray, G. (ed.), *The Anglican Canons 1529–1947* (Church of England Record Society, 6, 1998)

Buckinghamshire Dissent and Parish Life, 1669–1712, ed. J. Broad (Buckinghamshire Record Society, 28, 1993)

Bunyan, John, *Grace Abounding to the Chief of Sinners with Other Spiritual Autobiographies*, ed. J. Stachniewski with A. Pacheco (Oxford, 1998)

Burges, Cornelius, *Two Sermons Preached to the Honourable House of Commons . . . 17 Nov. 1640* (1641)

Burnet, Gilbert, *Discourse of Pastoral Care* (1692)

Burnet, Gilbert, *A History of My Own Time*, ed. O. Airy
(2 vols, Oxford, 1897–1900)

Calamy, Edmund, *England's Looking Glass* (1642)

Calamy, Edmund, *A Sermon Preached before the House of Commons . . .
November 17 1640* (1641)

Calendar of State Papers Domestic

Cardwell, E., *Documentary Annals of the Reformed Church of England.
1546–1717* (2nd edn, 2 vols, Oxford, 1844)

Cardwell, E., *A History of Conferences* (Oxford, 3rd edn, 1849)

*A Catalogue of Letters and Other Historical Documents Exhibited in the
Library at Welbeck*, ed. S.A. Strong (1903)

Chadwick, Daniel, *A Sermon Preached in the Church of St Mary in
Nottingham* (1698)

The Letters of John Chamberlain, ed. N.E. McClure
(2 vols, Philadelphia, 1939)

Charges to the Grand Jury 1689–1803, ed. G. Lamoine (Camden Society,
4th series, 43, 1992)

Chichester Diocesan Surveys 1686 and 1724, ed. W.K. Ford (Sussex
Record Society, 78, 1992)

*Churchwardens' Accounts of S. Edmund and S. Thomas, Sarum,
1443–1702*, ed. H.J.F. Swayne (Wiltshire Record Society, Salisbury,
1896)

*Churchwardens Presentments (Seventeenth Century): Part 1,
Archdeaconry of Chichester*, ed. H. Johnstone (Sussex Record
Society, 49, 1947–8)

Cleveland, John, 'Epitaph on the Earl of Strafford', *Poems* (1647)

*A Collection of Cases and Other Discourses Written to Recover
Dissenters* (2nd edn, 1694)

Collinges, John, *Vindiciae Ministerii Evangelici* (1651)

Corbet, John, *An Account Given of the Principles and Practices of Several
Nonconformists* (1680)

The Correspondence of Henry Hyde, Earl of Clarendon, ed. S.W. Singer
(2 vols, 1828)

The Clarke Papers, ed. C.H. Firth (Camden Society, new series, 4 vols,
49, 54, 61, 62, 1891–1901)

The Correspondence of Sir James Clavering, ed. H.T. Dickinson (Surtees Society, 178, 1967)

The Diaries of Lady Anne Clifford, ed. D.J.H. Clifford (Stroud, 1996)

The Autobiographies and Letters of Thomas Comber, ed. C.E. Whiting (2 vols, Surtees Society, 156–7, 1941–2)

The Compton Census of 1676: A Critical Edition, ed. Anne Whiteman (1986)

The Writings and Speeches of Oliver Cromwell, ed. W.C. Abbott (4 vols, Cambridge, Mass., 1937–47; reprinted Oxford 1988)

Defoe, Daniel, *A Tour Through the Whole Island of Britain*, ed. P.N. Furbank and W.R. Owens (New Haven, Conn., 1991)

The Diary of Sir Simonds D'Ewes 1622–24, ed. E. Bourcier (Paris, 1974)

Dod, John, and Cleaver, Robert, *A Godlie Form of Household Government* (1612)

Durham Parish Books (Surtees Society, 84, 1888)

Eikon Basilike, ed. P.A. Knachel (1966)

Episcopal Visitation Book from the Archdeaconry of Buckinghamshire, 1662, ed. E.R.C. Brinkworth (Buckinghamshire Record Society, 7, 1947)

Episcopal Visitation Returns for Cambridgeshire, ed. W.M. Palmer (Cambridge, 1930)

Episcopal Visitations in Bedfordshire, 1706–1720, ed. P. Bell (Bedfordshire Historical Record Society, 81, 2002)

Essex Correspondence, ed. C.E. Pike (Camden Society, 3rd series, 24, 1913)

The Diary of John Evelyn, ed. E.S. de Beer (5 vols, Oxford, 1955)

Fagel, Gaspar, *A Letter wrote by Mijn Heer Fagel* (1687)

Foreness, E., *A Sermon Preached at Manchester* (1683)

Gardiner, S.R. (ed.), *The Constitutional Documents of the Puritan Revolution 1625–1660* (3rd edn, Oxford, 1906)

Gilpin, Richard, *The Temple Rebuilt* (1658)

Gough, Richard, *The History of Myddle*, ed. D. Hey (Harmondsworth, 1981)

The Remains of Denis Granville, ed. G. Ornsby (2 vols, Surtees Society, 37 and 47, 1860 and 1865)

A Journal of the Life of the Ancient Servant of Christ John Gratton (1720)

The Diary of John Harington, ed. M.F. Stieg (Somerset Record Society, 74, 1977)

Letters of Lady Brilliana Harley, ed. T.T. Lewis (Camden Society, old series, 68, 1854)

Matthew Henry, *The Life of the Rev. Philip Henry*, ed. J.B. Williams (1825)

Diaries and Letters of Philip Henry, ed. M.H. Lee (1882)

The Autobiography of Oliver Heywood, ed. J.H. Turner (4 vols, Brighouse, 1882–5)

Oliver Heywood's Life of John Angier of Denton, ed. E. Axon (Chetham Society, new series, 97, 1937)

H., J., *The Life of the Reverend Mr George Trosse* (1714)

The Diary of Lady Margaret Hoby, 1599–1605, ed. D.M. Meads (1930)

Hunter, J., *The Rise of the Old Dissent Exemplified in the Life of Oliver Heywood* (1842)

Inspections of Churches and Parsonage Houses in the Diocese of Worcester in 1674, 1676, 1684 and 1687, ed. P. Morgan (Worcester Historical Society, new series, 12, 1986)

Remarkable Passages in the Life of William Kiffin, Written by Himself, ed. W. Orme (1823)

James I: Political Writings, ed. J.P. Sommerville (Cambridge, 1994)

The Diary of Ralph Josselin 1616–1683, ed. A. Macfarlane (1976)

Kenyon, J.P. (ed.), *The Stuart Constitution 1603–1688: Documents and Commentary* (Cambridge, 1966)

The Life of Richard Kidder, ed. A.E. Robinson (Somerset Record Society, 37, 1922)

Lancy, Benjamin, *Five Sermons* (1668)

The Works of William Laud, ed. W. Scott and J. Bliss (Oxford, 7 vols, 1847–60),

Sir Peter Leicester, *Charges to the Grand Jury*, ed. E. Halcrow (Chetham Society, 3rd series, v, 1953)

Lidgould, Charles, *A Sermon Preach'd in the Cathedral Church at Ely* (1699)

The Correspondence of John Locke, ed. E.S. de Beer (8 vols, Oxford, 1976–89)

The Diary of Roger Lowe of Ashton in Makerfield, Lancashire 1663–1674, ed. W.L. Sachse (1938)

Memoirs of Edmund Ludlow, ed. C.H. Firth (2 vols, Oxford, 1894)

Luttrell, Narcissus, *A Brief Historical Relation of State Affairs 1660–1714* (6 vols, Oxford, 1857)

The Diary of John Manningham, ed. J. Bruce (Camden Society, old series, 99, 1868)

Marshall, Stephen, *A Sermon Preached before the Honourable House of Commons . . . 17 November 1640* (1641)

The Life of Adam Martindale, ed. R. Parkinson (Chetham Society, iv, 1845)

The Diary of John Milward MP, ed. C. Robbins (Cambridge, 1938)

The Minute Book of the Men's Meeting of the Society of Friends in Bristol 1667–1686, ed. R. Mortimer (Bristol Record Society, 26, 1971)

The Minute Book of the Wirksworth Classis 1651–1658, ed. J.C. Cox (Derbyshire Archaeological and Natural History Society, 2, 1880)

The Minutes of the First Independent Church (now Bunyan Meeting) at Bedford 1656–1766, ed. H.G. Tibbutt (Bedfordshire Historical Society, 55, 1976)

The Letter-Book of John Viscount Mordaunt 1658–60, ed. M.H. Coates (Camden Society, 3rd series, 69, 1945)

The Entering Book of Roger Morrice 1677–91, ed. M. Goldie (6 vols, Woodbridge, 2006)

Diary of Thomas Naish, ed. D. Slatter (Wiltshire Archaeological Society, 20, Devizes, 1965)

Nedham, Marchamont, *A True Case of the State of the Commonwealth* (1654)

The Autobiography of Henry Newcome, ed. R. Parkinson (2 vols, Chetham Society, 26, 27, 1852)

Newsletters from the Archpresbyterate of George Birkhead, ed. M.C. Questier (Camden Society, 5th series, 12, 1998)

The London Diaries of William Nicholson, Bishop of Carlisle, 1702–1718, ed. C. Jones and G. Holmes (Oxford, 1985)

[Parker, Henry], *A Discourse Concerning Puritans* (1641)

The Diary of Samuel Pepys, ed. R.C. Latham and W. Matthews (11 vols, 1970–83)

Letters of Humphrey Prideaux, ed. E.M. Thompson (Camden Society, new series, 15, 1875).

Proceedings of the Short Parliament of 1640, ed. E.S. Cope and W.H. Coates (Camden Society, 4th series, 19, 1977)

Proposals for a National Reformation of Manners (1694)

The Diary of Abraham de la Pryme, ed. C. Jackson (Surtees Society, 54, 1870)

The Records of a Church of Christ in Bristol, 1640–1687, ed. R. Hayden (Bristol Record Society, 27, 1974)

The Records of a Church of Christ Meeting in Broadmead Bristol (1640–1687), ed. E.B. Underhill (Hanserd Knollys Society, 1847)

Records of the Churches of Fenstanton, ed. E.B. Underhill (Hanserd Knollys Society, 1854)

The Rector's Book, Clayworth, ed. H. Gill and E.L. Guilford (Nottingham, 1910)

Reformation and Revival in Eighteenth-century Bristol, ed. J. Barry and K. Morgan (Bristol Record Society, 44, 1994)

The Memoirs of Sir John Reresby, ed. A. Browning (2nd edn, revised by M.K. Geiter and W.A. Speck, 1991)

Reynolds, Edward, *Joy in the Lord* (1655)

Reynolds, Edward, *The Peace of Jerusalem* (1657)

R[ogers], T[homas], *Lux Occidentalis* (1689)

The Diary of Samuel Rogers, 1634–1638, ed. T. Webster and K. Shipps (Church of England Record Society, 11, 2004)

The Diary of John Rous, ed. M.A.E. Green (Camden Society, old series, 66, 1856),

The Diurnal of Thomas Rugg 1659–1661, ed. W.L. Sachse (Camden Society, 3rd series, 91, 1961)

The Diary of Dudley Ryder 1715–16, ed. W. Matthews (1939)

The Journal of William Schellinks' Travels in England 1661–1663, trans. and ed. M. Exwood and H.L. Lehmann (Camden Society, 5th series, 1, 1993)

The State of the Church in the Reigns of Elizabeth I and James I, ed.
C.W. Foster (Lincoln Record Society, 23, 1926)

Shaw, John, 'Autobiography' in *Yorkshire Diaries and Autobiographies of the Seventeenth and Eighteenth Centuries* (Surtees Society, 65, 1877)

Shaw, Joseph, *Parish Law* (1733)

Speck, W.A., 'An Anonymous Parliamentary Diary 1705–6', *Camden Miscellany XXIII* (Camden Society, 4th series, 7, 1969)

Tanner, J.R. (ed.), *Constitutional Documents of the Reign of James I* (Cambridge, 1952)

Taylor, S. (ed.), *From Cranmer to Davidson: A Church of England Miscellany* (Church of England Record Society, 7, Woodbridge, 1999)

Tewkesbury Churchwardens' Accounts 1563–1624, ed. C.J. Litzenberger (Gloucestershire Record Society, 7, 1994)

The Diary of Ralph Thoresby, ed. J. Hunter (1830)

A Collection of the State Papers of John Thurloe, ed. T. Birch (7 vols, 1742)

Tracts on Liberty of Conscience and Persecution, 1614–1661, ed. E.B. Underhill (Hanserd Knollys Society, 1846)

The Life of the Reverend Mr George Trosse, ed. A.W. Brink (Montreal, 1974)

Two East Anglian Diaries, 1641–1729, ed. M. Storey (Suffolk Records Society, 36, 1994)

Turner, G.L. (ed.), *Original Records of Early Nonconformity under Persecution and Indulgence* (3 vols, 1911–14)

Turner, Jane, *Choice Experiences* (1653)

The Diary of Thomas Turner 1754–1765, ed. D. Vaisey (Oxford, 1984)

Memoirs of the Verney Family in the Seventeenth Century, ed. F.P. and M.M. Verney (2 vols, 1925)

Visitation Articles and Injunctions of the Early Stuart Church, ed. K. Fincham (2 vols, Church of England Record Society, 1 and 5, 1994, 1998)

'Visitations held in the Archdeaconry of Essex', ed. E. Pressey, *Transactions of Essex Archaeological Society XXI* (1933–4)

The Diary of the Rev. John Ward, ed. C. Severn (1849)

Dr John Warner's Visitations of the Diocese of Rochester, 1663 and 1670, ed. F. Hull (Kent Archaeological Society, 1, 1991, parts 3, 4, 5)

Wentworth Papers 1597–1628, ed. J.P. Cooper (Camden Society, 4th series, 12, 1973)

Whalley, Peniston, *Episcopacy* (1661)

Williams, E. (ed.), *The Eighteenth-century Constitution* (Cambridge, 1960)

Wolseley, Charles, *Liberty of Conscience* (1668)

Woodhouse, A.S.P. (ed.), *Puritanism and Liberty* (1938; 2nd edn, 1974)

Wootton, D. (ed.), *Divine Right and Democracy* (Harmondsworth, 1986)

Secondary works

Abernathy, G.R., 'The English Presbyterians and the Stuart Restoration', *Transactions of the American Philosophical Society*, (new series, LV, part 2, 1965)

Acheson, R.J., *Radical Puritans in England 1550–1660* (1990)

Addleshaw, G., *The High Church Tradition* (1963)

Addy, J., *Sin and Society in the Seventeenth Century* (1989)

Allison, C.F., *The Rise of Moralism: The Proclamation of the Gospel from Hooker to Baxter* (1966)

Amussen, S., *An Ordered Society: Gender and Class in Early Modern England* (Oxford, 1988)

Anderson, P.J., 'Sion College and the London Provincial Assembly, 1647–1660', *JEH*, 37 (1986)

Ashton, R., *The English Civil War* (1978)

Ashton, R., *Counter-Revolution: The Second Civil War and its Origins 1646–48* (New Haven, Conn. 1994)

Aston, M., *England's Iconoclasts: I – Laws against Images* (Oxford, 1988)

Atherton, I., Fernie, E., Harper-Bill, C., and Smith, H. (eds), *Norwich Cathedral – Church, City and Diocese, 1096–1996* (1996)

Atherton, I.J., 'Viscount Scudamore's "Laudianism": The Religious Practices of the First Viscount Scudamore', *HJ*, 34 (1991)

Aveling, J.C.H., *The Handle and the Axe: The Catholic Recusants in England from Reformation to Emancipation* (1976)

Aylmer, G. (ed.), *The Interregnum* (1972)

Aylmer, G., and Cant, R., *A History of York Minster* (1979)

Aylmer, G., and Tiller, G. (eds), *Hereford Cathedral – A History* (2000)

Bahlman, D.W.R., *The Moral Reformation of 1688* (1957)

Bailey, J., *Unquiet Lives: Marriage and Marriage Breakdown in England, 1660–1800* (Cambridge, 2003)

Baker, J.W., '*Sola Fide, Sola Gratia*: The Battle for Luther in Seventeenth-century England', *The Sixteenth Century Journal*, 16 (1985)

Barbour, H., *The Quakers in Puritan England* (1964)

Barnard, T.C., 'Reforming Irish Manners: The Religious Societies in Dublin during the 1690s', *HJ*, 35 (1992)

Barnard, T.C., 'Protestants and the Irish Language, c.1675–1729', *JEH*, 44 (1993)

Barnard, T.C., *A New Anatomy of Ireland: Protestants in Ireland 1649–1770* (New Haven, Conn., 2003)

Barry, J., and Brooks, C. (eds), *The Middling Sort of People: Culture, Society and Politics in England, 1550–1800* (Basingstoke, 1994)

Bauman, R., *Let Your Words be Few: Symbolism of Speaking and Silence among Seventeenth-century Quakers* (Cambridge, 1983)

Beaver, D.C., *Parish Communities and Religious Conflict in the Vale of Gloucester 1590–1690* (Cambridge, Mass., 1998)

Beddard, R.A., 'Observations of a London Clergyman on the Revolution of 1688–9: Being an Excerpt from the Autobiography of Dr William Wake', *Guildhall Miscellany*, 11 (1967)

Beddard, R.A., 'Vincent Alsop and the Emancipation of Restoration Dissent', *JEH*, 24 (1973)

Beddard, R.A., 'The Privileges of Christchurch, Canterbury: Archbishop Sheldon's Enquiries of 1671', *Archaeologia Cantiana*, 87 (1972)

Beddard, R.A. (ed.), *The Revolution of 1688* (Oxford, 1991)

Bennett, G.V., *The Tory Crisis in Church and State 1688–1710: The Career of Francis Atterbury, Bishop of Rochester* (Oxford, 1975)

Bennett, G.V., and Walsh, J.D. (eds), *Essays in Modern English Church History* (1966)

Bennett, J., 'Conviviality and Charity in Medieval and Early Modern England', *P&P*, 134 (1992)

Bennett, M., *The Civil Wars in Britain and Ireland 1635–1651* (Oxford, 1997)

Berg, J. van den, *The Idea of Toleration and the Act of Toleration* (1989)

Berman, D., *A History of Atheism in Britain* (1988)

Bernard, G.W., 'The Church of England, c.1529–c.1642', *History*, 75 (1990)

Best, G.F.A., *Temporal Pillars: Queen Anne's Bounty, the Ecclesiastical Commissioners and the Church of England* (1964)

Bettey, J.H., *Church and Community* (1979)

Bettey, J.H., *The English Parish Church* (1985)

Bettey, J.H., *Church and Parish* (1987)

Bolam, C.G., Goring, J., Short, H.L., and Thomas, R., *The English Presbyterians: From Elizabethan Puritanism to Modern Unitarianism* (1968)

Bossy, J., *The English Catholic Community 1570–1850* (1975)

Bossy, J., *Christianity in the West 1400–1700* (Oxford, 1985)

Bossy, J., *Peace in the Post-Reformation* (Cambridge, 1998)

Boulton, J.P., 'The Limits of Formal Religion: The Administration of Holy Communion in late Elizabethan and early Stuart London', *London Journal*, 10 (1984)

Bozeman, T.D., 'The Glory of the Third Time: John Eaton as contra-Puritan', *JEH*, 47 (1996)

Brace, L., *The Idea of Property in Seventeenth-century England: Tithes and the Individual* (Manchester, 1998)

Brachlow, J., *The Communion of Saints: Radical Puritan and Separatist Ecclesiology 1570–1625* (Oxford, 1988)

Braddick, M., *State Formation and Social Change in Early Modern England c.1550–1700* (Cambridge, 2000)

Bradley, R., 'The Failure of Accommodation: Religious Conflict between Presbyterians and Independents in the Westminster Assembly 1643–1646', *Journal of Religious History*, 12 (1982)

Bradshaw, B., and Morrill, J. (eds), *The British Problem, c.1534–1707: State Formation in the Atlantic Archipelago* (Basingstoke, 1996)

Bradshaw, B., and Roberts, P. (eds), *British Consciousness and Identity: The Making of Britain, 1533–1707* (Cambridge, 1998)

Bremer, F., *Congregational Communion: Clerical Friendship in the Anglo-American Puritan Community, 1610–1692* (Boston, Mass., 1994)

Bremer, F., *John Winthrop: America's Forgotten Founding Father* (Oxford, 2002)

Bremer, F., and Webster, T. (eds), *The Encyclopedia of Puritanism* (Santa Barbara, Calif., 2006)

Brewer, J., *The Sinews of Power: War, Money and the English State, 1688–1783* (1989)

Brockett, A., *Nonconformists in Exeter, 1650–1875* (1962)

Brown, K., *Kingdom or Province? Scotland and the Regal Union, 1603–1715* (Basingstoke, 1992)

Buckroyd, J., *Church and State in Scotland 1660–1681* (Edinburgh, 1980)

Burgess, G., *The Politics of the Ancient Constitution: An Introduction to English Political Thought 1603–42* (1992)

Burgess, G., *Absolute Monarchy and the Stuart Constitution* (New Haven, Conn., 1996)

Burgess, G. (ed.), *The New British History: Founding a Modern State 1603–1715* (1999)

Burgess, G., 'Was the English Civil War a War of Religion? The Evidence of Political Propaganda', *HLQ*, 61 (2001)

Burke, P., *Popular Culture in Early Modern Europe* (1978)

Burns, A., Fincham, K., and Taylor, S., 'Reconstructing Clerical Careers: The Experience of the Clergy of the Church of England Database', *JEH*, 55 (2004)

Burns, J.H., with Goldie, M.A. (eds), *The Cambridge History of Political Thought 1450–1700* (Cambridge, 1991)

Burns, W.E., *An Age of Wonders: Prodigies, Politics and Providence in England, 1657–1727* (Manchester, 2002)

Caldwell, P., *The Puritan Conversion Narrative: The Beginnings of American Expression* (Cambridge, 1993)

Canny, N., *From Reformation to Restoration: Ireland 1534–1660* (Dublin, 1987)

Capp, B.S., *The Fifth Monarchy Men* (1972)

Capp, B.S., *The World of John Taylor the Water Poet* (Oxford, 1995)

Capp, B.S., *When Gossips Meet: Women, Family and Neighbourhood in Early Modern England* (Oxford, 2003)

Carlson, E.J., 'Good Pastors or Careless Shepherds? Parish Ministers and the English Reformation', *History*, 88 (2003)

Carpenter, E., *The Protestant Bishop: Being the Life of Henry Compton, 1632–1713, Bishop of London* (1956)

Champion, J.A.I., *The Pillars of Priestcraft Shaken: The Church of England and its Enemies, 1660–1730* (Cambridge, 1992)

Champion, J.A.I., *Republican Learning: John Toland and the Crisis of Christian Culture, 1696–1722* (Manchester, 2003)

Chatfield, M., *Churches the Victorians Forgot* (Ashbourne, 1979)

Claydon, T., *William III and the Godly Revolution* (Cambridge, 1996)

Claydon, T., *William III* (2002)

Claydon, T., and McBride, I. (eds), *Protestantism and National Identity: Britain and Ireland, c.1650–c.1850* (Cambridge, 1998)

Cliffe, J.T., *The Puritan Gentry: The Great Puritan Families of Early Stuart England* (1984)

Cliffe, J.T., *Puritans in Conflict: The Puritan Gentry During and After the Civil Wars* (1988)

Cliffe, J.T., *The Puritan Gentry Besieged, 1650–1700* (1993)

Clifford, A.C., *Atonement and Justification: English Evangelical Theology 1640–1790* (Oxford, 1990)

Coffey, J., *Persecution and Toleration in Protestant England 1558–1689* (Harlow, 2000)

Cogswell, T., Cust, R., and Lake, P. (eds), *Politics, Religion and Popularity in Early Stuart Britain* (Cambridge, 2002)

Cohen, G.H., *God's Caress: The Psychology of Puritan Religious Experience* (New York, 1986)

Collins, J.R., 'The Church Settlement of Oliver Cromwell', *History*, 87 (2002)

Collinson, P., *The Elizabethan Puritan Movement* (1967)

Collinson, P., 'A Comment: Concerning the Name Puritan', *JEH*, 31 (1980)

Collinson, P., *The Religion of Protestants: The Church in English Society, 1559–1625* (1982)

Collinson, P., *English Puritanism* (Historical Association, 1983)

Collinson, P., *Godly People: Essays on English Protestantism and Puritanism* (1983)

Collinson, P., 'The Jacobean Religious Settlement: The Hampton Court Conference', in H. Tomlinson (ed.), *Before the English Civil War* (1983)

Collinson, P., 'The Church and the New Religion', in C. Haigh (ed.), *The Reign of Elizabeth I* (Basingstoke, 1984)

Collinson, P., 'The English Conventicle', *SCH*, 23 (1986)

Collinson, P., *The Birthpangs of Protestant England: Religious and Cultural Change in the Sixteenth and Seventeenth Centuries* (1988)

Collinson, P., *The Puritan Character: Polemics and Polarities in Early Seventeenth-century English Culture* (W.A. Clark Memorial Library, Los Angles, 1989)

Collinson, P., 'Shepherds, Sheepdogs and Hirelings: The Pastoral Ministry in Post-reformation England', *SCH*, 26 (1989)

Collinson, P., 'Ecclesiastical Vitriol: Religious Satire in the 1590s and the Invention of Puritanism', in J. Guy (ed.), *The Reign of Elizabeth I: Court and Culture in the Last Decade* (Cambridge, 1995)

Collinson, P., and Craig, J. (eds), *The Reformation in English Towns, 1500–1640* (Basingstoke, 1998)

Collinson, P., Ramsay, N., and Sparks, M. (eds), *A History of Canterbury Cathedral* (Oxford, 1995)

Como, D.R., *Blown by the Spirit: Puritanism and the Emergence of an Antinomian Underground in Pre-Civil-War England* (Stanford, Calif., 2004)

Como, D.R., 'Women, Prophecy and Authority in Early Stuart Puritanism', *HLQ*, 61 (2001)

Como, D.R., 'Predestination and Political Conflict in Laud's London', *HJ*, 46 (2003)

Como, D.R., and Lake, P., 'Puritans, Antinomians and Laudians in Caroline London: The Strange Case of Peter Shaw and its Contexts', *JEH*, 50 (1999)

Connolly, S.J., *Religion, Law and Power: The Making of Protestant Ireland* (Oxford, 1992)

Coolidge, J.S., *The Pauline Renaissance in England: Puritanism and the Bible* (Oxford, 1970)

Cooper, T., *Fear and Polemic in Seventeenth-century England: Richard Baxter and Antinomianism* (Aldershot, 2001)

Coster, W., *Baptism and Spiritual Kinship in Early Modern England* (Aldershot, 2002)

Coward, B., *Oliver Cromwell* (Harlow, 1991)

Coward, B., *The Stuart Age: England, 1603–1714* (Harlow, 1994)

Coward, B., *The Cromwellian Protectorate 1653–59* (Manchester, 2002)

Coward, B. (ed.), *A Companion to Stuart Britain* (Oxford, 2003)

Cragg, G.R., *Freedom and Authority: A Study of English Thought in the Early Seventeenth Century* (Philadelphia, 1975)

Cragg, G.R., *From Puritanism to the Age of Reason* (Cambridge, 1950)

Cragg, G.R., *Puritanism in the Period of the Great Persecution 1660–1688* (Cambridge, 1957)

Crawford, P., *Women and Religion in England 1500–1720* (1993)

Cressy, D., *Literacy and the Social Order: Reading and Writing in Tudor and Stuart England* (Cambridge, 1980)

Cressy, D., *Bonfires and Bells: National Memory and the Protestant Calendar in Elizabethan and Stuart England* (1989)

Cressy, D., *Birth, Marriage and Death: Ritual, Religion, and the Life-cycle in Tudor and Stuart England* (Oxford, 1997)

Cressy, D., *Travesties and Transgressions in Tudor and Stuart England* (Oxford, 2000)

Cressy, D., 'Conflict, Consensus, and the Willingness to Wink: The Erosion of Community in Charles I's England', *HLQ*, 61 (2001)

Cressy, D., and Ferrell, L.A. (eds), *Religion and Society in Early Modern England: A Sourcebook* (1996)

Croft, P., 'The Religion of Robert Cecil', *HJ*, 34 (1991)

Croft, P., *King James* (Basingstoke, 2003)

Cross, C., *Church and People 1450–1660* (1976; 2nd edn, 1999)

Cross, C., *Urban Magistrates and Ministers* (1985)

Cross, C., 'The Genesis of a Godly Community: Two York Parishes, 1590–1640', *SCH*, 23 (1986)

Currie, R., Gilbert, A., and Horsley, L. (eds), *Churches and Churchgoers: Patterns of Church Growth in the British Isles since 1700* (Oxford, 1977)

Cust, R., 'Anti-Puritanism and Urban Politics: Charles I and Great Yarmouth', *HJ*, 35 (1992)

Cust, R., and Hughes, A. (eds), *Conflict in Early Stuart England: Studies in Religion and Politics, 1603–42* (Harlow, 1989)

Cuming, G., *A History of Anglican Liturgy* (1969)

Davies, A., *The Quakers in English Society 1655–1725* (Oxford, 2000)

Davies, H., *Worship and Theology II: 1603–90* (1975)

Davies, J.E., *The Caroline Captivity of the Church: Charles I and the Remoulding of Anglicanism* (Oxford, 1992)

Davis, J.C., *Fear, Myth and History* (Cambridge, 1986)

Davis, J.C., 'Religion and the Struggle for Freedom in the English Revolution', *HJ*, 35 (1992)

Davis, J.C., 'Against Formality: One Aspect of the English Revolution', *TRHS*, 3 (1993)

Davis, J.C., *Oliver Cromwell* (2001)

Dawson, J., 'Calvinism and the Gaidhealtachd in Scotland', in A. Pettegree, A. Duke and G. Lewis (eds), *Calvinism in Europe 1540–1620* (Cambridge, 1994)

De Krey, G., *A Fractured Society: The Politics of London in the First Age of Party 1688–1715* (Oxford, 1985)

De Krey, G., *London and the Restoration, 1659–1683* (Cambridge, 2005)

Delbanco, A., *The Puritan Ordeal* (Cambridge, Mass., 1989)

Dent, C., *Protestant Reformers in Elizabethan Oxford* (Oxford, 1983)

Dever, M., 'Moderation and Deprivation: A Reappraisal of Richard Sibbes', *JEH*, 43 (1992)

Dever, M., *Richard Sibbes* (Macon, Ga., 2000)

Doelman, J., *King James I and the Religious Culture of England* (Cambridge, 2000)

Dolan, F.E., *Whores of Babylon* (Ithaca, NY, 1999)

Donagan, B., 'The Clerical Patronage of Robert Rich, Second Earl of Warwick, 1619–1642', *Proceedings of the American Philosophical Society*, 120 (Philadelphia, 1976)

Donagan, B., 'Did Ministers Matter? War and Religion in England 1642–9', *JBS*, 33 (1994)

Donagan, B., 'Puritan Ministers and Laymen: Professional Claims and Constraints in Seventeenth-century England', *HLQ*, 47 (1984)

Donagan, B., 'The York House Conference: Laymen, Calvinism and Arminianism', *Historical Research*, 64 (1991)

Doran, S., and Durston, C., *Princes, Pastors and People* (1991)

Dow, F., *Cromwellian Scotland* (Edinburgh, 1979)

Dow, F., *Radicalism in the English Revolution* (1985)

Duffy, E., 'Primitive Christianity Revived; Religious Renewal in Augustan England', *SCH*, 14 (1977)

Duffy, E., 'The Godly and the Multitude in Stuart England', *17C*, 1 (1986)

Dugmore, C.W., *Eucharistic Doctrine in England from Hooker to Waterland* (1942)

Dunn, R., and Dunn, M. (eds), *The World of William Penn* (Philadelphia, 1986)

Dures, A., *English Catholicism, 1558–1642* (1983)

Durston, C., *The Family in the English Revolution* (Oxford, 1989)

Durston, C., *Godly Governors: The Rule of Cromwell's Major Generals* (Manchester, 2001)

Durston, C., and J. Eales (eds), *The Culture of English Puritanism, 1560–1700* (Basingstoke, 1996)

Dymond, D., 'God's Disputed Acre', *JEH*, 50 (1999)

Eales, J., 'Sir Robert Harley KB (1579–1656) and the Character of a Puritan', *British Library Journal*, 15 (1989)

Eales, J., *Puritans and Roundheads: The Harleys of Brampton Bryan and the Outbreak of the English Civil War* (Cambridge, 1990)

Ellis, S.G., and Barber, S. (eds), *Conquest and Union: Fashioning a British State, 1485–1725* (1995)

Emerson, E.H., *English Puritanism from John Hooper to John Milton* (Durham, NC, 1968)

Emmison, F.G., *Elizabethan Life: Morals and the Church Courts* (1973)

Every, G., *The High Church Party 1688–1718* (1956)

Ferrell, L.A., *Government by Polemic: James I, the King's Preachers, and the Rhetoric of Conformity, 1603–1625* (Stanford, Calif., 1998)

Ferrell, L.A., and McCullough, P. (eds), *The English Sermon Revised: Religion, Literature and History 1600–1750* (Manchester, 2000)

Fielding, J., 'Opposition to the Personal Rule of Charles I: The Diary of Robert Woodford, 1637–1641', *HJ*, 31 (1988)

Fincham, K., 'Prelacy and Politics: Archbishop Abbot's Defence of Protestant Orthodoxy', *Historical Research*, 61 (1988)

Fincham, K., *Prelate as Pastor: The Episcopate of James I* (Oxford, 1990)

Fincham, K., 'William Laud and the Exercise of Caroline Ecclesiastical Patronage', *JEH*, 51 (2000)

Fincham, K., 'The Restoration of Altars in the 1630s', *HJ*, 44 (2001)

Fincham, K., '"According to Ancient Custom": The Return of Altars in the Restoration Church of England', *TRHS*, 13 (2003)

Fincham, K. (ed.), *The Early Stuart Church, 1603–42* (Basingstoke, 1993).

Fincham, K., and Lake, P., 'Popularity, Prelacy and Puritanism in the 1630s: Joseph Hall Explains Himself', *EHR*, 111 (1996)

Finlayson, M.G., *Historians, Puritanism and the English Revolution: The Religious Factor in English Politics before and after the Interregnum* (Toronto, 1983)

Firth, K., *The Apocalyptic Tradition in Reformation Britain 1530–1645* (Oxford, 1979)

Fitzpatrick, B., *Seventeenth-century Ireland: The Wars of Religion* (Dublin, 1998)

Fletcher, A., *A County Community at Peace and War: Sussex 1600–1660* (1975)

Fletcher, A., *Gender, Sex and Subordination in England 1500–1800* (New Haven, Conn., 1995)

Fletcher, A., *The Outbreak of the English Civil War* (1981)

Fletcher, A., *Reform in the Provinces: The Government of Stuart England* (New Haven, Conn., 1986)

Fletcher, A., and Roberts, P. (eds), *Religion, Culture and Society in Early Modern Britain* (Cambridge, 1994)

Fletcher, A., and Stevenson, J. (eds), *Order and Disorder in Early Modern England* (Cambridge, 1985)

Ford, A., 'Dependent or Independent? The Church of Ireland and its Colonial Context, 1536–1649', *17C*, 10 (1995)

Ford, A., *The Protestant Reformation in Ireland, 1590–1641* (Frankfurt, 1987: reissued Dublin, 1997)

Ford, A., Milne, K., and McGuire, J.E. (eds), *As by Law Established: The Church of Ireland since the Reformation* (Dublin, 1995)

Foster, A., *The Church of England 1570–1640* (Harlow, 1994)

Foster, S., *Notes from the Caroline Underground: Alexander Leighton, the Puritan Triumvirate and the Laudian Reaction to Nonconformity* (Hamden, Conn., 1978)

Fox, A., *Oral and Literate Culture in England 1500–1700* (Oxford, 2000)

Foyster, E.A., *Manhood in Early Modern England: Honour, Sex and Marriage* (1999)

Freist, D., *Governed by Opinion: Politics, Religion and the Dynamics of Communication in Stuart London 1637–1645* (1997)

French, K.L., Gibbs, G.G., and Kumin. B. (eds), *The Parish in English Life 1400–1600* (Manchester, 1999)

Gaskill, M., *Crime and Mentalities in Early Modern England* (Cambridge, 2000)

Gaunt, P., *Oliver Cromwell* (Oxford, 1996)

Gentles, I., *The New Model Army in England, Ireland and Scotland, 1643–1653* (Oxford, 1992)

George, C., and George, K., *The Protestant Mind of the English Reformation* (1961)

Gibson, W.J. (ed.), *Religion and Society in England and Wales 1689–1800* (Leicester, 1998)

Gilbert, A.D., *The Making of Post-Christian Britain* (1980)

Gillespie, R., *Devoted People: Belief and Religion in Early Modern Ireland* (Manchester, 1997)

Gittings, C., *Death, Burial and the Individual in Early Modern England* (1984)

Glassey, L.J.K. (ed.), *The Reign of Charles II and James VII and II* (Basingstoke, 1997)

Goldie, M.A., 'James II and the Dissenters' Revenge: The Commission of Enquiry of 1688', *BIHR*, 66 (1993)

Goldie, M., and Spurr, J., 'Politics and the Restoration Parish: Edward Fowler and the Struggle for St Giles Cripplegate', *English Historical Review*, 109 (1994)

Goring, J., *Godly Exercises or the Devil's Dance? Puritanism and Popular Culture in Pre-Civil War England* (1983)

Gowing, L., *Domestic Dangers: Women, Words and Sex in Early Modern London* (Oxford, 1996)

Gowing, L., *Common Bodies: Women, Touch and Power in Seventeenth-century England* (New Haven, Conn., 2003)

Greaves, R.L., 'The Puritan-Nonconformist Tradition in England 1560–1700: Historiographical Reflections', *Albion*, 17 (1985)

Greaves, R.L., *Deliver Us from Evil: The Radical Underground in Britain, 1660–1663* (Oxford, 1986)

Greaves, R.L., *Enemies Under His Feet: Radicals and Nonconformists in Britain, 1664–1677* (Stanford, Calif., 1990)

Greaves, R.L., *John Bunyan and English Nonconformity* (1992)

Greaves, R.L., *Secrets of the Kingdom: British Radical from the Popish Plot to the Revolution of 1688–89* (Stanford, Calif., 1992)

Greaves, R.L., *Glimpses of Glory: John Bunyan and English Dissent* (Stanford, Calif., 2002)

Green, I., *The Re-establishment of the Church of England 1660–1663* (Oxford, 1978)

Green, I., 'The Persecution of "Scandalous" and "Malignant" Parish Clergy during the English Civil War', *English Historical Review*, 94 (1979)

Green, I., ' "Reformed Pastors" and *Bons Curés*: The Changing Role of the Parish Clergy in Early Modern Europe', *SCH*, 26 (1989)

Green, I., *The Christian's ABC: Catechisms and Catechizing in England c.1530–1740* (Oxford, 1996)

Green, I., *Print and Protestantism in Early Modern England* (Oxford, 2000)

Gregg, E., *Queen Anne* (1980)

Gregory, J., *Restoration, Reformation and Reform, 1660–1828: Archbishops of Canterbury and their Diocese* (Oxford, 2000)

Grell, O.P., Israel, J.I., and Tyacke, N. (eds), *From Persecution to Toleration: The Glorious Revolution and Religion in England* (Oxford, 1991)

Greyerz, K. von (ed.), *Religion and Society in Early Modern Europe* (1984)

Griffiths, P., Fox, A., and Hindle, S. (eds), *The Experience of Authority in Early Modern England* (Basingstoke, 1996)

Haigh, C., 'Anticlericalism' in C. Haigh (ed.), *The English Reformation Revised* (Cambridge, 1987)

Haigh, C., *English Reformations: Religion, Politics and Society under the Tudors* (Oxford, 1993)

Haigh, C., 'Communion and Community: Exclusion from Communion in Post-Reformation England', *JEH*, 51 (2000)

Haigh, C., 'The Taming of Reformation: Preachers, Pastors and Parishioners in Elizabethan and Early Stuart England', *History*, 85 (2000)

Haigh, C., 'Success and Failure in the English Reformation', *P&P*, 173 (2001)

Hair, P. (ed.), *Before the Bawdy Court* (1972)

Hall, R., and Richardson, S., *The Anglican Clergy and Yorkshire Politics in the Eighteenth Century* (Borthwick Paper, 94; York, 1998)

Haller, W.H., *Liberty and Reformation in the Puritan Revolution* (1963)

Haller, W.H., *The Rise of Puritanism* (1938; reprinted Philadelphia, 1972)

Hambrick-Stowe, C., *The Practice of Piety: Puritan Devotional Disciplines in Seventeenth-century New England* (Chapel Hill, NC, 1982)

Hamilton, D.B., and Strier, R. (eds), *Religion, Literature and Politics in Post-Reformation England* (Cambridge, 1996)

Harris, F., *Transformations of Love: The Friendship of John Evelyn and Margaret Godolphin* (Oxford, 2002)

Harris, F., and Hunter, M. (eds), *John Evelyn and his Milieu* (2003)

Harris, T., *Politics under the Later Stuarts: Party Conflict in a Divided Society 1660–1715* (Harlow, 1993)

Harris, T. (ed.), *Popular Culture in England, c.1500–1850* (Basingstoke, 1995)

Harris, T. (ed.), *The Politics of the Excluded, c.1500–1850* (Basingstoke, 2001)

Harris, T., *Restoration: Charles II and his Kingdoms 1660–1685* (Harmondsworth, 2005)

Harris, T., Seaward, P., and Goldie, M. (eds), *The Politics of Religion in Restoration England* (Oxford, 1990)

Haydon, C., 'Samuel Peploe and Catholicism in Preston, 1714', *Recusant History*, 20 (1990)

Haydon, C., *Anti-Catholicism in Eighteenth-century England* (Manchester, 1993)

Hayton, D.W., 'Robert Harley's "Middle Way": The Puritan Heritage in Augustan Politics', *British Library Journal*, 15 (1989)

Hayton, D.W., 'Moral Reform and Country Politics in the Late Seventeenth-century House of Commons', *P&P*, 128 (1990)

Hayton, D.W., *Ruling Ireland, 1685–1742* (Woodbridge, 2004)

Heal, F. (ed.), *Of Prelates and Princes* (1980)

Heal, F., *Reformation in Britain and Ireland* (Oxford, 2003)

Heal, F., and Holmes, C., *The Gentry in England and Wales 1500–1700* (1994)

Herlihy, K. (ed.), *The Irish Dissenting Tradition 1650–1750* (Dublin, 1995)

Herlihy, K. (ed.), *The Religion of Irish Dissent 1650–1800* (Dublin, 1996)

Herlihy, K. (ed.), *The Politics of Irish Dissent 1650–1800* (Dublin, 1997)

Herlihy, K. (ed.), *Propagating the Word of Irish Dissent 1650–1800* (Dublin, 1998)

Hibbard, C., *Charles I and the Popish Plot* (Chapel Hill, NC, 1983)

Hill, C., *Puritanism and Revolution* (1958)

Hill, C., *Society and Puritanism in Pre-revolutionary England* (1964)

Hill, C., *Antichrist in Seventeenth-century England* (Oxford, 1971; revised, 1990)

Hill, C., *The World Turned Upside Down* (1972)

Hill, C., *Change and Continuity in Seventeenth-century England* (1974)

Hill, C., *A Turbulent, Seditious, and Factious People: John Bunyan and his Church 1628–1680* (Oxford, 1989).

Hill, C., *The English Bible and the Seventeenth-century Revolution* (Harmondsworth, 1993)

Hindle, S., 'The Shaming of Margaret Knowsley: Gossip, Gender and the Experience of Authority in Early Modern England', *Continuity and Change*, 9 (1994)

Hindle, S., *The State and Social Change in Early Modern England c.1550–1640* (Basingstoke, 2000)

Hindle, S., *On the Parish? The Micro-politics of Poor Relief in Rural England c.1550–1750* (Oxford, 2004)

Hirst, D., 'The Failure of Godly Rule in the English Revolution', *P&P*, 132 (1991)

Hirst, D., *England in Conflict 1603–1660* (1996)

Hoak, D., and Feingold, M. (eds), *The World of William and Mary: Anglo-Dutch Perspectives on the Revolution of 1688–9* (Stanford, Calif., 1996)

Hobbs, M. (ed.), *Chichester Cathedral: An Historical Survey* (Chichester, 1994)

Hodgetts, M., 'The Yates of Harvington, 1631–1696', *Recusant History*, XXII (1994)

Holden, W.P., *Anti-Puritan Satire 1572–1642* (1954)

Holifield, E.B., *The Covenant Sealed: The Development of Puritan Sacramental Theology in Old and New England* (New Haven, Conn., 1974)

Holmes, C., *Seventeenth-century Lincolnshire* (Lincoln, 1980)

Holmes, G., *British Politics in the Age of Anne* (1967)

Holmes, G. (ed.), *Britain after the Glorious Revolution, 1689–1714* (1969)

Holmes, G., *The Trial of Doctor Sacheverell* (1973)

Holmes, G., *Religion and Party in Late Stuart England* (1975)

Holmes, G., *Augustan England: Professions, State and Society 1680–1730* (1982)

Holmes, G., and Speck, W.A. (eds), *The Divided Society: Party Conflict in England 1694–1716* (1967)

Hoppit, J., *A Land of Liberty? England 1689–1727* (Oxford, 2000)

Horle, C.W., *The Quakers and the English Legal System 1660–1688* (Philadelphia, 1988)

Horwitz, H., 'Religious Reunion during the Exclusion Crisis', *JEH*, 15 (1964)

Horwitz, H., *Parliament, Policy and Politics in the Reign of William III* (Manchester, 1977)

Houlbrooke, R., *Death, Religion and the Family in England 1480–1750* (Oxford, 1998)

Houston, A., and Pincus, S. (eds), *A Nation Transformed: England after the Restoration* (Cambridge, 2001)

Hughes, A., 'Thomas Dugard and his Circle in the 1630s: A "Parliamentary–Puritan" Connexion?', *HJ*, 29 (1986)

Hughes, A., *Politics, Society and Civil War in Warwickshire 1620–60* (Cambridge, 1987)

Hughes, A., *Godly Reformation and its Opponents in Warwickshire, 1640–1662* (Dugdale Society Occasional Papers, 35, 1993)

Hughes, A., *The Causes of the English Civil War* (Basingstoke, 1991; 2nd edn, 1998)

Hughes, A., *'Gangraena' and the Struggle for the English Revolution* (Oxford, 2004)

Hunt, A., 'The Lord's Supper in Early Modern England', *P&P*, 161 (1998)

Hunt, W., *The Puritan Moment: The Coming of the Revolution in an English County* (Cambridge, Mass., 1983)

Hunter, M., *Science and Society in Restoration England* (Cambridge, 1981)

Hunter, M., 'The Problem of "Atheism" in Early Modern England', *TRHS* 5th series, 35 (1985)

Hunter, M., *Robert Boyle Reconsidered* (Cambridge, 1994)

Hunter, M., and Gregory, A. (eds), *An Astrological Diary of the Seventeenth Century: Samuel Jeake of Rye 1652–1699* (Oxford, 1988)

Hunter, M., and Wootton, D. (eds), *Atheism from the Reformation to the Enlightenment* (Oxford, 1992)

Hurwich, J., 'Dissent and Catholicism in English Society: A Study of Warwickshire, 1660–1720', *JBS*, 16 (1976)

Hutton, R., *The Restoration* (Oxford, 1985)

Hutton, R., *Charles II* (Oxford, 1989)

Hutton, R., *The Rise and Fall of Merry England: The Ritual Year* (Oxford, 1994)

Hutton, R., 'The English Reformation and the Evidence of Folklore', *P&P*, 148 (1995)

Hutton, R., *The British Republic 1649–1660* (Basingstoke, 1990; 2nd edn, 2000)

Ingram, M., 'Religion, Communities and Moral Discipline in Late Sixteenth- and Early Seventeenth-Century England: Case Studies', in K. von Greyerz (ed.), *Religion and Society in Early Modern Europe* (1984)

Ingram, M., *Church Courts, Sex and Marriage in England 1570–1640* (Cambridge, 1987)

Isaacs, T., 'The Anglican Heirarchy and the Reformation of Manners 1688–1738', *JEH*, 33 (1982)

Israel, J. (ed.), *The Anglo-Dutch Moment: Essays on the Glorious Revolution and its World Impact* (Cambridge, 1991)

Jackson, C., *Restoration Scotland 1660–1690* (Woodbridge, 2003)

Jacob, W.M., *Lay People and Religion in the Early Eighteenth Century* (Cambridge, 1996)

Jenkins, G.H., *Literature, Religion and Society in Wales 1660–1730* (1978)

Jenkins, G.H., *The Foundations of Modern Wales 1642–1780* (Oxford, 1987)

Jenkins, G.H., *Protestant Dissenters in Wales, 1639–1689* (Cardiff, 1992)

Jenkins, P., *A History of Modern Wales, 1536–1990* (1992)

Jones, J.R. (ed.), *Liberty Secured? Britain before and after 1688* (Stanford, Calif., 1992)

Jones, N., *The English Reformation* (Oxford, 2002)

Jordan, S., 'Gentry Catholicism in the Thames Valley, 1660–1780', *Recusant History*, 27 (2004)

Katz, D., *Sabbath and Sectarianism in Seventeenth-century England* (1988)

Keeble, N.H., *Richard Baxter: Puritan Man of Letters* (Oxford, 1982)

Keeble, N.H., *The Literary Culture of Nonconformity in Later Seventeenth-century England* (Leicester, 1987)

Keeble, N.H., *The Restoration: England in the 1660s* (Oxford, 2002)

Kelsey, S., 'The Death of Charles I', *HJ*, 45 (2002)

Kendall, R.T., *Calvin and English Calvinism to 1649* (Oxford, 1979)

Kennedy, D.E., *The English Revolution 1642–1649* (Basingstoke, 2000)

Kenyon, J.P., *Revolution Principles: The Politics of Party 1689–1720* (Cambridge, 1986)

Ker, N., and Perkin, M. (eds), *A Directory of the Parochial Libraries of the Church of England and the Church in Wales* (2004)

Kermode, J., and Walker, G. (eds), *Women, Crime and the Courts in Early Modern England* (1994)

Key, N., and Ward J., 'Divided into Parties: Exclusion Crisis Origins in Monmouth', *English Historical Review*, 115 (2000)

Kidd, C., 'Religious Realignment between the Restoration and Union', in J. Robertson (ed.), *A Union for Empire* (Cambridge, 1995)

Kishlansky, M., *A Monarchy Transformed: Britain, 1603–1714* (Harmondsworth, 1996)

Knappen, M.M., *Tudor Puritanism* (Chicago, 1939)

Knighton, C.S., and Mortimer, R. (eds), *Westminster Abbey Reformed 1540–1640* (Aldershot, 2003)

Knights, M., *Politics and Opinion in Crisis, 1678–81* (Cambridge, 1994)

Knights, M., *Representation and Misrepresentation in Later Stuart Britain* (Oxford, 2005)

Knott, J., *The Sword of the Spirit: Puritan Responses to the Bible* (Chicago, 1980)

Knott, J., *Discourses of Martyrdom in English Literature 1563–1694* (Cambridge, 1993)

Kroll, R., Ashcraft, R., and Zagorin, P. (eds), *Philosophy, Science and Enlightenment in England 1640–1700* (Cambridge, 1992)

Lacey, A., *The Cult of King Charles the Martyr* (Woodbridge, 2002)

Lacey, D.R., *Dissent and Parliamentary Politics in England 1661–1689* (New Brunswick, NJ, 1969)

Lake, P., *Moderate Puritans and the Elizabethan Church* (Cambridge, 1982)

Lake, P., 'William Bradshaw, Antichrist and the Community of the Godly', *JEH*, 36 (1985)

Lake, P., 'Calvinism and the English Church 1570–1635', *P&P*, 114 (1987)

Lake, P., 'Feminine Piety and Personal Potency: The "Emancipation" of Mrs Jane Ratcliffe', *17C*, 2 (1987)

Lake, P., *Anglicans and Puritans? Presbyterianism and English Conformist Thought from Whitgift to Hooker* (1988)

Lake, P., 'Serving God and the Times: The Calvinist Conformity of Robert Sanderson', *JBS*, 27 (1988)

Lake, P., 'Richard Kilby: A Study in Personal and Professional Failure', *SCH*, 26 (1989)

Lake, P., 'Puritanism, Arminianism and a Shropshire Axe Murder', *Midland History*, 15 (1990)

Lake, P., *The Boxmaker's Revenge: 'Orthodoxy', 'Heterodoxy' and the Politics of the Parish in Early Stuart London* (Manchester, 2001)

Lake, P., and Como, D., '"Orthodoxy" and its Discontents: Dispute Settlement and the Production of "Consensus" in the London (Puritan) "Underground"', *JBS*, 39 (2000)

Lake, P., and Questier, M., 'Puritans, Papists and the "Public Sphere" in Early Modern England: The Edmund Campion Affair in Context', *Journal of Modern History*, 72 (2000)

Lake, P., and Questier, M. (eds), *Conformity and Orthodoxy in the English Church c.1560–1660* (Woodbridge, 2000)

Lake, P., with Questier, M., *The Antichrist's Lewd Hat: Protestants, Papists and Players in Post-Reformation England* (New Haven, Conn., 2002)

Lamburn, D.J., 'Petty Babylons, Godly Prophets, Petty Pastors and Little Churches: The Work of Healing Babel', *SCH*, 26 (1989)

Lamont, W.M., *Godly Rule: Politics and Religion 1603–1660* (1969)

Lamont, W.M., *Richard Baxter and the Millennium* (1979)

Lamont, W.M., 'The Rise of Arminianism Reconsidered', *P&P*, 107 (1985)

Lamont, W.M., *Puritanism and Historical Controversy* (1996)

Larminie, V., *Wealth, Kinship and Culture: The Seventeenth-century Newdigates of Arbury and their World* (1995)

Larner, C., *Enemies of God* (1980)

Larner, C., *Witchcraft and Religion* (1984)

Laslett, P., *The World We Have Lost* (2nd ed., 1971)

Leedham-Green, E.S. (ed.), *Religious Dissent in East Anglia* (Cambridge, 1991)

Legg, J.W., *English Church Life 1660–1833* (1914)

Lehmberg, S.E., *Cathedrals under Siege: Cathedrals in English Society, 1600–1700* (Exeter, 1996)

Lindley, K., *Popular Politics and Religion in Civil War London* (Aldershot, 1997)

Liu, T., *Puritan London: A Study of Religion and Society in the City Parishes* (Newark, Del., 1986)

Lund, R.D., *The Margins of Orthodoxy: Heterodox Writing and Cultural Response 1660–1750* (Cambridge, 1995)

McAdoo, H.R., *The Spirit of Anglicanism* (1965)

McClendon, M.C., Ward, J.P., and MacDonald, M. (eds), *Protestant Identities: Religion, Society and Self-fashioning in Post-Reformation England* (Stanford, Calif., 1989)

McClain, L., 'Without Church, Cathedral, or Shrine: The Search for Religious Space among Catholics in England, 1559–1625', *Sixteenth Century Journal*, 33 (2002)

MacClure, M., *The Paul's Cross Sermons 1534–1642* (Toronto, 1958)

MacCulloch, D., *The Later Reformation in England, 1547–1603* (Basingstoke, 1990)

MacCulloch, D., 'The Myth of the English Reformation', *JBS*, 30 (1991)

McCullough, P., *Sermons at Court: Politics and Religion in Elizabethan and Jacobean Preaching* (Cambridge, 1998)

MacDonald, M., 'The Fearfull Estate of Francis Spira: Narrative, Identity, and Emotion in Early Modern England', *JBS*, 31 (1992)

MacDonald, M., and Murphy, T., *Sleepless Souls: Suicide in Early Modern England* (Oxford, 1990)

McDowell, N., *The English Radical Imagination* (Oxford, 2003)

Macfarlane, A., *Witchcraft in Tudor and Stuart England* (1970)

McGee, J.S., *The Godly Man in Stuart England: Anglicans, Puritans and the Two Tables, 1620–1670* (New Haven, Conn., 1976)

McGiffert, M., 'God's Controversy with Jacobean England', *American Historical Review*, 88 (1983)

McGrath, A.E., *Justitia Dei: A History of the Doctrine of Justification* (Cambridge, 1986)

McGregor, J.F., and Reay, B. (eds), *Radical Religion in the English Revolution* (Oxford, 1984)

MacInnes, A.I., *The British Revolution 1629–1660* (Basingstoke, 2005)

Mack, P., *Visionary Women: Ecstatic Prophecy in Seventeenth-century England* (Berkeley, Calif., 1992)

McLachlan, H., *Socinianism in Seventeenth-century England* (1951)

Malcolmson, R.W., *Popular Recreation in English Society 1700–1850* (1979)

Maltby, J., *Prayer Book and People in Elizabethan and Early Stuart England* (Cambridge, 1998)

Marchant, R.A., *The Puritans and the Church Courts in the Diocese of York 1560–1642* (1960)

Marchant, R.A., *The Church under the Law: Justice, Administration and Discipline in the Diocese of York, 1560–1640* (Cambridge, 1969)

Marcombe, D., and Knighton, C.S. (eds), *Close Encounters: English Cathedrals* (1991)

Marcus, L.S., *The Politics of Mirth: Jonson, Herrick, Milton, Marvell and the Defence of Old Holiday Pastimes* (Chicago, 1986)

Marsh, C., *Popular Religion in Sixteenth-century England* (Basingstoke, 1998)

Marsh, C., *The Family of Love in English Society, 1550–1630* (Cambridge, 1994)

Marsh, C., ' "Departing Well and Christianly": Will-making and Popular Religion in Early Modern England', in E.J. Carlson (ed.), *Religion and the English People 1500–1640* (Kirksville, MO., 1998)

Marsh, C., ' "Common Prayer" in England 1560–1640: The View from the Pew', *P&P*, 171 (2001)

Marsh, C., 'Sacred Space in England, 1560–1640: The View from the Pew', *JEH*, 53 (2002)

Marshall, P., *Beliefs and the Dead in Reformation England* (Oxford, 2002)

Marshall, P., *Reformation England 1480–1642* (2003)

Martz, L., *The Poetry of Meditation: A Study in English Religious Literature of the Seventeenth Century* (1962)

Mather, F.C., 'Georgian Churchmanship Reconsidered: Some Variations in Anglican Public Worship 1714–1830', *JEH*, 36 (1985)

Matthews, A.G., *Calamy Revised* (Oxford, 1934)

Matthews, A.G., *Walker Revised* (Oxford, 1948)

Mayers, R.E., *1659: The Crisis of the Commonwealth* (Woodbridge, 2004)

Meadows, P., and Ramsay, N. (eds), *A History of Ely Cathedral* (Woodbridge, 2003)

Meldrum, T., 'A Women's Court in London: Defendants at the Bishop of London's Consistory Court, 1700–1745', *London Journal*, 19 (1994)

Merritt, J.F. (ed.), *The Political World of Thomas Wentworth, Earl of Strafford, 1621–1641* (Cambridge, 1996)

Merritt, J.F., 'Puritans, Laudians, and the Phenomenon of Church-building in Jacobean London', *HJ*, 41 (1998)

Merritt, J.F., 'The Cradle of Laudianism? Westminster Abbey, 1558–1630', *JEH*, 52 (2001)

Miller, J., *Popery and Politics in England, 1660–1688* (Cambridge, 1973)

Miller, J., *James II: A Study in Kingship* (Hove, 1978)

Miller, J., *The Glorious Revolution* (Harlow, 1983)

Miller, J., *After the Civil Wars: English Politics and Government in the Reign of Charles II* (Harlow, 2000)

Miller, P., *The New England Mind: The Seventeenth Century* (Cambridge, Mass., 1939; reprinted 1954)

Milton, A., *Catholic and Reformed: The Roman and Protestant Churches in English Protestant Thought, 1600–1640* (Cambridge, 1995)

Milton, A., 'Licensing, Censorship and Religious Orthodoxy in Early Stuart England', *HJ*, 41 (1998)

Milward, P., *Religious Controversies of the Jacobean Age: A Survey of Printed Sources* (1978)

Mintz, S., *The Hunting of Leviathan* (1962)

Mitchison, R., *Lordship to Patronage: Scotland 1603–1745* (1983)

Mitchison, R., and Leneman, L., *Sexuality and Social Control: Scotland 1660–1780* (1989)

Mole, N., 'Church-building and Popular Piety in Early Seventeenth-century Exeter', *Southern History*, 25 (2003)

Moody, T.W., Martin, F.X., and Byrne, F.J. (eds), *A New History of Ireland, Volume 3: Early Modern Ireland, 1634–1691* (2nd edn, Oxford, 1991)

Moore, S. Hardman, 'Sexing the Soul: Gender and the Rhetoric of Puritan Piety', *SCH*, 34 (1998)

Morgan, J., *Godly Learning: Puritan Attitudes towards Reason, Learning, and Education, 1560–1640* (Cambridge, 1986)

Morgan, N., *Lancashire Quakers and the Establishment* (Halifax, 1993)

Morrill, J., *The Revolt of the Provinces: Conservatives and Revolutionaries in the English Civil War 1603–42* (Harlow, 1976)

Morrill, J.S., 'The Church in England, 1642–9' in Morrill, J.S. (ed.), *Reactions to the English Civil War* (Basingstoke, 1982)

Morrill, J. (ed.), *Oliver Cromwell and the English Revolution* (1990)

Morrill, J. (ed.), *The Scottish National Covenant in its British Context 1638–51* (Edinburgh, 1990)

Morrill, J.S. (ed.), *The Impact of English Civil War* (1991)

Morrill, J., *The Nature of the English Revolution* (Harlow, 1993)

Morrill, J., Slack, P., and Woolf, D. (eds), *Public Duty and Private Conscience in Seventeenth-century England* (Oxford, 1993)

Mullan, D.G., *Episcopacy in Scotland: The History of an Idea, 1560–1638* (Edinburgh, 1986)

Mullan, D.G., *Scottish Puritanism 1590–1638* (Oxford, 2000)

Mullett, M., 'Conflict, Politics and Elections in Lancaster, 1660–1688', *Northern History*, 19 (1983)

Mullett, M., *Sources for the History of English Nonconformity 1660–1830* (British Records Association, Archives and the User, 8, 1991)

Mullett, M., *Catholics in Britain and Ireland 1558–1829* (Basingstoke, 1998)

Murphy, A., *Conscience and Community: Revisiting Toleration and Religious Dissent in Early Modern England and America* (Philadelphia, 2001)

Nuttall, G.F., *Visible Saints: The Congregational Way 1640–1660* (Oxford, 1957)

Nuttall, G.F., *Richard Baxter* (1965)

Nuttall, G.F., *The Holy Spirit in Puritan Faith and Experience* (Oxford, 1946; reprint Chicago, 1992)

Nuttall, G.F., and Chadwick, O. (eds), *From Uniformity to Unity* (1962)

O'Day, R., *The English Clergy: The Emergence and Consolidation of a Profession 1558–1642* (1974)

Ohlmeyer, J. (ed.), *Political Thought in Seventeenth-century Ireland; Kingdom or Colony?* (Cambridge, 2000)

Owen, D., *The Records of the Established Church in England* (1970)

Packer, J., *The Transformation of Anglicanism 1643–1660* (1969)

Pailin, D.A., *Attitudes to Other Religions* (1984)

Parker, K.L., *The English Sabbath: A Study of Doctrine and Discipline from the Reformation to the Civil War* (Cambridge, 1988)

Patterson, C.F., 'Corporations, Cathedrals and the Crown: Local Dispute and Royal Interest in Early Stuart England', *History*, 85 (2000)

Patterson, W.B., *King James VI and I and the Reunion of Christendom* (Cambridge, 1997)

Paul, R.S., *The Assembly of the Lord: Politics and Religion in the Westminster Assembly* (Edinburgh, 1985)

Peck, L.L. (ed.), *The Mental World of the Jacobean Court* (1991)

Pennington, D., and Thomas, K.V. (eds), *Puritans and Revolutionaries* (Oxford, 1978)

Peters, R., *Oculus Episcopi: Administration in the Archdeaconry of St Albans 1580–1625* (Manchester, 1963)

Pettit, N., *The Heart Prepared: Grace and Conversion in Puritan Spiritual Life* (New Haven, Conn., 1966)

Phillips, J., *The Reformation of Images* (1973)

Prestwich, M. (ed.), *International Calvinism* (Oxford, 1985)

Pruett, J., *The Parish Clergy under the Later Stuarts: The Leicestershire Experience* (Urbana, Ill., 1978)

Quaife, G.R., *Wanton Wenches and Wayward Wives* (1979)

Quaife, G.R., *Godly Zeal and Furious Rage* (1987)

Questier, M., *Conversion, Politics and Religion in England, 1580–1625* (Cambridge, 1996)

Questier, M., 'Loyalty, Religion and State Power in Early Modern England: Romanism and the Jacobean Oath of Allegiance', *HJ*, 40 (1997)

Questier, M., 'What Happened to English Catholicism after the English Reformation?' *History*, 85 (2000)

Quintrell, B.W., 'The Royal Hunt and the Puritans 1604–5', *JEH*, 31 (1980)

Ramsbottom, J.D., 'Presbyterians and "Partial Conformity" in the Restoration Church of England', *JEH*, 43 (1992)

Reay, B. (ed.), *Popular Culture in Seventeenth-century England* (1985)

Redwood, J., *Reason, Ridicule and Religion* (1976)

Reedy, G.J., *The Bible and Reason: Anglicans and Scripture in Late Seventeenth-century England* (Philadelphia, 1985)

Reedy, G.J., *Robert South 1634–1716* (Cambridge, 1992)

Richardson, C.F., *English Preachers and Preaching 1640–1670* (1928)

Richardson, R.C., *Puritanism in North-west England: A Regional Study of the Diocese of Chester to 1642* (Manchester, 1972)

Rivers, I., *Reason, Grace and Sentiment* (2 vols, Cambridge, 1991)

Rohr, J. von, *The Covenant of Grace in Puritan Thought* (Atlanta, Ga., 1986)

Roots, I., *The Great Rebellion 1642–1660* (1966)

Rose, C., *England in the 1690s* (Oxford, 1999)

Rowlands, M. (ed.), *English Catholics of Parish and Town 1558–1778* (Catholic Record Society, 1999)

Rupp, G., *Religion in England, 1688–1791* (Oxford, 1986)

Russell, C., *The Crisis of Parliaments* (1971)

Russell, C., *Parliaments and English Politics 1621–1629* (Oxford, 1979)

Russell, C., *The Causes of the English Civil War* (Oxford, 1990)

Russell, C., *The Fall of the British Monarchies 1637–1642* (Oxford, 1991)

Schochet, G.J., *Patriarchalism in Political Thought* (Oxford, 1975)

Schwartz, H., *The French Prophets: The History of a Millenarian Group in Eighteenth-century England* (Los Angeles, 1980)

Scott, D., *Quakerism in York 1650–1720* (Borthwick Paper, 80; York, 1991)

Scott, J., *England's Troubles: Seventeenth-century English Political Stability in European Context* (Cambridge, 2000)

Seaver, P.S., *The Puritan Lectureships: The Politics of Religious Dissent, 1560–1662* (Stanford, Calif., 1970)

Seaver, P.S., *Wallington's World: A Puritan Artisan in Seventeenth-century London* (Stanford, Calif., 1985)

Seaward, P., *The Restoration 1660–1688* (Basingstoke, 1991)

Sharpe, J., 'Last Dying Speeches: Religion, Ideology and Public Execution in Seventeenth-century England', *P&P*, 107 (1985)

Sharpe, J., 'Scandalous and Malignant Priests in Essex: The Impact of Grassroots Puritanism', in Jones, C., Newitt, M., and Roberts, S. (eds), *Politics and People in Revolutionary England* (Oxford, 1986)

Sharpe, J., *Instruments of Darkness: Witchcraft in England 1550–1750* (1996)

Sharpe, K., *The Personal Rule of Charles I* (New Haven, Conn., 1992)

Shaw, W.A., *A History of the English Church during the Civil Wars and under the Commonwealth* (2 vols, 1900)

Sheils, W.J., *The Puritans in the Diocese of Peterborough, 1558–1610* (Northamptonshire Record Society, 30, 1979)

Sheils, W.J., 'Oliver Heywood and his Congregation', *SCH*, 23 (1986)

Shell, A., *Catholicism, Controversy and the English Literary Imagination, 1558–1660* (Cambridge, 1999)

Shepard, A., and Withington, P. (eds), *Communities in Early Modern England* (Manchester, 2000)

Shriver, F., 'Hampton Court Revisited: James I and the Puritans', *JEH*, 33 (1982)

Simon, I. (ed.), *Three Restoration Divines: Barrow, South and Tillotson* (2 vols, Paris, 1967–76)

Slatter, M.D., 'The Court of Arches', *JEH*, 4 (1953)

Smith, D., *A History of the Modern British Isles 1603–1707* (Oxford, 1998)

Smith, M.G., *Pastoral Discipline and the Church Courts: The Hexham Court 1680–1730* (Borthwick Paper, 62; York, 1982)

Smith, M.G., *Fighting Joshua: A Study of the Career of Sir Jonathan Trelawney* (Redruth, 1985)

Solt, L.F., *Church and State in Early Modern England* (Oxford, 1990)

Sommerville, J.C., *Popular Religion in Restoration England* (Gainsville, Fla., 1977)

Sommerville, J.P., *Politics and Ideology in England 1603–1640* (1986)

Sommerville, J.C., *The Secularization of Early Modern England: From Religious Culture to Religious Faith* (Oxford, 1992)

Spaeth, D., *The Church in an Age of Danger: Parsons and Parishioners, 1660–1740* (Cambridge, 2000)

Spalding, J.C. 'The Demise of English Presbyterianism 1660–1760', *Church History*, 28 (1959)

Speck, W.A., *Tory and Whig: The Struggle in the Constituencies 1700–1715* (1970)

Speck, W.A., *Reluctant Revolutionaries: Englishmen and the Revolution of 1688* (Oxford, 1988)

Spinks, B.D., *Sacrament, Ceremonies and the Stuart Divines: Sacramental Theology and Liturgy in England and Scotland 1603–1662* (Aldershot, 2002)

Spufford, M., *Contrasting Communities: English Villagers in the Sixteenth and Seventeenth Centuries* (Cambridge, 1974)

Spufford, M., *Small Books and Pleasant Histories: Popular Fiction and its Readership in Seventeenth-century England* (Cambridge, 1981)

Spufford, M., 'Can We Count the "Godly" and the "Conformable" in the Seventeenth Century?' *JEH*, 36 (1985)

Spufford, M. (ed.), *The World of Rural Dissenters, 1520–1725* (Cambridge, 1995)

Spurr, J., *The Restoration Church of England, 1646–1689* (New Haven, Conn., 1991)

Spurr, J., *English Puritanism, 1603–1689* (Basingstoke, 1998)

Spurr, J., *England in the 1670s: 'This Masquerading Age'* (Oxford, 2000)

Spurr, J., 'The English "Post-Reformation"?' *Journal of Modern History*, 74 (2002)

Stachniewski, J., *The Persecutory Imagination: English Puritanism and the Literature of Despair* (Oxford, 1991)

Stoyle, M., *From Deliverance to Destruction: Rebellion and Civil War in an English City* (Exeter, 1996)

Stranks, C.J., *Anglican Devotion* (1961)

Stromberg, R.N., *Religious Liberalism in Eighteenth-century England* (1954)

Suggett, R., 'Festivals and the Social Structure in Early Modern Wales', *P&P*, 152 (1996)

Sykes, N., *Old Priest and New Presbyter* (Cambridge, 1956)

Sykes, N., *From Sheldon to Secker* (Cambridge, 1959)

Targoff, R., *Common Prayer: The Language of Public Devotion in Early Modern England* (Chicago, 2001)

Tate, W.E., *The Parish Chest*, 3rd edn (1969)

Temperley, N., *The Music of the English Parish Church* (Cambridge, 1979)

Thomas, K.V., *Religion and the Decline of Magic* (1971)

Thomas, S., 'Religious Community in Revolutionary Halifax', *Northern History*, XL (2003)

Todd, M., 'An "Act of Discretion": Evangelical Conformity and the Puritan Dons', *Albion*, 18 (1986)

Todd, M., *Christian Humanism and the Puritan Social Order* (1987)

Todd, M., 'Puritan Self-fashioning: The Diary of Samuel Ward', *JBS*, 31 (1992)

Todd, M., *The Culture of Protestantism in Early Modern Scotland* (New Haven, Conn., 2002)

Tolmie, M., *The Triumph of the Saints: The Separate Churches of London, 1616–49* (1977)

Tomlinson, H. (ed.), *Before the English Civil War* (1983)

Toon, P., *God's Statesman: The Life of John Owen* (1971)

Trotter, E., *Seventeenth-century Life in the Country Parish* (1919; reprinted 1968)

Tuck, R., *Thomas Hobbes* (Oxford, 1986)

Tuck, R., *Philosophy and Government 1572–1651* (Cambridge, 1993)

Twigg, J., *The University of Cambridge and the English Revolution 1625–1688* (Woodbridge, 1990)

Tyacke, N., *Anti-Calvinists: The Rise of English Arminianism, c.1590–1640* (Oxford, 1987)

Tyacke, N., *The Fortunes of English Puritanism 1603–1640* (1990)

Tyacke, N. (ed.), *The History of the University of Oxford IV: Seventeenth-century Oxford* (Oxford, 1997)

Tyacke, N. (ed.), *England's Long Reformation 1500–1800* (1998)

Tyacke, N., *Aspects of English Protestantism, c.1530–1700* (Manchester, 2001)

Underdown, D., *Pride's Purge* (Oxford, 1971)

Underdown, D., *Revel, Riot and Rebellion: Popular Politics and Culture in England 1603–1660* (Oxford, 1985)

Underdown, D., *Fire from Heaven: Life in an English Town in the Seventeenth Century* (1992)

Usher, R.G., *The Reconstruction of the English Church* (1910)

Vallance, E., 'Loyal or Rebellious? Oaths of Association 1584–1686', *17C*, 17 (2002)

Vallance, E., 'Preaching to the Converted: Religious Justification for the English Civil War', *HLQ*, 65 (2002)

Wakefield, G.S., *Puritan Devotion: Its place in the Development of Christian Piety* (1957)

Wallace, D.D., *Puritans and Predestination: Grace in English Protestant Theology, 1525–1695* (Chapel Hill, NC, 1982)

Walker, D. (ed.), *A History of the Church in Wales* (1976)

Walker, D.P., *The Decline of Hell* (1964)

Walker, E.C., *William Dell, Master Puritan* (Cambridge, 1970)

Walsh, J.D., Haydon, C., and Taylor, S. (eds), *The Church of England c.1689–c.1833: From Toleration to Tractarianism* (Cambridge, 1993)

Walsham, A., *Church Papists: Catholicism, Conformity and Confessional Polemic in Early Modern England* (1993)

Walsham, A., 'The Parochial Roots of Laudianism Revisited: Catholics, Anti-Calvinists and "Parish Anglicans" in Early Stuart England', *JEH*, 49 (1998)

Walsham, A., *Providence in Early Modern England* (Oxford, 1999)

Walter, J., 'Confessional Politics in Pre-Civil War Essex: Prayer Books, Profanations, and Petitions', *HJ*, 44 (2001)

Walzer, M., *The Revolution of the Saints: A Study in the Origins of Radical Politics* (Cambridge, Mass., 1965)

Warne, A., *Church and Society in Eighteenth-century Devon* (Newton Abbot, 1969)

Watkin, E.I., *Roman Catholicism in England* (1957)

Watkins, O.C., *The Puritan Experience* (1972)

Watt, T., *Cheap Print and Popular Piety, 1550–1640* (Cambridge, 1991)

Watts, M.R., *The Dissenters: From the Reformation to the French Revolution* (Oxford, 1978)

Webster, C., *The Great Instauration: Science, Medicine and Reform 1626–1660* (1975)

Webster, T., *Stephen Marshall and Finchingfield* (Chelmsford, 1994)

Webster, T., 'Writing to Redundancy: Approaches to Spiritual Journals and Early Modern Spirituality', *HJ*, 39 (1996)

Webster, T., *Godly Clergy in Early Stuart England: The Caroline Puritan Movement, c.1620–1643* (Cambridge, 1997)

Weiner, C.Z., 'The Beleaguered Isle: Elizabethan and Jacobean Anti-popery', *P&P*, 51 (1971)

White, B.R., *The English Separatist Tradition* (Oxford, 1971)

White, B.R., *The English Baptists of the Seventeenth Century* (1983)

White, P., *Predestination, Policy and Polemic: Conflict and Consensus in the English Church from the Reformation to the Civil War* (Cambridge, 1992)

Whiting, C.E., *Studies in English Puritanism from the Restoration to the Revolution, 1660–1688* (1931; 2nd impression 1968)

Whiting, C.E., *Nathaniel Lord Crewe Bishop of Durham (1674–1721) and his Diocese* (1940)

Wilcher, R., *The Writing of Royalism, 1628–1660* (Cambridge, 2001)

Willen, D., 'Godly Women in Early Modern England: Puritanism and Gender', *JEH*, 43 (1992)

Williams, G., *Welsh Reformation Essays* (1967)

Williams, G., *The Welsh and their Religion* (1991)

Williams, G., *Renewal and Reformation: Wales c.1415–1642* (Oxford, 1993)

Winship, M.P., *Seers of God: Puritan Providentialism in the Restoration and Early Enlightenment* (Baltimore, Md., 1996)

Woodhouse, H., *The Doctrine of the Church in Anglican Theology 1547–1603* (1954)

Woolrych, A., *Commonwealth to Protectorate* (Oxford, 1982)

Woolrych, A., *Soldiers and Statesmen* (Oxford, 1987)

Woolrych, A., *Britain in Revolution 1625–1660* (Oxford, 2002)

Worden, B., *The Rump Parliament* (Cambridge, 1974)

Worden, B., 'Toleration and the Cromwellian Protectorate', *SCH*, 21 (1984)

Worden, B., 'Oliver Cromwell and the Sin of Achan' in D. Beales and G. Best (eds), *History, Society and the Churches* (Cambridge, 1985)

Worden, B., 'Providence and Politics in Cromwellian England', *P&P*, 109 (1985)

Wright, S., 'Easter Books and Parish Rate Books: A New Source for the Urban Historian?', *Urban History Yearbook 1985*

Wright, S. (ed.), *Parish, Church and People* (1988)

Wrightson, K., *English Society 1580–1680* (1982)

Wrightson, K., and Levine, D., *Poverty and Piety in an English Village* (1979; revised edn, Oxford, 1995)

Wykes, D.L., 'Religious Dissent and the Penal Laws: An Explanation of Business Success?', *History*, 75 (1990)

Wykes, D.L., *Lay Religious Belief: The Spiritual Testimonies of Early Eighteenth Century Presbyterian Communicants* (Leicester, 1996)

Wykes, D.L., ' "To Revive the Memory of Some Excellent Men": Edmund Calamy and the Early Historians of Nonconformity' (1997)

Yates, N., *Buildings, Faith and Worship* (1991)

Yule, G., *The Independents in the English Civil War* (Cambridge, 1958)

Yule, G., *Puritans in Politics: The Religious Legislation of the Long Parliament 1640–1647* (Abingdon, 1981)

Zakai, A., 'Religious Toleration and its Enemies: The Independent Divines and the Issue of Toleration during the English Civil War', *Albion*, 21 (1989)

Unpublished dissertations and studies

Byford, M.S., 'The Price of Protestantism: Assessing the Impact of Religious Change in Elizabethan Essex: the Cases of Heydon and Colchester, 1558–94' (Oxford University D.Phil., 1988)

Craig, A.G., 'The Movement for the Reformation of Manners, 1688–1715' (Edinburgh University PhD, 1980)

Dillow, K., 'The Social and Ecclesiastical Significance of Church Seating Arrangements and Pew Disputes, 1500–1740' (Oxford University D.Phil., 1991)

Till, B.D., 'The Ecclesiastical Courts of York 1660–1883: A Study in Decline' (typescript, Borthwick Institute, York, 1963)

Wrightson, K., 'The Puritan Reformation of Manners with special reference to the Counties of Lancashire and Essex 1640–1660' (Cambridge University PhD, 1973)

Index